A GUIDE TO COUNTRY LIVING

A GUIDE TO COUNTRY LIVING

Edited by

P. D. N. EARLE,

Managing Director
The Country Gentlemen's Association Ltd.

THE COUNTRY BOOK CLUB
Newton Abbot 1973

New revised edition published by
David & Charles (Holdings) Limited
in association with the Country Gentleman's Association

This edition was produced in 1973 for sale to its members
only by the proprietors, Readers Union Limited, PO Box 6
Newton Abbot, Devon, TQ12 2DW. Full details of
membership will gladly be sent on request

Reproduced and printed in Great Britain
for Readers Union by Redwood Press Limited
Trowbridge, Wiltshire

ACKNOWLEDGEMENTS

I must acknowledge my great debt to my colleague, Major G. W. Anderson, M.C., who, as Editor of the C.G.A. Magazine for over thirty years built up the records which formed the basis for this book.

I must also thank Miss Leslie Elliot, whose patient research added to the reference files and kept them up-to-date, and Mr. W. J. Weston, who for so many years answered the Legal queries set out in the pages which follow. Invaluable also have been the contributions made by the Managers of the C.G.A.'s own professional departments on Taxation, Accountancy, Estate Duty, Architecture and Insurance, Messrs. K. Raw, A. E. Brooke, A. Silverwood and R. W. Denham.

Finally, I must thank the Members who contributed so many of the interesting and amusing items themselves, Alex Graham, who illustrated this edition with such wit, and my wife who helped and encouraged me.

A GUIDE TO COUNTRY LIVING

INTRODUCTION

In the offices of the Country Gentlemen's Association in Regent Street reposed an accumulation of information going back over many years. These files—irreverently called the Department of Useless Information—are the fruit of answering queries from Members of the Association, and represent the distillation of years of painstaking research. My task has been to extract what I think may be of interest to Members of the Association and the general public, who are country-dwellers. Queries which were received fell into discernible patterns and this Guide has been arranged accordingly.

This second edition has been extended and revised. The information should be valid as at date of publication but errors doubtless will occur. For these I apologise in advance.

Many of the questions have more than one answer. This is because an answer might be given and published in the Association's magazine. Readers would disagree or proffer alternative advice. These alternatives have been included. The reader of this Guide is welcome to choose for himself.

The material in this Guide is only an indication of the vast amount of material which had to be examined for inclusion. The Country Gentlemen's Association continues in its work and one of its functions is to answer Members' queries, no matter how bizarre.

As a reflection of human nature much of interest and even hilarity can be gleaned from reading between the lines. By far the largest cause for queries is boundary and territorial disputes with neighbours. One might be forgiven for suspecting that the average country-dweller *enjoys* disputes with his or her neighbour. Perhaps one could formulate an Earle's Law "Neighbours, with contiguous boundaries, are natural enemies and cannot be friends."

A second large selection of queries fall under the heading of eradication. Human beings living in the country seem bent on killing every natural living and growing thing in sight.

It is perhaps a truism to say that judging from these two unhappy characteristics alone, mankind is probably the most lethal and selfishly destructive creature that has ever inhabited this planet.

The tendency to fight with other human beings outside one's own boundary and destroy all other natural inhabitants within it, when the possible population increase of the world is taken into account, bodes ill for both humanity and all other living creatures.

CONTENTS

EXPLANATION OF CONTENTS

Each section is arranged alphabetically and there is an Index at the back of the Book.

The first two sections, as stated, deal with 'Indoor' and 'Outdoor (and Animal)' queries on a 'do-it-yourself' basis. Where animals are concerned, questions, especially on dogs, often involve giving addresses of breed societies or breeders, which it was felt logically should be included in the Outdoor (and Animals) section.
to this is where animals are concerned, questions, especially on dogs, often involve giving addresses of breed societies or breeders, which it was felt logically should be included here.

'Legal and Professional' queries involved legal questions and professional in the sense of questions which would normally be answered by Accountants, Chartered Surveyors, Tax Specialists and Solicitors.

'General' deals with questions of where to obtain goods or service from others. It is the reverse side of the coin to the two sections of a 'do-it-yourself' nature. It caters for those who have gone to live in the country but still believe the metropolis holds the answer to problems. As my grandmother would say 'When in doubt—a fast car and London!'

INDOOR

*This section comprises questions and suggested
'self-help' solutions*

Aga Cooker – Converting

I find our Aga very good to cook on but I would prefer something more labour saving as far as fuel is concerned. Can one dispose of these cookers second-hand or shall I have to throw it away?

Aga cookers and Agamatic water-heaters (solid fuel) can be easily converted to oil— There is no need to scrap them—we had both the above converted to oil a year ago for a cost of £150.

Alabaster – Mending

I have an alabaster figure about three feet high which fell and broke in two. Do you know how or where she could be mended?

We suggest that next time you come up to London you might like to take it in to Chinamend, who tell me that they would be able to mend alabaster. Their address is 54 Walton Street, London SW2. Telephone 01-589 1182.

Alabaster Stain

Is there any way of restoring to alabaster the translucency which it has lost by being overheated? I have an electric pendule consisting of a 16-in. alabaster bowl. The 200-w lamp when altered some months ago was hung almost touching the bottom of the bowl so that a disc of alabaster under the lamp now appears dead white in daylight and opaque (in just the same way as gypsum when heated). Of course, at night the light of the lamp fails to penetrate the alabaster and the mark appears as a brown-black area.

We think that the heat from the light bulb may have permanently affected the texture of the stone. You might possibly try to have it repolished.

Angora Wool – Curing Fluff

How do you prevent shedding from angora wool garments?

Put the garments in a plastic bag. Place in a refrigerator overnight. The effect lasts for 24 hours.

Apple Juice – Unfermented

Can any member give me the recipe for plain unfermented apple juice as sold under various names, such as 'Apella' etc? I have a great many unwanted apples and have made apple wine which was fairly successful, and cider which definitely was not.

A simple recipe for making apple wine is to be found in a book called *Easy made Wine and Country Drinks* by Mrs. Gennery-Taylor. She does add at the end that the apple juice does not turn into wine for a week or so after making and is all right for children to drink. We do not know of a recipe whereby the apple juice can be kept and not ferment, but obviously there must be one.

Aspidistras

I have just been given a potted-up aspidistra plant. Although quite big it is a shoot off a plant which I happen to know is a hundred years old at least. I have never looked after an aspidistra before and would be grateful if you could advise me on special treatment it should receive. Amount of watering, any feeding, does it really do any good to wipe its leaves with milk or tea, and finally does the sun do it harm or should it be kept in a darkish corner?

Aspidistras are exceedingly tough plants and will withstand almost any kind of treatment. It is, however, worth treating them well.

We assume that it has been given to you potted into a suitable compost, but if you ever have to repot it – which should be done if the present pot becomes very full of roots – use John Innes No. 2 Compost and do the repotting in March. You should give it plenty of water from March to October and from October to March just enough to keep the compost from becoming bone dry. It is best to use tepid water. About twice during the March/October period give liquidire. Wiping the leaves with milk and water does give them a gloss, but we consider it preferable to wipe them with warm water to which a drop or two of a detergent has been added. This will keep the leaves free from dust and enable them to 'breathe'. The plant should be kept out of direct sunlight, but in as light a position as possible; a north window is ideal. Preferably it should be in a room where the temperature does not drop below 50 degrees F.

Bats – 1

How can I get rid of bats in my roof? They seem to live in the space between the slates and the lining of insulating boards, but there is a line of droppings below the ridge of the roof.

This information from a member may serve your purpose. 'Some years ago numbers of bats lived behind the plaster of the porch here, getting in through the cracks between the timbers and the plaster; they made such a mess on the step below that one day I took a bee smoker, with the usual smouldering corrugated paper which I used for the bees, and blew the smoke into all the cracks I could see; at least 100 bats came out in about 10 minutes, and a week later, repeating the dose, there were only about half a dozen, since when I have had none there for 20 years.'

Bats – 2

Referring to the recent letter regarding bats, although I doubt if I can be of assistance, he might be interested in a similar experience I had last year. The house concerned, in Norfolk, is about 100 years old and the roof is of pantiles laid on lath and plaster. At that time the occupier complained his existence was being made unbearable owing to bats appearing all over the house in rooms and passages, and we decided the only thing to do was to strip the roof, remove the lath and plaster, felt and retile it. When this was done large numbers of

bats were dislodged from the roof, and there has been no recurrence of the trouble since the work was completed. It was significant to note that all the roof timbers were in perfect condition, being completely free from attack by any of the wood-boring beetles. This fact was felt to be of particular interest, as practically every other building in this district is seriously infected by these pests, and I have been told that the presence, on a roof, of an appreciable number of bats will keep it entirely free from attack by these beetles.

Bats – 3

I have just discovered what appears to be a bat, clinging to the ridge board in the roof space of my house. I am unable to find how it got in. Could you please advise me how to dispose of the creature, for while it has cleared all the spiders, its droppings are a nuisance.

The only way to get rid of this bat would be to catch it, release it outside and block up the point of entry, but as you are unable to find where it is getting in, we would really advise you to leave the creature alone. It is commonly believed that bats not only keep spiders at bay but also wood devouring beetles, and are therefore quite a valuable asset in one's roof. Surely one bat cannot create a great deal of droppings under the rafters, and if you were to spread, for instance, newspapers underneath it would be very easy to dispose of any such droppings from time to time without too much trouble.

Bats – 4

Can anyone tell me how to rid our parish church of bats please?

There are several methods of getting rid of bats which are all equally effective. One method is to choose a fine warm summer evening at dusk when the bats are on the wing and block up any holes through which they return to their sleeping quarters with small mesh wire netting or other materials. If this is not possible bats can be fed through the winter with a rat virus. Burning sulphur in the roof has been known to clear them away. Another method is to take a bee smoker, with the usual smouldering corrugated paper used for bees, and blow the smoke into all the cracks you can see. The bats will fly out within minutes, and if there are still some left after a week, repeat the process.

Bats – 5

I can assure you that a stuffed tawny owl, placed on a pole about 12 ft from the ceiling of the church (if bats are inside the church) or hung from a beam (if bats are in the belfry!) will keep bats away.

Bats – 6

Can you tell me where such a stuffed owl can be obtained? We have suffered from the nuisance for decades and the local pest officers have been unable to provide a remedy.

You should be able to obtain this from Edward Gerrard & Sons, 1 Ferdinand Place, London, N.W.1. They can often be obtained very cheaply at junk shops or auction sales.

Beer – Home Brewed – 1

We want to try and make a home-brewed beer that is more like a lager than the recipes we have tried previously. Could any of your readers, or you yourselves, give us any information that will result in a lighter, drier, or more sparkling and more alcoholic beer, such as the Spanish 'San Miguel?

We suggest that you write for advice to the Good Housekeeping Institute, Chestergate House, Vauxhall Bridge Road, London SW1.

Beer – Home Brewed – 2

I would like to make Beer at home and wonder where I might obtain a recipe, can you help?

We suggest that you contact: The Amateur Wine-Makers' Association, North Croye, The Avenue, Andover, Hants, who will be able to supply recipes for Beer and also for Wine, and advise you on the equipment you will require.

A recipe is: To make 2 gallons in a crock.

(1) Boil up ¼ lb of dried hops in a cloth in a large saucepan for 30 mins (simmer).

(2) Remove hops, stir in ½ lb tin of golden syrup.

(3) Decant into crock, add water to fill.

(4) When cooled to warm, stir in carton of brewers' yeast.

(5) Cover. After four days remove yeast and syphon into bottles.

(6) Drinkable after seven days.

Ingredients such as golden syrup from a grocer. Easy. Hops (dried) from a herbalist. More difficult. Brewer's yeast from a brewery. Do NOT use dried yeast from a chemist. The beer will taste horrible.

Beetles – Furniture

I have recently been finding very tiny beetle-like insects running about on my furniture. They are too small to see clearly, but they certainly have legs, and I think wings.

Are they destructive, can anybody tell me, and if so, what steps should be taken to destroy them? They seem to disappear into cracks and crevices when disturbed.

From the description you have given us of the insects we would suggest that you should get in touch with Rentokil Laboratories Ltd, Felcourt, East Grinstead, Sussex (Telephone East Grinstead 23661) promptly and ask them to advise you.

Billiard Room

Would you please inform me what minimum measurements a room should be to house a half-size, three-quarter-size and full-size billiard table?

We give below the minimum measurements necessary for a room to accommodate various sizes of billiard tables:

Size of table	Minimum size of room
12' x 6'	22' x 16'
10' x 5'	20' x 15'
9' x 4' 6"	19' x 14' 6"
8' x 4'	18' x 14'
7' x 3' 6"	17' x 13' 6"
6' x 3'	16' x 13'

These sizes are based upon giving a cue space around each table of 5'. The length of a billiard cue is 4' 10". Even with the smaller size tables 7' and 6', although slightly shorter cues can be used, you will require 5' cueing space to avoid damage to any furniture, or what you have available in the room.

Blackcurrants

I may well have blackcurrants surplus to bottling and jamming needs. Could these be made into juice and would this keep several months? I suppose an alternative might be to make syrup—any help and information you can give would be appreciated.

We recommend the following recipe: Blackcurrant Syrup. Boil 2 pounds of sugar with a scant pint of water for 10 minutes. Add 2 pounds of ripe blackcurrants and boil for 10 minutes more. Then press through muslin placed over a sieve, re-boil the liquid and bottle it. Use for flavouring purposes or dilute with water for a drink. For further information you could try contacting the Good Housekeeping Institute, Chestergate House, Vauxhall Bridge Road, London, S.W.1.

Boot Cream

Could you please send me a recipe for boot cream?

The following recipe is very effective; 1 pint wood turpentine (not turps substitute), 1 lb beeswax, 1 pint water, 1 oz potassium carbonate. *Method*: Heat, but do not boil the turpentine, and in it melt the beeswax by cutting the latter into small pieces. Boil the water and in

it dissolve the potassium carbonate; mix the two solutions, while still hot, in a large bottle and shake vigorously when a pale yellow creamy fluid will be produced. The potassium carbonate acts as an emulsifying agent which is essential to produce the creamy consistency required. This is also a good polish for furniture. You might like to try a smaller quantity before committing yourself to the nearly 3 pints given above, but it is important to adhere to the above proportions.

Bottle Cutting

How does one get the bottoms off bottles? You put oil in the bottle and then put a red-hot poker through the neck into the oil, or you put hot water in the bottle and plunge the bottle into cold water, or you put cold water into the bottle and plunge the bottle into hot water, but the bottom does not come off. How on earth do you do it?

It seems that you have already got all the methods for taking the bottoms off bottles fairly well taped. Some people put a red-hot wire around the place to be cut, but we think that if you use a diamond first to scratch a circle, you might find any of the methods more effective. What do you want to get the bottoms off for? For Heaven's sake?

Brass Cleaning

Would you please give me some advice on the best way to restore heavily tarnished brass? I have some brass car lamps (about 60 years old) with many nearly inaccessible places to reach with a cloth and I am wondering if there is any liquid, proprietary or which can be made up, in which articles of brass can be immersed without damaging the metal.

Half a lemon dipped in salt and rubbed on the article should remove the tarnish, or vinegar and salt used the same way. Oxalic acid (which is poisonous) and a weak salt-water solution is effective. First wash the brass in an ammonia solution to remove surface dirt. Clean brass with the oxalic acid and salt mixture. Wash carefully to remove all traces of it, and polish with a sweet oil on a soft cloth.

Bumps in the Night

When my father had a very old house in Sussex for some time they were disturbed by mysterious sounds at night, but could not discover for quite a long time what was the cause. The noise came from the back stairs near the kitchen. Then finally they discovered the culprit was a rat carrying a potato in its four paws and rolling with it. The potatoes were kept in an alcove just up the back stairs from the kitchen.

I have never doubted my father's story, but have never heard of any other similar instance. In fact my own personal experience is that the potatoes have always been eaten on location! Perhaps there may be other evidence of rats, or perhaps some similar sort of animal, conveying potatoes in this way?

I believe that, in fact, rats are quite well known for this sort of thing and I seem to remember reading somewhere that they would steal eggs without breaking them by holding them on their stomachs whilst lying on their backs and allowing their colleagues to haul them over rough ground to safety where the egg presumably would be devoured.

Cleaning Brass

Can you please tell me how to clean an old brass lamp which has been lacquered and has some corrosive patches on it?

An effective cleanser can be prepared by combining weak acid with salt immediately before it is required for use. Oxalic acid (poisonous) and salt are extremely effective, but vinegar and salt make a good substitute. Be sure to wash the metal thoroughly afterwards. First wash the brass in an ammonia solution to remove surface dirt. Clean the brass with the oxalic acid and salt mixture. Wash carefully to remove all trace of it. Polish with sweet oil on a soft cloth. For ancient brasses in bad condition it is often better to consult museum authorities and to be guided by their opinion.

Carpet Cutting

I am wanting to lay some carpets, and feel I may be in difficulties when it comes to cutting. Can you give me any hints, and is it necessary to have special scissors? If so, where do I get them, and also is any special tool needed for laying linoleum?

We are advised that you should not use scissors. A very sharp knife or an old cut-throat razor are useful for this purpose, and the carpet should be cut on the underside. A 2 in. hem should be left to turn under and tack. Stretch the carpet as tightly as possible first. For linoleum there is a special knife, which is slightly hooked at the end and can be obtained from any hardware shop, but again the practical thing is to ensure that the knife or instrument used is very sharp. Linoleum should be scored first before it is cut.

Carpet Store

I have a number of quite valuable carpets which are about to be put into store, where they are likely to remain for two or three years. Can you let me know how they should be treated against attack by moths. I hear that there is a process called moth-proofing, but I do not know whether it affords a real guarantee of immunity, nor how expensive it is. Do you consider that the normal procedure of moth-balling and sewing up in Hessian is a reasonably sure protection?

You would be unwise to send them to a store without having them thoroughly moth-proofed first of all. In fact, we suggest that you get the storage people to do this for you and charge for the service, so that when you remove your carpets you would have a claim against them for negligence if any deterioration occurred. Whatever you do, keep the bill for this extra service and any other correspondence until you are quite satisfied that the carpets are returned to you in their original condition. The normal procedure of moth-balling is not too effective for storage over a long period.

Cats – Damage to Furniture

How can one stop a cat sharpening its claws on upholstery?

Various correspondents have suggested remedies from speaking sharply to the cat each time, to batting it with a newspaper. The consensus seems to be that a cat needs to do this and that a considerate owner will contribute a sharpening board or log for the cat's use. According to the consensus such cats show their gratitude by leaving your upholstery alone.

Cat Scratching

Has any member discovered a way of preventing cats ruining chair-covers and other upholstery by scratching? I have a proprietary artificial 'scratching post' impregnated with catnip and said to be the delight of all felines, but my two turn up their noses at it and prefer the backs of armchairs.

It seems that you have already done everything possible to provide an alternative for their activities. The only thing left is to scare the cats every time they begin their scratching by hitting them with a rolled-up newspaper or cloth— fear is the only real deterrent for any animal.

Chimney – Incessant Smoking

We have moved into an old house where the chimney smokes incessantly it seems to us, but worst when the wind is from the south-west. The local builder says that the previous owners were always tinkering with the chimney, which has been extended in height and had various cowls fitted, apparently without improvement. Can you suggest anything?

A member who cured several smoking chimneys on his estate said that you must first establish the worst quarter for the wind, which may vary from chimney to chimney. Any handy-man can then effect a cure.

Cut a hole in the side of the chimney facing the wind direction which gives most trouble. Make the hole as low down as possible but sloping upwards into the vent of the chimney. To make a neat job, insert a field drainpipe in the hole and make good around it. The wind blowing into the hole causes a draft upwards; the stronger the wind, the better the draft. Put wire mesh in the pipe to keep birds out.

The Member says that this method is too simple and inexpensive to appeal to builders, who prefer scaffolding, labourers (with mates) for maintaining Union rates of tea consumption!

Chimney Sweeping

I would be very much obliged if you could advise me as to the best way of sweeping a chimney burning exclusively wood.

To sweep a chimney burning exclusively wood, we think you will find the following satisfactory: obtain a bunch of stiff holly, tie it as tightly as possible and have it rather larger in diameter than the chimney flue. Fix a rope to it and take the two ends, one to the top of the chimney and the other to the bottom (in the fireplace). One man at the top of the chimney pulls the bunch up and the man at the fireplace pulls it down several times. This should be done twice a year.

China Repairs

Can you recommend an adhesive which I can use for mending broken cups, plates, etc., and which will be impervious to reasonably hot washing-up water? I have tried several, unsuccessfully.

In reply to your request for information about a good adhesive for mending broken cups, etc., which will stand hot water, we regret to inform you that nothing seems really effective for this purpose other than riveted china, which is of course ugly. We have, however, found some information in the *Antique Restorers' Handbook* which you may find useful: 'It will be found by experience that fixatives should be used in the smallest quantity consistent with the provision of an unbroken film over the surfaces to be jointed. If too much adhesive is used the object of its use will be defeated, as the excess will tend to hold the pieces apart and the join will be weak. A certain amount of pressure is necessary to hold pieces in contact until the fixative has hardened. Sufficient pressure should always be exerted to squeeze any excess fixative out of the join. One of the main reasons for failure is the disturbance of the pieces before the adhesive has properly hardened, and a good deal of patience needs to be exercised in this direction. A proprietary adhesive sold under the name 'Fortafix' is extremely useful for repairing pottery and porcelain. The maker's directions for use need to be followed carefully. An ordinary glue may be made waterproof by adding linseed oil to hot glue in the proportion of 1 part of oil to 8 parts of glue. If $\frac{1}{2}$ oz. of nitric acid for each 1 lb. of glue is added, the glue will remain liquid.'

Cider – Home-made

Can you give me a recipe for making Cider? I have a lot of windfalls each year and would like to use them up.

The first step is to wash the apples, remove any pieces of stalk or leaf, and cut away any diseased parts, after which the apples must be reduced to pulp. The best way to do this is to pass them through the household mincer, which means that first they must be cut into pieces of a size the mincer can handle.
Preparing the Pulp
The pulp is then placed in a suitable container – wood, glass, porcelain, earthenware, but not metal – and an equal quantity of boiling water added. In this condition the pulp should stand for about 14 days, during which time it must be stirred at least once daily.

Make sure the container has a suitable cover, which will allow the gas formed during fermentation to escape and at the same time exclude the wasps and flies which will be attracted.

A loose piece of wood is probably best,

or, if the mouth of the container is small enough, a plate or saucer.

Don't use a cover of pine or other strongly smelling wood or the cider will quickly acquire the same smell.

When fermentation has ceased (that is, in about 12 or 14 days) the pulp is strained through a muslin bag. A good dodge here is to turn a chair upside down on the edge of the table and tie the corners of the muslin to the chair legs.
Draining the Pulp
If you want the cider as clear as possible it must drip through the muslin in its own time, which generally means leaving it overnight; but if you don't mind a cloudy drink, the draining can be hastened by pressing the pulp through the muslin, in which case the job will be over in a few minutes.

At this stage don't expect to see sparkling cider. What you will have will be a dirty-looking brown liquid. This must stand for at least two months before it is usable, by which time a thick sediment will have formed and the cider itself will have largely cleared.

The cider is now returned to the container that was used for the pulp (it has, of course, been scoured out in the meantime) and the necessary amount of sugar is added.

Some sugar is desirable in all cases to encourage fermentation, the amount need not exceed a half pound for each gallon of cider.

If sweet cider is required more sugar must be used, although a certain amount of sweetening can be obtained by adding saccharin about a month later, when the initial fermentation is over. The saccharin tablets should be dissolved in a little hot water before adding to the cider.

At the end of about two months the 'brew' can be bottled.

By that time there will be a crust on the surface of the liquid and a sediment at the bottom of the container and the process of bottling so as to exclude both of these therefore requires a little knack, though it is not a difficult matter. If it happens that some of the sediment becomes stirred up, put the container on one side for 24 hours and try again.

The whole process is quite simple and the cider produced in this way can be remarkably good.

Made during September it should be fit to drink at Christmas.

Cider Vinegar

Is there any simple recipe for making Cider Vinegar from windfall apples?

We are afraid that we do not know of a recipe for Cider Vinegar, but we will publish your letter in the magazine, and this will undoubtedly bring forth numerous such recipes.

I used the recipe for Cider given above and the result was 2 gallons of Cider Vinegar.

It sold well at the local Cancer campaign bazaar!

Cigars – Resuscitation of

I am perturbed. I inherited a box of cigars from my father who died ten years ago; these were given to him by Lord Ismay some years previously; reputedly they had been given to Lord Ismay by Sir Winston Churchill. Such provenance suggests they are about twenty years old.

Obviously I am an inadequate host: last evening three of these cigars were, gracefully, rejected by a guest who was dining with me. To me this was sad; my guest was eminently sensible.

Do I throw the whole box away: Could any of your members tell me how I can resuscitate them conveniently?

Your guest was probably quite right to refuse a cigar. We contacted Dunhills, and they say that such an old cigar would be unsmokable. If they had been kept in a humidor they would have lasted all right, but otherwise they would not.

The only treatment now is to place them spread out in an open south-west window in the sun so that the cigars can pick up the moist content of the breeze. Dunhills still doubt whether this can work after so long, but it might be worth a try.

Coal Briquettes – Home-made – 1

Can you please tell me what to do with a quantity of anthracite dust collected from my fuel store before it was refilled? This is a recurring problem and no one
wants the stuff. I feel I should be able to make use of it, but there is always too much to be used in damping down the fire overnight and so forth.

We wonder whether you have tried making your anthracite dust into briquettes, which can be done by mixing the dust with sawdust, glue and water and pressing it in a simple home-made wooden press. The briquettes should then be stored in a dry, well aired place before use. Care must be taken not to use too much moisture, since the mixture should be sufficiently 'tacky' to set hard for handling.

Coal Briquettes – Home-made – 2

What is the best way of making briquettes from coal dust to burn on an open coal fire indoors?

We would suggest you purchase a machine which will make these briquettes. Two firms supply this inexpensive piece of equipment, they are: Wm. Penn Ltd., 585 High Road, Finchley, London, N.12, and E. Higgs Foulkes & Co., 557–565 Barking Road, East Ham, London, E.6. The price of it is around 37½p. to 50p. mark, including postage.

Coffee Making

I found the following information at the back to a drawer and doubtless many who appreciate good coffee would like the secret. The prescription can be slightly abbreviated.

A Good Cup of Coffee

Sir—There are only two kinds of coffee beans known to English commerce: (1) *Coffea arabica,* which is aromatic, and (2) *Coffea robusta,* which has a very fine appearance but no aroma whatsoever, and is imported from rubber plantations for adulterant purposes: it costs 6d. a pound, and is very dear at the price—to the connoisseur-consumer.

Arabica may come from Mysore, Brazil, Costa Rica, Kenya, Jamaica or a dozen other places. Its flavour varies slightly according to its source of origin. *De gustibus non est disputandum.* The

Jamaican is the dearest and possibly the best; very little of it is grown; it is worth 2s. a pound wholesale, in the green berry, or less, according to the size of the beans. Some connoisseurs think that the smallest and cheapest grade is the best to buy— more aroma for your money; but the middle or largest grades are easier to roast uniformly. 'Peaberry' coffee is simply an abortion.

The point is that, to be good, *arabica* must be grown at about 3,500 feet—as it is grown in the Blue Mountains of Jamaica. Below 2,000 feet it is little better than *robusta*.

Having bought it, you should keep your green beans for at least a year to dry thoroughly; they always arrive in England damp from the barbecues and the sea voyage. You can't roast a wet bean; you merely cook it as you cook the dottle in your pipe. New season coffee improves five per cent per month for twelve months, just as sardines improve with keeping for a couple of years. It is a scientifically proved fact that by keeping the beans you increase the store of aroma in their constituent cells. It can be bought in barrels or bags of about 120–200 pounds. Two friends buying and splitting a barrel will obviously have a year's supply of two pounds a week and save money appreciably by paying little more than half the retail price.

Roasting: This is a very delicate and vital part of the business. Don't over-roast. If you do, you will lose all the fine flavour and make it bitter. Frenchmen and Spaniards always roast it until black and 'sweaty'—to make it go further. That is why 'coffee' spells 'poison' in those hyper-thrifty and unenlightened countries. English people still think 'French Coffee' is a term of eulogy. It is really the exact opposite.

Coffee should only be roasted till it cracks; when ground, it should be a chestnut brown, not so dark as chocolate. As for adding chicory—leave that to criminals.

Grind it about half as fine as tooth-powder. Any good grocer will roast and grind your beans for 3d. a pound in lots of two pounds at a time. It is as well to see it done and see that you get your own back unless you have a grocer whom you can trust. If you are par-ticular, you will learn to roast it your-self, twice a week at least, and grind what you are going to use every day. A small gas-roaster is quite cheap and easy to install. Remember that ground coffee soon dissipates its aroma. To keep it for days in a paper bag is about as wise as keeping cigars or tea in the same way on the kitchen mantel-piece.

Now for the making—and the vital secret. The ideal, you will admit, is to have it taste as it smells, when perfectly roasted and ground in the tin. This is as ludicrously easy and incredible as 'washing in Jordan.' Take a common French two-decker *cafetiere* made of copper, aluminium or tin. The enthu-siast will have one of copper, electro-plated inside. Put in plenty of ground coffee on the dividing sieve. ('Plenty' means a heaped tablespoonful for each large cup that your *cafetiere* will hold.) Damp this with a drop of cold water; press and ram it tightly down; and then *fill the top compartment full to the brim with cold water*. Let it drip through; it should take 20–25 minutes at the out-side. Then remove the grounds and the top compartment holding them and merely heat (don't boil) as much of the resultant liquid as you want for im-mediate use to the hottest temperature the human mouth will stand. You can heat some of the brew for breakfast; some for after lunch; some for after dinner. It keeps perfectly good in the cold liquid for twelve hours; but it deteriorates if kept longer, as Eau de Cologne does if left uncorked.

Once boiled it is spoiled; for the aroma depends on a very volatile essen-tial oil. That is why you should fling any 'machine' of the American 'Brew' type into the dust-bin hastily. Coffee will not stand being distilled like Stockholm Tar. The Americans drink more coffee and make it more villain-ously than any nation in the world.

Drink it as hot as you can—with sugar if you like; either black or with a little thick cream. Coffee made thus is nectar: it is also powerless to keep you awake at night, for the cold water leaves the dangerous element unextracted. You will find it greets the palate with a soft caress; not with a percussive blow, as even the best restaurant coffee does.

Can Anyone Tell Me How to Rid Our Parish Church of Bats, Please?

(See page 4)

And the exquisite flavour will hang on the tongue for a good half-hour.

Readers who do not know this way of making coffee will think the whole of the above is a subtle and silly jest. It isn't. You just try it once, and you will never use any other method. It is an old Dutch secret, carried by the Dutch to the Cape and thence to Jamaica by Miss Knollys. She taught it to Mrs. Quin, who made the coffee at the Jamaican stall at Wembley, for which people queued up all day long. And, thank heaven, Miss Knollys also taught it to me, which made a voyage to Jamaica really worth while.

After all, it is only common-sense; even an English cook knows better than to put an 'essence' into a jelly and then let it boil. You can choose between having the aroma of your coffee disseminated about the house or having it in your cup. And you will agree (if you are a real coffee-lover) that this priceless revelation alone should induce anyone to subscribe to the *Spectator* for at least ten years in advance.

Cleaning Antique Copper

Please could you suggest some method for cleaning up a fairly filthy antique copper kettle? The smoke and grime is caked on and in places the metal itself is corroded.

If the kettle is caked with grime, we would suggest soaking it in a weak ammonia solution, and then scrubbing it with cold water and a Brillo pad. Dry it quickly and then polish it with something like Duroglit. If the metal is corroded there is not much you can do, unless you wish to take it to a professional electroplater, who might be able to do something.

Copper Plate Foliage

I have been told that it is possible to copper plate foliage, etc. Have you any details of the process?

We regret that we do not know anything about this process. Copper plates are very sensitive and perhaps if foliage were placed on a copper plate and pressed in the manner used by etchers an impression might be obtained.

You can buy Aerosol sprays nowadays which might do the trick.

Coral – Cleaning

I have one or two pieces of coral which some members of the family brought back from the Pacific many years ago but which have now got rather dirty. Can any member suggest a way by which these could be brought back to their natural colour?

In reply to your member (Cumberland) who wishes to clean coral, may I relate my experience.

Six months ago I set up a Marine Aquarium and it was essential that coral was sterile before the fish were introduced.

I used 'Brobat' in proportion 1 of Brobat to 3 of water and immersed the coral totally for three days.

After that it is necessary to rid the coral of the very persistent smell of Brobat. This can be done by flushing it in a bucket under a slow running tap for at least 24 hours.

Coral comes out brilliantly white except for one muddy coloured specimen which turned a vivid crimson.

Shells such as conch, whelk, oyster, added as 'scenery' were unaffected in colour by the sterilising mixture.

Decanters – Broken Stoppers

Can anyone tell me how to get a broken stopper out of a glass decanter, and how to repair it?

The proper procedure to remove a broken stopper is this:
(1) Put the decanter vertical in a reasonably warm place, eg, the kitchen. Place a few drops of penetrating oil (not lubricating oil) around the broken edge of the stopper. Leave for 12 hours. (2) Fix the end of the piece of good string to some firm structure, not a tap or a door handle, because if you do you will pull it off. (3) After 12 hours place two or three blankets on the floor at the site of operations. (4) Grasp the decanter firmly in the right hand (unless you are left-handed, in which case reverse instruc-tions). Grasp the free end of the string

in the left hand, coil it around the neck of the decanter two or three times and maintain gentle pressure on the string with the left hand; move the decanter rapidly back and forth between the fixed structure and the left hand. This, by friction, generates heat on the neck of the decanter, but not on the broken stopper. When quite warm up-end over the blankets, tap lightly with the hand. Out comes the stopper undamaged. Tap of course the body not bottom of the decanter. To repair, join the two pieces of stopper with clear Bostik. Follow instructions. To prevent (which is alleged to be better than cure). (a) Never replace stopper of a washed decanter until both it and the stopper are at the same temperature. This may take three hours. (b) Always after partaking of a filled decanter, before passing to the left, rotate the mating surface of the stopper between the forefinger and thumb. (There is no lubricant to equal a little human sebum.) It may excite some comment from initial hosts, but upon explanation, you will find that you are invited again.

Decanters – Cleaning – 1

Can you advise on getting cloudy marks off the inside of a decanter after it has been in use some time and has been emptied?

Various methods have been suggested by Members:
(a) Fill the decanter with a mixture of a tablespoon of salt to a quarter-pint of vinegar and leave to soak. Shake occasionally, rinse when clear and dry with a dust-free cloth.
(b) Use a good dentifrice powder, a heaped tablespoonful to a half-tumbler of warm water, then as above.
(c) Use silver sand instead of dentifrice powder.
(d) Use stinging nettles head downwards in the decanter, which should be filled with water. Leave to soak and agitate occasionally until clean.

Decanters – Cleaning – 2

The old method of shaking the decanter filled with water and shot is very tiresome. It is much easier to pour in some bleach such as is used in most households. I have found this instantly effective.

Deep Freezing

I should be most grateful if your Culinary Expert would inform me what is the theoretical and practical virtue of the 'blanching' operation, which we are assured is essential to the storage of garden vegetables in a domestic deep freeze. Are there any disadvantages or dangers in putting raw fresh peas, beans, etc, into the polythene bags without this process?

The value of the blanching operation lies chiefly in the destruction of enzymes. Freezing stops bacterial growth but does not entirely stop enzyme activity. The latter develops unpleasant flavours in vegetables. The colour and texture are also affected so that freezing raw vegetables produces a poor result. Scalding for a short time destroys the enzymes. It also shrinks the vegetables a bit so that they take up less room in the freezer. Incidentally, adding sugar to fruit has the same effect of cutting down enzyme activity. There is no actual danger in freezing 'unblanched' raw vegetables, but the results are not very satisfactory.
    Good Housekeeping Institute.
Editor: I don't agree. We have found blanching a waste of time.

Drainage Troubles

About thirty years ago when I modernised this seventeenth century house I put in septic tank drainage designed to cope with the number of bathrooms, basins, sinks, and w.c.s then installed. During the last ten to fifteen years another bathroom and w.c. have been added and we have fitted washing and washing-up machines. There is no doubt that the quantity of detergent going down the main drain has increased substantially. The septic tank effluent is no longer fairly pure water and I have had to fit what is in effect a cesspit to cope with it. Furthermore every few months the run of the main drain (4-inch pipes) gets blocked with a white deposit. It seems that this is solidified detergent which has caught somewhere in the drain – perhaps at the joins in the pipes – and then built up until it blocks the system. It can always be cleansed fairly easily with drain rods, but that is a messy and unpleasant job, and I would like to find a cure. Have other C.G.A. members had similar experiences? Will detergent stop the micro-organisms in the septic tank working in the manner intended? Would putting an acid down the drain periodically dissolve the deposits of detergent, if such is the trouble? I would be grateful for the experience of other members and effect. I wonder whether any of your readers has had a similar problem and can suggest any possible remedy.

Effects of Drain Solvents etc.

Soap, drain solvents, and other mild cleaning or disinfecting solutions used for normal household purposes cause no trouble in the tank. Constant use in large quantities, however, and disinfected wastes from the sickroom may prove harmful.

Wastes from milk rooms, strong chemicals used in sterilising equipment or in photographic work, and the wastes from filters or water softeners not only reduce bacterial action but also cause abnormally rapid accumulations of sludge and clogging of the tile lines.

Drainage – Care and Maintenance of Septic Tanks – 1

How can one prevent a white deposit forming in a septic tank and pipes and apparently disrupting the whole process of drainage?

A septic tank when first used does not need starters, such as yeast, to promote bacterial action. A good septic tank normally requires no maintenance other than a yearly inspection and an occasional cleaning. Frequency of cleaning depends on the capacity of the tank and the quantity and composition of the sewage. Tanks of the size recommended—500 gal-

lons to 1,000 gallons capacity—may require cleaning at intervals of 3 to 5 years.

The tank should be cleaned when 18 to 20 inches of sludge and scum has accumulated. If a drain has not been provided, sludge may be removed by bailing or by pumping with a sludge or bilge pump. It is not necessary to remove the entire liquid contents. Burial in a shallow pit or trench with at least 18 to 24 inches of earth cover at a point remote from water sources is the most practical method for disposing of these wastes.

A septic tank is intended to handle sewage only. Coffee grounds and ground garbage may be included if there is an ample supply of water for flushing and the tank is cleaned more frequently than would otherwise be done. The size of the tank should be increased at least 25 per cent if these materials are included in the sewage.

Do not use matches or an open flame to inspect a septic tank, as the gases produced by decomposing sewage may explode and cause serious injury.

Drainage – Care and Maintenance of Septic Tanks – 2

I suffer similarly from the white deposit. In my view nothing, other than physical clearing with rods is any use. The deposit appears to be the result of the combination of detergents and the long run of small-bore pipe always associated with such systems.

Septic tank systems have first of all a tank into which all sewage and domestic waste water collects. This should be of such capacity that it will not, in the first instance start to overflow into the filter bed until the contents of the tank have 'digested' and been broken down by bacterial action into a filthy, grey sop without many large lumps. This effluent is overflowed into a gravel filter bed, where it, initially, encourages the growth of bacteria which feed on the (to us) unpleasant elements, leaving only the water to flow away clear.

The bacteria live in a jelly of their own making, which coats the stones of the filter bed. The purpose of the stones is to provide the maximum area of bacterial jelly within the box of the filter bed. Unfortunately even if all is well, and it may not be, the bacterial jelly grows and blocks the spaces between the stones and the bacterial filter fails or nearly fails, to work. In large public sewage works the status quo is maintained by switching the flow to come out of a number of filter beds. On those which are left to dry out, the 'jelly' dies and dries, and the bed is then ready for further service. 'Private' septic tank filter beds just stop working properly when the bacteria choke them.

In case anyone wonders how it then is that there is not very widespread and gross pollution by ineffective septic tanks, the answer seems to be that the effect of the flow of water down a stream on the polluted effluent is incredibly beneficial.

I have effluent from an antique plant of very dubious efficiency discharging into a stream in my land. This plant now deals with something like four times the number of houses for which it was originally designed by the Local Authority who own them.

A few years ago, I was very concerned at the state of the stream in a dry season because my horses drink from it. My own professional adviser invoked the River Board and the responsible Local Authority. Tests of the water downstream of the outfall showed that there was no pollution above legally acceptable limits, though very close to it, owing to the lack of water, it was greater than what was acceptable. The digesting chamber was pumped out immediately and there was a further clearance after which increased flow of the stream dealt with the problem of pollution very close to the outfall, which produced an unpleasant smell but, 100 yards further down it did not affect the horses.

Drainage – Care and Maintenance of Septic Tanks – 3

There can be no doubt that detergents do prevent bacteria working in the manner intended in septic tanks.

Detergents gradually solidify and build up eventually blocking drain pipes in various places: my most recent and unsuspected place was the 'H' intake pipe into the septic tank. Draining rods can be pushed through the pipes and appear to clean them. My experience is that they merely make a hole through the detergent deposit. To remove the deposit, it is necessary to fit a rubber disc, which exactly fits the pipe, onto the end of the rod.

A successful cure is to put about $\frac{1}{4}$ lb. of washing soda crystals in sinks or other places where detergents are used and to pour a kettle of boiling water on the crystals. This should be done at least twice a week. It is a slow but effective cure. After a year of this treatment, the improvement in the outflow from my sinks is quite remarkable: furthermore, the usual crust is back once again on the surface of the liquid in my septic tank.

However, your correspondent and practically everyone else with a septic tank is unlikely to suffer thus because detergents and disinfectants inhibit the bacterial growth necessary to deal with the sewage. In fact, a septic tank system will not work unless the quantity of disinfectants is extremely small compared with the volume of water and then only if no detergents are used, since they adversely affect the desired bacterial growth in the filter bed.

The white deposit complained of is not, in my own case, detergent, but fat, both domestic and (owing to very hard water) soap curds. It coats the pipes and physical cleaning with rods will dislodge it, but it should be intercepted and removed from the system. If not, it will wedge in the pipes and produce further blockage.

Attacking with solvents involves blocking the pipes downhill and filling with solvent and subsequent disposal without affecting the functioning of the digesting tank and filter bed, and I think this is impractical. Dosing sink water with soda, etc., if it does anything, does more harm than good because near where it enters the pipe, it does remove deposits, it frequently allows the subsequent flow to detach solid lumps of the fatty lining which turn and block the pipe.

As a general principle, frequent rodding is the preferred method. Replacement of the drainpipe with larger pipe of oval section to give a better scour with small flows would help but is no doubt impractical on ground of cost. Total baning of detergents will, owing to its unpopularity within the household, be equally impracticable, though it would restore lost function in the filter bed. It would also still leave fat deposits taking place, though they would be nearer the kitchen drain and more concentrated.

Fingers – Cracked – 1

Some year or so ago you published a letter about cures for cracked fingers, recommending mustard and vaseline. I should like to place it on record that it is excellent. All the other cures mentioned in the letter I had tried and though they were effective for a short time their efficiency did not last. The simple mustard and vaseline mixture I have used ever since I read your recommendation and it keeps my hands in order. In the past they have been dreadful.

Fingers – Cracked – 2

As we have received so many enquiries about the cure mentioned in the letter published in the July issue on cracked fingers, we thought members might like to have the recipe. Mix together equal quantities of dry mustard and vaseline.

Firewood – From Limes

A lime tree has been blown down in a recent gale. Can you please tell me if it can be used for firewood, and, if so, how long will the logs have to be stacked before being fit to burn?

Lime makes first-class firewood. It should be cut up and stacked for some 3–4 months, and it will then be ready for burning.

Firewood – Logs for – 1

My aunt used to recite a rhyme about firewood. Can anyone recall it? It is most useful when selecting firewood.

Logs to burn; logs to burn;
Logs to save the coal a turn.

Here's a word to make you wise

When you hear the woodman's cries;
Never heed his usual tale
That he's splendid logs for sale,
But read these lines and really learn
The proper kind of logs to burn.

Oak logs will warm you well,
If they're old and dry;
Larch logs of pinewoods smell,
But the sparks will fly.
Beech logs for Christmas time;
Yew logs heat well;
'Scotch' logs it is a crime
For anyone to sell.

Birch logs will burn too fast;
Chestnut scarce at all;
Hawthorn logs are good to last
If cut in the fall.
Holly logs will burn like wax,
You should burn them green;
Elm logs like smouldering flax,
No flame to be seen.
Pear logs and apple logs,
They will scent your room;
Cherry logs across the dogs,
Smell like flowers in bloom,
But ash logs all smooth and grey,
Burn them green or old;
But of all that come your way,
They're worth weight in gold.

Firewood – Logs for – 2

Beechwood fires are bright and clear
If the logs are kept a year.
Oaken logs burn steadily
If the wood is old and dry.
Chestnut's only good, they say,
If for long it's laid away.
But ash new or ash old
Is fit for a Queen with a crown of gold.

Birch and fir logs burn too fast,
Blaze up bright but do not last.
Make a fire of elder tree,
Death within your house you'll see.
It is by the Irish said
Hawthorn bakes the sweetest bread.
But ash green or ash brown
Is fit for a Queen with a golden crown.

Elmwood burns like churchyard Mould,

E'en the very flames are cold.
Poplar gives a bitter smoke,
Fills your eyes and makes you choke.
Applewood will scent your room
With an incense-like perfume.
But ash wet or ash dry.
For a Queen to warm her slippers by.

Firewood – Sparks from

*Can you please tell me why pinewood
logs tend to throw sparks, and whether
anything can be done to prevent or
minimize this, such as ensuring that the
wood is cut when the sap is done, or
that only well-seasoned logs are used?*

It is well known that pine is very prone
to sparking owing to the large proportion of resin in the wood. This could
only be minimized by seasoning or de-
laying its use for firewood as long as
possible. Undoubtedly it would be better
to cut trees for firewood in the autumn
or winter when the sap has ceased to
flow.

Flagstones – Cleaning

I have flags here of a hardish blue-grey
stone, commonly used in the locality.
All that is done to them is to wash with
clean water, but I have heard that some
of the locals used to wash occasionally
with milk (wipe over, that is) to give a
shine. I have some of the same stones
laid in a courtyard, these having come
from a nearby cottage which was
demolished for road widening. A few
of these have flaked and produce dust,
and I thought that they were naturally faulty, but would not now be surprised if it is not being exposed to the
weather. I have used silicone water-
proofing on the ham stone on the outside
of this house where it is exposed to
driving S.W. winds, and had excellent
results as regards waterproofing. I would
suggest that if the flags which are crumb-
ling were to be coated with a similar
compound (it is quite colourless and
sinks into the stone like water) it would
be possible to wash off the dirt without
wetting the stone to make it crumble.

Flies – Plague of – 1

*Each year we have trouble with flies
getting into the first floor rooms of our
house, usually during the latter part of
October and the month of November,
and even though windows are kept tightly
shut and are reasonably well fitting they
still seem to find a way in. This year
there have been so many flies, and even
with constant use of insecticide killing
off thousands of them, I am tempted to
write and ask you if you know the reason
for this trouble and whether you are
aware of any method of tackling it.*

We cannot understand why you are
getting such a swarm, unless they have
found suitable breeding conditions in
your area this summer and are now
seeking warm winter quarters. One of
our members found that an area beneath
the windows of his house facing south
was a breeding ground for thousands of
flies' eggs. Although this was filled in and
sprayed, the flies still continued to swarm
there on a warm day. Fly-killer only
killed the flies but left the eggs to germinate. He did, however, have some success
with an aerosol called " Moth Doom "
which had to be applied from time to
time.

Flies – Plague of – 2

I was interested to read the letter concerning a plague of flies getting into
first-floor rooms. We had the same
trouble on south-facing upstairs windows.
We tried everything, finally found the
answer. Hermetically fitting screens outside the windows, of very fine gauze
which hardly shows. Nothing else was
any use at all.

Flies – Plague of – 3

I was interested to read of the Member
who suffers from a plague of flies. If his
house has sash windows, as ours has,
I think he will find that the flies live
and breed inside the sashes, coming in
and out by the holes up and down which
the sash cords go. We finally solved our
problem by pouring Residual D.D.T.

down the holes by means of a squeezy bottle. We had to do it frequently at first, but in the end we succeeded completely, but we still do it occasionally, to be on the safe side.

Flies – Plague of – 4

I have been interested in reading letters concerning plagues of houseflies. We have a small holiday bungalow in Cornwall, and in early October we suffer from thousands of houseflies which come to nest in window sashes, cupboards, and any other dark corner they can find.

We have tried Flit and a D.D.T. spray but without completely eradicating them. I noted in one letter that " Residual D.D.T." applied at regular intervals proved effective. I have been unable to obtain this stuff locally. Can you tell me where and how it can be found?

The residual D.D.T. mentioned in a letter published was Murphy Residual D.D.T.

Footnote—In view of bad publicity D.D.T. has recently suffered we would recommend Vapona Strips, which you can hang in a room and which last for several months.

Fly-trap – Baiting

I have a Victorian glass fly-trap and I would like to know what mixture was used to bait it. So far I have tried treacle and water, which went bad without a single fly being entrapped.

I remember a glass fly-trap in my childhood in the early 1900s which was baited with stale beer and sugar.

The fly-trap was similar in shape to the old-fashioned glass bedroom water bottle, with the bottom cut out and the rest curled inwards and upwards to make a sort of circular trough about an inch deep and an inch or so across, and stood on three glass feet. Flies and wasps crawled underneath and flew upwards, and after drinking were unable to escape by normal straight flight. Ours had at one time a glass stopper but this got lost and the hole at the top was closed with a cork. My recollection is that it was very effective.

Cut Flowers – Make last

In the flower stem there are a great number of very thin tubes, as fine as a hair. They are called capillaries. Through these capillaries the water is conveyed from the vase to the leaves and flowers. This is essential to compensate for the water which regularly evaporates from the flower and the leaves and to dissolve and convey food to all parts of the plant. So we must see to it that these capillaries are always open, when we put flowers in the water. This is done by cutting a small piece from the stem, thus making an open wound.

Splitting the stem does not open the capillaries. By crushing the stem with a hammer the capillaries are closed. Cutting a piece off with scissors also causes a narrowing or closing of the capillaries.

An oblique cut made with a sharp knife causes the least damage to the capillaries. The cutting is necessary, because during the transport from the florists or from your garden to your house the capillaries take up air instead of water. The part filled with air must be cut away, because the air has caused the capillaries to shrivel and so hampers the absorbing process.

Drooping of flowers is caused by an insufficient supply of water. In normal water thousands of infinitesimally small impurities are formed, which cause clogging of the capillaries.

A new crystal solution from Holland (Chrysel—obtainable from all large florist shops) keeps the water clean and the capillaries open. Moreover, it contains nourishing components so that the flowers continue to grow normally, spread their fragrance and keep their colours.

Cut flowers in the country are not quite such a problem as in towns where they may cost twice as much and last half as long, but now with this substance or plant food it is possible to keep cut flowers as fresh in the vase as they would on the plant, and in addition it keeps the water clear and odourless. It is not necessary to change the water if the vase is kept topped up with the solution. Once made from the crystals the solution will keep for weeks in a corked bottle. A further advantage is that the plants retain their colour. Roses in bud, placed in this solution, will come to full bloom without any of the buds dropping. Lilacs and dahlias will not wither even in warm rooms. Cut flowers are placed in rooms which can never possess the same light or heat to which the plant has become accustomed when growing, and flowers in plain water, moreover, miss the natural growing elements which can now to a greater extent be supplied by these flower crystals.

Leaves

If you wish to preserve leaves, the best way is to stand them for a couple of weeks in a solution of half glycerine and half boiling water, well shaken to ensure good mixing. This method, however, will always turn them a rich brown. If you let the stems stand in the solution too long or use too much glycerine, they sometimes 'sweat' the glycerine through the leaves making them sticky and unpleasant. You may need some experience before you learn how to avoid wasting the glycerine. Another good rule is to choose leaves that are tough and strong, as you will find some of the more delicate ones break up when dry.

To dry the flowers, hang them in bunches, up-side-down, in a dry, airy place. Do not imagine that you can achieve the desired colour of shape by leaving them in a damp place, such as an old potting-shed or cellar. They will only go mouldy or lose their colour, and, if you try to dry them in the sun they tend to bleach. A large cupboard, an empty room or open shed will all do, but remember to keep them away from damp, sunlight, and if possible, dust. Pick your flowers just before they reach full maturity. Peonies, for instance, with petals too far open, fall apart when they are dry; but if you pick them in bud they will lack colour and be inclined to hang their heads. This rule applies even to seedheads. Do not wait until sorrel goes a beautiful rich red-brown, pick it while still green, it usually goes brown as it dries, and will not then scatter its seeds all over your table.

It is fairly safe to say that double flowers dry better than single ones, though many of the single ones have very attractive seedheads.

Flowers – Drying and Preserving

Roses can be preserved by picking them in the budding stage, just before the petals open. Dip the severed ends in hot wax and then wrap the complete rose and stem in tissue paper. They can then be stored in this condition for several months.

Delphiniums can be preserved for several months if the tall spikes are cut, to the length required, when in full bloom but before any of the petals begin to fall. The stems should then be hung upside down so that the moisture in the stems flows back to the flowers. When the stems and blooms are completely dry, they should be very carefully handled. The petals will not fall off and the colour will remain, although slightly faded, for several months.

Flowers – Everlasting

None of the flowers that we grow are in the true sense of the word 'everlasting' and when this descriptive word is used horticulturally, it is generally in a comparative sense. Several genera (mostly belonging to the natural order Compositae) produce flowers of a tough papery consistency, which, if gathered, and hung downwards in a dry, clean place before they are fully expended will dry well, and retain their form and colour for a long time if placed in dry vases, after their stems have been hardened by the drying process.

Everlasting Flowers
Ammobium (Everlasting sunflower).
Helichrysum (Everlasting flower).
Xeranthemum (Immortelle).
Several varieties of all the above.

"Foxing" in Prints and Drawings

Can you tell me how I can get rid of some brown spots that have appeared on some prints of mine?

'Fox' marks are the reddish-brown spots to be seen on prints, drawings, and old paper generally. The exact cause of these marks is difficult to determine, but damp is a predisposing factor. There are a number of ways of dealing with the trouble, all more or less effective.

Immersion in a fairly strong solution of sodium chlorate, followed by washing in clean water, has often been used with success. A solution of equal quantities of hydrogen peroxide and absolute alcohol applied with a fine brush will often deal with the trouble.

If in doubt send the pictures to a restorer. Local antique dealers will probably recommend someone. If not ask for an address from the Association of British Picture Restorers, 43 Albemarle Street, London, W1.

French Polishing

Can you give me any information on French polishing of furniture; is there anybody who teaches this? I was looking for a part-time occupation. I do not know if it involves long training or if it is a paying proposition.

You will find that French polishing should never be used on antique furniture. For new wood one should obtain a perfect surface with fine glass paper. The surface should then be very lightly oiled with linseed oil. French polish can then be applied using small quantities applied with a wadding covered with an old soft covering cloth. Very little polish should be applied at a time. When the first coat has hardened it should be rubbed down again with very fine glass paper and the process repeated until a high polish is obtained. The polish can be obtained ready for use from a paint shop. Undoubtedly you will require a lot of practice before you become an expert in the process. Whether it is a paying proposition or not will depend upon the time it takes to do the job and the value you set on your own services.

Furniture Polish – Recipe

I have a clock, I think Regency period, either walnut or walnut veneer, it is about 1 ft. high, maker Brockbank & Atkins. The wood has become very dry, probably due to central heating. What should I do with it?

Many modern polishes put a wax finish on furniture, which eventually prevents oil ever getting into wood. We gave a recipe for a mixture which feeds the wood and keeps it from drying out in sun or central heating. It is as follows: One part best vinegar, two parts boiled linseed, one dessertspoon of methylated spirits to each pint of the above mixture. Shake well in a bottle before and during use. Apply in small quantities at a time.

(*See also* page 38.)

Furniture Scratches

How can I get rid of some scratches on my furniture, also some rings?

To remove the scratches use Topps scratch cover polish and new type pen applicator. To get rid of the rings use Topps Ring-Away.

Cigarette ash will remove ring marks equally well.

Method: Put a damp cloth into a full ash-tray, picking up the ash and apply as if polishing.

Furniture Storage

If it is desired to store upholstered furniture in the cellar, the question arises as to whether the formation of mould and general damp on the upholstery can best be dealt with by (i) some device to absorb the humidity of the air, (ii) improved ventilation to create an air-current, or (iii) space-heating. If (iii) is the answer then the point arises as to the minimum temperature to be maintained to ensure that under conditions of normal British winter humidity the moisture can be retained in the air and not imparted to absorbent surfaces such as upholstery. Can you perhaps inform on this?

We have contacted several organizations on your behalf concerning the storage of upholstered furniture in a cellar, but we have not received a satisfactory reply. It appears that the use of substances to extract dampness from the atmosphere such as 'Silicagel' are an uneconomical proposition. The only solution is to see that the cellar is properly ventilated and heated and of these two factors the most important is ventilation. Heating should be supplied by a regulator heater or oil stove, and the necessary attendance on these would ensure regular inspection of the furniture to see if the upholstered surface is being kept dry. Some form of ordinary sheeting over the furniture is necessary, but plastic sheeting may only result in dampness by condensation.

Furniture – Sunbleached

How can I restore the colour of my furniture, which has been exposed to the sun?

We suggest you use the following recipe: 1½ pts. linseed oil, 2 tablespoons of draught vinegar and 2 tablespoons of turpentine. Shake well each time before applying with soft rag. Boiled linseed oil is most essential and can be obtained at all ironmongers.

Game – Hanging

Can you give me some general rules about hanging game?

It is almost impossible to lay down any definite time for hanging game as so much depends on individual taste, the state of the weather, the condition of the birds, and the storing accommodation. Most game birds should be hung for a certain length of time, otherwise they will taste little different from the ordinary poultry. A young bird will not require so long hanging as an old one, and one that is badly shot or bruised in any way will not keep well.

The condition of the weather will affect game very much, dry cold weather being much better for keeping purposes than close or damp days, when the birds need to be watched closely as it may go

bad very quickly. When game is hung it should be unplucked and undrawn. For all practical purposes game is ready for cooking when the tail feathers will come away easily when pulled, but it must be remembered that if it is required to taste high when cooked it should smell, disagreeably so, beforehand.

Wild ducks and other water fowl should be used fresh. Their flesh is of a very oily nature and soon turns sour; in cold dry weather they can be kept only a few days. Small birds too, such as snipe and woodcock, that are cooked without being drawn, should not be kept for long.

A rabbit should be used fresh, and must be paunched at once. If it has to be kept a day or two the skin must not be removed until just before the rabbit is to be cooked; this prevents the flesh becoming dry. Tie two of the feet together and hang up on a hook in the larder.

Times for Hanging Game, etc.

Venison	...	...	14 to 20 days
Hare ...	...	...	7 to 10 days
Pheasant	...	...	2 to 3 wks.
Grouse	...	...	3 to 7 days

Gilding

Leaf-gold is applied to a number of surfaces, usually by means of gold-size, which is a weak glue especially adapted for the purpose, made from boiled linseed oil and ochre.

Picture and mirror frames are prepared by covering the wooden base with several coatings of a mixture of whiting and size. When this has hardened, it is covered with a thin coating of gold-size on to which the leaf-gold is pressed. It then receives a final coat of size or varnish.

For water-gilding the work is first sized. When this is dry the leaf is laid on with water. It is finished with a coat of varnish as before. The term water-gilding has also been applied to a kind of gilding in which the gold is first reduced to a fluid state by dissolving in mercury.

Fire-gilding is effected by applying an amalgam of gold with mercury to the object, afterwards volatilizing the mercury with heat.

Gold-gilding on silver is effected by dissolving gold in aqua regis. A piece of rag is dipped into the solution, burnt, and the ashes rubbed on the silver. In this way the metal is deposited as finely divided particles.

Gilding sometimes needs burnishing. An agate or bloodstone burnisher is commonly used, the work afterwards being washed over with vinegar. Since a burnisher improves with use, a second-hand one is usually the most desirable.

In electro-gilding, the most modern process, leaf gold suitable for the restoration of the sort of gilded articles to which it can be applied is purchased in 'books' containing the sheets interleaved with tissue. They are extremely thin and both skill and practice is needed to apply them. The amount of gold in a book containing 25 leaves each 3¼ in sq, amounts to about 4 grains. Can be obtained in several shades.

Gilt Frames – Cleaning

I have before me an old copy of Mrs. Beeton 'New Edition 1869' and find what might interest you.

(2467) To brighten Gilt Frames.

Take sufficient flour of sulphur to give a golden tinge to about 1½ pints of water and in this boil 4 or 5 bruised onions or garlic which will answer the same purpose. Strain off the liquid and with it, when cold, wash with a soft brush any gilding which requires restoring and when dry it will come out as bright as new work.

This recipe I tried on an old picture frame and found it did no harm and cleaned the gilt very well.

Glasses – Chipped

Is there any method of taking out or rubbing down chips on the drinking edge of glasses? Perhaps you could recommend if this is at all possible or a firm which deals with this?

If the chip is not too deep, and you are very careful, this can be ground down by hand on a double-sided oil stone, finishing off with the smooth side and

using plenty of oil. The rough side will cause minute splintering when used. If you feel that you cannot tackle the job yourself, you could try contacting one of the following professional glass repairers: F. W. Aldridge, Ltd., 2, Ivy Road, London, E.17. (Tel Leytonstone 3717.) G. Garbe, 23 Charlotte Street, London W1 (Tel. Museum 1268.)

Glass – Chipped

Do you know of any method to make a chipped glass good?

You can rub the edge of the glass very gently all around with a sheet of fine sand paper if the chip is only a slight one. If larger, it would be better to have it done professionally by a firm such as Thomas Goode, South Audley Street, London W1.

Glasses – Remedy to Stop Cracking

Do you know of any remedy to stop glasses cracking in hot water?

Place the glasses in a pan of cold water and gradually bring them to the boil – and keep boiling for one or two minutes before removing This can be done with glasses of any quality and will (or should) cure them for life.

Suggest you try with Woolworth glasses before your best Waterford!

Glass Decanter

If the stopper of a glass decanter gets broken off at the neck whilst in the decanter and nothing is left outside to catch hold of, how can the broken portion be extracted?

The thing to do is to hold the decanter under a hot-water tap until the glass is warmed through and then, holding it upside down, tap the neck gently with a heavy piece of wood. Under no circumstances must you hit the bottom of the decanter, as this action will only drive the stem further in. You can also try using easing oil, leaving it to stand for

Chimney—Incessant Smoking

(See page 8)

quite a while before tapping the neck again as previously suggested.

Glass Decanter – Removing Stopper

I was amused by your reply and advice on broken stoppers of decanters having dealt with the matter for several friends. If your advice is followed and works, which it seldom does, the broken fragment falls to the sink or basin and is damaged, so that subsequent repair is impossible. The proper procedure is this: (1) Put the decanter vertical in a reasonably warm place, e.g., the kitchen. Place a few drops of *penetrating oil* (not lubricating oil) around the broken edge of the stopper. Leave for 12 hours. (2) Fix the end of a piece of good string to some firm structure; not a tap or a door handle because if you do, you will pull it off. (3) After 12 hours place two or three blankets on the floor at the site of operations. (4) Grasp the decanter firmly in the right hand (unless you are left-handed, in which case reverse instructions). Grasp the free end of the string in the left hand, coil it around the neck of the decanter two or three times and maintain gentle pressure on the string with the left hand; move the decanter rapidly back and forth between the fixed structure and the left hand. This, by friction, generates heat on the neck of the decanter, but not on the broken stopper. When quite warm up-end over the blankets, tap lightly with the hand. Out comes the stopper undamaged. Tap of course the body, not the bottom of the decanter. *Repair:* Join the two pieces of stopper with clear Bostik. Follow instructions. *Prevention* (which is alleged to be better than cure, although as a doctor I doubt it). (a) Never replace stopper of a washed decanter until both it and the stopper are at the same temperature. This may take three hours. (b) Always after partaking of a filled decanter, before passing to the left, rotate the mating surface of the stopper between the forefinger and thumb. (There is no lubricant to equal a little human sebum.) It may excite some comment from initial hosts, but upon explanation you will find that you are invited again.

Glass – Cloudy Marks

Can you advise me how to get white cloudy marks off the inside of a decanter?

You could try using hydrofluoric acid. Pour in a sufficient quantity of dilute acid (2 per cent is suitable) and allow it to remain for half a minute. Subsequently pour off the acid and rinse the glass with copious amounts of running water. Stinging nettles are also effective. Stuff head first into the decanter full of water and swizzle around every 30 minutes and it goes in a few hours.

Grimed Glass – Cleaning – 1

Having lately modernized a cottage and replaced a cracked skylight with grimed glass obtained from Carlisle station roof, which is being entirely re-roofed, I wondered how to clean it. The glass having been in use for more than 100 years was black with soot from the trains and from numerous factory chimneys in Carlisle. The glass was opaque with fine lines running down it, making a corrugated surface on the outside. To clean the glass *soak* well for at least quarter of an hour with undiluted paraffin. Wash off with hot water. The glass I obtained from the station had this treatment and became as clean as new glass. The man who cleaned the glass for me said tractor vaporizing oil or diesel oil would be equally effective.

Grimed Glass – Cleaning – 2

I see that a Member asks how to clean grimed glass. Has he tried the really marvellous cleaning power of snow? When the snow is thawing it should be very firmly brushed or rubbed off, and it is astonishing the amount of dirt that comes with it.

Gluwein

Can you please give recipes for hot

Gluwein, which is popular in Swiss-Austrian ski-ing resorts. It varies considerably in different places.

We suggest that you try the following recipe: 3 sugar lumps, 1 slice lemon, 1 slice orange, 1 clove, 1½ pints claret, small piece cinnamon stick. Put all ingredients in a saucepan and slowly bring just to the boil. Strain and serve at once.

Gold Plate – Cleaning

I would be grateful for any advice you can give me on the cleaning of gold plate.

Gold is best cleaned with soap and water, because if it is reasonably pure it will not tarnish. Tarnish which will not yield to this treatment means that other metals are also present. Ammonia solution applied with a soft rag will probably be all that is necessary in such cases.

A more drastic treatment is immersion in a 5 per cent solution of potassium cyanide (quantum vis). The object should not be left overlong in the solution, and after removal should be thoroughly washed in running water to remove all traces of the cyanide. We must warn you that this substance will dissolve gold in course of time.

Gold Leaf – How

I am anxious to learn the technique of gold-leafing wooden and metal objects and wonder if you can put me in touch with a person or reference book who or which would give me the necessary information.

We regret to say that we do not know of any book or person who could be helpful; of course, gold-leafing is a specialized job done by craftsmen. Gold leaf can be bought in books from a reputable colourman, and the following information may be of interest: 'Leaf-gold is applied to a number of surfaces, usually by means of gold-size, which is a weak glue especially adapted for the purpose, made from boiled linseed oil and ochre. Picture and mirror frames are prepared by covering the wooden base with several coatings of a mixture of whiting and size. When this has hardened it is covered with a thin coating of gold-size on to which the leaf-gold is pressed. It then receives a final coat of size or varnish. For water-gilding the work is first sized. When this is dry the leaf is laid on with water. It is finished with a coat of varnish as before. The term water-gilding has also been applied to a kind of gilding in which gold is first reduced to a fluid state by dissolving in mercury. Fire-gilding is effected by applying an amalgam of gold with mercury to the object, afterwards volatilizing the mercury with heat. Cold-gilding on silver is effected by dissolving gold in aqua regia (one part nitric acid to three parts hydrochloric acid). A piece of rag is dipped into the solution, burnt, and the ashes rubbed on the silver. In this way the metal is deposited as finely divided particles.'

Ham – Home-cured

Fifty years ago I used to stay in Yorkshire and much enjoyed locally cured hams. The flesh was brick coloured and had a marked tang in taste. Recently I purchased a so-called York ham and it tasted just like boiled bacon. Can you tell me where I can obtain a ham with a tang or, alternatively, a recipe for curing a ham to produce the same result?

Here is an old Yorkshire recipe: 100 lb meat, 21 lb brown sugar, 4 gallons water, 8 lb common salt, 2 oz saltpetre. Place the salt, sugar, saltpetre and water in a large pan. Bring to the boil and skim until quite clear, then allow to cool. Place the meat in a clean, hardwood barrel. Add the brine. Cover closely and weight the cover down to keep the meat under the brine. The meat does not require any turning or handling during curing. No good purpose will be served by placing a layer of salt in the bottom of the barrel. It would be preferable to make up a fresh supply of brine if there is any reason to think that the pickle is not strong enough. As regards the length of time that the meat must be kept in the pickle, you may be sure that the brine has not strength enough to overcure, but it has sufficient strength to keep the meat for any length of time. The time that it is left in pickle should depend to a large extent on the strength of cure desired. One day to the lb is reckoned for immediate use, but twice this time will be required if better keeping bacon is wanted. When taken out of pickle wipe and hang out of doors to dry. If liked, the meat after it has been cured sufficiently may be smoked with good hardwood sawdust. Wrap it in calico and store it in a cool, dry atmosphere so that it keeps well. The meat will keep indefinitely in the pickle, but will not keep long after it is removed from pickle. It is better to dry-salt bacon when wanted to keep for any length of time.

Mrs. Beeton has numerous recipes in her Cookery Book.

Heat and Paintings

I am shortly moving to a house where central heating by means of radiators is installed. I should be glad of expert advice as to whether such heating will adversely affect eighteenth century portraits if hung above, or in the vicinity of such radiators. The portraits are in reasonable condition and have been recently re-varnished.

Some little risk is associated with bringing pictures into a centrally heated house. It would be a wise precaution to keep the pictures away from the radiators as far as possible (especially avoiding hanging them immediately above them) and it is also sometimes advisable to have a bowl or tray of water in the room which will increase the relative humidity by evaporation.

Heat Stains

I shall be obliged if you will kindly advise me on a problem we have at my church school-room – a stone-built building with a slated roof, in use every Sun-

day afternoon and three or four times a week in the evening. Last autumn we had the room redecorated – ceiling distempered white and the walls pale-green oil-bound distemper and at the same time the old coal-burning Tortoise stove was dispensed and four gas wall heaters installed, fixed approximately 8 ft up on two walls. Within a few weeks during last winter I observed the ceiling flaking badly and the upper part of the walls going black, and by now the walls are in a very dirty state and in an unsightly condition. Previously, when we used the coal-burning stove the walls never got into this state. I shall be glad if you will kindly give me your opinion as to whether this is due to condensation and lack of ventilation through the gas fumes. We propose to redecorate the room again very shortly, and before doing so we would like to have expert advice on how to avoid further discoloration and what type of wall paint to use.

You will find that gas, electric, and hot water heating apparatus if placed against walls will often cause heat stains. The only thing to minimize this effect is to put a shield over the apparatus in order to deflect the fumes. Should you use a wall paint, then we suggest that this should be of the washable variety and cleaning should be done fairly frequently to avoid any chemical from the stains eating into the paint surfaces.

Ink Stains – How to Remove

There are some ink stains on a new carpet. How can I remove them?

You do not say whether it is ball-pen ink that was spilt or ordinary ink, so I am taking it that it was ordinary ink, and would recommend the following method:

'Sponge the soiled part, using the lather only of a detergent on a white cloth, and then wipe with a dry cloth. If it is a light coloured carpet, it may be treated very carefully by sponging with a liquid made up of 1 part hydrogen peroxide and 2 parts ammonia. This will remove some of the colour from the carpet, and then a weak solution of the dye the same colour as the carpet is needed and should be applied lightly, using an old tooth brush.'

I am afraid this stain will be very obstinate as it has been allowed to dry.

Ivory – Maintenance

I have just brought back from West Africa some small hand-carved ivory figures. Is any treatment of these desirable or necessary to maintain them in good colour and condition?

Ivory is extremely brittle and requires careful handling. It is dangerous to soak it in water, but it can be wiped with a damp sponge. It can also be cleaned and polished with powder pumice or whiting applied on a damp cloth or soft brush.

Jackdaws – Getting Rid of Them

1. Burning sulphur or other noxious fumigant in the fire of the chimney selected by the birds. The birds will tend to come back unless the fumigation is constantly repeated and where there are many disused chimneys this method is hardly practical.

2. Wiring the chimneys. Some who have tried this for years have found it most unsatisfactory. The birds constantly succeeded in breaking through or displacing the wire. Often the snow accumulated on the wire netting and blocked the chimney. Moreover, if the chimneys are very tall scaffolding is required to do the wiring effectively. As constant replacement is necessary if there are many chimneys, this method is not a practical one.

3. Alarm clock. Fix an alarm clock to the end of an 8 ft pole, and set the alarm to go off at 3 am and push it up the chimney. For those whose nerves will stand the strain of such an early shock this seems a simple and practical suggestion.

Personally we've had a family of jackdaws nesting in one of our chimneys for years and they do no harm. We regard them as old friends.

Lacquering Door Knockers

I wonder if it would be possible to obtain advice on lacquering of door knockers and brass handles exposed to the weather? I would appreciate any help or advice you can give.

We recommend that you use a paint called " Joy." This is applied sparingly on to a clean surface. Alternatively you could try an aerosol lacquer called " Ormolac," or Goddard's new long-term brass cleaner. This is not a lacquer, but the brass stays clean for a considerably longer time than if the usual type of brass cleaner is applied. It must be remembered that no lacquer is scratch-resistant, and when the handles need to be re-lacquered you must remove the old lacquer with acetone.

Lacquer – Restoration of Moulding

The best material for modelling small replacements has to be found by experience, but plaster of Paris suitably coloured with a " lacquer " paint would probably be as effective as anything.

On articles to which it can apply, a good cleaning and polishing paste can be made from flour and olive oil. It should be applied with a soft pad, wiped off, and the article polished with a soft silk rag.

Lavender – Distillation

Several ingenious methods are employed to extract the aromatic oils from the plants ; the principal one is distillation —the heating of the plant tissues to the point where the volatile oils vaporise, to be cooled and condensed in the still ; this is usually done in the presence of boiling water or steam ; and when the vapours condense the oil is readily separated from the water, with which it will not mix. Alternatively, the oils may be extracted by solvents such as alcohol or simply expressed by pressure. A delicate process, employed to capture unsullied the fragrance of jasmine, takes advantage of the fact that the odorous oil is both volatile and soluble in fats ;

fresh blossoms are laid on trays of lard, and as the oil is released it is caught and held, to be extracted and concentrated later ; this method is called in France *enfleurage.*

Lavender cutting is done in July or August, as the plants come into flower, and should be carried out as early in the day as possible, before the sun evaporates the fragrant oil ; the plants yield best in dry, sunny summers. After drying in the shade the flowering tops are distilled with boiling water, but from an acre of lavender only about twenty pounds of oil are obtained each season, for a ton of flowers may yield only ten pounds of oil—truly a precious harvest.

Leather Bindings – Preservation

I have some leather-bound books, the leather finish has become very dry, and in some cases is flaking off.
Could you please tell me the best method of treating the leather for preservation?

There is leather preservative called the 'British Museum Leather Preservative' which is a formula originally made up by the British Museum containing lanolin, etc. This is a liquid and is inflammable so cannot really be put in the post, but can be bought at a bookbinding firm called Sangorski & Sutcliffe of 1 Poland Street, London, W.1.

Leather Polish

With reference to the letter on Leather Polish, I have found the following formula to be quite successful: 1 pint wood turpentine (not turps substitute); 1 lb. beeswax ; 1 pint water ; 1 oz. potassium carbonate. *Method :* Heat, but do not boil the turpentine, and in it melt the beeswax by cutting the latter into small pieces. Boil the water and in it dissolve the potassium carbonate, mix the two solutions, while still hot, in a large bottle and shake vigorously when a pale yellow creamy fluid will be produced. The potassium carbonate acts as an emulsifying agent which is essential to produce the creamy consistency your correspondent requires. I have also found this to be a good polish for furniture.

Leather – Preserving – 1

I have some military leather which I wish to store away for my son, now aged 2. Can you recommend any preservative which will keep the leather supple for a further 18 years without losing the shine in the end?

We contacted the Leather Institute, and they say that the length of time you wish to store leather is immaterial as long as the conditions are right ; also it is unnecessary to put anything on it to preserve it. Make sure that where you store the leather is not air-tight—leather likes air, and needs a current of air, even if it is very slight. The storage place must not be damp. It would be better not to store it in direct light, as leather tends to fade. It is advisable to inspect it at least once a year to see that it is all right. The Institute tell us that they have some leather which is 3,000 years old and has never had anything done to it, and has kept perfectly well.

If you have any further queries, we suggest you contact the Curator, Museum of Leathercraft, 9 St. Thomas Street, London SE1.

Leather – Preserving – 2

My son was recently commissioned and I have been able to pass on to him not only a Sam Browne ca. 1910, but sword ca. 1930 and a pair of mess Wellingtons which had belonged to my father—who retired around 1906, so heaven knows how old they really are. The leather is magnificently supple and the shine impeccable.

Some time between 1906 and 1910 my mother polished them with wax and put them away in an old hat box. In 1968 they emerged as if time had stood still.

Leaves

Do you know of a method to preserve leaves ?

The usual method of preserving leaves is to stand them in a jug containing two parts water to one part glycerine. Leave for about 3 weeks, then put them under a carpet or mattress, to flatten them. The important thing is to pick the leaves before they cease to suck up moisture and to crush the ends of the stems to help them to draw up the glycerine mixture.

Lemon Squash

How can I make Lemon Squash with a low calory recipe?

We suggest that you write to the Good Housekeeping Institute, Chestergate House, Vauxhall Bridge Road, London, S.W.1. Alternatively, there are many good cookery books for slimmers in which you should be able to find a good recipe.

Unique Liqueur?

Some forty years ago, I inherited from a relative a full-sized and sealed bottle of a liqueur called 'Monastere' Liqueur. At the time, I was informed that this Distillery was no longer in production. I have never seen a reference to this liqueur in a catalogue and I wonder what is the interest or value of such a bottle? The bottle, which is still intact, is the same size and shape as a 'Dom Benedictine' bottle.

Mahogany – Repolishing – 1

I have an old mahogany dressing table which is solid, not veneered. The polish, in particular on the table top, has been damaged many years ago by rain and sun light at an open window. The appearance is of faded patches where pools of rain sat and pock-marks where the drops stood.
I would like to repolish the table top myself. What methods are there for the complete amateur with nothing but elbow power and enthusiasm?

Since the dressing table is solid it may be better in the long run to plane or sandpaper the surface to its original wood if the present stains are not too deep.

This wood would take a high polish.

If you prefer to make your own polish a good recipe is as follows: 16 parts bees-wax, 4 parts resin, 1 part Venice turpentine. Melt the ingredients in a double sauce-pan over a low flame. Remove from the heat and allow the mixture to cool. Whilst still warm stir in 12 parts of turpentine. Add a little colouring if desired. Many of the proprietary polishes may be better than anything you could make yourself. You could try 'Antiquax' or Goddard's Furniture Cream.

Mahogany – Repolishing – 2

In reply to a letter you suggested a member should sand or plane the top of his mahogany dressing table. This is a difficult and tedious job besides removing all semblance of age from the furniture. By far the easiest way of improving old furniture is to remove the old polish with paint stripper, and repolish; either with wax, slowly building up a good finish over a period of time, or by a thin layer of French polish to seal the wood before waxing. Any stains (ink, burns, water, etc.), which remain after stripping can be removed with diluted oxalic acid, applied with wire wool and elbow grease! Oxalic acid can be obtained from most chemists and diluted with boiling water; use fairly strong for dark stains. Apply with fine wire wool, always use *with* the grain not across, and leave at least four hours to dry before applying wax or polish. Please dissuade your readers from planing or sanding – especially in the case of antiques as this renders them virtually valueless.

Mahogany – Repolishing – 3

I had a walnut dressing table in a similar condition – badly bleached by sun and rain. I was told of a wood dye called *Joy*, made for oak, mahogany, walnut, ebony, etc., by Turnbridges Ltd, London SW17, which would restore it. I found it worked beautifully. Painted on, left to dry, then repolished with a good furniture cream. A small bottle costs 2s., is ample for several applications if more than one is required. The member might like to try this simple remedy and if not pleased could then plane as suggested.

Mahogany – Repolishing – 4

I was most interested to read the letter and reply on repolishing mahogany in the January 1967 magazine. Last year at home in England I had a very similar mahogany dressing table. I rubbed it down most carefully and sanded it with an attachment to a power drill till it was beautifully smooth. I then carefully built up many fine layers of polish using only antiquax till it was a joy to behold! However, it is close to the wash-basin and try as I might I could not prevent some drops of water falling on it. All of them (even those which can hardly be seen at the time) quickly developed white stains which were very hard to remove. Is there anything I could no to alter the polish or seal it in some way without spoiling its beauty?

We think you may have to start all over again, using the process described in your letter. There are some wood polishes on the market which claim to preserve polish but we cannot, of course, vouch for their efficiency. We have heard of a substance called *Seal*, but this may possibly be for vinyl and other tiling, therefore it may not be applicable for wood. Some very high and durable finishes for mahogany can be obtained by using clear Polyurethane varnishes, but you may not approve of this type of finish.

Mahogany – Repolishing – 5

With reference to an enquiry regarding the sealing of mahogany against water. I have a table of this timber which is left out day and night on my patio in this very humid climate, and which suffers wetting from rain and condensation from cold drink glasses – entirely without blemish. It is sealed with Ronseal (obtainable from any good store) a polyurethane material which can be easily applied by the amateur, and which can provide a finish anywhere between high gloss and dull matt, merely by mixing a little powdered china clay with the Ronseal before application. The duller

the finish required, the more china clay should be added.

Mahogany – Repolishing – 6

With reference to resurfacing of old wood, my experience may be of interest. I have a fine William and Mary marquetry table – the wood was Sussex bleached, the inlaid flowers were scarcely visible. I took a chance and stripped to the wood with an electric sander and gave a coat of polyurethane which looked awful so I rubbed down with fine wire wool for an hour or more and then polished with pure wax using a lamb's wool mop to my drill. Result marvellous and the extraordinary thing is that the clear transparent polyurethane varnish brought back the rich colouring of the wood and grain.

Mahogany – Repolishing – 7

White marks on polished mahogany caused by water or tea, etc, can be removed by applying a paste of salt and olive oil; leave it on for 20 to 30 minutes, then wipe off and polish as usual. The sooner this paste is put on after the damage the better. The paste can be left on longer in cases where the damage has not been treated at once; if left on too long it tends to darken the wood.

P.S. – I have dealt with cups of hot tea spilt on the tablecloth on an old mahogany table and treated an hour later after the party, successfully.

Marble – Cleaning

Some years ago you answered a query on how to clean the surface of marble. I should be most grateful if you could repeat this information.

Ancient marble must be cleaned with care, because the surface develops a patination with age which should not be lightly regarded. White marble will not be harmed by washing with a good quality soap and water applied with a medium-hard brush. For pieces of lesser importance, a little ammonia can be added to the water. Stains can often be removed with a 5 per cent solution of oxalic acid. Oil-stains will usually yield to a paste made from powdered kaolin mixed with benzene, which should be laid over the stain. The area immediately underneath the paste will need repolishing. Petrol, alcohol, acetone, and benzene are all safe to use as stain removers. Chloroform will remove bees-wax. Acids attack marble and should not be used. Soap and water can be deleterious to some coloured marbles, and their use is a matter for experiment.

Marble Slab –Cleaning

I have a marble slab which is stained extensively with blood from a butcher's shop. Can the stains be permanently removed? I am told that stains which are removed return again; is there anything that will prevent this?

We feel that you will have great difficulty in getting rid of these stains. The porosity of marble differs according to the variety. Some marble definitely 'sweats' under certain atmospheric conditions so that stains may disappear and reappear. Unless the marble slab is of particular value we think that it would be far better for you to get another slab and scrap the old one. They can often be picked up quite cheaply in builders' yards or junk shops.

Meals – Easy-to-make

Could anyone advise me where to get some recipes for easy-to-make meals? I am a bachelor living alone.

I should like to reply to the Member (Lancs.), who enquired about Easy-to-make meals.

A few years ago, the *Daily Telegraph* published a pamphlet by Bon Viveur entitled 'Cooking for One'. This is very easy to follow.

There is also a book called *Everyday meals for Invalids* by May Tremel, published by Stanley Paul and Co. Ltd. I cannot say if this book is still obtainable. In spite of its title, the book contains many good recipes, easily prepared for one person.

I write from experience, for I am an old bachelor myself.

Medlar Jelly

I was surprised to see in your reply to an enquiry the statement that medlars are only used for eating raw. A delicious jelly is made from them, the recipe for which is as follows: Put ripe medlars into a pan, cover with water and stew till reduced to pulp (about two-thirds of their original bulk). Strain through a jelly bag. To every pint of liquid add ¼ lb. sugar and boil till it sets. Tie down in small pots like jam. This jelly should be a lovely rosy pink, quite clear, and we think it is one of the best accompaniments to vanilla ice-cream, as well as to all the usual breads, etc. This recipe is pre-war. Nowadays I find a little extra sugar seems necessary.

Mirrors over Fireplaces

I see in an article on Fire Protection that mirrors should not be fixed over open fireplaces. This, of course, is where they are usually put. Is this an old wives' tale or is there a logical explanation? I am intrigued to know what it is.

The answer is that this is purely a precautionary measure against accidents by fire. We cannot stress too strongly how dangerous it is to place a mirror directly over a fire; a person has little option but to lean over the fire in order to look at themselves in it. More accidents occur in the home than anywhere else. Let us do our best to avoid them.

Moths – Cedar Repellant

I have a query concerning the use of cedar wood as a protection against moths.

Is there any truth in the old supposition that trunks, chests of drawers, wardrobes, etc., made of cedar wood provide adequate protection against moths?

I have heard that this is so, but I have never observed it for myself or met anyone who could confirm it. You will appreciate that large pieces of furniture or trunks made of cedar wood are rarities on their own account. I cannot remember ever encountering anything larger than a cigar-box.

Muffins – Recipe

Ingredients: ¼ lb. plain flour, ½ oz. yeast, 1 tablespoonful sugar, 1 oz. margarine, ½ pint milk, 1 egg, pinch of salt.

Method: Cream together the yeast and sugar. Add the margarine melted in the warm milk and well-beaten egg. Pour this mixture over flour and pinch of salt.

Cover, set in a warm place to 'prove'. Grease a tin or griddle, place as many muffin rings as required, drop the mixture, allowing 2 spoonfuls to each, and bake till the muffins are firm on top. Lift the rings and turn the muffins, which should be allowed to cool before being toasted, split and buttered.

Needlework Sampler

I have in my possession a child's needlework sampler done, apparently, in silks on linen and dated 1794. Although this has been securely framed under glass, after such a long period of time it has become dirty and discoloured. I wonder if you could advise me as to cleaning and restoration, as I hesitate to attempt the washing of a fabric over 170 years old.

The textile department of the Victoria and Albert Museum tell us that as long as the colours of the silks do not run you would be able to wash it by hand – before this date the coloured silks were not fast dyes, but by 1794 they were using fast dyes, so yours should be all right. To test the colours, damp a piece of cotton wool and try each colour to see if any comes off. If it does not, then you can wash it gently by hand, or we understand that the Royal School of Needlework undertake this work. If the colour comes off, you will have to have it dry cleaned and a good firm for delicate work such as this is: Lilliman & Cox Ltd, 14 Princes Street, Hanover Square, London W1.

Noise

I live in an old Georgian mansion that is well built and the problem of noise does not often arise, but there is one particular case that is proving difficult to overcome. Two rooms are separated by large and heavy mahogany doors 1¾ in. in thickness, with a space of 2 ft 3 in between the doors. As it is not desired to have access to the rooms through these particular doors, I have had one of them sealed, then on the inside of this door I was advised to hang – in curtain fashion – a roll of glass wool. I then enclosed the glass wool with a sheet of Treetex or Celotex (a soft boarding about ½ in ihick). The space between the original doors is now used as a wardrobe. After carrying out the above work I regret to say that I am worried by the noise from a TV set and a radiogram used in the adjoining room by an elderly couple who, through some deafness, have the volume louder than I would have it. Do you advise putting a second thickness of the glass wool and another sheet of soft boarding? Or is there some better method of insulating against sound?

The precautions you have taken are quite right and we wonder if the noise is coming directly through the walls or perhaps through ventilator bricks via the flooring or some other unnoticed aperture. If space permits you could try the effect of a small air space about 1 in. or more between your layers of insulating material.

Oil Painting – Cleaning

I recently acquired an oil painting which is covered with dirt and thick varnish. It is most unlikely to be valuable, being painted on board of Victorian date, but I would like to clean it enough to see some of the underlying picture. Can you please tell me how to clean enough of it to be able to decide whether it is worth sending to a professional cleaner?

We have consulted the Chief Restorer at the National Gallery on how best to clean an oil painting. He does not advise an amateur to attempt this, because it calls for a great deal of skill and experience, but he says you could try washing down the surface with a very little soap and water 'like a small boy washing his neck,' without getting the picture wet. When it is dry put on a layer of thin varnish. This will clarify the picture and you can then decide if you want to clean it yourself. This can be done with a mixture of one part of weak acetone to five parts of white spirit, but again the Chief Restorer cannot guarantee any good result and does not recommend it to the amateur. Acetone fumes are of course poisonous, and care should be taken when using it. We suggest that you may like to practice first on a picture that you are quite sure is valueless, in order to gain some experience.

Ormolu – Cleaning

Could you please tell me how best to clean ormolu mountings on clocks and furniture?

Ormolu castings can usually be cleaned by scrubbing with soap and water to which a little ammonia has been added, rinsing in clean water, and drying well before replacement. Occasionally it will be found that such castings have been coated with a shellac varnish to save the trouble of cleaning. This it does at the expense of appearance, and before the metal can be cleaned the varnish must be removed with a solvent. Ormolu castings are sometimes gilded, in which case they need to be washed with care, and a soft brush. If the gilding has worn off in patches, regilding is indicated. If the dirt is obstinate, brush the surface with a solution made from: 2 parts alum, 65 parts nitric acid, and 250 parts water. As soon as the gilding is clean, wash carefull and dry.

Ormolu – Gilding

Do you know of any preparation which I could use to gild ormolu?

We suggest you try Treasure Gold, which is sold at good art shops. It is quite expensive – about £1 for 5 cc. The gold is in very finely divided dust form – possibly collordale carried in a medium of hard wax. The gold coloured wax is rubbed over the part to be treated with a finger or small soft pad. This can subsequently be burnished to match the original.

Treasure gold comes in various shades between copper and silver.

Paint Brushes – Cleaning

Can anyone tell me how to get hard paint out of last year's paint brushes? Soaking in turps substitute does not seem to work.

An old country recipe is to boil up the bristle part of the brushes in cheap vinegar until they become soft.

Paint Removing – 1

I have a Georgian mahogany table that has been painted white. I intend to try and remove this with paint remover, but am not sure how to polish or treat it once I have got the paint off. Would you be good enough to let me know what to do?

We have been in touch with an expert on antiques and great reservations were expressed about restoring this table if it is genuine Georgian.

What needs to be done is for paint remover to be applied and the paint removed with nothing more radical than wire wool. There is considerable danger of scoring the surface if any more drastic implement is used. Our expert advised that as this is the most expensive part of the work and it takes a great deal of time, you would be well advised once the table has been cleaned down to take it to a french polisher and have it french polished professionally. Our expert's main advice was to have the restoration done by a professional restorer because of the risk of doing irreparable damage.

Paint Removing – 2

Could you please give me some advice on stripping varnished pine doors and skirtings? There is a great deal of moulding so that scraping or sanding presents a real problem.

The wood has also been stained and we wish to remove this to achieve the

Can You Suggest Any Treatment for Woodworm?

(See page 49)

natural wood finish. Is there a safe bleach for this purpose?

We suggest you buy some paint stripper which can be bought at any ironmongers. As far as removing the stain from the door we think you will have to sand it down, either with emery paper or wire wool, and it might be a good idea to experiment on the door to see what is effective.

Paint Removing – 3

I have recently purchased a Queen Anne house in which two rooms are pine panelled. The panelling at present is painted with at least three coats of cream paint. It is my intention to strip the paint and leave the panelling in its natural state. Could you suggest the best way of stripping the paint and dressing the pine panelling to give a smooth finish?

We think any good paint stripper would be the best thing to use, although it will probably require several applications. The use of a scraper, except very carefully, should be avoided. Light sandpapering, using a fine grade, after the paint has been removed should give the surface you require, and if you wish to darken the wood a little then we would suggest a light dressing of linseed oil.

Panelling – Oak – 1

I have some oak panelling in the hall which has gone a lovely silvery grey, but is very dry and obviously wants feeding. Can you please tell me what to use, if possible without darkening it too much?

An application of linseed oil or a mixture of turpentine and bees-wax should be applied. Here is a good recipe: 1½ pints linseed oil, 2 tablespoons draught vinegar, 2 tablespoons turpentine. Shake well each time before applying with a soft rag. Boiled linseed oil is most essential, and can be obtained at all ironmongers' stores.

Panelling – Oak – 2

With reference to the letter concerning treating oak panelling, I can only suggest from experience of teak, not oak, that linseed tends to darken the wood. In India we had a lot of furniture made of Indian teak, and to begin with it was a wonderful silver grey. Unfortunately it had to be stored for various periods during the war, and we treated it liberally with linseed in hopes of preventing warping and splitting. The wood is now almost the colour of mahogany.

I remember my old bearer producing a marvellous patina when the furniture was new with 'heel-ball' (which I think is a pure wax), lemon and water, also plenty of 'elbow grease.'

Parquet – Reviving Wood Block Floors

Parquet wood block floors can normally be revived by sanding the old surface to bring out the natural beauty of the wood below. If the floor is an old one then the blocks will probably be about ¾ in thick, so the slight reduction won't be missed.

The sanding of the old surface can be done by hand with some sandpaper wrapped around a building brick, but this can be a tedious and rather lengthy job. Better to use an electric floor sander which can usually be hired from a local builder or floor laying firm. Alternatively you may be able to get a reasonable quotation for having the job done for you.

Once the sanding is done and a new layer of wood is exposed the surface should be sealed with a proprietary sealer to seal up the pores in the wood and afterwards apply a good wax polish.

Don't overdo the application of the polish—a little at a time is all that is required.

Pewter – Cleaning of – 1

I have a modern pewter rose-bowl the inside of which has become stained or corroded as a result of having flowers in it. The bowl comes from Williamsburg, Virginia, and the cleaning instructions were 'soap and water', but the stains do not yield to them. Can you suggest any safe treatment?

Whiting may serve your purpose. If not you could try a mild abrasive.

Pewter – Cleaning of – 2

Would you please advise me on how to clean a pewter tankard which is very blackened with age.

The black on your pewter tankard is what the collectors call the Patina, and most dealers and collectors would be horrified if you made it bright and clean. An occasional wash in warm soapy water is all it should have. Another method for cleaning really heavily soiled pewter, if so desired, is to apply powdered whiting mixed with a few drops of oil and then rub up with a soft leather.

Pheasants by Mail

In an article Mr Gaslee advocates packing game that is to be sent by post in a stout box. In the course of my life I have sent and received quite a lot of game of various sorts none of which has even been parcelled in any way, nor to my knowledge suffered in transit. Surely it is cheaper and easier to attach a label to the bird's neck and post it like that. This also takes care of the ventilation problem. I should be interested to know if others also parcel their game and if this is done to preserve the game from damage or the Post Office staff from temptation?

So far as your letter is concerned, I cannot agree that his method is the best. Nevertheless, he has found it acceptable over a long period and so no doubt he will continue with it. Not only, to my mind, is there the question of possible damage to the birds (and the new parcel sorting machines really are vicious), but there is a risk that the label will come off. I am pleased all has gone well for him with this method, and wonder if others have been as lucky.

John Gaselee.

As far as I know labels have always worked with pheasants sent to me. My wife would be delighted to confirm safe receipt if anyone is in doubt, and would like to send her one.

Editor.

Pictures – Cleaning – 1

Some time ago you recommended cleaning pictures with a product called Klinos. Do you still recommend it, or has some more recent discovery succeeded it?

Quite frankly, we feel that the safest method of cleaning a painting for an amateur is to use a damp piece of cotton wool and distilled water. This can do no harm at all, whereas one does not know what is in the cleaning products on the market and one could easily do some damage by using strong acids and detergents.

Windsor and Newton make a product called Winton which is sold for 7s 6d a bottle, but I am afraid we have not tried this at all.

Pictures – Cleaning – 2

I feel I must challenge one of your statements in your published reply to 'Cleaning Pictures'.

As one who has been conserving oil paintings for a good many years, I can assure you that to use cotton-wool swabs and distilled water may well do very considerable damage: if the picture is in a certain condition, i.e. an old one, which will be covered in 'Craqueleur', and where the varnish film has deteriorated. Moisture will seep through to the support and loosen the paint-layer more than it may be already. This incidentally will not readily be observable.

To 'clean' an old oil painting it is necessary to remove the discoloured varnish, and to do this is a highly skilled art. I should have thought, then, that the best advice you can give any future enquirer is to apply to The Secretary, The Association of British Picture Restorers, 43/44 Albemarle Street, London, W1, who will put the picture owner in touch with a suitable restorer at far less cost than if he had approached a picture dealer. And the picture will not suffer!

(*See also* Oil Painting – Cleaning, page 33.)

Pipes

I have some pipes running through my loft which are always getting frozen up each winter. Is there some way of permanently lagging them?

Melt an equal quantity of vaseline and paraffin wax together, and, after wiping the pipes perfectly dry, apply with an old brush a thick coat of this mixture while it is hot. An old lamp or torch will easily keep it in a liquid state. You will find that, no matter how cold the weather may get, the frost cannot penetrate this coat of grease.

Furniture Polish – 1

Can you give me a good recipe for furniture polish?

16 parts bees-wax
4 parts of resin
1 part of Venice turpentine.

Melt the ingredients in a double saucepan over a low flame. Remove from the heat and allow the mixture to cool. Whilst still warm, stir in 12 parts of turpentine. Add a little colouring if desired.

A polish for dining table tops calls for 1 quart of cold-drawn linseed oil, which must first be strained and then gently simmered for 10 minutes. One-quarter of a pint of spirits of turpentine should then be added to the oil and the polish is ready for use. This will produce in course of time a brilliant finish which will resist heat from dishes and plates.

(*See also* page 21.)

Furniture Polish – 2

I have found that 1 part best vinegar, 2 parts boiled linseed, 1 dessertspoon (approx.) methylated spirits to one pint of the above. Mix in bottle. Shake well before and during use. Use a little at a time and *rub well in*. This mixture *feeds* the wood, and keeps it from drying out in sun or central heating. Many modern polishes put a wax veneer on the furniture, which effectually prevents any oil ever getting into the wood.

Pork Sausages – Recipe

I wonder if you can give me a recipe for home-made pork sausages?

The following recipe is very satisfactory, but you may like to vary the seasonings once you have tried it a couple of times: Put through the mincer 2 lb lean pork, 1 lb fat pork, 1 lb fresh breadcrumbs. Add ½ oz pepper, 1 oz salt, ¼ oz sage, pinch of nutmeg and pinch mace. Put through the mincer a second time and fill into casings.

New Potatoes – Cooking

For 30 years we have grown new potatoes and tried many varieties. In the end we have come back to Sharpe's Express as having the best flavour. Now, however, these potatoes always break up in boiling. Can anyone tell me what is the reason?

No, but if you steamed them they would not crumble.

Pot-pourri

How do you make Pot-Pourri?

This is made in two different ways: by a dry method and a moist. The first is easier and quicker, but the moist process is better, giving a sweeter, and more enduring result.

In the dry method the rose petals are completely dried; preferably on sheets of paper in an airy room. The lavender and sweet geranium leaves and any other ingredients are also made quite dry.

In the moist process the material is only partly dried, so that it has a tough, leathery consistency; it is then put into a well-glazed jar, a good handful at a time, pressed down and sprinkled with a salt mixture, consisting of equal parts of bay salt and common salt. The bay salt, which is sold in lumps, is roughly pounded, so that some of it is quite small and some the size of peas, and is mixed with the common salt.

Materials. The usual materials for potpourri are: rose petals for a good half or more of the whole bulk, sweet or scented geranium, sweet verbena, bay leaves and lavender. If a preponderance of rose petals is secured the exact proportions of the rest do not matter; the supply is sure to vary from year to year. Anything may be added which has a lasting fragrance from possessing some kind of essential oil.

How to make. If the pot-pourri is made on rather a large scale it is convenient to prepare the different ingredients in separate jars. But everything is treated alike in being put into the jars, salted and pressed. The layers should be about ½ in thick after pressing, and the salt over each layer should be enough to show evenly all over without actually covering. It is important that the roses should be picked when free from rain or dew; they should be just full blown, but not overblown; the petals are picked off and separated, and laid out in a room to become half dry. No definite time can be given for this but it usually takes from two to three days. The leaves of the sweet geranium are torn into strips, and take about as long to dry as the rose petals. Bay leaves, lavender and sweet verbena have less natural moisture; they can be put straight into the jars without any special drying. The material is not only pressed down in the jars as it goes in, but must also be weighed down by means of a wooden disc that nearly fits the inside of the jar, and a stone or other weight. The wooden presser may have to be in two pieces if the jar narrows at the neck. When all is ready a mixture of spices and sweet gums is prepared; a suitable quantity for a bulk of two-thirds of a bushel would be: Mace, Cloves, and Cinnamon, half an ounce of each, all pounded; and violet powder, a quarter of a pound. The prepared rose petals would be found to be in close, flaky masses that must be carefully broken up by hand and well mixed up with all the rest and with the spice mixture. The same spice mixture can be used for both kinds of pot-pourri.

Prints – Stains

I have a number of framed prints, many large ones, which are showing small yellow spots (presumably damp). I would like to know (a) *whether these spots can be eradicated; (b) whether such work must be professional; (c) whether, if not, what can be done at home to help? And further, I know that prints have been out of favour for many years. Mine were mostly collected at the turn of the century and are mostly signed. I believe I am right in saying that only a small number are signed and that these are called 'first impressions' and are more valuable than others. (d) Are they today of any value at all? (e) Is it worth spending any money on them?*

For the yellow spots we would suggest immersion in a fairly strong solution of sodium chlorate, followed by washing in clean water. A solution of equal quantities of hydrogen peroxide and absolute alcohol applied with a fine brush will often deal with the trouble.

This work can be done yourself but if the prints are really valuable it might be best for them to be done professionally. We would suggest you get into touch with Sotheby's at 34 New Bond Street, London, W.1, telling them what your prints are and the condition they are in, and they will be able to advise you as to their value and the advisability of restoring them yourself. They will be able to suggest a suitable restorer if this is necessary.

Sanding – Floor-boards

I should be grateful if you could give me some information about polishing ordinary floorboards. I gather that instead of staining the boards and then polishing, which is never very satisfactory, there is a process called sanding, and I wonder whether you could let me know how this is done. I believe this makes the boards a light honey colour, and then one can polish them and the result is permanent.

Sanding is done by a power machine which may often be hired locally, probably from advertisements in your local press. After sanding, it is necessary to put on a sealing component, which the sanding firm will recommend.

Silver-Tarnish

We are going abroad for some time

and have to store various silver things. Can you give me any advice on storing this silver and plate properly so that it does not become spotted or deteriorate in any way.

It is best to store the silver in absolutely clean, dry tissue and brown paper (dry this in an airing cupboard for a couple of days) in a dry atmosphere. We have also heard that it can be kept quite bright if it is enclosed in an air-tight polythene bag.

Sloe Gin – 1

During the war whilst stationed in Northern Ireland I made excellent sloe gin: ⅓ pricked sloes, ⅓ sugar, ⅓ gin, and 3 kernels from sloes slightly crushed put into one container. I only made three wine or gin bottles full, but it really was good; *do not use almond essence,* you will be surprised at the tremendous strength and fragrance of almond from the kernels.

Sloe Gin – 2

My family have used the following recipe for sloe gin for the past 60 years: 1 quart sloes (cleaned and stalked), 16 oz. best candied or loaf sugar, 1 oz. sweet almonds, ¼ oz. bitter almonds, 1/12 oz. Jamaica pepper corns, 1 clove, ½ gallon Plymouth gin. Shake or stir on way three times a week for ten weeks, strain and bottle. Keep at least a year before using.

Sloe Gin – 3

I have been making this for some 15 years and the method is as follows: prick the sloes and drop them into the jar, add the gin, add the sugar and shake up every day for a week or so. Leave it for two or three months, decant it, and drink it. Now as to proportions, I only make a bottle or so of it, and for small amounts the quantities are 1 lb. sloes, 1 pint gin, 12 oz. sugar. The amounts are not critical, except possibly for the sugar, and for the sort of quantity you are thinking about it would be 4 lb. sloes,

3 bottles gin (nearly 4 pints), and 3 lb. sugar. I have supervised the making of this for a neighbour who makes this sort of quantity, and I have got an idea that it does not come out so well when made in larger quantities. I always make it in gin bottles, and I think mine tends to be better than my neighbour's. A convenient quantity for a gin bottle is ½ lb. sloes, ¼ pint gin, and 6 oz. sugar, which just about fills the bottles to the shoulders. When I first made this the only sort of sugar available was ordinary granulated and this was quite satisfactory, but nowadays I use demerara, which I think is better. I have never used candy sugar simply because it was not available when I first started making it. I made some one year with honey, but we could not see that it was any different from that made with sugar, but there was nothing wrong with it. I should go easy on the almond essence; I have tried this and it only needs two or three drops to the pint. Better still is to grind up two or three bitter almonds and drop in, but I should not do this if you think it is too cloying. Incidentally, if you leave the sloes in the gin for a long time you get a slight almond flavour from the sloes, presumably from the kernels.

Smell Remover – Hands

A useful tip for people who have to handle fish, rabbits, poultry, onions, is to add half a teaspoonful of ordinary mustard powder to the soap lather on your hands when washing them.

Smoke Box – For Meat or Fish – 1

Could you please tell me how I can obtain a design of a Smoke Box suitable for home use for smoking fish or meat. Information on this processing would also be appreciated.

These are obtainable from H. Hardy Brothers (Alnwick) Ltd, 61 Pall Mall, London, SW1. The make is called the Abu Smoke Box, and is suitable for smoking both fish and meat. It consists of a square metal enamelled box, mounted on a stand under which is inserted a small fuel container. The box contains a lattice and a lid.

To smoke, first gut, clean and dry the fish then amply rub in salt. Sprinkle a level layer of sawdust over the bottom of the oven. Put the lattice into its right position then lay the fish or other food-stuff on the lattice and shut the lid. When grilling leave ½in. opening in the lid. Fill the fuel container with methylated spirit, put it exactly under the fire ground and light the asbestos wick. In approximately eight minutes the fire has extinguished itself and the fish is ready to eat. This special form of 'pressure smoking' gives a delicious smoked fish, fat and juicy. The smoker can also be used for grilling purposes – an altogether splendid little device for anglers who like to smoke their fish out of doors.

Smoke Box – Home-made – 2

I wonder if any of your readers could help with advice as to how to make a small 'smoker' for smoking fish such as herrings, mackerel, etc.?

Use a bottomless barrel and some bricks. Place a sheet of iron on the bricks and leave openings at the sides for smoke to enter. Make a sawdust fire (oak or ash preferred) and keep it smouldering gently. Hang fish from rods across the top of the barrel and place a damp sack over the top.

Sparrows in Roof

I should be most grateful if you could tell me how to prevent sparrows from nesting in our roof, which is made of stone tiles. They get through the inter-stices.

You might try covering the roof with small-meshed wire netting, as is done with thatched roofs. Sometimes it is pos-sible to cement the lower edges of the tiles, but we think this remedy is none too good, because unless the work is properly done rain water may back up against the cement filling and force its way under the tiles. The only other sug-gestion we can offer was one sent in by a member who managed to stop sparrows from burrowing in his thatched

roof by placing long sticks thickly coated with ribbons of DAK rat-catching paste at strategic points on the roof.

Squirrels in Lofts – 1

S.O.S.—Save Our Sleep! For many months we have been invaded by squirrels in our loft. Ours are of the grey variety with, I'm con-vinced, hob-nailed boots. They so far have chewed through a lead main water pipe (which flooded the bathroom), eaten cwts of poly-styrene sheeting and are having, for dessert, fine portions of our beams, etc. We have tried several deterrents, including smoke bombs, used primarily for wood-worm. I have put rat poison down. But, they still come regularly and do a Fred Astaire routine during the night.

So, Sir, that is our problem. Do you know of a solution?*
*Quick—please!

I am glad to see that your sense of humour has not deserted you in spite of such travail. I was on the point of suggesting that far from having Fred Astaire you might have got Ginger Rogers stashed away in your loft.

However, to be serious—squirrels are difficult to get rid of and if you shut a large cat in your loft they can be quite aggressive and the poor cat might come off worse. The real solution is to find some method of keeping them out, if you can find out where they are getting in. If they are invading under the eaves the best thing to do is to get some fine mesh wire netting and block up all access so that they cannot get inside. Firstly you have to make sure that there are no 'tap dancers' trapped in the loft before you close it off.

I take heed of your warning about putting a cat in the loft. What could be worse than having a badly mauled pussy around the house.

Experiments have been tried with wire mesh but, unfortunately, we have a sort of mock Tudor style house with eaves all over the place—in addition to which we had a large room built in the roof some time back which means that certain holes are inaccessible and are therefore unblockable. Can any member suggest a solution?

Squirrels in Lofts – 2

Now about our friend (your March magazine issue) with squirrels in the belfry. Perchance a near neighbour of mine was similarly visited—and I make something of a hobby of this kind of headache.

Here we placed a break-back rat-trap in the loft. In fact, the squirrel won a Pyrrhic victory: it must have died the day after we went away for three weeks summer holiday. The atmosphere in the loft had to be seen to be believed—and nearly could. Our friend would probably succeed similarly if he put down something tasty for a day or two and then baited with it.

I think a more certain victory, though sticky, would be by using bird-lime. This material, of course, ceased to be so-called on the passage of a certain law, but was still sold as rat-lime. Messrs. Youngs, Misterton, Somerset, used to stock that and every kind of countryman's trap and gadget—and I have always found them excellent to deal with. In this instance, it should probably be smeared on 12 in. square pieces of newspaper, and these possibly arranged round a tasty morsel. The poltergeist would then, I suppose, appear to have changed from clogs to bare feet.

Lastly, acetylene would probably do the trick—provided you could be out of the house for a few hours. Being slightly less dense than air penetration down from the loft would be minimal unless there was something peculiar about the house air circulation—a matter which should certainly be checked. Anyhow, the stink is so strong that they would know if there was any serious concentration. Carbide is still obtainable, I think, and fairly easy to use.

The rat-lime is probably the best bet.

Squirrels in Lofts – 3

A simple and much less inhuman method than rat-lime is to place in the loft a 10 or 15 gallon oil drum with straight sides, half-filled with water. Then a baited piece of wood 10 in. by 1 in. by $\frac{1}{4}$ in. is delicately balanced on the edge of the drum over the water. Outside the drum the free end of the billet should be supported on something solid, say a box on end.

The principle is that the squirrel walks along the see-saw to get the food and falls in the water and drowns.

The depth of the water must be kept deep enough to prevent the squirrel reaching bottom, so as to spring out.

Over the years we have caught many squirrels (but no rats) in this way, and we always keep the gadget set up for emergencies. School-boyish but infallible! We use bread for bait.

Squirrels in Lofts – 4

While acknowledging that 'The Association accepts no responsibility for opinions expressed', I was so horrified at the directions on this subject, that I was astonished at your printing them.

We all admit that grey squirrels are a pest, but what is wrong with keeping one's loft (as we keep ours) properly protected with wire netting? I fully appreciate that pests must be dealt with, and that, regrettably, this often involves unavoidable suffering. But to go about my day's business, or settle down to my night's rest, aware that in my very house or on my own premises some poor creature was, quite unnecessarily, struggling for its life, I could not. I should regard myself as heavily to blame that, through my negligence, it ever got in.

Squirrels in Lofts – 5

I was surprised and disgusted to read a letter about a method of drowning squirrels in a tin. This, surely, is a most cruel and inhuman method of solving the simple problem of keeping squirrels out of a loft. The intelligent method is, of course, to block up the holes into the loft by which they gain access, as such holes will certainly provide access for other life.

I was surprised, too, that the Editor thought it proper to reprint the letter and now expect this letter of criticism to be published. The so-called 'school-boyish' method above must be answered as being one which would be found repulsive by most people, and surely not one advocated by the CGA.

Stains – Removal of

Can you tell me if there is any known solvent which might help in removing

old uric acid stains from cloth material
used in nursery furnishings?

There is something new on the market
called 'Biotex' which claims to remove
stains such as this. We have not tried it
at all, and we should have thought that
if the stains are old there would be little
you could do about it, except perhaps
dye the material a darker colour.

Stone – Cleaning

*One of the paraffin stoves which we use to
heat our small church burst into flames some
weeks ago and has left the wall in the vicinity
very black. The wall is faced with a very
porous light colour stone, not unlike sandstone. What should we do in order to clean
without damaging?*

We suggest you experiment by washing
the surface of the stone with warm water
containing 10 per cent ammonia. This
should dissolve the grease in the soot into a
soapy solution which can then be wiped off
with clear water. Great care should be
exercised in order not to damage the surface.

Stone Flags

*I should be grateful for any information
about how to clean a stone-flagged
kitchen floor now that people no longer
scrub on hands and knees. My flags
always look dirty no matter how we
mop and scrub them with a long-handled
brush.*

Frankly we do not hold out much
hope of obtaining any reasonable results
with long-handled scrubbing brushes.
Have you considered having the existing
flag stones covered over by some more
manageable surface which can be easily
cleaned by a long-handled mop?

Talking of long-handled mops a friend
of ours was approached by her new char
who said, 'Where's the Easi-Squeezie?'
'There isn't one,' our friend replied. 'It's
a case of Kneezie-weezies.'

(*See also* page 18.)

Stucco

*I want to cover some ugly red brick
additions to my home with stucco. Can
you suggest how I should do this?*

The character of the background on
which the stucco is to be applied governs
to a large extent the strength of the
mixes to be used. In addition it is essential that the surface to be rendered
should provide a good key and be well
cleared of dust or anything likely to prevent a satisfactory bond.

If the stucco is to be applied to brickwork, for example, the joints of the
brickwork should be raked out to a
depth of approximately ¼ in. and the
whole surface thoroughly cleaned before
the rendering coat is applied. Before
applying the first coat the brickwork
should be damped sufficiently to ensure
a proper bond between the background
and first coat. When possible the work
should be started on the shady side of
the building and continued round
following the sun, so that the stucco does
not dry out too rapidly.

In exposed positions stucco is applied
in three coats, and a typical mix for
brickwork can be as follows:

Spatterdash Coat: 1 cement, 3 coarse
and mixed with sufficient water to give
the consistency of thick slurry. This
should be dashed or thrown onto the
walls to give a thin nobbly uneven surface. This must be allowed to become
white dry before the application of the
next coat.

Straightening Coat: Composed as
follows: 1 Portland Cement, 2 hydrated
lime, 8 sand. This coat to be evened
with a straight edge (not trowelled) and
scratched up to form a key. Should be
allowed to dry before finishing coat is
applied.

Finishing Coat: Composed as for
straightening coat, trowelled up and
finished to required texture, when the
coat has partly set.

The straightening coat should not exceed ⅜ in. thick or be less than ¼ in. The
finishing coat should not be less than
3/16 in. thick or more than 5/16 in.

Various textures can be worked on the
finishing coat as required and colour
effects can be obtained by the use of
coloured cements.

A useful booklet, giving further information on the subject, is obtainable

free on application to: The Cement and Concrete Association Ltd., 52 Grosvenor Gardens, London, S.W.1, and is entitled "External Rendering."

Sword – Cleaning

I have a number of English and Indian Swords and Pathan knives which have been stored and got rusty. Please tell me how to clean them. Emery paper leaves them unsightly scratched. Can you recommend (a) any powder or liquid, and (b) any liquid to paint them with after I have removed rust so as to preserve them against the sea air here?

If you use the very finest quality sand-paper it will not scratch the surface. Sometimes a kitchen scouring powder will have the same good result. It is possible to purchase a liquid varnish from almost any ironmonger, which will then form a lacquer over the surface to keep rust from getting in, but in the course of time this does tend to yellow.

Table Mats – To Make

I should very much appreciate your advice on making the type of table mats which are so popular now, namely, those made of hardboard on which pictures are painted. In particular I should like to know how to ensure that the picture adheres firmly and how and with what to draw the gold edging surrounding the picture.

We think that you will find these are done with special machinery which applies heavy pressure. You could however experiment yourself by using any good hardboard or plywood and *Evostick* (which is a very strong glue) and as much pressure as possible, a hand press would be best in fact. After the glue is thoroughly dry, the mat surface could be glaze varnished by using one of the new polyurethane clear varnishes, which should be obtainable from any good ironmonger or art shop, if not they can be purchased from boat stores. Good gold paint must be obtained from an art shop such as Reeves and can be applied with a thick nib drawing pen, although we believe there is a special wheel device which is used by professionals for such work.

Tapestry – Cleaning

Where can I obtain advice on how to clean some very old tapestry which has become very dirty through dust settling over a period of years upon it?

The Victoria and Albert Museum suggests using a hand suction cleaner, applying this carefully to the back of the canvas. The front could be treated in the same way, but in view of the fragile condition it would be advisable to cover the hanging first of all with a fabric mesh such as a piece of embroidery canvas with an open weave; this method will free superficial dirt; but there would be no remarkable improvement in the general condition.

The ideal method would be to wash the embroidery if this could be done without risk of breaking the threads. It is, however, very important to make sure beforehand that the colours are fast. This can be done by testing small areas. Only soft water (preferably distilled) should be used. A soap known as saponin gives particularly good results.

Alternatively dry cleaning methods are indicated but without examination of the physical condition of the hangings it is difficult to give a safe opinion on either of these methods.

Thatch – Fireproofing

I have been given the following receipt for fireproofing a thatched roof:

'In 50 galls. of water dissolve: 28 lb. of Ammonium sulphate, 14 lb. of Ammonium carbonate, 7 lb. of Boracic acid, 7 lb. of Borax, 7 lb. of Alum.

Spray liberally on the roof.'

Can you please tell me what is the effective 'life' of this mixture? Also whether an insurance company would make any reduction in its premium if this treatment is carried out?

The life of the mixture concerned should last about three years according, of course to how much rain and severity of winter may affect it.

The Insurance Company will not make any reduction for fire-proofing thatch. We can, however, recommend an Insurance Company which offers very advantageous rates for thatched property if you would like to have their address.

Thatched Roofs – Bird Damage

I am having trouble with my thatched roof. It was covered with nylon net, but in the course of time and winds, the net has broken, and birds are now stripping all my roof. The point I am hesitant about is whether I can claim this repair on my house insurance policy? I have a comprehensive policy.

We see that you have a comprehensive policy on the buildings of your home and therefore if the damage to the net has been caused by a storm then we feel that you have a justifiable claim under your building insurance policy. Any claim will normally be subject to you paying the first £15. In addition the question of betterment may well arise.

On the other hand if the net was broken through normal wear and tear and gradual depreciation then unfortunately you would have no claim on your policy.

We do not feel that the company would entertain any claim for the damage now being caused by the birds stripping the roof.

Timber – Fireproofing

May I ask what methods are now common or recommended to give fire resistance in the treatment of timber?

As a simple chemical, the most commonly used is mon-ammonium phosphate, and that is the basis of a great number of fire resistant processes. There are two entirely different methods of making wood fire-resistant. One is impregnation, in the same way as you would use a preservative, in a pressure cylinder. The second method is by painting with a fire-resistant compound having a silica base, or another type of base; the former is rather heavy and

thick and adds to the weight of the timber, but gives a good fire resistance. There are dozens of fire proofing compounds. A few are used on a large commercial scale, but most of them are based on the same chemical. Borax is another chemical used—and boracic acid.

Tortoiseshell – Polishing

I have a recollection of a recipe for polishing tortoiseshell; could you please tell me the method?

Tortoiseshell can be cleaned safely with warm water. The surface is brought to a fine polish by using a buff, the wheel of which is covered with a cloth and charged with whiting. A power tool buffing wheel can be used for this purpose.

Trophies

I have a fairly large room which is 'decorated' with a great number of animal heads, some of which are very fine. These were all stored away in attics during the war and for fifteen years after the war, and many are showing signs of being moth-eaten and powdery. It would be impossible for me to afford to have them re-done. Is there any known method of spraying on some sort of preservative which would at least preserve them in their present condition and stop them deteriorating further?

The only moth-proofer that we know of in spray form is a product such as Cooper's Moth Proofer Aerosol. When sprayed, articles are protected for a period of about twelve months.

Trout – Smoking

How do you smoke Trout?

Scale the fish, split down the back, remove the head and all backbone except for a short portion at the tail. Clean and dry well, rub with a mixture of equal parts of salt and Jamaica pepper and allow to stand for 24 hours. Drain well, rub two or three times with a mixture of 1 lb. salt, 3 oz. brown coarse sugar, and 1 oz. saltpetre; allow to stand two days and repeat. Stretch fish on sticks, and hank it by tail in a smoking chamber. This can be improvised by using a bottomless barrel and some bricks. Place a sheet of iron on the bricks and leave openings at the sides for smoke to enter. Make a sawdust fire (oak or ash preferred) and keep it smouldering gently. Hang fish from rods across the top of the barrel and place a damp sack over the top. Time of smoking depends on how long you expect the fish to keep. Smoke 24 hours to keep it two to three weeks and three days for four weeks or longer. Small trout can be smoked fresh without preparation but should not be kept long.

(*See also* Smoke Boxes, page 40.)

Tweeds – Waterproofing

I find that when tweeds – particularly the soft Harris ones – are dry-cleaned, they return with a harshness in the cloth caused by the loss of the natural wool grease. Would it be practicable, in your opinion, to replace this grease by making up a solution of lanolin in a solvent such as ether, and immersing the suit in this? Have you any ideas of proportions?

There are several waterproofing substances for cloth on the market, usually obtainable from marine stores such as Captain Watts, of Albemarle Street, London W1, but these may not be suitable for your purpose. Your idea of mixing a solution of lanolin sounds very interesting, but it would be wise to experiment on a very old coat or a small section of the cloth such as an elbow. We cannot suggest the proportion of ether to lanolin, but in any case we think you should contact the Wool Council with your idea and obtain their expert advice since they undoubtedly maintain a laboratory for tests such as this.

Tweed – Cleaning

Although not yet a member of your admirable association I frequently have the pleasure of reading your journal. I was interested in an issue in which a member was mentioning harshness of tweeds after dry cleaning. For what it is worth, sir, I would suggest that it is practically always best to have Harris and equivalent tweed cleaned by the French (or wet) method and it will then be found that the material will 'bloom' afterwards and will have no suggestion of harshness whatsoever.

Varnish – Remover – 1

We have two lacquered copper trays which we want to polish. How do we get the lacquer off them, please?

Try using acetone (i.e., nail-varnish remover).

Varnish – Remover – 2

Reference the use of acetone to remove varnish. Most expensive and the acetone dries so quickly a film of cellulose is left. The trade use boiling caustic soda which I find is best. Have had experience over trays, furniture, fire screens and the like. Prewar I got short instruction privately on cellulose spraying. As a result I introduced it to the Army, where in command at Didcot Ordnance Depot actually showing the workshop staff how to handle the equipment. We ended up with 14 spray plants, mostly used for oil-based paint. My own plant I use on my yacht – oil paint – car, coloured cellulose and distemper in house. All my furniture is cellulosed also gilt picture frames, ornaments, etc., and articles of metal that do not get handled. (Above to put myself in the picture.) Boiling caustic soda is the best and cheapest way of removing old, clear or any cellulose if the article will stand it. The most difficult job is to cellulose furniture that has been french-polished – say a table, one scrapes the polish off, but it has gone into the grain of the wood, and all oil and grease must be removed. To clean filigree metal after removing the cellulose I have to take it to the trade who dip it in nitric acid for 1½ to 2 seconds. I cannot brush it on in that time. If longer it goes green. I have used 'Brushing Belco' – obtainable in cycle shops, it is cellulose with a retarder to allow time to apply with a brush. Quite good – expensive. At Didcot we mixed sand and oil paint and did a quarter of a million 'tin hats', two men running down a row of 50 at a time about two minutes. Previously by brush, two to three minutes per hat.

Varnish Removal

I have a small round Victorian table, mahogany, and it has been heavily varnished at some time. Would it be possible to strip off the varnish and re-polish – if so how would I do it?

If you do not mind going right down to the bare wood then any proprietary paint remover such as 'Stripit' will do the job. The instructions should be obeyed very carefully and the varnish can then be removed with a brush, but not scraped off or you will damage the surface of the wood and will have to smooth it again with sandpaper. The Antique Restorers' Handbook recommends the following furniture polish which may be suitable for your purpose: 16 parts of bees-wax, 4 parts of resin, 1 part of Venice turpentine. Melt the ingredients in a double saucepan over a low flame. Remove from the heat and allow mixture to cool. Whilst still warm, stir in 12 parts of turpentine. Add a little colouring if desired. A polish for dining-table tops calls for 1 quart of cold-drawn linseed oil, which must first be strained and then gently simmered for ten minutes. One-quarter of a pint of spirits of turpentine should then be added to the oil and the polish is ready for use. This will produce in course of time a brilliant finish which will resist heat from dishes and plates. There are also proprietary french polishes on the market which can be applied from the bottle.

Vellum – Cleaning

Can you tell me how to clean a vellum lampshade?

Make up a solution of one tablespoon-ful of pure soap flakes with one tablespoonful of water (mix well together so that the soap dissolves) and two tablespoonfuls of methylated spirit. Use a soft cloth to apply this solution then rinse it away with a second cloth moistened with methylated spirit.

If this does not work we are afraid we know of no other way of dealing with the problem, except to try with petrol.

Veneer – Repairs to

Can you advise me on how to repair a veneer surface that has become blistered through heat?

Blisters are caused by heat or damp, usually the former. The best way to lay them down is to cut them through the centre with a razor blade. A little glue can then be worked under the loose veneer with the tip of a thin blade, the spot being covered with oiled paper and subjected to heavy pressure until dry. The repair should then be almost invisible.

It is, of course, impossible to glue a veneer back to the carcassing if dust and dirt has penetrated beneath it. In this case it is usually advisable to cut around the blister in such a way as to raise a small flap. This will make it possible for all dust to be cleaned away.

For curved surfaces it is generally advisable to shape a block to follow the curve and to use this to apply the necessary pressure. A sheet of oiled paper between the pressure-block and the veneer will prevent adhesion due to any surplus glue being squeezed out.

Rough-cast Wall

I should be pleased to have advice on what I should use to clean a white rough-cast wall which has now a marked greenish-tinge. I suppose this to be due to a fungus growth in this very damp weather. Plants grow at the foot of this wall, therefore I could use nothing likely to be injurious to them. I should be grateful for any help you can give.

We think that you will find cleaning this a very difficult proposition and even if you use a detergent and water such as is used for cleaning buildings in cities it will still affect plant life unless the surface fluid can be diverted. We suggest that ordinary lime wash is the best solution and the small amount of lime which falls upon the ground may even be beneficial to the plants. Some very good exterior wall coverings with a cement base can be purchased. As an alternative, you could rub the greenness off as well as you can with a stiff wire brush and apply Dimanin. Care should be taken to avoid Dimanin falling on plants.

Walnuts – Preservation of – 1

How does one preserve walnuts? My old tree has a good crop, but the kernels always go mouldy.

There is considerable variation in the keeping qualities of different varieties of walnuts, so yours may be of a kind which 'naturally' tend to go mouldy. You should let the nuts reach full maturity and preferably fall of their own accord in October. If you are troubled by squirrels taking the nuts, pick them in October or shake the tree to bring them down.

Spread the nuts out for a day or two in a shed to dry and then remove the husks. After this thoroughly clean the nuts by scrubbing gently with clean water and spread out to dry in a warm airy place. The best way is to spread them out on wire trays so the air can circulate round them. Once dry store them in clean sand. It is a good idea to sprinkle salt on each layer of nuts before putting on the layer of sand. If kept too long in a dry atmosphere the kernels tend to shrivel and the addition of salt helps to retain a moderate moisture content.

Walnuts – Preservation of – 2

I have always found that they keep perfectly for up to two years, stored in a wooden barrel or box if placed in alternate layers with peat moss liberally sprinkled with salt. The nuts do not shrivel since the salt attracts moisture, neither do the shells go mouldy.

Water Deposits – Cleaning off

I should be most grateful if you can advise on the best way to remove water deposits on crystal flower vases and bowls. The water here is exceptionally hard, the rim it leaves is from chalk or lime. All usual liquid household products are useless.

There are various systems. One way is to use hydrofluoric acid, pouring in a sufficient quantity of dilute acid (2 per cent is suitable) and allowing it to remain for half a minute. Subsequently pour off the acid and rinse the glass with copious amounts of running water. One member has suggested a method he has found very successful. This is to fill about one-fifth of the bowl with lead shot – about No. 6, obtainable from any gunsmith – and then half fill with water. Vigorous shaking will then do the trick and the shot can be kept for further use. An easier method is to pour in some bleach such as is used in most households. This is usually instantly effective.

Weathercocks – Lightning Conductor

Can you tell me whether weathercocks on the top of a house are any more likely to draw lightning than, say, TV aerials? I have a weather vane made by Pearce's which I brought here on removal from our old house where it was on the roof of the stable. There is no place here where it will catch the wind other than the roof of the house. It is only a small house, but each gable end has a chimney stack, and, apart from the effect of smoke, the chimney stack would rather detract from its appearance. The most suitable spot is at a roof junction in the middle of the house, where it would be slightly lower than the tops of the chimneys. If you have any experience in such matters and there is no more fear of it attracting lightning than the chimneys themselves, I may as well have it put up, but there is no fear of my have a lightning conductor fitted.

Our expert advises that any metal object projecting into the atmosphere simulates a lightning-conductor component. A weathercock is the equivalent of an air terminal rod but has no down conductor to carry the current to ground. A television aerial has a wire leading to the set, and through it to earth via the electrical installation, but it is quite inadequate to carry a lightning discharge safely, so that consequential damage will occur in both cases if the building is struck. Neither can be said to 'attract' lightning, other than within a very localized field, viz, if the building is struck it is usually the highest point that takes the discharge, and of course the higher the object the greater the risk. The safest way in both cases is to provide an earthed conducting path externally.

Window Cleaning

To clean glass to make it better than new, put two teaspoonfuls of sugar in 1 pint of paraffin and allow to stand for 24 hours.

Apply this mixture on a cloth with some pressure, polish off, and later a film of white will show.

A final polish and the glass will be like new.

It is possible to apply this to filthy glass without previously washing dirt and slime off, but the glass is easier to clean if lightly washed first.

Wine – Home-made – Book on

I never succeed in making good home-made wine. Can you recommend a book on this?

Try *Guide to Better Wine-making for Beginners* by Mrs. Tritton, published by Faber.

Wines – Recipes

I have a surplus of blackberries, currants and raspberrys, and would like to make them into wine. Can you give me a recipe for these fruits?
Currant Wine

To every gallon of water put 4 lb of loaf sugar and 4 lb of currants clean picked from the stalks and bruised. Put the currants into half the water and the sugar into the other half, let it stand one

day and night and then strain the currants through a hair sieve. Put all together and let it stand one day to ferment, and then put into a barrel with no spurge hole and leave unstoppered till it has done working.

Raspberry Wine

Choose sound, ripe fruit, bruise it down into a measure and then turn it into a crock. Add an equal measure of cold water. Leave it for 24 hours. Strain through a jelly bag and leave to drip overnight. To each quart of juice add a pound of sugar. Stir occasionally until sugar is dissolved. Pour into a cask. Cover lightly, until fermentation ceases. Bung tightly. Keep for about three months before bottling.

Blackberry Wine

Measure your blackberries and bruise them. Then cover with boiling water, allowing one quart of water for each quart of fruit. Let the mixture stand for 24 hours stirring occasionally. Strain the liquid on to white sugar, allowing one pound of sugar to each quart of blackberries. Stand, or stir, the mixture until the sugar dissolves. Keep for a year and then bottle.

Wood – Hardening Surfaces

How can a dining-room table, made from a large piece of old furniture, be hardened to prevent it being easily scratched? Neither French nor wax polish has proved to be effective.

Strictly speaking, wood, if it is a variety which can be hardened, should be exposed to the weather for about seven years. I assume that the questioner means 'how can a non-scratch surface be produced?' I know of no application which produces a glass-hard surface on wood, but after light sandpapering I have found that two coats of Ronseal (clear) gives a surface which is very resistant to scratches on furniture and floors. Usual disclaimer.

Woodworm – Treatment

Can you suggest any treatments for woodworm and dry rot?

For treating furniture attacked by worm or beetle or for timber affected with dry rot, several proprietary preparations are on the market. Messrs. Cuprinol Ltd provide various solutions.

'Heppels Fluid' is a similar product for treating woodwork attacked by furniture beetle. This liquid is supplied by Regent Chemists Ltd, 70 Vauxhall Bridge Rd., SW1. Another suitable proprietary preparation called Benzine-Benzol is supplied by Messrs Baiss & Co, 274–276 Ilderton Road, London SE15. None of these preparations appears to damage the surface of furniture.

Woodworm – Alder as a Trap – 1

We are troubled in this old Tudor house with woodworm of various sorts and furniture beatle in nearly all rooms. Disinfection would be beyond our means even if it were possible, which I doubt. Some months ago I read an article or letter saying that if one put a block of alder wood, of the right age, in rooms and changed these annually, the beetles would always lay their eggs for preference on this alder and gradually disappear. Can you put me on to someone who could tell about the way to do this, when to change the wood, etc.

We are rather inclined to think that the use of alder as an inducement for woodworm to lay their eggs is rather an old wives' tale. It is possible that woodworm may have been attracted by this wood, but we feel that it is unlikely that they would go around looking for it.

Woodworm – Alder as a Trap – 2

Some years ago I cut down an alder and my gardener put it on the bonfire. Three times I retrieved it for burning in the house and each time he took it back to the bonfire. When I remonstrated he said that an alder should never be brought into a house. He was old and has now died, and I thought it was just an old wives' tale. But there is often summat in it, and it would be interesting if anyone had the real answer.

Woodworm – Alder as a Trap – 3

With regard to the letter in the August issue on woodworm, I entirely disagree with the editor's remarks! It has certainly helped me over three years. I now buy blocks of alder 6 in by $\frac{3}{4}$ in by 1 in from my wood merchant and drill holes 1/16th in in them each year. Sixty pieces of alder only cost approx. £1.

Editor: The gardener knew his firewood rhymes i.e. 'Make a fire of alder tree, Death within the house you'll see!

Making Yoghourt.

My wife, after successfully making daily yoghourt for many years past, has recently encountered failure of setting. She uses Eden Vale plain as culture and either fresh or dried milk gave the same result.

Perhaps a member could provide a hint in remedy please.

Failure *may* be due to using milk from cattle fed with antibiotics. This is a subject which Ministry of Agriculture and C.G.A. should have explored in much greater depth and detail. It may explain cases reported of children developing infections from bacteria, which are insensitive to therapeutic doses of antibiotics.

OUTDOOR (AND ANIMALS)

This section comprises questions and suggested 'self-help' solutions

Acre Sizes – Differing

Several years ago you published in the C.G.A. Annual Diary a list showing the different sizes of an acre of land in various counties in England. If I remember rightly an acre of land in Cheshire was equivalent to approximately 1¼ acres in say Warwickshire. I should be most grateful if you could supply me with a copy of this land measure.

We cannot find the list you refer to and, in fact, came to the conclusion initially that you were pulling our legs. However, I have spoken to Major Anderson, our old editor, and he is not absolutely sure that there might not be something in what you say.

It is true that the Irish acre is different—but this, of course, is only to be expected; but an Irish member tells me that this is because they leave out a certain amount for the walls in Ireland.

Perhaps one of our members may know the answer.

An Irish acre is equivalent to approximately 1 and 3/5ths English statute acres. Although Irishmen do not like to be reminded of it, the Irish acre was in fact invented by Cromwell, who when allotting land to his soldiers in Ireland instructed them to step seven paces to the perch instead of the recognised 5·5 yards; a pace in this instance apparently being synonymous with a yard, instead of a mere 30 in. as now.

The Irish acre is the standard measurement of land in the East of Ireland, but strangely is practically unknown in the West, where it is replaced by the statute acre.

I understand there are other 'local' acres, in particular a Kentish acre, but I am not qualified to speak on this subject.

A Member from Birmingham has come up with the following answer to your query:

Statute Acre	1·000
Scotch Acre	1·26118
Cheshire Acre	2·1157
Lancashire Acre	1·61983
Northumberland Acre	1·2245
Devon Acre	·8273
Irish or Plantation Acre	1·61983
Welsh Acre	2·000

Adders

Is there a cure for getting rid of adders (snakes)?

The only thing is to find out if possible where they breed (probably on a sunny bank) and kill the lot, young and old, by gas if you have any, such as was used in destroying rabbits, or else with gun shot.

Agricultural Training

I would like your advice on behalf of an 18-year-old boy who is leaving school in December. He has three A-levels, two B-levels and one D-level, possibly all in science. He wishes to work on a farm for 12 months prior to going to a university to study agriculture. Could you let me know the best way of obtaining a position on a mixed stock and arable farm?

You should approach the National Agricultural Advisory Service in the area in which your friend wants to work. Your local one is at Beeches Road, Chelmsford. They usually have a list of approved farms who will take students in every area and should be able to fix him up with something suitable.

Alder and Elder

Can you please tell me if an elder tree and an alder tree are the same thing. If not, could you roughly describe an alder tree and tell me its most natural habitat.

There is a distinct difference between an alder and an elder tree. The alder has a distinctive, rather elegant growth, with slender horizontal branches and dark foliage, heavy, but not densely distributed over the tree. In spring before the leaves appear, when rusty catkins hang down from every twig, it looks as if it belonged to a Japanese drawing or design. In the early post-glacial ages, when marshy land was widespread alder appears to have been a dominant tree throughout Britain. Now it only survives as a wild tree in places such as the Norfolk Broads and moist valleys of Wales and Scotland, where it forms small woods in association with birch, ash and oak. Its frequent use for holding river banks against erosion makes it a familiar feature of the landscape, and it is also often seen as a close narrow fringe on the water's edge of meres and lakes. The elder is such a commonplace shrub or tree that it hardly merits any description. It is particularly noteworthy for its clusters of flowers and berries.

Algae – In Pond

I have a pond in the garden but the water has turned green and looks unpleasant. Can I clear this in some way?

This is a natural happening and is caused by quantities of a single celled floating plant known as Algae. This tiny plant only thrives in water which is exposed to plenty of light. When other water plants are growing profusely in the pond the Algae is choked out. If the water is emptied out and the pond refilled the water would turn green again within a few days. The best method of clearing the water is to introduce some water plants especially some which float on the surface. The surface leaves will shade out some of the sun and so help to clear the water. The top could be covered with duck weed or by water lily leaves. Once the water cleared the duck weed could be flushed off with a hose.

Algae – Clearance of

Tell me if there is a preparation which will prevent algae growing on York stone paving and oak garden seats.

We suggest you treat them with deosan hypochlorite, which is not poisonous to vegetation.

Ant Hills

In one of my fields over the last five years, several ant-hills which were present have increased to such enormous proportions as to become a serious nuisance. I feel that the ordinary proprietary ant killers would be insufficient to cope with the trouble and would welcome any advice you can give me to help exterminate them. I would point out that cattle

graze in the field during the summer months.

Experts whom we consulted about your problem suggest that it would be advisable to harrow or flatten the ant-hills by some means then treat the area with Murphy Chlordane Worm-Killer at the rate of use recommended for controlling worms. Chlordane is very effective as an ant killer but it is essential to keep grazing cattle out of the treated area for at least three weeks after treatment and longer if there is no rain after treatment to wash Chlordane into the soil. In the circumstances it might be advisable to delay treatment until the cattle are removed from the field at the end of the summer.

Apple Trees – Beating

Could you tell me what is the best time of year and the correct procedure for beating an apple tree in order to make it yield fruit? Although I cannot remember the details, about forty years ago I watched my father and the gardener beat an old apple tree in our garden near the Vale of Evesham: the following season the tree was laden with fruit! Some ten years later, I saw an experiment at Long Ashton Research Station for the same purpose but, instead of beating the apple tree, an incision was made in the bark: again, I do not remember – (a) how or when the operation was carried out, or (b) whether it was as successful as the beating. However, I clearly recollect telling the demonstrator at Long Ashton about the beating and, somewhat to my surprise, he admitted the old method was often very effective.

We have consulted our Fruit Nursery about this matter; they are very old-established and knowledgeable about the treatment of fruit trees, both now and in the past, but they have never heard of this custom, although it used to be thought that a walnut tree bore better if beaten. The incision in the bark is most probably ring-barking. This is done by removing a ring of bark ¼ in. wide around the trunk of the tree about 2 ft. from soil level. This checks the growth of the tree and encourages the formation of fruit buds. It is done in April or May (in England of course!) and the cut should be painted over with pruning paint. A less drastic form of this is to remove the bark in two semi-circles on opposite sides of the trunk, one 3 to 4 inches above the other. A further modification is knife-edge ringing which is simply placing the blade of a sharp knife against the bark and drawing it around the stem.

Apple Trees – Pollinators

What would be suitable pollinators for Cox's Orange Pippins? In our garden we have Blenheim Orange, Allington Pippins, Cockle Pippin, and Bramley. Will any of these fertilise the Cox? If not, what will and what is the maximum distance that the Cox should be from this other tree?

Suitable pollinators for Cox's are Worcester Pearmain, James Grieve and Bramley. Trees should be planted 30 ft. apart.

Apple Trees – Spraying

I have an orchard of old apple trees, in the main they are Bramleys, Blenheim, and Russet, they all have the normal diseases of an old, untended orchard. I am planting new trees in the gaps.
Can you give me a simple spray programme? Summer/winter, new/old trees? I would be most grateful if you can help me in this matter.

It is very difficult to give a 'simple' spray programme for amateur orchards. One can give a number of routine sprays, but it is quite on the cards that these would guard against pests or diseases that are not present anyhow and fail to control the one thing that was present in your orchard.

Apart from giving a regular winter wash with Thiol (listed on page 283 of the C.G.A. 1969 Annual Price Book), our advice would be to spray only against specific pests and diseases whose presence has been noted. We think that you will find that good cultivation and pruning of the old trees, together with natural predators, will keep a good many ills at bay.

We will always be pleased to advise on specific remedies for specific troubles.

Artichokes

Do you know of anywhere I can obtain artichoke tubers?

If you apply to Thompson & Morgan, The Nurseryman, Ipswich, or Kathleen Hunter, Wheal Francis, Callestick, Cornwall—they will be able to help you.

Asparagus

The article in the July *CGA Magazine* gives invaluable help to both shopper and housewife when making a choice of types of asparagus after it is grown.

But it could confuse rather than clarify the growers choice of crown which will produce the type of 'spears' he wants, or how, and where, he can obtain them.

There are no 'varieties' of asparagus simply because the crowns being of separate sexes, the constant interchange of inherited characters between male and female precludes the possibility of there being *groups* of individuals within the species *all* of which possess similar characters (just as no two of our children are alike, or two calves or lambs). But, by selective pedigree breeding we can, and have been able to, produce pedigree bred 'breeds' or 'strains' in which the individuals are similar in many characters, but not in all. Hence the differences between a true variety and a 'strain'. As crowns can be improved as cattle have been I suggest the choice between a 'so-called' variety and a pedigree bred strain is not a difficult one. The only species which has been cultivated is the edible species *A. officinalis* for consumption as a vegetable.

The great diversity in types is entirely due to the diversity of soil, climate, method of cultivation, and taste preference, in the countries where grown. 'Argenteuil' means only that it is the type growers in this district prefer. The imported 'Lauris' and 'German White' are, as so called 'varieties' are, the 'cultivars' and derivatives of *A. officinalis*. The flavour of the white (blanched) stems is distinct from that of the same stem when it is exposed to light and becomes green. If the white flavour is preferred all the grower does is to earth up the stems (as celery is blanched) or, if his soil is warm, dry sand, plant the crowns deeper and cut the shoots when they appear above the soil. 'Anglais', English asparagus, is *not* always thin, although much grown in the Evesham district is. The pedigree bred 'strain' K.B.F. named Kidner's Pedigree when given the Award of Merit by the Royal Horticultural Society, produces on well aerated soils, even larger spears than the French 'Lauris' with the great advantage of not only the tips being tender, but also having a delicious pith which extends into the white stem. When the stems are cooked, cut off, split open and the pith scraped out and eaten by itself it provides a delicious 'white' flavour asparagus, as well as another dish of delicious green tips, each of which are the perfect dish for the epicure.

Do you know of a grower of asparagus?

A. W. Kidner, Asparagus Farm, Lakenheath, Suffolk, produces asparagus.

Azaleas

I should be grateful if you could give me any information on azaleas, i.e., the best way of keeping the indoor potted variety in flower from year to year (e.g., amount of water, heat and pruning).

If you have bought an azalea from a shop, then it has been bought from Belgium especially for forcing by the nurseryman and it is not expected to last more than one year. The nurseryman at any rate hopes you will not keep it too long, as he wants to sell you another next Christmas. If you haven't a greenhouse it is not easy to keep the plant going indoors, the bese thing you can do is to plant it, pot and all, in the garden in late May after all fear of frost has passed, in a sunny bed. Keep it well watered—feed it with liquinure (high in potash) every fortnight or so and then bring it in the house late in September and keep it in a sunny room. If you have a greenhouse, then from June to November the temperature should be 40–45° F., and from November to June 60–

65° F. Repot firmly after flowering every two years and syringe once a day after flowering until the pots are put outside. Read *The A.B.C. of the Greenhouse,* which will give you more information on this subject.

Badgers in the Wood – 1

Recently on old badger has occupied a fox earth in our wood, and is now tearing up our lawns looking for insect life presumably. Short of drastic measures, can any member kindly say what other means will drive the animal away?

To prevent a badger from tearing up your lawn is a little difficult. Perhaps a smelly herbicide spray or some lawn fertiliser may put it off. If it works at night, which is presumably the case, you could try the effect of occasionally flashing a powerful torch to drive it off.

Badgers in the Wood – 2

For some time now there has been a badger set in the copse adjoining my house and their digging has spread to my lawns and flower-beds. The damage is increasing to such an extent that I must get them removed. The last thing I would wish is that they should be harmed; is it possible to have them removed to another area and if so who might undertake the task?

With regard to the badgers we would suggest that you contact the RSPCA, who will be able to remove them for you.

Bamboo Canes – 1

Can you please tell me (1) the correct time of year to cut bamboo canes, and (2) is there any special care to be taken in drying them?

Bamboo canes can be cut any time in the autumn, although many people leave the removing of other stems until early April. Be careful to remove the growths from close to the ground line, never shortening a shoot half way, for it must be cut clean away at the base. Drying should be done, if possible, in a cool-covered place, with the stems laid flat on the ground.

Bamboo Canes – 2

Can any of your readers help me with the problem of marketing large quantities of bamboo? Some has grown to a considerable height and sticks are sometimes of quite 2 in. diameter.

Bark Nibbling – 1

Can you please advise me how to prevent ponies from nibbling the bark of trees? We have two ponies running with Dexter cattle in a park where there are a number of old oaks, chestnuts and other trees. Can you say whether such nibbling causes damage to the growth of the tree and whether creosote applied over the affected part will stop the ponies doing it?

We certainly think that such nibbling causes damage to the growth of a tree and may even kill it. Do not use diluted creosote. Creosote cannot be diluted and it is not good for trees. Some obnoxious substance such as Foxorine might prove effective.

Bark Nibbling – 2

I was interested to read your remarks on bark nibbling. I experienced the same trouble some time ago with my three ponies running in a small paddock with some trees in it. My ponies, however, only barked the trees when they themselves were deficient in minerals. The ponies now have free access to a supply of 'mineral nuts' in the paddock and they do not attempt to bark the trees in any way. I consider that prevention is better than cure!

Beekeeping

Could you please give me some advice on what books I can get on bees, as I in-

tend to start keeping them this summer, but know very little about how to manage them, etc.

We suggest two leaflets, *Advice to Intending Beekeepers* published by the Ministry of Agriculture, Fisheries and Food, and *Do You Keep Bees or Would You Like To?* by the British Beekeepers' Association.

We also suggest that you might write to the General Secretary of the British Beekeepers' Association, whose address is O. Meyer, 55 Chipstead Lane, River-head, Sevenoaks, Kent, to see if there is a representative in Ireland who could help you.

Bindweed – Eradication of

We are much troubled with bindweed in our garden. We have been trying to eliminate this by spot painting with 'S.B.K.' but while this does seem to set the weed back, it does not seem to be 100 per cent successful. Can you suggest any better treatment?

We consider that, in principle, the method of control you are adopting against bindweed is the most satisfactory. We note that although the growth has been checked, the weed has not been killed, and this frequently happens when the roots are well established, as is often the case with this weed. If there is a considerable amount of underground root system, further growths shows up in different places, and the main point to remember with this 'spot' treatment is that several regular applications are needed before the weed can be kept under control or cleared. The best results are obtained when the weed foliage and shoots are young, and small, and when such growth is new. If you can concentrate on this aspect of the treatment, and repeat two or three times quickly, we feel that you will have more positive results. S.B.K. is very suitable for this purpose, although the same principles apply to any other selective weed-killer used for this purpose. In some cases, the makers of these products suggest using double strength solution and this can be done for spot treatment, so

long as care is taken to avoid foliage of
cultivated plants being wetted, and also,
any drift of the weedkiller, must be carefully avoided. Where the weed is growing between border or other plants, then
these points are especially important.

Bird Boxes – 1

*I have a number of bird nesting boxes of
conventional shape about my garden and
woodland. House sparrows have invaded
them. What is the diameter of hole
which will admit tits, wrens, etc., but will
keep the sparrows out, and is a circular
hole in the best shape?*

There is little you can do about
changing the size of the holes. Tits are
larger than sparrows, and these latter can
squeeze into almost anywhere. We
would suggest that you make a small
perch outside the box and hang fatty
foods on it, such as bacon rind and pea-
nuts, in the hope that a number of tits
will congregate and keep away the sparrows. You are right in assuming that
a circular hole is the best shape for the
entrance to a bird box.

Bird Boxes – 2

The House Sparrow, which is likely to be
the cause of the problem, is larger than any
of the Tits, although the Great Tit rivals it.
It is therefore possible to provide boxes
with holes small enough to suit the Tits
while discouraging the Sparrows, if not entirely excluding them. I have had considerable success in this field in my own
garden.

The solution I am inclined to suggest is
that two types of nest box be provided.
Boxes for Tits with small holes (2–2·5 cms.
diameter) such that Sparrows could only
enter them with difficulty or after enlarging
the hole with their beaks, and boxes with
larger holes (3·5–4 cms. diameter) specifically
for Sparrows. Careful siting of these boxes
may also help. This is the method I have
employed with good results.

Birds – Crashing Into Windows

For some time now carrion crows have
*been flying straight into some of the
windows of the house here, crashing
against the glass, often leaving behind a
mess of blood and feathers. We have
tried to stop this practice by hanging
things in front of the windows, but they
only change their target to another window not obstructed. Can you give us
any reason for their behaviour, and tell
us of a way to stop their antics? As a
last resort we shall have to destroy them.*

We have made a series of inquiries
without much luck. However, most
cases we have heard about of birds flying into glass is because there is a window on the far side of the building, and
thinking there is a clear passage through
they fly straight on. Should this be the
case, a trellis work either inside or outside, and/or curtains have been the only
effective way of dealing with it. It does
appear from other instances that this
only occurs at certain times of the year,
but one cannot be certain of this.

Bird Damage – 1

*For two years running blue tits have
attacked and eaten all my wisteria buds,
as early this year as late February. Consequently I am left with the leaf, but not
the flower. We have tried Glitterbangs
and also putting up a dead kestrel-hawk
that my keeper shot, but all to no avail.
Can you or any of your correspondents
suggest any remedy that will be effective? It is very fine old wisteria covering
two sides of the house, and it would
need miles of cotton-thread to cover it,
but this, I feel, is not practical.*

In the past we have published remedies
against bullfinches, which include such
things as black cotton, stuffed hawks,
etc., all of which you have tried. Another
member suggested a solution of renar-
dine and paraffin, but although this was
successful with his fruit bushes, another
member who tried the same remedy did
considerable damage to the buds probably by using the mixture in the wrong
proportions. Another of our members
says he flies two or three brilliant red
flags on very pliable bamboo canes and
he states that no birds will come near
his blossoms or buds.

Bird Damage – 2

For some years now damage by birds of various kinds, in the garden, has been increasing. At one period we had extensive damage by pigeons, but shooting with a 4.10 and an air rifle have reduced this menace. The damage by small birds, principally sparrows and bullfinches, so far as one can see, and more especially the latter, is mounting rapidly. In 1965 spraying with Morkit protected about 50 per cent of the fruit blossom and some gooseberries, but all the forsythia and some other flowering shrubs were badly damaged.

In 1966 we used little spraying with Morkit and substituted black Scaraweb which was certainly as effective as Morkit in protecting the buds and young shoots of fruit trees and flowering shrubs but it did so much damage to leaf buds, etc., and was so difficult to remove that we decided against its use this year.

We have therefore used Morkit again and, before the heavy rains of a fortnight ago, we used it and had preserved a large number of buds on fruit and other trees. An examination last weekend, however, has shown that we have now lost most of the buds on the gooseberries and blackcurrants, all those on pear, and plum trees, all those on the early apples, all those on flowering peach and cherry trees, all those on a sweetly scented tree the name of which we do not know, all those on forsythia, weigela and even mock orange (philadelphus) so that the garden is going to be shorn of flowering trees right into July and the only things we shall have will be magnolia, rhododendrons and azaleas. Not only have the birds taken out the flower buds, but, so far as we can see, except for about two leaf buds at the end of long stems of the trees, all of them are completely defoliated and if they have any leaf at all, will have less than about 20 per cent of normal leaf.

I have always been very much in favour of conservation and am very interested in birds, but depredations on this scale have got to be tackled.

In 1964 we had kept a top net on the fruit cage but in that year a late snowfall

caught on the net and collapsed the whole thing so that that method of protection of the early buds on fruit trees is too expensive!

We certainly think that you have done everything possible to preserve your buds and at present we are at a complete loss to suggest any new preventive measures. We will, however, publish your letter since some of our members may be able to help with suggestions.

Bird Damage – 3

A member recommends that the netting of a fruit cage should be removed during the winter months. This is bad advice if redcurrants or gooseberries are grown inside the cage, as the worst damage to these fruits from bullfinches and sparrows occurs between mid-November and the end of March. Blackcurrants are damaged during March, or April, if the spring is a late one. These bushes must be protected during these months if there is to be any hope of their fruiting. The normal recommended spray programmes can be depended on to keep the pests in check.

Bird Damage – 4

I can contribute a suggestion only to the problem in the last paragraph above. The netting of a fruit cage should be removed either from the side or the top during winter months to allow birds to destroy pests. The top net is the most practicable if made of fish net. I have used two types of cage. The easiest is a long one ten feet wide. The netting overlapping the sides by a foot or two is rolled on a rod, and unrolled along the 'roof' at the latest possible moment. It can be kept from sagging by cutting the uprights diagonally in criss-cross fashion. The margin of the netting hanging down over the edge of the upright wire-netting sides is an effective seal though an occasional hook is useful. In the autumn the roof net is easily rolled up (from inside the cage) and stored for the winter. The other type of cage was too wide for this procedure and I had to roof it in sections with overlapping nets. The overlapping margins had to be tied at intervals and this was more trouble but the same general procedure was followed.

Bird Damage – 5

May I suggest scattering Quaker Oats on the lawn regularly, and the birds will leave the garden in peace?

Bird Damage – 6

We have recently had our house here re-thatched with Norfolk reed. We are concerned to find that the birds are now attacking it in several places. The work was carried out during our absence abroad, and completed by about May. The reed appears in some places to be of poor quality and to have been put on too loosely. We would like to be put in touch with the best authority you can recommend on reed thatching, and preferably someone from outside this area who can inspect and give an impartial opinion and in the event of his finding inferior material and/or workmanship, superintend the rectification of such by the thatcher concerned.

It is sometimes necessary to cover thatch with fine wire netting to protect it from birds. It is possible that some air-borne insects were attracted to the thatch, thus causing the birds to arrive and attack it. We do not know of any authority whom you could consult, but the following firm is well-known for its thatching work: Norfolk Reed Thatchers Ltd., Loudwater Land, Loudwater, Herts.

Bird Scarers – Silent

Please advise me where I can obtain details of the silent scarer.

The firm to contact who have developed the silent bird scarers are The Merrydown Wine Co., Ltd., Horam Manor. Horam, Sussex. They apparently have three different types: a 'hawk', a balloon and one with 300 ft. of cable. Perhaps you would like to write to them and ask for details.

Bird Scarers – Starlings

I have known two cases of severe starling infestation; one in this county completely destroyed a small game covert; the other in Devonshire was in a large shrubbery which was rapidly becoming poisoned in spite of burning sulphur candles, letting off occasional shots, etc. The owner then had the correct idea that all living creatures need to sleep and proceeded to install automatic detonating gear to go off fairly frequently during the night. Before long the starlings gave their nests up as a bad job and vacated the shrubbery for a quieter neighbour's premises!

Blanket Weed

For anyone who is troubled with blanket weed, I have for years used copper sulphate which is much more effective for this purpose. Correct mixing is essential and is best done by the local chemist who is accustomed to this kind of work. It must also be carefully distributed. Used this way it is harmless to fish and plants. If fish have spawned, it is best to examine the blanket weed for fish eggs which will be found in it in great quantities.

Blight – American

I have some old apple trees which still fruit very well. Some have what I believe is called 'American Blight' – a white fur. I recall my father scrubbing small trees with paraffin many years ago, but presume there must be some easier ways now. These trees are large and old fashioned so this treatment is not entirely suitable. Can you please suggest a solution if indeed one is necessary?

'American Blight' or 'Woolly Aphis' can cause considerable harm to apple trees. It results in loss of vigour because the insects concealed under the 'wool' suck the sap of the tree. They also make wounds in the trunk and branches through which canker can attack the trees. The best control on large trees is to spray thoroughly and forcibly with liquid Malathion. The dilution rate is 1 fluid oz. in three gallons of water. Forcible spraying is necessary so that the liquid can penetrate the 'wool'.

Blueberries

I am very interested in the idea of culti-vating blueberries. The soil at my pre-sent house is very acid and damp: at present the ground is covered with heather, tufty fine grass, conifers and silver birch—rhododendrons and azaleas grow wild and the soil is very sandy. Could you put me in touch with some-one who can supply young bushes, and also can you give me information on cultural details?

By blueberries we presume you mean the *Vaccinium myrtillus,* commonly called the bilberry or wortleberry. The fruits are bluish-black in colour, and have a slight bloom on them. They are rounded and usually a third of an inch across. They grow as bushy decidu-ous shrubs, about 12 to 18 in. high as a rule, and they flower in May. The bushes should be planted 2 ft. apart each way, preferably in November and December, and if the ground is lacking in humus it is a good thing to fork in some well-rotted compost. On the other hand, as your soil is sandy, it seems, you could fork in sedge peat at a bucketful to the sq. yd. if compost is not available. The fruits are usually available from the middle of August to the beginning of October, so the picking can be spread over a long period. As regards those who could supply the bushes, I would try Messrs. Stewarts Nurseries of Fern-down, Dorset, and Messrs Thompson and Morgan, the nurserymen of Ipswich.

Gardening – Books on

I am anxious to purchase a compre-hensive gardening book for my wife's use, principally. It should have full details of most horticultural practices, particularly growth of strawberries, asparagus and various fruits, perhaps on a small commercial scale. If you are able

to recommend any book which might be suitable I would be grateful if you would let me have its name and publisher. If there is a selection of suitable books, their price might also be of interest.

We think that the best comprehensive gardening book is *The Amateur Gar-dener,* by A. G. L. Hellyer, published by Collingridge at 35s. This gives accur-rate instructions for almost every type of plant. For details of growing fruit the best guide is *The Fruit Garden Dis-played,* a Royal Horticultural Society's Publication costing 9s. and obtainable from the R.H.S., Vincent Square, Lon-don S.W.1 (postage 2s.). There is an ex-cellent series of Penguin Gardening Handbooks produced in conjunction with the R.H.S., and a list of these can be obtained from the R.H.S.

Bracken – Clearance

I shall be glad if you will kindly let me know the best method of clearing a site covered with bracken.

Where it is not practicable to eradicate bracken by ploughing, tractor-drawn crushers or cutters may be employed. This is a much cheaper method than hand labour. To achieve success, how-ever, cutting or breaking must be carried out repeatedly and should be combined with the application of lime and ferti-lizers to stimulate the growth of the grass. If it is not possible to plough or cut the whole infested area, efforts should be concentrated on dealing thoroughly with the advancing edges of a colony, in which case spraying with sulphuric acid twice in the season is an alternative to repeated cutting. An annual dressing of sodium chlorate will take the place of two applications of acid, but unfortu-nately sodium chlorate is too expensive for large-scale use.

Most important of all, new colonies of bracken should be destroyed as soon as they appear. In such cases, a dressing of sodium chlorate, repeated once the next year, will usually ensure a complete kill of bracken.

Buckthorn

Will you tell me, please, how to propagate purging buckthorn?

The propagation of purging buckthorn can be done by taking cuttings under glass in September or by layering branches in March.

Budgerigars

I have just been given two budgerigars, and wondered where I might be able to obtain more information about them, or if there is a book on the subject.

There are two places which might be able to help you. They are: Budgerigar Information Bureau, Orchard House, Orchard Street, London, W.1, and Cage and Aviary Birds, Dorset House, Stamford Street, London, S.E.1. An excellent book on the subject is Homing Birds, by the Duke of Bedford and L. G. Collins, obtainable at bookshops or from Cage Birds, by Raymond Sawle, Bird Curator, London Parks.

Bulrushes

We have a lily pond some acre or so in extent, with a fine show of water lilies. But it is being increasingly invaded by bulrushes, which have grown up through the water lilies, and will I fear ultimately destroy them by strangulation. If any other member has had this problem and has solved it (short of pulling up each bulrush by hand from a boat), I should be grateful to know the answer. Any selective weedkiller which would kill the bulrushes would, so far as I know, certainly kill the water lilies also.

It seems that the only thing to do is to pull them out by hand or cut them off below the surface with a water scythe.

Cage Birds

I would like information about Mynah birds and where I can obtain one.

A book that might help you is 'Cage and Aviary Birds,' published by Farmer and Stockbreeder Publications, at Dorset House. Several firms who specialise in foreign birds advertise there and will be able to supply birds at a more reasonable price than expensive Pet Shops.

Camellias

We are pulling down an old, unheated conservatory which houses four large and one smaller camellia tree, the former about 16 ft high, the latter about 8 ft. They will have to go outside in the garden, but we are not sure of the best site. We have a totally enclosed walled garden, so that the trees could have any aspect – it has been suggested that they would be better on a north wall, so that after a frost they do not thaw too quickly. Of course they cannot be right up against any wall, as 'they are not trained. Any suggestions as to their acclimatization would be welcome.

As you have a walled-in garden, I do not think that you need worry at all about the aspect or position. Camellias are far hardier than people imagine. There is something in what you say about keeping the sun off the blooms should they be touched by the frost during the night, but in view of the general shelter provided by the wall-in garden, I am fairly sanguine that all will be well, and that they will not need acclimatizing.

Camomile Lawn

I am endeavouring to establish a camomile lawn and should appreciate some advice concerning the treatment of it. The lawn is a small one, about 15 yd by 5 yd and the plants were put in last autumn. They are doing well, and only here and there is there ground to be seen between them. I am keeping the area weeded and a few plants have flowered. The general appearance is healthy but untidy. I do not know at what stage and to what extent I should cut the lawn. In fact I should be glad to be told the appropriate treatment now and in the future.

We would advise you not to allow the

camomile to flower, so cut the plants down to within an inch or so of soil level, even if you have to do this job by hand. It may be that the lawn needs feeding, and you can give it a fish manure at the rate of 3 oz to the sq yd. It would be best to cut the lawn regularly from September onwards.

Caper Spurge

An enquiry regarding Caper Spurge (Euphorbia lathyrus) has come to us from a Scottish member.

This is a biennial plant. It is raised from seed sown outdoors in April or May, the plants being put in their flowering positions in the autumn. It will flower the following year and then die, but once established, it seeds itself very freely and can, in fact, become a nuisance.

It is a somewhat full plant about 2 ft high with leathery dull green leaves and insignificant greenish flowers. It is claimed that the roots give off some secretion that moles dislike and that the animals will not tunnel ground where the Caper Spurge is planted.

Seed can be obtained from Messrs. Thompson and Morgan, Ipswich.

Carnation Growing

I want to grow carnations commercially under glass on a large scale. Can you recommend a book on the subject?

The Ministry of Agriculture has a publication known as " Carnations under Glass ", Bulletin 151, published by H.M. Stationery Office, price 3s.

Cat's Fur

Can you tell me how to disentangle matted lumps of fur on a half-Persian cat? We have a very beautiful tom-cat, doctored, who is very keen on hunting in long grass and woods. He has long and very thick creamy-coloured fur, fine in texture, and to my horror, I discovered the other day that, under a sleek surface, it is a mass of tightly matted lumps. I have tried combing, but it is obviously very painful and the scratches and struggles of the cat make it impossible to get much result. When the weather gets warmer should I just cut out the lumps and hope the hair will grow in long again, and then pay more attention to daily grooming?

You have really supplied your own answer to the problem when you ask if you should pay more attention to daily grooming. The cat should not have been allowed to get into this condition – and correct daily grooming would have prevented it. You should get a steel toothed comb to remove the dead fur and this is especially important in the spring when the cat will be shedding its winter coat. The matter portions should be teased out with the end of a pair of scissors or cut out altogether if the hair has become too badly matted. Some assistance from a second person holding the cat whilst the grooming is being done would doubtless be necessary. Since the cat would seem to have been allowed to get into a very bad condition, we would suggest that the grooming operation is done in instalments. Those matted lumps *must* be got rid of and daily grooming minimises the risk of fur balls.

Cats – Breeding Siamese

Now my husband has retired, we have moved to a house in the country. As a hobby, I would like to breed Siamese cats. Where can I get information about this and where can I find the name of a reliable local breeder to buy the kittens from?

The Cat Information Centre, 69 New Oxford Street, London, W.C.1, has the names and addresses of the club secretaries representing the 12 most popular breeds of pedigree cats in Britain. These are the Siamese (Sealpoint and Colourpoints), Blue Persian, Abyssinian, British Blue, Burmese, White Longhair, Cream and Blue-Cream Longhair, Chinchilla, Colourpoint, Rex and Manx. The Centre will send you a free information card giving details of correct care for a Siamese and the name of your nearest breeder.

Cats – Feline Smells

Have you any nostrum for removing the very persistent smell of cat pee?

In answer to your enquiry for nostrums to remove cat pee smells, we would refer you to the Ministry of Science and Technology Pamphlet No. 736/542/B/vi/17/(Cat) and the Feline Waste Products (Liquid) Disposal Order of 1956 as amended in 1963 Section 1(i)/A. These documents give much useful advice on this problem. We are informed that Ministry technicians have established that the persistence of feline liquid waste product odour is in direct proportion to the age, sex and breeding of the animal. An old male alley cat being at one end of the persistence (P) scale with an odour (O) duration of more than fifty days, while a young, female Burmese or Abyssinian will have a P/O of only a few hours.

Ministry experts tell us that the cheapest antidote for feline P/O is a simple decoction of liquorice (the Italian variety Liquorici Tutti Quanti is the best) though the English or French variety (Gateau Pomfret or Pontefract Cake, so called from its medieval Latin derivation Pongus—a Smell and Fractus—broken or dispersed). Boil 1 lb. of liquorice in a pint of diesel oil and you'll be amazed at the result. In less persistent cases, applications of Chanel No. 5 to female cats or Faberge Brut to toms will be found to be very efficacious. Care should be taken not to give Chanel No. 5 to tom cats as it is liable to turn them queer. We are told that a useful gipsy remedy consists simply of omitting to send the family vests and socks to the laundry for two months. Instead heat them gently at a temperature of 90 degrees until their odour cancels out the feline P/O.

Cats – Training

I wonder if any member has any information or knowledge of how cats could be trained or deterred from crossing a busy road; in my case the cats have acres of fields but seem to like the road best.

Unfortunately we know of no way to stop your cats from crossing the road, but we will endeavour to publish your letter in the Magazine to see if any of our members can come up with a solution.

In reply to the letter from a Gloucestershire Member, I suggest he tries, as we have done successfully, to convert his cats to spending the night indoors, as the tragedies all occurred during darkness. Withhold food during the day, call the cat at dusk and offer it its favourite food, and puss will quickly settle to this routine. If worried about the cat's capacity to last the time, provide a sand tray.

In a lifetime with cats I have found it difficult to stop them doing what they fancy, but I asked the tenant of our shoot what he had done to protect his young birds from our three hunting cats.

He gave me two names, Ripello and Renodin, being repellants which he spreads to keep off cats and foxes. He thinks they have been successful.

Could you perhaps put one of these along your ground which borders on the main road?

Chestnuts – Spanish

Could you please tell me how Spanish chestnuts may be preserved in their natural state as picked up, with the idea that they could be used for roasting and so on during the winter? This year we have vast quantities of very large chestnuts, equal in fact in size to those one buys in the shops imported from abroad. Normally we find that after a week or two they seem to dry up, shrivel and spoil.

I have had no difficulty in keeping Spanish chestnuts and using them for roasting during the winter. First of all, of course, they should be gathered from the ground when they are fully ripe, then they should be stored in the dark in a room where it is not too dry so that the nuts will not shrivel, and not too moist so that they will not rot. Most storehouses, lofts and the like, tend to be on the dry side. We do most storing in a well-built shed with an earth floor, because the latter seems to supply the right amount of moisture for the atmosphere. Of course, as a rule wire netting has to be laid down over the earth floor to prevent the rats getting in.

Chicken – Dropsy in

I keep about 20 hens (RIR and LS) on free range on grass of about ¼ acre, and over a period of some months have lost four, all apparently from dropsy. I believe there is no cure, but can you advise a prevention? The land, though ample, has carried hens for many years. It has been limed this year.

Dropsy is usually the outward symptom of either egg peritonitis, through unlaid eggs falling into the belly cavity or tumours associated with the leucosis complex or fowl paralysis. If the latter – and to some extent it also applies to the former – the only way to avoid it in future is to buy pullets from strains which are reasonably resistant to the leucosis complex, and do not suffer from ovarian breakdowns. To some extent, also, you can assist by rearing any chicks as far away from any older stock as possible.

Chinchillas

I am collecting information about breeding chinchillas (for a relative shortly returning from abroad). Can you put me on to pamphlets or literature, which also give up-to-date financial aspects? Is there a chinchilla association in this country?

The organisation which you might like to contact is The British Chinchilla Breeders' Association ; the Secretary is Miss E. L. Spooner-Lillingstone, 1 Manor Drive, Bathford, Somerset. She is very helpful and would send you all the information you want to know.

We also suggest that anyone breeding chinchillas for their skins should be very careful before investing money in such a project since the English market for such skins is not very established, and it literally requires hundreds of well matched skins to make a fur coat, which means considerable wastage and lower prices for inferior skins. Breeders of course are only too pleased to sell pairs to people and to encourage them to start farming chinchillas, but it is a risk with quite a lot of money involved usually.

Chinchillas – Snags

Please advise your Sussex member to tell her friend to have nothing whatever to do with chinchillas. An attempt to make money out of them cost me about £1,000 which I could ill afford, and prices were better then than they are now. Feed prices have recently increased, apparently as the result of devaluation, and the most successful breeder I know has recently decided to give up as a result.

The only market for chinchillas has always been the States, and it has been a complicated business to get skins there. Whether there is still any demand I doubt, as good skins are now fetching only two to three pounds, which is quite uneconomic. It would be utter folly to start trying to make chinchillas pay now.

Chinese Geese

Please can you tell me if Chinese Geese are good to eat?

We can assure you that Chinese Geese, unlike Chinese eggs, are very good to eat.

Christmas Trees – Commercial

I should be grateful if you would be good enough to advise me about the growing of Christmas trees for profit.

With regard to Christmas trees the best variety to grow is Norway spruce, and under average conditions the following planting distance is 3 ft. by 3 ft. on your soil is probably best. If, however, you are growing these trees for the purpose of thinning them out in stages you can reduce this planting distance considerably. They can then be marketed from 18 in. high, thinning each year until they attain 6 ft. or more in height. It is impossible for us to tell you what price you will obtain for your trees, because this fluctuates according to supply, and we cannot anticipate the market for years ahead. The cultivation is fairly simple once the trees are established. Prices received by growers vary from year to year according to the state of the market.

Christmas Trees

How can I keep down the grass in a plantation of Christmas trees I am growing without damaging the trees and without too much expense?

Geese will do this for you if there is a reasonable amount of grass for them to eat. They will not hurt the trees.

Clay Soil

Three years ago I began to make a kitchen garden out of a long-neglected field. The soil is heavy Essex clay, and in spite of all my efforts to lighten it with compost, etc., it is as " puggy " as ever in wet weather and concrete-hard in a dry summer. I have been told that I could use sifted coke ash, of which I have a large supply; but it seems to me that it must be detrimental to plant life, as coke before combustion contains sulphuric acid. I would appreciate your comments.

It takes a very long time, usually 15 years or more, before such soil can be improved. Of course, it would help matters if you could make vast quantities of really well-rotted compost and use it at the rate of 75 tons to the acre as I once did on a market garden in Kent. I must add that I prefer adding organic matter so that the humus can be built up and then the living organisms in the soil will do the work. However, there is not anything particularly wrong in coke ashes providing the coke has been fully consumed, but do not, whatever you do, use coal ashes which can be poisonous and harmful.

Club Root – in Vegetables

We have suddenly started to get club root on a lot of our vegetable plants. Could you please let me know what causes it and how we can prevent it affecting any more, as we have already lost a crop of spring and other winter vegetables?

Club root is caused by a slime fungus. It can attack all members of the brassica family (cabbages, cauliflowers, brussels sprouts, turnips) and also ornamental plants belonging to the natural order Cruciferae (wallflowers, stocks, etc.). It can also, unfortunately, live in the soil without a host plant for up to five years.

Where plants are badly affected they should be dug up and burned and if possible no brassicas should be grown on that bit of ground for three years. If you walk on or dig a piece of ground where the disease has attacked you should clean soil off your shoes and implements to avoid transferring the fungus to other parts of the garden. Also try and keep the ground clear of all weeds belonging to the Cruciferae (shepherd's purse, charlock, etc.). Liming the ground at 4 oz. per sq. yd. will also help.

To protect brassicas themselves the roots should be dipped in a paste made by mixing 1 lb. of calomel dust with about ⅓ pint of water before planting them out.

Cobnuts

I have approximately four acres of silver birch and bracken scrub (a few oaks). It has been suggested that to clear this and grow cobnuts would be highly profitable, as once the cobnuts are planted little attention is required, and the harvesting and sale of the crop are simple operations. Your comments, please.

There are several problems connected with the growing of cobnuts. First of all, of course, I would not be certain whether the ground is suitable. Secondly, you would have to make sure that there are no squirrels in the vicinity, especially the grey ones, for they will quickly strip the trees of nuts and are the main pest at the moment. Thirdly, there is the terrible pest of the nut weevil, which tunnels into the nut, and regular spraying will have to be carried out to control this pest. To say that little work is required in connection with the trees is of course not true, for there would be the winter and summer pruning to carry out each season, and there is the suckering to do each year. If nuts were as easy to grow as you suggest, then of course they would be a very popular crop, whereas at the present time they are a dying industry. For further details read the *A.B.C. of Fruit Growing*, published by the English Universities Press.

Cocksfoot

Can you suggest a method of removing cocksfoot grass from a lawn other than that of digging it out?

There is no way of getting rid of cocksfoot grass from a lawn, other than digging it out.

Couch Eradication

I should be glad to receive your advice regarding the best method of eradicating couch grass from pasture land used for grazing ponies. I have received particulars from you of Dowpon Grass Killer, which would appear to be one answer to this problem, but before using this I should be glad to know if you would recommend any other procedure. The area in question is approximately one acre.

At present there is no method of controlling couch grass which is growing in a grass sward, as it is one of the most resistant grass species to grass-killing chemicals—due in the main to its underground rhizome system. If the pasture is well manured and utilized the couch will not increase. Couch often spreads from hedge bottoms, ditches, etc., and the use of a dalapon in such situations is advisable where couch is a problem. When the pasture is ploughed the couch can be controlled by chemical plus cultural methods.

Cox's Origin – Apples

Please settle a local argument. What is the origin and date of the Cox's Orange Pippin apple? Who was Cox and why the Orange? Is there now such a fruit as a plain Cox's apple? Is there any truth in the dictum that in a genuine Cox's Orange Pippin the pips should rattle in a ripe specimen when shaken? Is it not a fact that the Cox's Orange Pippin varies widely in colour, juice, flavour and pip rattling depending on the district or soil in which it is planted?

The apple Cox's Orange Pippin was raised in 1830 by a Mr Cox. He was a brewer in Bermondsey and retired to Colnbrook Lawn near Slough in Buckinghamshire where he devoted himself to gardening. Cox was a chance seedling and the parentage is not known for certain, but it is believed that the pip from which it arose came from a Ribston Pippin. The 'Orange' in the name refers to the colouring of the ripe fruit.

It is true that *all* apples when they are fully ripe should rattle when they are shaken. Another way of telling when they are fully mature is that the pips should be a very dark colour. When actually picking apples the best way of telling if they are ready is to lift the fruit gently in the palm of the hand and see if it parts easily from the spur.

It is a fact that THE Cox's Orange Pippin varies widely in flavour. This is dependent on soil, situation, culture, and also on the rootstock onto which they are grafted. There are also different 'varieties' of Cox, some better than others.

Crayfish – 1

I wonder if you or any member have any experience of catching fresh water crayfish? Any information about baits, type of trap, etc., would be welcome.

I am afraid we have no knowledge of how to catch fresh water crayfish, but members may be able to help.

In the Far East one threw a dead dog in a river with a string attached and removed it later plus crayfish. First find a dead dog! . . .

Crayfish – 2

When a boy I caught many hundred crayfish. The best method is to tie a lump of raw liver on the end of a string and lower gently under the bank of the

stream. The crayfish is quite easy to
see. When it takes hold jerk it out on
to the bank.

Crayfish – 3

In the 'thirties we used to catch crayfish by the following method: Use four
or six flat nets made from iron circles
about 14 in to 16 in wide covered with
netting or wire netting of smallish mesh.
Attach four cords or wires about 18 in
long leading into one cord of the length
required to sink the net to the bottom of
the stream and have enough slack to pin
to the bank with a stake. Tie a piece of
'high' kipper firmly in the middle of the
net. Lower the net with the aid of a
long stick with a fork at the end into a
suitable place in the stream. Place the
nets at convenient intervals. When the
last net is in place return to the first
and retrieve it with the long stick, and
with luck wou may find up to a dozen
crayfish sticking to it! They should,
unfortunately be boiled alive with plenty
of salt, and eaten cold with mayonnaise.

Crayfish – 4

The most effective way I know of catching crayfish is to make up a large bundle
of pea-sticks or twigs, with two or three
large stones and some rotten meat in the
middle of the bundle. Tie a string to
the bundle and throw it into the stream;
the crayfish will work their way into the
sticks to get at the meat and will remain
entangled there when the bundle is removed.

Crayfish – 5

These delicious crustacea, known in
Sweden as kräfta, can be caught in small
lobster pots which unfortunately cannot
be obtained, to my knowledge, in the
U.K. However, there are other methods
although the bait requires some skill in
election and like all fishing, there is a
bit more to it than just dropping a trap
in the water.

Crayfish – 6

Crayfish, when alarmed, dart rapidly
backwards. All that is required is to
lower a butterfly net about a foot behind
them and then create some disturbance
in front either with a stick or dropping
a stone in the water. If you are lucky
they shoot straight into the net.

Croquet Lawn – Size of

*I am having difficulty in finding out the
correct measurements of a croquet lawn, in
particular the correct hoop and stick spacings.
I know the outside measurements. Can you
please provide me with the correct hoop and
stick spacings?*

A croquet lawn should be 28 yd. by 35 yd.
and the hoop and stick spacings should be
7 yd. in from both sides at the corners.

Cucumbers

*Can you tell me what makes cucumbers
bitter?*

Cucumbers become bitter when they
are pollinated. Pollination is not necessary for the formation of the fruit, so
male flowers should be removed as soon
as they are seen.

Cuttings

*How do you raise cuttings in polythene
bags using vermiculite?*
Is a hormone used at the same time?

It is a very simple matter to put the
vermiculite in a seedbox or polythene
container, and then having given it a
good watering just to push the cuttings
into this material. You will find that
they will root quite easily. You can dip
them first of all into a hormone powder,
but it is not really necessary.

Cypress

*My cypress trees have grown too high
for a fairly small garden. I estimate
that they have reached about thirty feet.*

You did not mention pruning in your letter and I would be most grateful if you could tell me how much pruning can be done without causing possibly undesirable effects. Is it possible to shorten the trees simply by lopping off the top few feet or would this result in growth in other directions which would prove troublesome?

Lawson cypress take kindly to pruning. You should prune the tree flush to the main stem and take care not to leave bits of branches standing out from the main trunk.

Deer – Close Season

Can you tell me the close time for deer?

Red Deer (Stag) May 1-July 31 ; (Does) March 1-Oct. 31. Fallow Deer May 1-July 31 ; (Does) March 1-Oct. 31. Sika Deer May 1-July 31.

Deer – Fencing Against

My garden is surrounded by woods, and last year newly planted shrubs and young trees suffered considerably from roe deer rubbing the velvet off their horns. Fencing is impracticable and I should welcome suggestions for protecting them effectively without being too unsightly.

The only method that we know of is either to erect deer fencing which is very expensive or to erect an electric fence which has been known to keep these creatures out. Unfortunately we cannot guarantee its effectiveness nor suggest any other method.

Deer – Control

We are bothered by deer who invade our spinneys and garden from surrounding countryside and do much damage. Can anyone advise us how to mitigate or prevent this trouble?

Mr. H. A. Fooks, of Hay Bridge, Bank of Ulverston, N. Lancs., is a consultant on Deer Management, and no doubt if you care to write to him he would be able to advise you.

Deer – Damage – 1

Where can I get some help and advice about controlling deer?

We suggest you contact the Secretary of St. Cuthberts Club, Mr. Frederick Ratry, Moor Place Farm, Bramshill, Hants (Heckford 269). The members are ardent stalkers and can control very large areas selectively.

Deer – Damage – 2

We have a garden adjoining St. Leonard's Forest and numbers of deer appear to take early morning walks through the garden, taking the choicest shoots from the roses, azaleas, etc., for their breakfast.
What can be done about these deer? They are multiplying rapidly both in and around the forest.
What says the law? Apparently the deer belong to no one.

Protection of your property against the incursion of deer is for the most part a matter of self-help; in Goodwood Park, for instance, are stretches of electrified fence designed to keep sheep in and the larger possible intruders out. The self-help extends to the shooting, even in the statutory close season, of trespassing deer on enclosed land. Section 10 of the Deer Act, 1963, which makes it a criminal offence to kill deer in the close season, makes an exception of 'the killing by means of shooting of any deer on any cultivated land if the shooter proves that his action was necessary to prevent serious damage to crops on that land.'
You will be aware, too, that under Section 98 of the Agriculture Act, 1947, the Minister of Agriculture may serve notice in writing requiring steps to be taken for the destruction of pests (deer being among them). If the deer in St. Leonard's Forest are in fact a menace to crops, the Minister could be invoked and asked to tell the Forest Authorities to take appropriate action. Are not the farmers adjacent to the Forest concerned?

Deer – Damage – 3

With reference to the letter in your July issue by a Sussex member, clearly control of the deer is the best way of minimising damage. I cannot imagine fencing other than proper deer-fencing, electrified or not, keeping deer out, and substances to paint around the garden to deter deer by smell or taste do not seem very effective. Control should always be done with a rifle used by an experienced person, and I think you are wrong to encourage garden owners to 'self-help' themselves by shooting. If they were fully experienced they would presumably do this anyway. If not they are likely to lean out of the window and pepper the deer with a shotgun, almost certainly wounding it in a most nasty manner. I suggest that you refer such complaints, which I have read in the CGA magazine before, to the British Deer Society, who can put the person concerned in touch with the local Deer Control Society.

With reference to your letter regarding deer damage, I would like to draw your attention to the above Control Society which was formed and is affiliated to the British Deer Society and is operating in your area. We are already controlling the deer on various farms in the St. Leonards area, and would be quite willing to assist you in any way we can. This is a completely voluntary organisation, and as such free of charge to landowners.

L. Preston, Hon. Sec., Surrey-Sussex Border Deer Control Society, Norwood Hill Orchards, Norwood Hill, nr. Horley, Surrey. Tel. Norwood Hill 439.

(*See also* page 178.)

Deer – Information

Where can I get information about deer?

We suggest you contact: The British Deer Society, 43 Brunswick Square, Hove 2, Sussex (Hove 38670).

Deer – To Keep

Would any of the readers be able to advise me how to induce a stray hind to stay on my rough grazing close to my house? She and her mate first appeared in the early months of 1958. Then they disappeared after eating our crocuses and a few shoots of hydrangeas in our garden! They left the narcissi and daffodils

alone. They have appeared again, but a less tolerant neighbour has shot the male because of their depredations—but my wife and I do not feel like that. The hind, very timid, of course, feeds on the grass bank within 100 yards of our house, and we should like her to stay there—or at any rate within the 50 acres of our immediate land. Can any of your readers advise how this could be achieved? Unfortunately we cannot afford to feed her all the time on crocus bulbs, but are there less expensive articles of diet which we could always set as a focal point for her delectation?

The best suggestion we have to offer is that you purchase some cattle nuts and scatter a handful or two where you wish the hind to feed. You might also leave a lump of rock salt there for her to lick or purchase a mineral salt block.

Roe Deer – to keep out

I have a problem with roe deer, and would like your advice about these deer, who live in the woods nearby, and spend most nights in my garden, feeding almost entirely on my roses, many of which have been killed by defoliation. I have about 200 rose bushes, and we were unable to pick a single bloom last summer—all eaten by deer. Their other main diet seems to be yew hedges and ground ivy— I have watched them browsing on these in broad daylight. The garden is 3 acres, and fencing against deer is virtually impossible without ruining the look of the garden (ha-ha walls, etc.); shooting them is only a short-term answer, as more would take their place.

Is there any means of repelling roe deer, either by chemicals or a type of scare-crow (or scare-deer)? I need hardly add that they also damage my trees, but curiously enough this is not a serious problem, as most of my woodlands have grown beyond that stage.

It would be best if you could contact your local Forestry Commission District Office, and their Game Warden would no doubt be able to give you some first-hand advice on this subject.

It would seem that the only lasting way of keeping them out is to put up a 7 ft. deer fence, but as you say, this would spoil the appearance of your garden. There are chemical deterrents, but these are not lasting.

We have spoken to the Forestry Commission Game Warden in the New Forest, and he suggested you should contact your local Game Warden in Northumberland, as so much depends on local conditions, and he feels sure he would be pleased to help you.

There is also the possibility of putting up an electric fence, which you might like to suggest to the Game Warden.

Devil's Stinkhorns

Can your Horticultural Adviser suggest a quick, certain, and lasting method of killing stinkhorns? I have quite a prolific but localized crop amongst rhododendrons, azaleas, brooms, and heaths within smelling distance of my house, and being the only smoker in the family I am generally expected to remove and burn those which attain full maturity and " out of the blue" whenever my back is turned. Not only am I getting extremely tired of this form of exercise but it seems that the more I scrape around and remove the young round ones the better the crop of the mature article. Also they definitely thrive in drought conditions, which seems odd. The extent of the problem can be measured by the fact that I have already bagged and burned around 100 so far this season from an area of 100 sq. yd. Neither a flame-gun nor weed-killer could be used in this particular area, and lime would not be popular with nearby azaleas, etc. Furthermore, the obvious remedy of encouraging the rest of my family either to take up smoking or alternatively to wear gas-masks is liable to lead to still further trouble. Any advice, short of employing an H-bomb, would be gratefully received.

The problem you have set does not seem solvable because of the proximity of the rhododendrons, azaleas, and the like. I can only suggest using a flame-gun.

Devil's Stinkhorns

I was interested to read the above letter and would like to make a suggestion. We used to be troubled with these stench horns, as they were known then, and we found that the way to deal with them was to knock them over with a stick, after which they immediately stopped smelling and dried up and withered away. They seemed to appear suddenly after a shower of rain.

Dewponds

How do you make a dew-pond?

The process is to hollow out the earth (say on the slope of a hill) to make a much bigger hole than the proposed pond. If the floor of the excavation is at all loose or fractured thoroughly consolidate by " punning " then cover with a layer of puddled clay, free from sand or earth, from 6 in. to 12 in. thick – the thicker the weakness of the foundation and the diameter of the pond. On that lay a layer of wheat straw, which is more permanent than oat or barley, to insulate ; on that another layer of clay, and pitch the top of this upper clay with a flooring of stones on edge ; the lower layer of clay is essential, if there is any fear of ground water.

An alternative might be concrete, adding 5 per cent of Pudlo to the cement, smoothing off the sides and floor, then use as an insulating material magnesia slabs or the like, being careful to fill all interstices ; 3 in. thick should suffice on the top of this another layer of concrete water-proofed Pudlo, and into this insert " pudding " stones to give a grip to the stock ; 6 in. of concrete should suffice for the bottom layer, whilst 12 in. may be preferable for the top one. After finishing, the whole floor should be kept covered with wet sacks for as long as possible until the concrete has completely consolidated and set, and its skin hardened ; 3 ft. depth of water is ample, and a few buckets to start helps.

Docks – Eradication

How can I get rid of a large patch of docks in my orchard?

S.B.K. or C.G.A. Brushwood killer are
effective but should be applied early in
the spring and again as docks are resist-
and and recur unless attacked in this
way.

Dogs – Basenji

Where can I get a Basenji?

One of the best known Basenji kennels
in this country is that owned by Miss
Veronica Tudor-Williams, of Matham
Manor, Molesey, Surrey (Tel. 1274);
who, if she has no stock for sale herself,
can probably advise you as to where a
good puppy can be obtained. Prices
vary according to the quality of the
puppy, but the average is between 8 and
10 gns. at eight to ten weeks of age. As
this is undoubtedly a coming breed it
might be a good plan to buy a bitch and
breed from her occasionally. Bitches,
too, are often more affectionate and kind
with children. When choosing a puppy
from a litter decide definitely the sex
required and then have the other puppies
removed ; watch the remainder at play
for a few minutes and select the boldest.
This, from the companion point of view
at least will be the best of its sex in the
litter.

As these dogs are usually silent they
would not be considered good watch-
dogs from the barking angle, but being
very intelligent and devoted would deal
with an intruder firmly. They make
excellent companions for children, but
being comparatively small (weighing 10
to 20 lb.) must be guarded from rough
handling by younger members of the
family.

It is hard to find a drawback to this
charming breed. It is handsome in
appearance, exceptionally clean by habit,
full of brains and humour, and a first
rate sporting dog into the bargain. The
breed is very old, and recognisable
examples are depicted in carvings found
in the Pharoah's tombs. Several Basenji
mummies were also found, embalmed
with loving care and buried with full
honours by a shrine to the dog god
Anubis. In more recent times they have
been greatly prized in the Congo regions
as hunting dogs.

Basset Hounds – Dogs

*A young German cousin of ours has
asked us to help him buy an English
Basset hound. Could you possibly give
me the name of a thoroughly reliable
breeder so that I could put our cousin
into direct touch?*

There is a breeder in Cheshire called
Mrs. B. Bowmer, of Waterloo House,
Waterloo Road, Poynton, Cheshire.

If you do not have any luck there, we
suggest you write to the Secretary of the
Basset Hound Club: Mrs. Seiffert, Basset, Weald Way, Caterham, Surrey.

Dog Beauty Salon

*Do you know of a reputable Dog Beauty
Salon in London?*

We suggest the following: Town and
Country Dogs, 35b Sloane Street, London, S.W.1.

Dogs – Bitch Deterrent

*Our dog will persist in paying court to
our neighbour's bitch. Is there any way
we can stop this?*

The dog will naturally "pay court" to
neighbouring bitches that are allowed out
to leave a trail of scent while they are
in-season. It is therefore up to the bitch
owners to keep their animals shut up for
the entire 21 days of the season if they
wish to avoid serenading male dogs. As
further precautions a strong-smelling disinfectant, such as Jeyes, can be sprinkled
in gateways, etc., and where the bitch
has been allowed in the garden for necessary purposes. There are tablets on the
market which are reputed to remove the
scent from a bitch, but these do not prevent mating. Anti-mate rubbed on a
bitch will deter most dogs (and humans
too!). As to Law and Etiquette: the
former does not relate to these circumstances (unless trespass with damage was
involved), and the latter, where it exists,
puts the onus on the owner of the bitch
which is the cause of the trouble. Fetch-

ing an errant dog which has been attracted from home by the scent of a bitch is surely quite as much of a nuisance to his owner, and this could be pointed out when complaints are made. To sum up, it would seem that responsibility lies entirely with the bitch owners, with whom, on this basis, one can perhaps reach an agreement that will make life more tolerable for all parties.

Dog – Books

Do you know of any books about Spaniels (English Springer), Setters, Poodles, and obedience training for dogs?

The titles of some books which are all obtainable from Foyles are: 'English Springer Spaniels', by Frank Warner Hill. 'Setters', by Marjorie Bilton. 'Obedience Training for Dogs', by Marjorie Gordon. 'Poodles', by M. R. Shelton and B. Lockwood.

Dogs – Bulldogs

I would like to buy a bulldog and wonder whether you have the name of any societies that might be able to help me in this area.

We contacted The Kennel Club and they suggested the following: South of England Bulldog Society, 39 Chasewater Avenue, Copner, Portsmouth. Or: The London Bulldog Society, Throgmore Cottage, Kenys Walden, Nr. Hitchin, Herts. Or: a breeder is Mr. F. Hadderll, Vine Cotage, Bottlesford, Woodborough, Pewsey, Wilts.

Bullmastiffs

Please let me know something of the habits, care, etc., of bullmastiffs, and suggest a good breeder.

The bullmastiff was originally bred as a gamekeeper's guard, and trained to down and hold poachers without injuring them. It is a breed of great charm and intelligence, but needs understanding and careful training from puppyhood if it is to be a satisfactory companion. Clearly, with such large dogs feeding plays an important part in their care. Puppies need codliver oil and calcium/vitamin D supplements, plus plenty of meat, offal, eggs, milk, and fish. The adult dog does better on three meals a day, as the large amounts of food required tend to cause digestive troubles if fed in great quantities at longer intervals. Suggested times are as follows: breakfast, meat soup, vegetables, and good dog biscuits (or wholemeal bread and milk); mid-day, fish, with a dessertspoonful of codliver oil; evening, meat. The total should give one-third bulk and *two-thirds animal protein*, 3 lb. of food in all. The breed society describes the dog as high spirited, reliable, active, alert, and enduring.

We suggest you contact: The British Bull Mastiff League, 43 Glebe Road, Hinckley, Leicestershire, its Hon. Secretary is H. P. Burton.

Dogs – Cairns

Do you know of any breeders of cairns in the Surrey area?

There are two that the Kennel Club recommend—they are: Mrs. M. Thompson, Fairy Cross, Sally's Mead, Lingfield, Surrey, and Mrs. J. Harding, 27 Brunswick Road, Sutton, Surrey (Mel 1051).

Dogs – Coat Loss – 1

My dog has lost all its coat and although I have tried various things which a vet has given none of these seem to do the trick. The vet says this is a diet deficiency.

The vet is probably right. Dogs fed on too much meat can lose their coats entirely. You should feed it on a sole diet of carrots for 14 days. You will find that it may not wish to participate in such an unappetising dish for anything up to three or four days but you must steel yourself against its complaints and you will find that this will bring back its coat in full and stimulate the growth. Cut down on the amount of meat you give it in future and we advise you to include a few carrots in its feed in order to maintain its coat.

Dogs – Coat Loss – 2

I was very interested in your reply to the member in Hereford whose dog had lost its coat. I have never seen carrots recommended before for the canine diet and should like to know what vitamin they contain.

I have a four-year-old Labrador to whom a carrot is the greatest reward she can be given. We have always noticed that while she is absolutely trustworthy left in the car with the household shopping, including the Sunday joint, she is not above going down to the barn to help herself to carrots kept there for the donkeys. She bites them raw, one after the other. In the past I have told her not to take the donkeys' rations, but after reading your advice I shall give her a regular share.

Dogs – Coat Loss – 3

I did not see your reply referred to in the above letter, so my remarks may merely duplicate yours.

I have a black curly-coat that, as a puppy, lost his coat almost completely and was really thriftless. Our vet eliminated what he could, e.g., the manges, vitamin deficiency, and allergies from collar material or dog-mat. So he arranged a visit to Liverpool University's experimental station in Wirral. There they were most helpful and assiduous, and finally diagnosed an allergy to beef and whale-meat protein. Although this eliminated a number of common proprietary dog-foods, we were lucky in that our local pet store discovered sources of rabbit meat and chicken offals at competitive prices, which, coupled with straight wholemeal biscuits, vegetables, and a vitamin supplement (when we remember) has completely restored our dog to health and his coat to the standard lustre of his breed.

I write this because the question of allergy is often overlooked in animals.

Dogs – Cocker Spaniels

Do you know of any breeders of cocker spaniels?

The Kennel Club recommend: Mrs. Carey, Ware Cottage, Denham Way, Maple Cross, Rickmansworth, Herts. (Rickmansworth 74216). Mrs. J. King, Oakhill Road, Stapleford, Abbotts, Nr. Romford, Essex.

Dog's Diet

We have two Border Terrier dogs aged about 6 years, one which carries no spare flesh weighing 17 lb., and the other about 26 lb. At the moment both dogs are rather itchy and shake themselves when patted or touched on the back. They scratch a certain amount but not a lot. They are usually fed twice a day with lights and a handful each of dog biscuits at each meal. Occasionally by way of variation we get a sheep's head for each of them, but this seems to aggravate the itchiness. When out for a walk or in the garden both dogs always eat a lot of grass, which I believe signifies a shortage of a certain vitamin. I feel that both this and the itchiness are probably due to diet and I should be glad of your advice on how best to effect a cure.

Management is probably the cause of the trouble with these dogs. Both are rather overweight, the heavier being nearly 10 lb. more than the standard for Border Terriers. Scratching points to diet deficiency as you suggest, and grass eating may be another symptom, or possibly due to indigestion. The following course should bring them into better condition. First of all bath both the dogs in warm water with mild soap, such as Lux toilet soap, and rub down briskly, so that they start with really clean, tingling skins. Give each six tablets of Vetzyme or Yestos brand yeast a day (these are palatable and readily eaten once tasted) and one teaspoonful of cod liver oil. The tablets may be reduced to two a day after about a fortnight. Try slightly stale brown bread instead of meal, and add to this gravy, cooked green vegetables or shredded raw carrot, and for the meat ration bullock's cheek, tripe, " melt " (spleen) or liver, giving a variety as available. Any good lean muscle meat is better fed raw. Two meals a day is correct but make the morning one lighter than the supper, which can be digested during the night. Lights should only be used occasionally as they are nearly valueless nutritionally. Plenty of walking exercise to encourage natural bowel action should complete the cure, and the dogs should be fit within a month or six weeks.

Dog for Family Pet

We are about to choose a bitch puppy for my 12-year-old son and would be grateful for your advice as to the rival merits of pugs and Basenjis, between which the choice lies. Obviously the prime requisite is good temper and reliability with children. We must also have a dog without a " one-man " temperament, for my son is at prep. school and the dog will therefore have to be more of a family pet. We already have large poodles, so any additional dog must be short-coated and clean and if possible as quick and intelligent as a poodle. There are many neighbouring dogs, so it must also be of a non-fighting strain. I like Boston Terriers but am doubtful of their temper with children. Perhaps you can suggest another medium-to-small sized breed we should consider, but please, nothing that yaps?

The pug is a charming companion for an adult but doubtfully suited to the rough and tumble of life with a child, as though sturdy enough they are inclined to suffer from heatstroke and other respiratory troubles due to their " push-faces." The Basenji is much tougher, with plenty of energy and quick intelligence. Though as with all breeds individuals may have fighting tendencies, the average Basenji is very gentle and, of course, does not yap. A bitch puppy now is a good investment as this is a coming breed and a litter will always sell. Boston Terriers are by descent part French Bulldog and part Old English Terriers (now extinct), and have temperaments as varied as those of their ancestors. Alternatively, a Beagle is suggested. Away from pack conditions these nice little hounds are very clean and good in the house and become devoted to the family. In some ways the hound temperament is better suited to the role of family dog, as opposed to " one-man " dog, as they become attached to all their immediate human relations, to other dogs in the house, and to the house itself, and this makes them less likely to pine in the absence of one member. Equally, this strong devotion must be recognized as it can cause fatal pining if everything familiar is lost to a hound. Beagles are highly intelligent and full of fun, and generally good-tempered ; but some strains are inclined to be nervy and a puppy should be chosen from bold parents of working stock.

Gun Dog – Hard Mouth

I shall be pleased to obtain advice regarding a young gun dog. This dog has a very good nose and will retrieve well, but it has a very hard mouth and tears the game he retrieves. Is there any way to soften the mouth or to teach it to be less strong with its jaws?

An inborn or acquired hard mouth is hard to cure. As the age and breed of this dog is not given it is difficult to assess the possibilities of re-training him ; however, matters may be improved by taking him off work and reverting to training with a dummy at first and then with a *cold* partridge, pigeon or rabbit—the wings of the birds being bound to the body with one or two strong rubber bands. A fast pick up will lessen the chances of the game being torn and this is facilitated by whistling the dog as he closes his jaws on the bird, while the handler retreats, thus increasing the dog's haste to return. The game brought to hand must be accepted slowly and gently, and acknowledged by congratulations and a pat or two. Eager young dogs often acquire a hard mouth if allowed to retrieve strong runners and so this should be avoided until they have learned sense with age and experience.

Dogs – Starting a Kennel

For many years I have bred and trained gun dogs. This I have done as a hobby in my spare time. Shortly I am retiring from my present employment, so I am considering starting up a kennels, so that I may continue with this work, running it as a business. Can you advise me how to start? Naturally it will involve a capital outlay for the building and buying of kennels, the buying of equipment and dogs, also a van or car. I would welcome the answers to the following questions: (1) Do I register the kennels officially, if so where? (2) How big a concern must it be to obtain official recognition? (3) As a business what tax relief could I expect, if any?

There are two accepted means of founding a kennel. (1) by purchasing one or two brood bitches in whelp; or (2) by obtaining one or two very high quality bitch puppies at the age of 8–12 weeks. Of the two, the first is the best and most expensive method. It is generally agreed that a stud dog is the last animal to buy. Until the kennel has a countrywide reputation at trials and shows it is much better to concentrate on a team of really good bitches, which can visit the best stud dogs at reasonable fees. The book "Modern Kennel Management," by O. Gwynne-Jones, is recommended. You will require planning permission if you are establishing a new kennels, especially in a residential area. You should approach the local planning authority before going too far to avoid disappointment. (1) The governing body of the dog world is the Kennel Club. Its headquarters is in Clarges Street, Piccadilly, London, W.1. It is useful but not obligatory to register a kennel name—a prefix or affix with the K.C. Home bred puppies may then carry this name and individuals that eventually win at trials or shows form a means of indirect advertising. Other official registration is not required, but planning permission may be necessary before kennels can be erected, and it is possible that bye-laws might effect kennels run as a business. Advice on both these questions can be obtained from the Surveyor's Department of the local council offices. If you are going to use a business name this has to be registered with the Registrar of Business Names. (2) No minimum is fixed by the K.C. (3) Tax relief should be obtainable on numerous counts, including car or van running costs, etc. The CGA's

accounting services would be helpful here and the reasonable fees charged repaid in the long run. Keep all bills, bank statements from the very start to save trouble later. Obviously, a long established reputation as a successful amateur breeder and trainer of gundogs is an asset but, while the new venture is in its initial stages it might be worth considering adding a kennel block for ordinary boarders in order to produce a quick and lucrative return for the capital outlay. If stables or other buildings suitable for conversion are not available, it will be found that ready-made sectional dog kennels are expensive. As an alternative it may be possible to buy ex-W.D. huts.

Dogs – Kerry Blues

Do you know of anyone who can advise me on good breeders of kerry blues?

We suggest you contact the Secretary of the Kerry Blue Association, J. R. Davy, Esq., 66 Park Hall Road, East Finchley, London, N.2 (TUD 1876). He does breed them himself as well.

Dogs – Lawn Damage

Over the winter my lawn has been greatly spoilt by my spaniel bitch urinating on it, and it is pock-marked with ugly yellow patches.
I have now devised a scheme to divert her off the lawn when she is put out, and I should be grateful if you could advise me as to whether there is any dressing to help remove these spots in the shortest time (I suppose the spots are mainly caused by the ammonia?).

The only thing we can suggest is for you to mix some grass seed and sprinkle over the patches, first scratching them over thoroughly, then roll. There is nothing that will get rid of ammonia.
Get a dog next time!

Dogs – Lucas Terriers

Do you know where I could obtain a Lucas terrier?

We suggest you contact Sir Jocelyn

Can You Recommend a Book on Training Dogs?

(See page 81)

Lucas's kennels: The Hon. Mrs. Plummer, Bonners, Pepprestock Road, Luton, Beds. (Markyate 260).

Dogs – Norwegian Bu-hund

We have recently acquired a Norwegian Bu-hund puppy and as we know very little about him I should be grateful for all the information you can give me concerning the breed.

The Norwegian Bu-hund is a Spitz breed and is mainly used in that country for herding: its other name is Norwegian sheepdog. It first came to general notice at Crufts Show shortly after World War II, but the numbers kept in this country are still limited; though anyone who has experience of these dogs find them gay, intelligent, and companionable and of smart appearance. Probably in common with other types of working dogs, which have recently become popular as household companions, careful training is necessary to prevent the adult animal becoming self-willed and difficult to manage. Given kind but firm handling during puppyhood, the Bu-hund should make a very nice dog to be proud of.

Dogs – Nose Colour Changes

My cavalier King Charles Spaniel has developed a brown nose. She is a Blenheim and as I am anxious to show her, I wonder if anything can be done to restore it to its original colour; it was black. Her age is 18 months and she has had a litter of pups. I should be most grateful for any advice you can give me.

Dogs with yellowish coats—yellow labradors, golden cocker spaniels, etc.—are more liable to develop brown noses than other breeds when they become adult. In some cases this is only seasonal, often occurring in hot sunny weather. In others it may be due to mineral deficiency, which is likely to be the case with this Blenheim bitch, as she has reared a litter. A course of yeast tablets and a mineral mixture will probably restore the pigment. "Vetzyme" yeast tablets are recommended, given like

sweets at the rate of 6 a day. The minerals may be obtained by adding Boots Chemists mineral mixture for small livestock to the drinking water, or by giving Phillip's "Stress" daily, this can be obtained from any good chemist.

The diet should contain a proportion of iron-rich foods such as liver and cabbage, both given with the stock in which they are cooked.

Dogs – Old English Sheep Dog

I would be glad if you would let me know how to care for the coat of an Old English Sheep Dog. We have just got one from some kennels, and the coat was terribly matted and had to be close clipped. How long should it take before the coat grows, so that it looks like a proper Sheep Dog again?

It should probably take about six months for your Sheep Dog's coat to grow out. He should be combed at least once a week to maintain the "pile." You should watch out for these dogs' eyes, which can't stand light, if the hair is cut away.

Just out of interest the address of the Secretary of the S.E. England Society for this breed is G. Gooch, Wraxall, East Farleigh, Maidstone, Kent. He is a breeder as is also Mrs. Earle, Chestnuts, Beckley, Sussex (my wife!).

Dog for Outside Work

I would appreciate some advice on the choice of a small working dog (not a house pet) and its training. It would be wanted chiefly for vermin extermination, and would have to live in a kennel, near the poultry yard. We keep chickens, ducks, and geese, many at liberty, and have lately lost a good number to rats. We do not like to leave permanent baiting points because the smaller "liberty" birds, bantams and chicks, can and do get into drainpipes and behind tiles to eat it with disastrous results. The geese live in a small orchard adjoining the

the poultry yard and it is not practicable to shut them up at night. Muscovies and ornamental ducks we have at liberty in the garden, but some Aylesburys for fattening are kept in a wide enclosure with straw bale house—and not by any means foxproof. We also have valuable parakeets in aviaries and have lost several lately to rats burrowing under or forcing a weak joint in the wire netting.

Could a small dog be trained to patrol at night and smell out during the day without doing too much damage? Our house dog, a bull terrier, has done great damage when " ratting," tearing matchboarding from the inside of the stables, ripping up floor boards, even pulling out the upholstery from a fine veteran car—though he does kill a rat occasionally. If unchained, could it be trusted to remain " within bounds" and not to frighten the poultry unduly (the bull terrier, though he doesn't chase poultry, loves to hurtle round corners at top speed, scattering the unsuspecting birds left and right).

Finally, what would be the best breed (and sex) for such work, hardy enough to be out all the year, and really " game"? We had considered a " Jack Russell" fox terrier, a Norfolk terrier, a King Charles spaniel, a miniature sheepdog, a sealyham, a beagle, and finally a gypsy lurcher. What would be the best age and sex and how should training start? Or is it much too much to expect a small dog to protect a four-acre holding from what is about exclusively nocturnal raiding? Your advice would be appreciated.

There is no breed of dog that would be ideally suited to your requirements, and neither a King Charles spaniel nor a Shetland sheepdog would thrive or be any use under these conditions. A Norwich or Parson Jack Russell terrier would be very game and keen on rats, and a Whippet Lurcher (whippet x terrier or x Bedlington) might be useful. However, like the bull terrier, all dogs are liable to do damage in the heat of the chase and could be disturbing to the poultry; and it is unlikely that a dog could be trained to patrol for rats and foxes at night without human supervision, and of course ratting at night would again disturb the birds.

The real answer might be the following: entrances to drain pipes fitted with half inch apart bars to form a grating; crevices, etc., in buildings to be stuffed with broken glass which is then cemented in; sheet metal strips (obtainable from ironmongers) attached to the lower and more vulnerable parts of aviaries, etc., where rats or foxes might be able to scratch or chew an entrance; and other places where cementing is impracticable can be packed with ordinary mothballs (which are obnoxious to rodents) or pepper dust, obtainable from seedsmen or chemists. " Foxorine," a harmless, but very obnoxious liquid to foxes could be used round the straw bale houses.

These suggestions cover defence measures. As to attack, any poisons to rats are obviously highly dangerous where domestic livestock are concerned, but the newer biological baits which produce epidemic diseases among rats are quite harmless to other stock. The local Pest Officer, M.A.F., can advise on this.

With regard to the foxes, if the neighbouring country is reasonably open and unwired, the local Hunt will welcome a note asking for help. Foxes not killed by the hounds will be disturbed and driven to better cover, and a contribution to " the cap" will be well repaid. Failing the Hunt, the Pest Officer will again prove useful.

Once the vermin have been got under control, a few cats would keep down rats better than any dog. Two or three male kittens can be obtained through a veterinary surgeon, the local R.S.P.C.A., or from a farm, and given quarters in one of the outbuildings. If reared with poultry from an early age they will be quite safe with them, and as they hunt quietly and mostly at night they will prove ideal ratters in a few months. Cats kept for rat control need to be large and the kittens will be better if neutered, and well fed each morning, with only a dish of milk provided at night. Neuters will not wander and can be relied upon to hunt their own ground.

A dog kennelled near the more remote poultry will keep off foxes at night, but from the point of view of humanitarianism and the law it should not be chained there permanently. It will keep its intelligence and gameness much better if it is allowed freedom and given good outdoor quarters.

Dogs – Papillions

Do you know of any breeder of papillions in this area?

The following are recommended by the Kennel Club: Mr. and Mrs. C. Garrod, Wild Wings, Ashtree Farm, Guyhirne, Wisbech, Cambs.

Dogs – Pekineses

Where could I obtain a white pekinese?

We suggest you contact the Secretary of the Pekinese Club, Mrs. L. Cole, 109 Sunnyhill Road, Streatham, S.W.16 (Streatham 4693). She has white ones, and sends all over the world. She is the world's best breeder, and is recommended by the Kennel Club.

Dogs – Pointers

Can you recommend a breeder of Pointers?

We suggest you contact the Secretary of the Short Haired German Pointer Club: Mrs. L. Petrie-Hay, Waidman Kennels, Bouts Lane, Inkberrow, Worcs. She also breeds them herself.

Dog Portraits

Have you got a list of artists who do Dog Portraits?

There are the following:
Mrs. H. de L. Panet (Truda Panet), 161 Wilton Road, Salisbury, Wilts. Tel. Salisbury 3615—Dogs and Cats in Pastel. Portraits completed in about two hours in client's home. 10 guineas (Unframed). Travelling expenses extra. Miss K. Shakleton, Beech Park, Clonsilla, Co.

Dublin, Eire. Tours of South England, charges very modest, likenesses very good. Miss Marjorie Cox, Somerden Green, Chiddingstone, Kent. Tel. Penhurst 285. Highly recommended, quick and reasonable. Miss Mary Browning, Parish House, Greatworth, Banbury, Oxon. Large clientele, locally and further afield. Highly recommended, reasonable. Mrs. Symes, Pie's Cottage, Sparsholt, Winchester. Well known.

Dogs – Magyar Puli

Could you inform me whether a breed of dog known as Hungarian Puli is obtainable in this country? I saw a specimen in the United States and was very attracted to the breed. I should also be grateful for any other information you could give me about this breed.

Available records do not show that the Puli has ever been bred in this country, or that even single specimens have been imported. The dogs have been recognized by the American Kennel Club for some twenty years, but Puli there are still regarded as rare oddities; and it is unlikely, by their very nature, that these dogs will ever become popular outside their native land. The breed is very old, probably more than a thousand years, and was bred to herd the semi-wild sheep of the plains. It has a thick woolly coat, lying in long matts from the hind-quarters, and is generally red and black colour. The head is somewhat poodle-like but with a shorter nose and ears that fold back. In size and weight it resembles a working beagle. Puli was never kept as pets but lived rough with their nomadic masters, and in consequence tend to be self-willed and liable to wander. With expense no object, it should be possible to obtain a specimen from America or from Germany.

Dogs in Road

I wonder if you can tell me of any effective way of preventing one's dogs rushing out of one's drive gate on to the road?

Do you know if a "cattle grid" is any deterrent, or is there any such similar device for dogs? I should be most grateful to hear of any suggestions you may have. We have had one dog run over on the main road already and are most anxious about the other dogs. I know, of course, that one could shut the gates, but the drive is a long one and it would be a great nuisance if no tradesman would come up to the house because he had to open and shut the gates every time.

An ordinary type of cattle-grid with flat bars is unlikely to stop a dog. If triangular bars were used this might be effective, but would be very rough going for vehicles. With expénse no object, there are electronic devices that open and shut gates automatically, but this sort of thing is presumably out of the question. The answer then seems to lie with the dogs and their management. One could ask why they rush down a long drive and out of the gate; are they pursuing the tradesmen or going hunting, or what? A trained dog will not usually leave the vicinity of its human owner, and perhaps a little attention to training may be needed. On occasions when the dogs must be left on their own it should be possible to arrange a stable yard or well-fenced area where they will be safe and yet have comparative freedom. A daily routine that includes a proper amount of exercise and definite meal times will often cure a bored dog's desire to wander.

Dogs – Training Book

Can you recommend a book on training dogs?

The Kennel Club recommend: "The Choice and Training of the Family Dog," published by the Popular Dogs Publishing Co. Ltd., 178-202 Great Portland Street, London, W.1.

Dogs – Training

We are having great difficulties in trying to train our 6 month old labrador not to foul in the garden. He can quite easily get out into the gravel lane outside and we have tried keeping him in for several days on end, walking him at hourly intervals up and down this lane. We have also tried picking up his droppings saying "bad dog" and carrying them out to the lane verge, where we pat him and say "good dog" as we do so. But still no luck—we hesitate to punish him as he's really a very intelligent dog (very easily house trained) with a sweet nature. Are we expecting too much of him, and should we wait until he's older? I am so afraid he will never learn if we let this go on for too long unchecked. I shall be so glad of some advice.

Too much is being asked of this puppy. Some individual dogs naturally seek a private place for this purpose without training, and most do not, and scolding may result in inhibiting the animal from relieving himself properly, which will cause internal upsets such as impacted anal glands. A daily tour with a shovel seems the only solution at present, not an arduous business, as the dog will pass droppings twice a day at most. Particular places favoured by the dog might be treated with CGA Foxorine, which could also be applied around flower beds and other more important areas. In time the dog may learn to go out into the lane for himself. A walk with plenty of galloping exercise, morning and evening, will activate bowel movement and perhaps form a habit, but, in fact, it is seldom possible to own a puppy and a spotless garden.

Dog Training – Residential

Can you recommend anyone who does training of dogs?

One person we know of is: Mrs. Porterfield, "Bowesmoore Kennels," Tile Kiln Lane, Bexley, Kent.

Dogs – Training to Gun

I would like some advice about training dogs to the gun, and also the name of a suitable kennels.

Dr. D. A. White, Camden House, Bletchingley, Surrey (Bletchingley 206), will advise people on this subject. The name of a Kennels is: Gun Dogs Kennels, Washwater, Newbury, Berks. (Newbury 848).

Gun-Dog Training – Book

I would be grateful if you could please advise me on a good book on gun dog training.

'Gun Dogs—Training and Field Trials', by Moxom, published by Popular Dogs at £1.62½. It is obtainable from Foyles or through your local bookseller.

Dogs – Training

Is there a book on the handling of Gundogs ?

Gilbertson and Page Ltd., of Hertford, Herts, have published a useful booklet entitled " The Handling of Gundogs During and After Training," by Lt.-Col. G. H. Badcock. (Price not known.)

Donkey Show Society

The Donkey Show Society has recently been inaugurated. It aims to serve all lovers of donkeys and is long overdue. As most people know, the number of donkey owners in Britain has increased tremendously year after year since people became more interested in them. At present nobody knows how many donkeys there are in this country, and no authoritative standards have been laid down, so there have been no pedigrees. The Society intends to start right away on a register of stallions, and hopes to record details of all donkeys in Britain. The principal object of the Society will be to encourage owners to show their pets at reputable shows, and already several horse and agricultural shows are holding donkey classes. We are fortunate in having Mr. R. S. Summerhays as our first president. He is one of the most famous authors of books and articles on the horse and shares his enthusiasm for donkeys with the rest of our council. I shall be delighted to

send a copy of the rules of the Society and further details to anybody interested. I particularly want to hear from donkey owners and secretaries of shows. This is a young society, as yet our funds are small, may I say that a stamped addressed envelope enclosed with any query sent to me would be greatly appreciated. Mrs. Walter Greenway, Hon. Secretary, The Donkey Society, Prouts Farm, Hawkley, Nr. Liss, Hants.

Donkeys

Where might I obtain a Donkey?

Robin S. Borwick, Esq., Ruffs Orchard Donkey Stud, Hawthorn Hill, Maidenhead, Berkshire, supplies pet donkeys—he generally prefers and has the smaller type of donkey; he is also helpful about queries you might have about donkeys. Or you might contact the Hon. Sec., National Equine and Smaller Animals Defence League, Blackwell, Carlisle. They do not sell donkeys but find good homes for them, a stable for the winter must be provided and animals supplied must not be bred from nor sold, but the League will always take back unwanted animals. They have branches all over the country.

Dowsing or Water Divining

Can you please say if there is such an association as the " Dowsers," and what their address would be?

Address of the British Society of Dowsers is York House, Portugal Street, W.C.2.

Drive – Planting Under Trees

Can you help me with my drive and surrounding land ? I have given up my garden and intend confining myself to improving and laying out my drive and land, which consists of a large rock garden to the sea front (Menai Straits) and the drive borders. The lower part of the land wants colour but has overgrowing trees, as has the drive avenue. Both want colour and I thought of hydrangeas; I have now no means of propagating them and those that I have in the open are doing well. Will they take on the lower land and under the overgrowing branches of the avenue of beeches on the drive? Can I get them reasonably ready for planting? And how should I go about it – I think I can use 50 to advantage. Also is there a book which I can find useful for my purposes? When replying will you let me know what to do with three or four hydrangeas which are making leaf, one in a large way, with only two or three flowers at ground level.

It is going to be very difficult to get anything to grow under beech trees. These invariably make the culture of other plants under them impossible. If there were any spaces not covered by the shade of these trees then probably hydrangeas could be established, especially if you dug in plenty of sedge peat at say two good bucketsful to the square yard. With regard to your hydrangeas that are not flowering, this may be due to lack of potash, and I would advise you to apply wood ashes for three or four feet around each bush at the rate of half a pound to the square yard. This could be lightly pricked in. The book you require is *The A.B.C. of Flowering Shrubs,* published by the English Universities Press and written by W. E. Shewell-Cooper. It gives full instructions as to how hydrangeas could be propagated.

Ducks – Information About

Can you recommend a book on the rearing and management of wild duck?

The Wildfowlers' Association of Great Britain and Ireland of 1/3 Harrington Street, Liverpool 2, publish a booklet entitled " Ducks galore ".

Duckling Rearing

Kindly advise me, if you will, about duckling rearing on a smallish commercial scale. (I know where to get the eggs.)

It sounds as though you also propose to hatch the eggs which, on a small scale, is usually unremunerative; but since you ask about rearing and not about incubation I will stick to some comments upon the former. In general you can rear ducklings with very much the same equipment as chicks, bearing in mind that a duckling needs twice as much room, is very active on its feet, and after a few days does not require so much heat as a chick. This means that the overhead, infra-red space heater in a draught-proof, rat-proof, house would be satisfactory; and the duckling could be reared intensively given the space. But they grow rapidly: a good type of Aylesbury should attain 6 lb. at ten weeks; and although frequently changes put them back and are costly, one move. to the outside is often justified. (If the area is also fox-proof they will do quite well in a straw bale shelter after a month.) The best food is a proprietary duckling mash, such as that sold by B.O.C.M., moistened and fed at intervals, because once a food is mixed with water it very quickly sours if left about and the ducklings pad it down. The item needing most attention is water. The ducklings must have water at all times: they must never be without. At the same time they should never be allowed to swim in it, at any rate to start with, because, oddly, they may drown. Although this is hardly the appropriate moment to mention it, ducklings are very subject to sunstroke: in other words, when outdoors after May they need handy shade, as also protection against storms.

Ducks – Muscovy

Where can I obtain information about Muscovy Ducks?

We suggest you contact: Lt. Col. A. A. Johnson, The Priory Waterfowl Farm, Ixworth, Sussex, who is an authority on this subject.

Ducks

I have a small lake, about three-quarters of an acre in area, and I wish to keep on it some very ordinary types of duck

*such as Mallard and small farm ducks.
Could you please inform me the best
way of obtaining some information
about this.*

We suggest that you contact the following organization, which will be able
to give you expert advice : The British
Waterfowl Association, Cash Lane,
Eccleshall, Staffordshire. An article on
waterfowl will soon be printed in the
magazine.

Ducks – Ornamental Wildfowl

As a commercial breeder of ornamental
wildfowl during the last ten years, I
would like to make the following comments on Major Grahame's article
'Ornamental Bird Husbandry' in the
February C.G.A. Magazine.

Major Grahame says that his pinioned
birds are protected by a 7 ft. high fox-
and cat-proof wire fence. When asked
by visitors if such a fence is necessary
the short answer is that for a large collection upward of 30 birds the expenditure
is justified. For people, however, with
comparatively limited space, who plan to
keep three or four pairs of birds, he
would definitely advise against erecting a
fox-proof fence.

Pinioned birds are completely at the
mercy of predators and I believe that the
practice of removing the last joint of one
wing is acceptable only if all birds are
going to be kept in a completely vermin-
proof area where they can look forward
to a greater expectation of life than their
counterpart in the wild.

I will not knowingly sell birds to anyone who is not prepared to fence them
safely. Where the garden is small and
a high fence an eysore I advise that the
birds be shut in an 'aviary' at night—a
routine they learn quickly. Such a wire-
netting pen can usually be tucked away
in a corner.

Ducks – Rearing Their Young

*My tame ducks never succeed in rearing
their young.*

I can readily understand your
puzzlement over ducks failing to rear
their young. Domestic ducks are all
descended from the Mallard except the
Muscovy. Initially, the wild Mallard
was tamed by the simple expedient of
feeding it and, knowing there was a
regular supply of food to hand the
Mallard stayed, becoming more and
more domesticated. Even today Mallard
are extremely easy to tame. By becoming domesticated the Mallard lost its
wildness, it was protected by its
" owners " from various predators and,
as it came to look more and more to
man for its food and its protection it
lost a part of its natural instinct.
Domestic ducks, initially by accident,
now by design, are bred *not* to go
broody, it automatically follows that
they also " forget " how to rear their
young. Mallard together with some
ornamental domestic breeds, notably
Black East Indian will, however, hatch
their own eggs, but mostly this is under
" controlled conditions " where the
question of protection from predators
does not arise as far as the ducks themselves are concerned, it being the job
of theirs to protect them from rats and
such like vermin by keeping them in
coops with wired runs etc. Thus the
domesticated Mallard is up to a point
unsuited to hatch and rear its young if
left to its own devices. Numerous wild
Mallard do successfully hatch and rear,
but many lose most if not all their ducklings, usually to rats and crows. Your
member only assumes the wild brown
duck was a Mallard, it might very well
have been a Mallard cross, the description brown leaves much to the imagina-
tion. There are a great number of
Mallard crosses around, caused through
the drakes flying into places where
domestic ducks are kept. Some of these
crosses whilst being able to hatch
successfully, just haven't a clue when
it comes to rearing their ducklings. The
very wildness of the duck in question
leads me to think it was a Mallard cross,
possibly with a domestic ornamental
variety such as a Call-duck, these crosses
can be pretty wild and shy without
having the natural sort of built-in
cleverness of a truly wild bird. I keep
a number of wild Mallard amongst
others here, some of these successfully
conceal their nests and one day appear
with a string of ducklings. I usually

leave them to their own devices as we keep the place clear of rats by heavily poisoning all around and constant shooting over the years has all but wiped out crows and rooks, to the extent that they seldom even fly over now, but give us a fairly wide berth as if they knew they would be shot at if they came near. These Mallards occasionally lose the odd duckling through their inability to count, often we hear one crying in distress, when we find it we either put it in a brooder or if we know where the parents are we take it to them. It is only man's effort to domesticate that has caused these ducks to lose their capacity to hatch and rear their young and it is only a matter of time before geese "acquire" this habit. A good poison to use is Raticate which I can definitely recommend, both for its effectiveness against rats as well as its harmlessness to domestic poultry, ducks and wildfowl, cats and dogs, geese, sheep, all from first hand experience.

Ducks –Keeping and Protecting

Can you give advice on how to keep ducks and ornamental fowl and protect them against predators?

There is only one main difficulty in keeping ornamental waterfowl, and it is not connected with the water; for ducks thrive on almost any pond provided it has shelving banks which cannot be dibbled away. The problem lies in protection for the birds, especially during the breeding season from foxes, cats, stoats, otters and from rats. It is necessary for duck to be pinioned, unless they are completely covered with netting. To keep birds full-winged adds to the expense, but also to the pleasure of seeing them fly, and if the netting is dipped in black varnish before purchase it is not unsightly. On the other hand, pinioned ducks do not suffer in consequence, and if done by cutting off the first joint of one wing with scissors before they are 24 hours old, it is quite painless. Feeding of adult stock is simple, throw a handful per duck of wheat and crushed maize into the shallow water where it cannot be taken by rats or sparrows, give

also stale bread, duck weed, lettuce or any fresh green food as available; and see that there is plenty of sharp gravel grit accessible.

Mandarins lay at the beginning of April and the average period of incubation is 29 or 30 days. It is best to mate the species in pairs (as an odd duck or drake can be a great nuisance). It is also advisable not to let a duck attempt to hatch her first brood, for the earliest duckling are liable to die of cold and exposure and lack of the natural insect life which is present later in the season. The eggs should therefore be removed as soon as laid, and a specially made "pot" egg inserted. When the complete clutch has been laid, all the dummy eggs can be removed and the duck will probably start laying again in about a fortnight.

Duck Weed

Will you please advise me how to remove duck weed from a lake, other than by keeping ducks?

We are not certain whether what you call duck weed is, in fact, this. Many people refer to the slimy green blanket seen on ponds as duck weed, which it is not. If you have the slimy green blanket you can get rid of this with a preparation called GLBX. On the other hand, if you have a green broadleaf weed you can get rid of it with a preparation called Reglone. We would point out that Reglone can, if great care is not taken, kill everything in the pond (lilies, fish, etc.).

Earthworms – 1

Can any of your readers give advice on obtaining and keeping a ready supply of earthworms? These are required for mole eradication, using strychnine, and the time-consuming job of digging for worms on each farm visited has become uneconomic; nor is it always possible to fit in the job when ploughing is taking place – which can sometimes speed up worm collection. Does anyone know of any commercial concern which can supply large quantities of earthworms?

If so, how can one best keep them alive in captivity? If not, how can one best breed earthworms and keep them alive?

Earthworms can be obtained in small quantities of say one hundred, or larger, from Mr Reynolds, of 10 Chaucer Road, Wellingborough, Northants.

They are packed in moss, and I find they will keep for two or three days provided week-ends are avoided.

Earthworms – 2

In answer to your correspondent's request for advice on the above, may I suggest he enquire of the Director of the Wildlife Sanctuary, Healesville, Victoria, Australia.

This sanctuary keeps in captivity specimens of the duck-billed platypus. These animals eat about twice their own weight in earthworms daily. As a result the sanctuary runs an earthworm "farm", a site for the breeding and upbringing of their own supply. The address is: The Director, Sir Colin Mackenzie Sanctuary, Badger Creek, Healesville, Victoria, Australia.

Earthworms – 3

To breed earthworms, you must first of all collect them. This has been done (by me) by building a 10 ft. by 10 ft. compost heap on a surface of bare earth. On this earth, when some material is ready for composting, spread several raw onions, well broken up; dried outside skins are best.

Then build an aerated compost heap – not just a pile of sodden grass or leaves: layer criss-cross with a few branches occasionally. Do not use any "activator". Dig a 1 ft. by 1 ft. ditch well outside for drainage, and cover heap with the earth.

Worms in thousands will travel, for miles, to lodge in the basement flat of this desirable residence, and if left undisturbed will of course breed there and go on doing so.

Do not initially disturb heap for 5–6 months so as to give the worms a chance to settle down, but after this repairs to the heap will of course be necessary. With a board or two across the centre the heap can be made in two easily operated sections.

Earwigs – Control of

How can I get rid of an absolute plague of earwigs in our garden and outbuildings?

These are difficult pests to control when they occur in large numbers. They feed chiefly at night and shelter during the day, and measures taken to reduce the available shelter would be useful. Any coarse vegetation in hedge bottoms or ditch sides near the garden should be, as far as possible, cleaned out and the weeds kept down. An insecticidal spray may be found useful in reducing their numbers, but they can be got rid of by trapping or poisoning. As a rule they can be trapped either in hollowstems such as pieces of bamboo or in inverted flower pots partly filled with dry hay, straw or moss. Another method is to trap them in match box lids. These are filled with crumpled paper, grass or other similar rubbish. By means of string they could be hung on the branches of shrubs. The earwigs take shelter in them in large numbers. The boxes can be collected at regular intervals and the earwigs, together with the rubbish, can be destroyed. In addition, balls of crumpled paper placed in the forks of branches will also provide shelter for large numbers of earwigs, and these also can be collected and destroyed at regular intervals. It is not suggested that this practice will entirely rid you of the pest but it should reduce their numbers.

Small Eggs

Would you be kind enough to let me have any advice you can give on the question of the large percentage of small eggs I am now getting from my R.I.R./ L.S. pullets? These were delivered to me on March 10 last as "on point of lay", which in fact they were. The number is 200. The birds are housed in a new deep litter house of suitable size and bedded on chopped straw. Deep litter meal is purchased and is in hoppers and ad lib., there is an adequate supply of both types of grit always available, there is also always a supply of fresh water. 2 oz. of wheat per head is given each evening. My last chit from the egg packing station read as follows: large ½ doz., standard 3 doz., mediums 18¼ doz., small 22 doz., extra small 4½ doz. In addition to the foregoing, approx. 6 doz. of the smallest used for cooking purposes in the school. I do feel that I am getting far too many small eggs at present, and any suggestions you may be able to make will be most acceptable.

Egg size is largely a matter of strain and breeding. But small eggs are more persistent with autumn hatched pullets than at other periods because they tend to mature earlier, through the action of spring light on the pituitary gland ; and if a pullet begins to lay at any time after four months it seems to take a longer time—in fact it may be until she is 10–11 months old—before she comes to her full grade of egg. Presumably you do not know when the pullets were hatched, so that you cannot find out if it is a matter of strain or too early maturing; in any case there is little practical action that you can take with the present stock of pullets. But there is one small point that you might bear in mind; egg size tends to drop in a period of very hot weather. This is prevented by first-class house insulation, plenty of water points, and possibly even wetting the mash.

Falconry

I wish to refer to the article entitled 'Falconry Past and Present' in which the author made certain statements which have no foundation in fact. He was referring to the attitude of the British Falconers' Club towards beginners to the sport of falconry. I enclose a pamphlet for your information which we send in reply to a first enquiry received from a beginner, presenting, I think, a fairly comprehensive outline of what is required for the commencement of falconry.

A great deal of time and expense is given in helping all beginners with the right facilities for the practice of the sport. We do not, however, advocate the keeping of such birds in towns as family pets, and thus, do not encourage these beginners.

It was the B.F.C. who instigated the proposed legislation restricting the importation of birds of prey and not the Government, for we are also very strong conservationists and would abhor the disappearance of any avian predator.

We shall be affected by the same restrictions as imposed upon any other falconer and furthermore have applied our own restrictions, namely, that we do not accept haggards (adult birds) only under exceptional circumstances reported to our Committee, as they represent the breeding stock of the world. We do not feel that falconry is doomed by these measures but that they are probably the salvation of falconry, affording protection and conservation to the various species.

From our modest annual subscriptions we donate regular yearly sums to certain bird protection societies and have a bounty system whereby we pay £5 to any gamekeeper who ensures that a nest of hawks is successfully reared.

If as stated only 25 per cent. of the present membership of the B.F.C. are active falconers and that the B.F.C. does not encourage beginners, then it would be logical to assume that the remaining 75 per cent of the membership are not even beginners, but in actual fact the members unable to practice falconry did so very successfully before I or the author were born.

The author also made the contradictory statements that falconry could not be taken up by anyone, but that on the other hand it is a sport that can be undertaken by the whole family as these birds make excellent pets and it was not essential to train them to hunt.

The natural function of these predators is to hunt and in this respect they do not have to be trained, but if on the other hand they are kept as pets for which they are totally unsuitable, then this is not falconry and the people who so keep them are not falconers and do not belong to the British Falconers' Club or for that matter in any other falconry organisation. We do not recommend anyone embarking upon the sport under the age of six-teen, and the picture of a terrified youngster with a Bateleur eagle being called to the fist in the incorrect manner – a hawk should always be called from behind with the rear of the arm presented to it – can do irreparable harm to the image of the sport.

In view of the bad type of publicity that falconry has attracted, the acquisition of illegally taken kestrels, many of which are found dead or dying, caught up by their trappings, plus the advertising of these birds in such journals as the *Exchange and Mart*, have at last induced the RSPCA to announce that they are opposed to falconry and in particular the increase in the number of people keeping these birds.

Finally, I should like to refer to the claim that there are a great many changes taking place in the sphere of training and the species being trained. According to Hartlings 'Bibliotheca Accipitraria' the sport of falconry has been traced back to the Hia dynasty in China to the year 2205 BC, not 4000 BC as stated, and since this time professional and amateur falconers have used the well tried methods of their forefathers. The two latest innovations to the sport have been the ring perch devised by our President, J G Mavrogordato, CMG, in the thirties and the ring screen perch by Herr Renz Waller, of Germany, in recent years, so there has in fact been little change over the centuries.

If, indeed, there are great changes being made, then I think it would have been more to the writer's credit to have written about these rather than attacking the traditional club of falconry in the British Isles.

C J Morley, Hon Secretary,
British Falconers' Club.

Fantails

I would like to keep Fantail Pigeons but someone has told me that wild pigeons will drive them away and that they will attack my kitchen garden.

We do not think that these are likely to stray or be attacked by wild pigeons. Opinions about this breed are rather mixed. Some people say that they are mischievous and cause a great deal of damage in the garden. All pigeons will damage a garden unless they are properly fed. The hardiness of pigeons depends entirely upon the stock from which they are bred.

The average housing provided for pigeons such as a small house on a pole, or a box about the size of a dog-kennel attached to a wall, is quite useless, unless the occupants are confined to a couple of birds or so. They are too small to be cleaned out properly, and the birds become infested with pests. It is far better to provide a proper aviary with the front facing south, something on the lines of a small portable shed, about 7 ft long by 6 ft by 6 ft; this would do for half a dozen pairs or more. It should be raised above the ground to keep out rats and cats, and it also needs ventilating and properly fitting out inside with perches and nest boxes. Pine or cedar sawdust is the best nest material. Upon arrival pigeons need to be kept shut up in the darkness for at least a fortnight and then let out for a few days in a wire enclosure so that they may become accustomed to outside feeding and their surroundings. They should then be willing to stay in the area of their own accord when released.

Farm Smells – Cure – 1

I live on a farm where the cow slurry is collected in a pit, and subsequently spread on the land. Obviously, the pit is cleared out every day or two, and both I and the farm hands suffer very much from the smell, which is overpowering and, when the wind is in a certain direction, almost unbearable.

Can you tell me if anyone has thought of producing any form of chloroform or similar deodorant for use in bulk on farms? And if not why not?

I shall be most grateful for any information and help you can give me.

I was tempted to suggest you applied large quantities of chloroform to your cows in which case the problem would presumably cure itself. Or perhaps one could buy chlorodyne in such vast quantities that the slurry-pit would suddenly find itself no longer required at all.

Seriously, however, no doubt you really meant chlorophyll, which is used to sweeten human breath and is given to dogs sometimes to increase their charms (but not to other dogs).

Presumably if such treatment could work it would have been tried by now. To kill a strong natural smell by applying an artificial one would be pretty impossible. We are really sympathetic to your plight. The only solution is to move the pit and/or the cows away from close proximity, or place them in a direction from which the wind seldom blows, i.e., due west. Other than that we can think of no solution.

Farm Smells – Cure – 2

Whilst journalistically amusing, your reply overlooks the fact that such a problem is well within the scope of the possible. May and Baker Ltd.—a supplier of yours—produce a range of 'Alamask' compounds for odour control. These are available through their distributors. One is specifically for sewage odour control and is widely used by local authorities and intensive farm units.

Steel Fencing Hurdles – Repair of

I want to straighten some steel fencing hurdles. Is there a special implement for doing this?

It seems impossible to find a tool which will do this work satisfactorily, but it has occurred to me that if you crossed two pieces of angle-iron, with a strong bolt at the junction, and laid on these a piece of iron such as a section of railway track cut to the length of the hurdle, you could then push this under the top bar and hammer direct on to it, thus straightening out each bar *in situ*. You would probably have to have two different sizes one for the top bar and one for the lower bar. The foot could rest on stout planks to avoid any driving into the earth. The whole thing when erected would look rather like the horse used for sawing logs.

Fencing Stakes

For many years I have bought peeled and pointed chestnut stakes for fencing. After *thorough drying out, these have been soaked in creosote for 48 hours, and after this treatment the 4 – 5 in. stake, whether round or split, has lasted about 15 years. Now I have my own Jap larch thinnings of similar size. Will this treatment of larch give me as good fencing stakes?*

Japanese larch will probably contain a higher proportion of perishable sapwood than chestnut, and will therefore be inherently somewhat less durable. However, soaking for 48 hours in creosote should result in a better standard of treatment in larch than in chestnut. Consequently we think that creosoted larch stakes should almost certain give a life of 15 years—i.e., similar to that now being obtained from creosoted chestnut ones.

Fig Trees

Can you recommend a book about growing figs out of doors?

Yes: "Figs out of Doors" by Justin Brooke published by Rupert Hart Davies.

Fish for Pond

I should be very grateful if you could tell me what kind of fish to put into a large natural pond approximately 2 ft. 6 in. at its greatest depth, with running but muddy water. There are a few brown trout in it, which have been there for years, but I would like to put in some more fish as the trout do not breed, possibly due to the mud. I find that 9 in.– 10 in. young trout are very expensive and if I put in smaller ones I am afraid that the old ones will eat them. Can you recommend any coarse fish which would do well in such shallow water and would any of them breed? Also could you please tell me where I can get them?

We have consulted the *Angling Times* concerning your pond, and they say that the mud is definitely the reason why the trout will not breed, and suggest that you clear the trout out and replace them with bream, tench, and perch. They also give this address, which might help you with further queries and from which you can buy these fish: Stanbridge Trout Farm, Great Stanbridge, Rochford, Essex.

Fisheries – Establishment of

I have a small fast flowing stream (never dry) forming the boundary to my property and eventually running into the sea.

Higher up a ravine there used to be a small dam which the previous owner allowed to fall into disrepair. Is it feasible if the dam were restored – it is not a wide one – to create a small pool for stocking with trout.

We suggest you contact the Fishery Management Services of Coventry, who would be able to advise you.

Flamingoes

I would like to know if it is possible to keep flamingoes in this country.

It is possible to keep flamingoes in this country provided you have a pond between 12 and 18 ins. deep in the centre, since flamingoes spend 95 per cent of their time in the water. A hut must also be provided for winter, but it does not necessarily have to be heated. They eat ordinary poultry mash and will also take shrimps to keep their colour up. You will also find that it is better to keep four flamingoes rather than two, as they like to be in a crowd.

Fleeces – Cleaning, Spinning, Weaving

I should be obliged if you could recommend a firm which would undertake the cleaning, spinning, weaving and dyeing of two sheep fleeces.

I know that some forty years ago this work was carried out by the Shvall Weavers of Haslemere, Sussex, but I do not know if they are still in business.

If you would like to contact Miss Dorothy Wilkinson, Kensington Weavers, 136 Kensington Church Street, London, W.8, she says she would be delighted to help you. She has been spinning for fifty years and could either do it herself or find

someone else. Perhaps you could tell her what kind of sheep they were so that she would have some idea of how many pounds you would get from the two fleeces; also whether you want it dyed and made up into tweed or worsted.

Eye Flies

I have recently bought a donkey, and find that the flies congregate around its eyes, causing great irritation. Also, it appears to have lice on its body. I should be very much obliged if you would advise on the treatment for both the above.

The treatment against lice consists of cleanliness and applications of DDT powders. Two applications are necessary at an interval of about 10 days. Grooming kit must also be cleaned. Flies which are attracted to the eyes of horses and donkeys are a common occurrence and it is often necessary to provide an eye fringe. A light application of paraffin or some other deterrent might be useful but it must not be applied where it can get into the animal's eyes.

Frost Damage Prevention in Orchards

I have been experimenting for six years on an extraordinarily economical method of staving off the April and May frosts from fruit blossom, and I have now got it 100 per cent efficient by using the following equipment for 1 acre of bush fruit. Initial lay-out, 1 acre: 50–60 gallon drums. These can be old, battered, rusty and leaky. Knock the tops off. Pierce 10 to 15 holes about ½ in. diameter extending from the bottom of the tin to half-way up. These allow for draught. These tins can often be obtained gratis as worn-out drums. Ingredients, 1 acre: Sawdust, 10 barrow loads; dry if possible, not sappy (can be obtained gratis from sawmills), heavy oil, 10 gallons. We use the heavy lubricating oil from sumps of lorries, etc. often poured down the drain by garages. Gas-tar 15 gallons. The above ingredients should all be thoroughly mixed together and must be turned over and over. We mix it in a shed earthen floor. In each of the drums, which are placed equi-distant throughout the acre, put one heaped-up shovelful of the mixture. This will fill the drum about quarter of the way up. Lay the drum on its side in case of rain. The drum can remain out indefinitely ready for the first frost and light-up. Torches for lighting. A light metal rod 3–4 ft long, with a bundle of rag or cotton waste secured to the end. This is soaked in paraffin just before lighting up. Procedure: two men and two boys lit up 3 acres of blackcurrants, 160 tins, 20 minutes. The boy carried the torch, lighted and held well overhead. The man carries a tin of paraffin and a cup. As each drum is reached the man throws half a cupful of paraffin into the drum. The boy touches it with the torch; it lights at once. Read the temperature 35°–36° went to bed still smouldering next morning.

Old Fruit Trees

I have a number of fine but old fruit trees in the garden. However, they all have shoots coming from the base or surrounding soil. Is there any known method of killing these off without harming the tree?

These should be cut off continuously as they appear. On the other hand, this is often an indication that fruit trees are past their best, and if it is the fruit you want, rather than the ornamental qualities of the trees, you should consider replacing them.

Gate – Oak Cleaner – 1

Can you please advise on the best way to clean an oak gate which has gone 'green' with lichen, etc., being sited under trees. As it is a presentation gate I would like to be sure it gets the right treatment. Also, is any preservative treatment recommended for interior oak panelling? We have some which seems in good condition but a bit dry.

First of all, try and scrub it with a bleaching powder. If this is unsatisfactory you may have to resort to sandpapering or wire brushing the wood, in which case you must be careful to avoid

scratches or raising the grain, and you should finish off the surface very smoothly with fine sandpaper. An application of linseed oil or a mixture of turpentine and beeswax might then help to prevent discoloration. The mixture will also do for your interior panelling, since we assume that you do not wish to use a preservative furniture polish.

Gate – Oak Cleaner – 2

I would be glad if you could offer advice on the following topic: I have an oak entrance gate which I purchased from the C.G.A. some five years ago. Initially I linseed oiled it thoroughly but after two years it looked very weathered. I then sanded it right down and gave it several coats of polyurethene varnish, but still the damp has got in, I presume, and lifted off the varnish. It now looks just as weathered as before. I want to be able to appreciate the wood, so am totally against painting it, in any case oak isn't very keen on paint from what I have seen. I should be most grateful for any suggestions you could offer.

Oak sometimes has a tendency to go almost black from exposure, and this may be due to the original seasoning of the wood. For instance, kiln drying cannot compare with seasoned wood which has probably taken two or three years to dry out. Many people believe that linseed oil is not a good material to use for the prevention of weathering, although it is better than nothing at all. There are some proprietary oils for wood on the market, such as teak oil, and we think there is one for oak, and possibly this can be obtained from your local ironmonger or a marine store. Your idea for using polyurethene varnish is good, but were you quite sure that the wood was absolutely dry before varnish was applied? It is possible too, that the damp has got in at the sharp edges where the varnish cannot really penetrate and which, of course, get the most wear; if these edges can be rounded a little before you varnish the gate the result might be more successful.

Another bad place for damp is at joins, and these should be carefully filled with wood stopper. Polyurethene too, requires light sanding down between coats to obtain a really mirror-like hard finish.

In reply to your correspondent who was concerned to preserve the appearance of his oak gate, you may care to recommend that he uses the new Rentokil clear water repellent finish which does not form a film and therefore cannot crack or peel, but allows the full texture of the grain to be seen and prevents swelling and shrinkage of wood, by stopping up-take of moisture. One or two coats should protect up to three years, and if it needs renewing it is only necessary to wipe off the dirt and apply another coat. There is also a pigmented cedarwood version of the water repellent finish and both types are intended for just this type of use on outdoor timber cladding, fences and sheds. They are available through ironmongers and hardware merchants at 33s a gallon or 19s yd for a ½ gallon can.

Gate Design

I have a pair of wheels from an old trap which I would like to incorporate in a pair of gates. I wonder whether you could suggest a suitable design, details, thickness of frame, etc. The idea was to use the gates in the post and rail fence of a paddock. The wheels are 44 in. in diameter, 1½ in. rims.

We suggest that you contact the Rural Industries Bureau, 35 Camp Road, London, S.W.19, since they are in touch with craftsmen who would be able to assist you in this matter.

Geese and Goslings

I have a pen of one gander, three geese, and fourteen goslings of April hatch. They are mainly Old English – nondescript lot. During the last three weeks the geese have been producing eggs at the rate of two or three a day – of excellent size. Is this unusual, and is it likely to have any effect on the normal spring laying next year? We already have over 30 eggs.

The average farmyard goose usually starts its laying cycle fairly regularly around mid-February, But this has been an abnormal year as you will have noticed. (It is not often that the writer can pick blooms of two of his kinds of clematis montana in mid-October as he has done this year.) But although it is an abnormal year for climatic conditions it is not abnormal for geese on occasion to lay in the autumn. I think it is possible that those that have laid now may delay their next cycle until March; but you can influence this to some extent by feeding well in January–February, particularly on a protein laying mash. You could also produce the same effect – as Aylesbury duck breeders do and turkey breeders, but it is hardly practical with geese – by artificial lighting.

Geese – As Mowers

I have a six acre field planted with nine thousand Xmas trees (Canadian Spruce) and have experienced great trouble in keeping the grass and weeds down. I am at present using an Allen Challenger which is very satisfactory.
However, my object in writing is to ask if there is any form of livestock – such as hens, ducks or possibly a donkey or sheep that would keep the grass down without harming the trees which are on average about three feet high?

The answer to your problem is geese – they would keep down the grass and not harm the trees.

Geese

Please could you let me have all the information possible on geese, especially: How many geese can one gander accommodate? How many eggs should be placed under one goose and are these left in the nest as laid? Where can I get a pamphlet on geese?

It is normal to mate a heavy type of gander, like a Toulouse-Embden cross, with three geese; but a lighter gander, like a Chinese, could be put with half a dozen. A goose will sit on 20 eggs without difficulty, but she tends to be an uncertain and sometimes rather clumsy mother, so it is best to make a certainty of hatching by placing the first 4–5 eggs under a broody hen, and perhaps repeating the process more than once before giving the goose a clutch to wind up with.

Geranium Plants

I have a fine bed of geraniums and I would like to preserve them for replanting next summer. Can you advise me as to the best way to keep them through the winter? I have no shed or greenhouse proof against hard frost.

If you have no shed or greenhouse proof against hard frost there will be risk of loss with the geraniums. The plants, or any cuttings taken, will have to be brought indoors, and although there may be some difficulty with watering in a dwelling-house room, we can see no alternative if there is no building, garage, etc. available other than the house itself. The best method is to lift the plants, cut the top growth back half way, and plant the 'stools', close together very firmly in boxes which are 4 in deep. Use a very light sandy compost. Very little water is needed, just enough to prevent the stems from shrivelling. Any dead leaves should be picked off. Keep the atmosphere as dry as possible. If the plants are kept where there is danger from frost, cover them with sacking, matting or similar dry material whilst the weather is severe. If you wish to take a batch of cuttings use the ends of the shoots, cut to about 4 in long. Leave the tip intact, trim through a leaf joint at the base, remove lower stems, and insert firmly in a mixture of half coarse sand and half loam in 3 in deep boxes. These can be kept on a window sill indoors and the same watering principles can be followed as described for the plants. Insert cuttings about 2 in apart and remove any dead leaves regularly. Pot up in early spring and keep indoors until frost danger is past. Cuttings will also need frost protection in winter, but should only be covered whilst the hard weather lasts. Here again, keep a dry atmosphere, or the cuttings will rot.

Goats – 1

I have some three acres of unfenced pasture backing on to my garden, and in order to keep the grass down it occurred to me that one or two goats tethered on a suitable length of rope might solve the problem. I envisage billy goats, since there would be no milking problem, and I have stables where they could be kept during hard weather.

Could you please advise me of the problems, if any, of keeping goats, and let me know how I would set about obtaining them. If they can be bought in the normal way, can you give me an idea as to cost. I should also like to know whether goats will be happy to live on grass with hay in the winter.

We suggest that you write to the Secretary, The British Goat Society, 5 Farnham Hall, Saxmundham, Suffolk. They publish leaflets on keeping goats, and would be able to advise you where to buy some, and the cost.

Goats, tethered on the unfenced pasture, would be a good way of keeping down the grass, and they would be quite happy living on grass, and hay in the winter.

Goats – 2

I have become interested in breeding goats, and wondered if you knew of any place where I could get information about these animals.

We suggest you contact the Secretary of the British Goat Society – Mr. Savage, 5 Farnham Hall, Saxmundham, Suffolk. This Society has a list of affiliated clubs throughout the country and they bring out a monthly journal and annual year book.

Goats – Billy

I have about ⅛ acre of ground which my house overlooks, which is in effect a continuation of the garden. This was infested by dock nettle and buttercup and very rough, so I have just had it levelled and grass sown.

I do not want to have to mow it – it

is too stony in any case — nor do I want to put up a fence to supplement the existing stonewall surround to keep animals in (unless I have to).

I am wondering whether a tethered goat would successfully keep the grass short, and whether it would eat dock and buttercup. If so, how many would I need and what looking after is necessary. If not, what would you suggest?

You could try a billy goat. It should have plenty of water and a house and be tethered. They tend to wind themselves up by the tether and would need some augmentation of their feed in winter especially. They eat the same sort of things as sheep, so a local supplier could advise you.

The number of goats depends upon the strength of the keep. You could start with one and see how he progresses and get another if he cannot keep down the grass on his own.

Goats or Ganders

I have read the correspondence headed 'Billy Goats' with much interest, as I have the same problem with a piece of ground, and would be grateful for the following further information.

Would the tether pole be too heavy for a woman of seventy to move on her own? The land is close to the house – is it possible to get a billy goat which does not cause an offensive smell in hot weather? Can you tell me where such a goat could be obtained, and the approximate cost?

Alternatively, I have been advised to have a tame gander. Do you think this would be better? If so, can you tell me where I could buy one, and whether it would be necessary to have its wings clipped?

We do not consider that a billy goat is suitable for dealing with a situation where it would have to be handled by a woman of seventy. Not only does the tether have to be driven into the ground because billy goats are so strong, but the goat itself might knock its owner down, which could be a serious matter for someone of that age. They also have a tendency to bolt the moment the tether

is lifted, and could thus prove very difficult.

We would advise you to purchase a pair of geese, and if these are not advertised in the local press, we suggest you ring up the local Ministry of Agriculture and ask whether they know of any farm who could let you have a goose and a gander for grazing purposes. You do not need to clip their wings if you put up wire netting to fence them in, and they will not try to get out as long as they have got enough to eat.

Goldfish – Disappearing

We have an artificial fishpond which contained about 25 goldfish, four of which were large – about 7 or 8 in. The other day we found that nearly all of them had disappeared and the water was covered with streaks of scum. We surmise that grass snakes had entered the water and eaten the fish. Would you say that this is correct, and, if so, can you suggest any means of preventing this in the future? We might mention that the only ones left, or at any rate visible, are small ones, and in that case the snake or snakes had eaten four of those large ones in addition to several small ones. Although herons have occasionally been seen flying over, this is a very rare occurrence and the presence of the scum streaks does not seem to point to them. But as a precaution would a few wires across the pond discourage herons should they be attracted?

We find it rather hard to believe that grass snakes would eat the fish, it may be that water-rats are responsible. This wires or nylon fishing line criss-crossed over the pond might discourage herons. For small ponds nylon net is used.

(*See* Herons, page 98.)

Goldfish Fungus

Can you tell me the cause and cure, if any, of goldfish fungus?

The fungus on goldfish is very well known and often shows itself in waters which are not very favourable to fish life. If the fish are very badly attacked it pays to destroy them, unless they are very valuable, and get a fresh lot, after improving conditions of the water. Sometimes the fish get so badly infected that they die off. The cause of the fungus appearing is that the spores are always present, just waiting a favourable time and condition to germinate.

If the fungus is not too prolific, the best treatment is to give the fish a salt bath, using a 10 per cent solution of common salt, putting the fish in a shallow dish of salt water and watching until they turn on their sides, then removing to fresh water. Another and better way, if it is possible, is to put them into fresh, clean running water for a period of weeks, when the fungus usually goes.

Goldfish – Retain Colour

I have a natural pond approximately half the size of a tennis court, fairly deep in the centre, which has water lilies in it. Some years ago I put in about two dozen goldfish of various sizes and they have multiplied every year, although I lost some of the big ones in that hard winter. These are a lot of pale coloured fish ranging from black to white. What is this caused by and what can one do to rectify it in order to retain the natural colour of goldfish?

It is very difficult to keep a good colour strain of goldfish in a pond of any size. These fishes originally came from bronze coloured fishes. Many youngsters do not change to the desired gold, but revert. If some of these are left in the pond to breed with the others, it is certain that each year less well-coloured fishes will be bred. If it is possible to catch the blackish ones they should be removed from the pond. The pale coloured ones are just a natural colour form and can appear amongst most strains of goldfish.

Gourds – Ornamental

Last year I grew some ornamental gourds for the first time in the hope that they would make a permanent decoration. I find, however, that the dark green on many is now turning a dull yellow and that many of them are going bad. The only treatment I have given them is to polish them with furniture polish.

Can you tell me whether there is a way of treating them so that they neither lose colour nor go bad, or whether gourds must be regarded as expandable?

We think that the trouble probably was that because of the wet cool summer last year your gourds did not ripen properly.

They should be picked when they are fully ripe and then dried slowly in a cool (but frost free) place out of direct sunlight. It is best to put them in a single layer on wire trays or slatted boxes so that the air can circulate freely.

When they are quite dry and hard paint them over with colourless varnish.

Given this treatment they should last for a considerable time.

Grass – Keeping Down

I am thinking of keeping sheep to graze sports fields, etc. I am a complete novice. I know nothing. Can you recommend a suitable pamphlet?

We think the best information on this subject for your purpose can be obtained by purchasing a copy of the Young Farmers' Club booklet about sheep. This can be obtained by writing to: The National Federation of Young Farmers' Clubs, 55 Gower Street, London, W.C.1.

Grass – Compost

For many years I have made good compost from pure grass clippings by the following method:

The pile is started on either earth, or, more usually, a small amount, say 5 per cent, of last year's heap. This is very rich in worms.

More or less by layers, it is built into a heap which, when rotted down, is 4 ft. high by 6 ft. wide, by as long as may be. After each mowing, a little Fertozan Special is usually sprinkled on to the heap. Controlled tests, to see whether this makes any difference, have not been made, since we do not feel it to be worth the risk of spoiling the heap.

Rotting is rapid till the autumn, but it stops when the weather gets cold. So that it all rots thoroughly, it is left till the following summer. Then any which is required as a top dressing for lawns is dried in the sun and screened. This must usually be done in August, to be sure of finishing it while there is any sun. The worms are killed, and it may be mixed with the desired amount of sand, which is about 50 per cent, depending upon the condition of the lawn to which it is to be applied.

I would like to see it covered with a sheet to stop the rain leaching the goodness out of it, between, say, November and May. Perhaps we shall manage that this year. No straw is used, and such straw-like things as hedge clippings and weeds tend to come all in the autumn. They are covered with a thin layer of grass clippings, next spring, to help them to rot down.

Grass Drying

What would you consider is the minimum acreage of grassland needed to economically maintain a 'Farmac' grass drier with an output of 4½–5 cwt. of dried grass meal per hour? Labour available, five men, and the necessary amount of harvesting implements and machinery. If possible could you also let me know how much the minimum acreage could be reduced by the employment of overhead irrigation?

It is difficult to say what is the minimum acreage of grassland which will economically maintain a 'Farmac' grass drier. Two points which occur to us at the outset are (a) that truly economical use of a grass drier does imply a fairly high degree of organization, and (b) that the make of drier mentioned has, to the best of our knowledge, been out of production for some time and that you are therefore presumably considering the use of a second-hand machine which might require a fair amount of expenditure on repairs and maintenance. To enlarge on point (a), whereas a few years ago (when imported feeding staffs were expensive and hard to come by) dried grass could be produced in a fairly casual way within the framework of normal farming operations and still show a profit, in present conditions the grass-drying operation must be planned almost on industrial lines (in miniature) to be competitive. It is normally necessary to have about 100 acres of grassland to ensure that a 4–5

cwt./hour drier is kept going. Without irrigation there would be times when no grass would be available whatever the acreage, particularly in a hot, dry summer. The effect of drought conditions can be partly alleviated by including some lucerne, or lucerne-cocksfoot mixture, in the acreage to be dried. We have no experience of the use of irrigation to keep up the production of grass for drying, but it might be possible with sufficient irrigation to reduce the necessary acreage to as little as half of that mentioned. However, before embarking on such a project you would be well advised to balance the irrigation costs against the costs of the acreage saved for other crops – making a conservative estimate for this saving – and against the present overall economic position of the dried-grass meal market.

Grassland – Management

I should be glad to have your advice on a question of grass management. We have one 4-acre and one 1½-acre field in grass. The grass is respectively three and two years old and in each field followed barley. The fields have been let to a farmer who has grazed cattle on them, free range. Each year in late spring artificial grass manure chosen by this farmer has been applied before his cattle were put on the grass.

There appears to have been a progressive deterioration in the quality of the sward with the appearance of coarser types of grass.

Can you say, please, what should be done now to make this grass sward recover some of its quality? Can this be effected by controlled grazing or should some other management be tried?

Finally can you recommend a readable book of 'Grass Farming'?

It is impossible to keep a grass sward in top class condition unless either it is very intensively and heavily grazed constantly throughout the growing season or it is mown once or twice during the season. However, the appearance of coarser grass is not necessarily a bad sign unless it is one of the weed grasses rather than a cultivated one.

I am afraid that at this distance the only practical suggestion I can make is that you try and get the farmer to cut the swards once at least in each year or you insist on him using an electric fence to divide the fields into paddocks and thus ensure much heavier grazing.

I am sorry to be unhelpful in this but I am sure you will appreciate that at this distance it is impossible to give detailed technical advice.

As far as a book on grass farming is concerned there are so very many and I would suggest that you try and obtain one of the official Young Farmers' Club booklets that should be obtainable at your local bookshop.

Grass – Rough

As I was not going to use my grass tennis court last year I kept a couple of rams on it in the early summer. The result was a thick mass of grass in the autumn, almost comparable to a coir doormat. As I want to use the court this year I tried to cut it, but nothing could compete. I have a flame gun. Should I burn it off with this; if so, when, or can you tell me of any chemical I can use?

We certainly think that a flame gun may be effective, especially if it is used during the winter months when the grass is dead and dry. It is very difficult to advise about the use of chemicals because these will kill all the grass and may prevent new growth for at least six months. One always gets this trouble with sheep when they graze grass, because they will only eat very short, sweet stems, and this, of course, encourages the growth of any of the more tussocky varieties.

Grass Tetany

I am having trouble with 'grass tetany' with a valuable Aberdeen Angus cow. This is apparently due to a shortage of magnesium. I am told that vitamin D would help the metabolism with Ca and Mg. Can you advise, please?

There have recently been some reports in the Press of apparent success of the use of vitamin D injections in Hypomagnesaemia, but the results were uncontrolled and only supported by general circumstantial evidence. There is no scientific evidence that this method is likely to lead directly to improvement in this disease. Vitamin D does, of course, help to maintain the calcium status of the blood, and may indirectly improve general vigour. Hypomagnesaemia is often associated with stress factors such as marked spells of cold weather or herd movements from one pasture to another, especially in spring time. It is a simple matter to treat animals for this disease. They should be given 2 oz. of Calcined Magnesite daily until the danger period is over or improvement is obvious. This can be given mixed with sugar beet pulp, or first laced with molasses and then added to some meal. Many country compounders prepare a special dairy mix containing enough of the magnesium salt to cover the daily requirements of a cow in every 4 or 5 lbs of food.

Ground Clearance

I am carrying out work of clearing a large area of pleasure grounds on this estate which has been rather neglected for some years. The work consists of removing a lot of elder, brambles and self-sown saplings preparatory to replanting with azaleas, rhododendrons, etc. The above growths are being pulled out or chopped off, but there is a large quantity of wild rhubarb, mares tail, and the tall, thick type of polygonum (not P. affine or P. baldschuanicum). One is bombarded with advertisements of modern weed killers; when asking if they are likely to prove effective before ordering a quantity, one is told they have no experience of the result. I wonder if you can suggest something to rid the ground of these growths? The soil is wet and sandy, but is being drained. Frost has withered the rhubarb and polygonum, so I propose waiting until the spring in the hope that I shall then know of a substance to apply which will act through the leaf. I have tried atlacide already, but I think this failed because the wetness of the area caused the strength to be so diluted.

We have found that the strongest of all the hormone type weed killers is S.B.K., made by Synchemicals. It kills brambles, stumps of trees, elderberry, and the like. It is important to remember that with a good many of these hormone type liquids you get the best results by using them when the plants are in full growth. They should always be mixed up in accordance with the instructions on the container, and generally speaking are first-class for use in the spring and early summer.

Ha-Ha –How to Build One

I want to build a ha-ha between the bottom of my garden and the beginning of the park to replace some unsightly railings and would be glad of your advice on this matter. I should like to know the dimensions required to exclude : (a) rabbits and hares; (b) cattle and horses.

Are there any drawbacks to constructing such a ha-ha in lower greensand?

The usual depth is 5 ft and the distance across the top 9 ft and the width at the bottom 4 ft. The bottom should be given a 'fall' so that the water can get away.

We know of no drawback to constructing in lower greensand.

A 9 in. brick wall with a concrete base, 2 ft wide and 9 in thick and a coping stone would be best. The wall should have weep-holes so that moisture from the soil at the back of it could trickle through and run into the bottom of the ha-ha, and get away in the direction of the fall. The sloping side of the ha-ha should be made at the angle of repose. It could be covered with turves if a good slope is given.

Hares – Damage by – Close Season

I have recently found two or three hares in my garden. What damage do these animals do to a farm or garden? Is there a 'close' season?

Like all rodents, hares can do quite a lot of damage in the garden. There is no close season, but hares are not allowed to be sold between March and July.

Hawthorns

I wish to transplant two large standard hawthorns, which have been in their present position for approximately ten years. I should be very grateful if you

can inform me what steps I should take to reduce the risk of transplanting these trees to a minimum.

We think that there will be considerable risk in moving large standard hawthorns. However, if you feel that you must do it early November would be the best time. Some six weeks before the actual move cut round the trees with a sharp spade about three feet away from the trunk. When you do move them chip inwards from this cut down and under the tree. You will probably have to sever some of the larger anchoring roots but these are not so important as the ball of fibrous feeding roots. Get the trees up with as large a ball of soil as possible and trim off any torn roots cleanly. Replant immediately, treading very firmly and staking securely.

Next year see that they never suffer from lack of water in dry periods and spraying the foliage daily with clear water in hot weather will also help. It may also be advisable to cut back some of the top growth to balance the loss of roots.

Hedgehogs

My boys brought home two baby hedgehogs which we are anxious to keep and they are for the moment thriving upon bread and milk. Should they have any addition to this diet, and upon what do they feed when adult? I should also like to know what damage, if any, they would do to the garden when we let them go.

A bread and milk diet will do for the time being, but hedgehogs are grub and carrion eaters, and we suggest, therefore, that you should add bits of raw meat to their diet little by little. They should not do much damage in any garden, but they should not be allowed in the house, since as a rule they are swarming with fleas once let out of doors.

Herons – Poaching by

I have a natural pond approximately 30 by 50 yards within one hundred yards of the house, in it are goldfish, carp, roach and the like.

Until recently we have never been troubled with herons, but within the last three months we have visits every night and morning by one who has been causing havoc to the fish population. In many cases the fish are just killed and left on the bank.

Have you any suggestions to scare them away. The bird, I understand, is protected. In any case I have no wish to shoot it.

The consensus of opinion is that herons will land on dry land and wade into water. The answer is therefore to stretch a single wire or some wire-mesh around the pond and prevent the bird getting into the water. Another solution is to build a hide for the fish of rocks. They will see the bird approaching and conceal themselves.

Holly Berries

I wonder if you or any of your readers can tell me how to preserve and protect our holly berries from the birds? This year we have an abundant supply of green berries, and already the birds have had a nibble or two. From our experience over the past couple of years, by the time these berries turn red in October or November, the birds will attack in force, and our fairly extensive area of holly bushes will be stripped bare.

We have tried netting and plastic covers, but these are expensive and not all that effective. I have heard of plastic spray, but have been advised that this, apart from making the holly sticky and unattractive, is also not all that effective.

As far as we know there is no really effective way of preventing birds from eating holly berries, which is their natural food in the late autumn, other than by netting. This is as you say expensive and unsightly. Members may have suggestions.

(They didn't!)

Holly Hedge

I have here a holly hedge, running up both sides of the drive for a distance of about 180 yards. Since I took this place over two years ago, I have cut it back once, and pruned it once. It is now *not quite so big as it was, but its dimensions are roughly 7 to 8 ft high and about 4 ft across. It is growing broader and more unmanageable at the top, and losing its foliage at the bottom. It now takes a quite unnecessary amount of labour and time and petrol to prune it, and I am anxious to reduce it to a more manageable size, say 4 ft high by 2 to 2½ ft across. This operation will presumably take a year or two to carry out, but I am anxious to get on with it as soon as possible. I can probably get the services of a big mechanical hedge cutter for at any rate part of the hedge. Would you very kindly advise on this operation in general, and in particular, when I should begin, and how many years will it take to get the hedge down to the above proportions without undue damage.*

This operation may take three years to carry out successfully. Cut back one side fairly hard in May of this year after all fear of frost is past. Do this preferably with a pair of secateurs. Then next year cut back the other side quite hard, in fact to the desired width, again using secateurs. The third year you can reduce the height of the hedge by about two feet, and if you wish do it again the following year lower still. We do not advise the use of the mechanical hedge cutter, since this never cuts to a 'joint' but just anywhere.

Holly Logs

A large ancient holly tree has been blown down in a gale. I believe it could be valuable. Can you advise me what to do?

Our Forestry expert advises that the chief uses for holly are as follows:

It is mainly used for inlay work and, when stained black, as a substitute for ebony in handles of teapots, brush backs, etc.; it is valued for the linings of cigarette and similar boxes.

It is also good for engravings, especially for calico printing, turnery (tool handles, etc.), clogs and in veneer for marquetry, and in Tonbridge ware.

Accordingly we would suggest to your reader that he contacts turnery workers and tool handle manufacturers and offers the timber to them.

In the meantime, we would suggest that he sticks the logs under cover, but not necessarily in an enclosed space, merely protecting them from rain, and raises them clear of the ground.

In view of the specialised uses of this timber we would not suggest that he cut them through and through, as the market may have their own special forms of requirements and, as such, it would be better to sell the logs in the round.

We should be pleased to supply your enquirer with likely sources of markets should he require them.

Hornets

Hornets started to build a nest in a tits' nesting-box which was attached to the wall of the house. Choosing a rainy night, we plugged the hole with cork, detached the nest-box and immersed it in a bucket of water. Upon examination, we found a small partly finished nest, a queen hornet with about a dozen ordinary hornets and a number of grubs and eggs in the cells. Since that young colony was destroyed, we have not seen a single hornet.

Horses Hooves – 1

I have two young thoroughbreds (5 years old and 4 years old) which have been running out since May last. Today the blacksmith came to shoe them after having been without shoes just over a month, and was of the opinion that the 4-year-old's feet were too broken to shoe. Can you recommend any treatment or regime which will encourage this horse's hooves to grow out quickly so as to be able to put shoes on him as soon as possible?

In general the rate of horn growth is directly proportional to the health and vigour of the animal. There is a good deal of disagreement as to the efficacy of remedies that in the past were used to encourage hoof growth, but there are many who believe that a number of oils are effective in this respect, especially cod liver oil, neat's foot oil, and whale oil. Therefore, a mixture of equal parts of these three oils could be prepared and applied by massage to the clipped coronet once daily. A little of the cod liver oil could be given in the nose bag of corn once daily to encourage growth from inside.

Horses Hooves – 2

I was given an excellent hunter that was unsound because he did not grow enough hoof to protect the frogs of his feet. My father had a thick layer of clay put on the floor of a large loose-box and stood the horse on this throughout the summer with the result that he grew proper hooves and was quite sound next season to the astonishment of his former owner and of the local blacksmith.

Horses – Treatment for Laminitis in

What is the best treatment for laminitis in horses?

Take off the shoes and replace them by thick wide-seated bar shoes. Keep the horse in a large box, with plenty of deep straw litter, taking care to remove all droppings and wet straw regularly. Give a physic ball, sloppy bran and green food only. Always keep the bowels open freely. Take the horse out for a few minutes leading exercise several times daily. Keep cold swabs over the feet. The more the horse lies down the better. After recovery, use the broad-seated shoes for a considerable time and only gradually commence faster work. Avoid trotting on hard surfaces till the cure is complete.

I recommend that you should consult a veterinary surgeon who specialises in treating horses. The Master or Secretary of your local Hunt will be able to give the name of a suitable vet.

Horses – Warts – 1

We own a thoroughbred chestnut gelding aged twenty-six years who is now in honourable retirement. Unfortunately, he has grown two large warts on the inside of his hind leg. These were 'tied off' but

"So They Caught You Too?"

(See page 111)

have grown bigger each time.

My veterinary surgeon, whose opinion I thoroughly respect, says that the condition can only be cured by an operation, and at this age would cause more distress to the horse than it would be worth – if, indeed, he survived it.

We are treating them with daily applications of permanganate of potash, but this does not seem to have very much effect. Can anyone suggest a cure?

Horses – Warts – 2

I have read with interest your letter about your old horse with two large warts on the inside of his hind leg. Do not laugh at this, but I have on several occasions cured warts on animals—and people—by the following procedure.

Take an apple, cut it in half and rub one half over and into the warts. Tie the apple together again with string (rather 'fiddly') and hang in a tree or bush. Do not touch the warts again, or if possible, look at them – but in due time when the apple has withered the warts will be gone. It is only fair to say that with one exception the warts cured have been small clusters, but I have cured one animal with large warts on his face spreading from his nose upwards towards his eyes. This was a D/S/H bull who as a yearling was to be shown at the Oxfordshire Show. He was operated on by my vet and won first and champion at the Show. The warts grew again and he was entered for the Royal, without telling my vet, I did the apple treatment. The warts went and the bull won. I afterwards told my vet, and I believe he used this treatment on a herd suffering from clusters of warts. I have myself used it on children and animals, and it has never failed.

Horses – Royal Cream

I am anxious to find out about the origins of the royal cream colours, that is the horses brought over by King George I from Hanover. The breed was kept up, and they used to pull the Gold Coach and the royal carriages up till 1914, when of course it became impossible to keep up the breed, as new blood from abroad could not be imported, and the Windsor Greys were the substitutes. I used to see the cream colours in Palace Yard, when they had brought the King to open Parliament. I would like to know how they were originally bred and how the breed was kept up in England for so long, and if they have any collaterals today in Vienna or other foreign countries, and what became of the old cream colours when they were superseded? I believe some of the horses in the Dolemites are cream-coloured.

This is a very interesting subject, and I am afraid one on which we have no information, and seem unable to find out anything about these horses. I telephoned to the press office at Buckingham Palace, and they said they would let me know if they have any information on them I would have thought it quite possible that someone in The Royal Mews might remember the horses, and I suggest that you write to them.

I was told, as a child in the pre-1914 period that use of the Hanoverian cream-coloured horses had already been ended because of their bad temper. The breed has not necessarily died out in this country; perhaps it is still to be found in the Home Park at Windsor.

Ivy

I have a flint wall which is covered in ivy. I have been advised (i) that I must cut the ivy away at the roots, (ii) that on no account must I cut the ivy away at the roots because it keeps the wall up. Can you give me a ruling on this apparently controversial subject.

The best person to advise you would be a local builder or perhaps you could ascertain for yourself whether the ivy is holding up the wall or not by removing a small section. If the wall underneath the ivy is dry after a severe downpour of rain then it is possible that the ivy is not only supporting the wall but preserving it as well. You may find that most of the ivy stems have not penetrated the interstices of the wall but are merely holding on to it by a lot of hairy surface roots. If you do decide to cut away the ivy then unless the rootlets can be torn off without damaging the wall it is better to let the roots and stems remain until they rot away, presuming, of course, that you have already cut the main roots.

Laburnum Seed – Dangers of – 1

Laburnum seeds are notoriously poisonous to fish in garden ponds. Are they as hazardous to dogs which have the run of a garden where laburnums grow? I am particularly anxious about the possible effect on a young puppy.

Laburnum seeds are highly poisonous, both to humans and animals. No dog to my knowledge would ever touch them. I have laburnums growing in my garden for years and no dog or cat has ever come to any harm.

Laburnum Seed – Dangers of – 2

Your Suffolk member and indeed the writer of the reply to his query may like to know that a case of fatal laburnum poisoning in the dog has been recorded in the veterinary literature. In this case the chewing of a branch was the cause.
Cases have been recorded in horses, cattle, pigs and of course humans.
The question was, however, about seeds.

Land – Reclaiming for Grazing

I want to reclaim for grazing about four acres of rough land which was originally pasture and orchard but has been allowed to run wild for some years.
The local branch of the Ministry of Agriculture inform me that a grant cannot be made either for fencing or clearance of weed etc., but only for ploughing which is impracticable on part of this ground.
Is this correct? It would seem to be an absurd ruling particularly as a grant can—I believe—be made for such items as a cattle grid which are a convenience rather than an essential for production.

I think there must be some misunderstanding between you and the Ministry as provided you are a registered agricultural holding, there is certainly grant available for both fencing and clearance of orchard

trees; this grant is in fact the Farm Improvement Scheme grant of 25 per cent plus an investment incentive of 5 per cent making a total grant of 30 per cent.

I am sure if you reopen discussions with the Ministry, you will find that assuming you are a 'prudent owner/occupier', then grant will be available to you.

Lavender –Drying of

We planted about two dozen dwarf lavender bushes in the spring and these are now developing and coming into flower. Could you please let me know the process by which lavender is dried and stored in sachets or small bags?

Pick the lavender when it is in flower, and lay it out on newspaper until dry (the whole flower including the stems). When it is dried, remove the flowers from the stalks and fill the sachets.

Lead Garden Ornaments – Mending

We have a pair of lead garden ornaments 23 in. high, one of them with both the leg and the arm broken off. We would like to repair it ourselves and wonder if you can advise how to do this. If this would be difficult, do you know where it could be taken for repair?

We have been advised that it is extremely difficult to mend these lead garden ornaments yourselves, as they are probably made of spelter, a type of zinc. If you could have them taken to the following firm they would be able to do the work for you. They are: Hawkins and Scuffell, 123 Camden Mews, London, NW1 (01-485 8946).

Leaf-Mould

A query about unsatisfactory leaf-mould, please: the heaps here are made up with oak and beach leaves, packed tightly into corrugated iron wire-fronted bins, the layers dressed with soil and 'Adco.' But even allowing twelve months for the heaps to mature, the leaves remain in much the same condition as when first put in – a solid mass, not friable.

Much depends upon the state of the

leaves when they were put into the compost heap. If they were dry then they would not disintegrate into good compost very quickly. We also assume that you carried out composting instructions very carefully by moistening the leaves, turning over the heap at regular intervals, and keeping the top of the heap covered with moist sacking. If this was done then the soil and 'Adco' should by now have made a satisfactory compost within the leaves.

Leatherjackets

Both my front lawn and my neighbour's have dull grey patches, while the rest looks none too healthy. My neighbour was told this was caused by leatherjacket grubs feeding off the roots of the grass. He dug up a small area of turves, and at a depth of 2 in. or so did find some brownish chrysalis about 1½ to 2 in. long. Until now we thought our front lawns were poor, as they faced south to the local beach.

Could these chrysalis be leatherjackets and, if so, would they spoil lawns? Is there any chemical which would reach them at the grass roots?

Without seeing the 'brownish chrysalis' we cannot be absolutely sure that they are leather jackets, but it sounds very much as if they are.

These larvae of the Crane Fly or 'Daddy-Long-Legs' can do very considerable damage to turf, and the best control is to water with chlordane wormkiller.

Lichen

Should lichen be removed from slate roofs? I have been told that lichen breaks the woodwork under the damp slates and that the lichen roots may penetrate to and cause the wood to rot. Is this true? If hypochlorite is applied to kill the lichen, must the latter then be scraped off?

Most people like to see this plant on roofs. If you kill the lichen you will find that the dead roots cling most tenaciously

and their removal hardly makes the trouble worth while provided there is no sign of any wood rot in the roof timbers.

Magnolias – Cultivation

I have recently acquired some ripe seeds from a matured magnolia bush, probably the variety conspicua. Could you please advise me on their sowing and general culture?

The usual practice for growing magnolias is to use cuttings and grafts for the better kinds or by layers in autumn for the common ones. They should be planted in spring in good friable loamy soil. If you use seeds you will have to grow these in the same manner as ordinary seeds and prick them out later on for replanting.

Manure – Pig

I should be grateful if you would kindly advise me of the best method of storing pig manure in order to get an early breakdown of the long straw and a more friable condition of the dung. Should it be stored under cover and should it be treated with any of the composting agents?

Treatment with composting agents will accelerate breakdown of the straw and add to its material value. It is better, too, if it is left in the open provided that it does not get too saturated and leached out by rain.

Marble – Preservation of White Statue in the Open Air

If the statue is in comparatively pure air in the country no special treatment is needed except washing down fairly frequently with clean water. Individual dirt marks can be removed by using mild soap and thoroughly rinsing afterwards.

If the statue is situated in a built-up area and is open to soot and acid deposit on the surface it would be advisable to treat the marble, when it is perfectly clean, by spraying with: (a) A colourless petroleum jelly dissolved into a thin liquid in synthetic turps—i.e., not genuine turps. (*b*) Cementone No 3 which contains these ingredients with paraffin wax, and is manufactured by Joseph Freeman Sons & Co Ltd, 96 Garrett Lane, Wandsworth, SW18. The resulting film on the marble will be non-drying, but will hold firmly to the surface and give good protection against acid-laden air or rain. From time to time it would be necessary to wash the marble with synthetic turps and respray as above. Hard-drying lacquer or varnish is not recommended.

Maypoles

Can any member tell me: (a) *how to make and rig a maypole;* (b) *how to dance around it?*

If the Devonshire Member consults Chambers Book of Days, he will find, under May 1st, a very full account of Mayday customs, with pictures of Maypoles, including the raising of one.

When I was a boy, there was a tall Maypole on the tiny village green of Paganhill, Nr. Stroud. At the appropriate time, streamers used to be attached to this and, on May 1st, children used to hold one end of the streamers and dance around it, the dancing being only what I may describe as here-we-go-round-the-mulberry-bush type.

The Devon Member could not do better than consult Sir Frederick Ashton, c/o The Royal Opera House, Covent Garden, London, W.C.2. His Maypole in 'La Fille Mal Gardée' is the best rigged and danced about of any I know.

Melon Frames

I have been growing melons in a frame but am in doubt over what one does with the lights of the frame. Are they on or off? A 9 in. mound plus the plant on top would reach the top of my frame or protrude. I should be obliged if you could help.

With regard to the lights on frames in which melons are being grown, after planting, keep the frames closed until it

is seen that the plants are growing freely. They can then be given a small amount of air, by opening the lights three or four inches during the day, but closing again at night. Later, usually about July, when the plants have reached full size, air can be given quite freely even to the extent of removing the lights completely during the day, but my own practice is to replace them at night, leaving them open about a foot. This is the procedure to be followed until the fruit is finally cut just as it begins to ripen. We suggest that you might stand the frames on a base of bricks to give more overhead room, or they could reduce the height of the mounds to 6 in. Either, or both, of these methods can be used, but if the frames are brick built, some of the soil can be taken out, to make allowance for the mounds.

Mice and Crocuses

I should be grateful if you could tell me whether there is any known means of protecting crocuses from field-mice. Is there any chemical solution in which the bulbs can be dipped before planting, which will deter the mice without harming the bulbs and which will remain effective during their whole period of growth?

Unfortunately there is no chemical solution into which bulbs may be put before planting in order to prevent the mice nibbling them. Some people have tried a solution of red lead with a little disinfectant such as Jeyes, but reports at the moment are not very encouraging. Using backbreaking traps set with marrow seeds has given the best results.

Midges – Eradication of

I live in an old stone house in a valley leading into the Yorkshire Moors, at the foot of the Pennines. We have a large garden surrounded by forest trees. There is a small lake of about two million gallons of running water maintained weed-free. Adjacent there is an old farmstead built in stone as a dairy farm,

but now converted to intensive pig rearing. A fast stream goes through both the
farm and gardens. Beyond, at the head of
the valley, about one mile distant, there
are three small domestic water storage
reservoirs. The valley has always, in my
lifetime, been apparently a breeding or
congregating ground for midges. On a fine
warm summer's day, especially in the
evening, the garden is infested with
plagues of midges. One morning from
nine o'clock until noon we had the
largest population of midges that I have
ever seen, the air being almost thick with
them all over the garden, particularly on
the farm side. Could you advise me: (1)
how to combat the nuisance of midges
spoiling outdoor enjoyment of the garden, and (2) how or where we might discourage their breeding?

First of all it is assumed that the midges
are not of the biting kind. Non-biting
midges breed in vast numbers in accumulations of fresh water where they live at
the bottom feeding on the detritus to be
found in the mud. As these creatures do
not come to the surface for oxygen and
only come out of the water when they
are ready to emerge as adult flies, it is
very difficult to deal with them, and this
is one of the more intractable problems
with which we are faced. There is no
satisfactory solution to the problem
where the water is running thus preventing draining the lake, other than the use
of DDT and other insecticides in certain
proportions. Your correspondent will not
find this method very satisfactory and
probably rather expensive. The larvae of
the midges are eaten by fishes, and it has
occurred to me that the lake may not
have sufficient of these animals and so an
introduction of bottom-feeding fish might
prove beneficial.

Marestail

Is there any known way of eradicating
marestail? If so, I should be grateful for
any information.

To the best of our knowledge there is
no certain way of destroying marestail.
We would think that continued treat-

ment with one of the Paraquat based
weed killers such as Weedol (or on a
larger scale Gramoxone W) might, by
constant destruction of the top growth
gradually 'starve out' the weed.

Mistletoe – Propagation of

Have you any idea where I can obtain mistletoe plants for grafting onto old apple trees?
I gather you can get them in France, but have
not heard of anywhere in the U.K.

To the best of our knowledge it is not
possible to buy mistletoe plants anywhere
in the United Kingdom.
We would have also thought that it would
be impossible to graft a fully grown plant of
mistletoe on to a tree. Mistletoe is a harmless
parasite in that it actually 'roots' into its
host tree, and we doubt very much if normal
grafting methods would succeed.
The way to establish it is to obtain some
ripe berries and rub them either into a
natural crack in the bark on the inside of
the branch, or else cut a small notch for
insertion. The most suitable month for
'sowing' the seeds is March, but you could
plant at any time.

Moles – Eradication of – 1

I would be most grateful for advice on
ridding my property of moles under the
lawn. I have tried the anti-mole stink
bombs without success and I have also
flooded their runs with a hose – but this
is not the complete answer.

This is one of the most difficult problems to deal with. Suggested remedies are
as follows:
1 Traps.
2 Mole catchers (try the local RDC).
3 Gassing by Topvil fuses.
4 Gassing – pipe gases from motor
  mowers into holes – two-stroke engines
  are best.
5 Insert Foxerine, Jeyes Fluid or Mothballs into the runs.
6 Insert empty bottles base down into
  the runs – the wind noise across the
  neck of the bottle is supposed to drive
  them away.
7 Stamping – moles are sensitive to
  vibration and stamping on the mole

holes may actually kill them.

8 Strychnine on worms inserted in the runs. This is a dangerous practice and other animals might be affected.

I have tried all these remedies with the exception of traps, and to encourage you, must admit that I have more moles in my lawn this year than I have ever had before. I am not, however, able to tackle the problem daily and I am sure that persistence is the real answer whatever remedy you use.

More recently I bought a trap and this actually works.

Moles – Eradication of – 2

In connection with your note on moles, an old remedy which I have tried over the last two years is to place small slices of lemon down holes about 6 in. to 8 in. deep in the lawn on grassed areas. If a grid of, say, 3 ft. square is made of holes over the lawn, this seems to have some effect, and I have not been troubled with unsightly mole hills for some time. They appear to have transferred their activities into the adjoining woodland. Disadvantage—lemons in bulk are expensive!

Moles – Eradication of – 3

Having read somewhere that moles will not go within 70 ft of Caper Spurge,* and having been told by a friend that experience had lead him to agree, I put in a few plants near the runs of my few moles and was surprised and delighted to find that they had departed within a week or two, presumably to the field next door from whence they had come.

Moles – Eradication of – 4

Some years ago I read, I think in your magazine, that moles can be kept at bay by planting a certain plant named *Euphorbia Lathyrus,** the seeds of which can be obtained from Thompson & Morgan, Ipswich, price about 1s 6d a packet. I planted these around my lawn and moles bothered me no more. A co-incidence perhaps, but worth trying for the expense of 1s 6d.

Euphorbia Lathyrus and Caper Spurge are one and the same thing. Personally, I don't find it works.

Moles – Eradication of – 5

Has anyone tried Chlordane worm-killer on his lawn – on the theory no worms no moles? I tried all your suggested remedies with no success, but since using Chlordane many years ago (applied once annually, in February) I have not been troubled.

Moles – Eradication of – 6

I was very pleased to read your note on the subject of moles. I can give him the answer, and that is to shoot them, and I am not joking. When I first bought Ranworth a full sized tennis court was disfigured with many molehills. The verandah overlooks this lawn, and therefore it was not difficult to see these animals working from time to time. They say that moles work at 4, 8 and 12 o'clock; whether this is true or not I do not know, but I remember killing them at roughly midday when I was having an aperitif on the verandah. I shot six of them, blowing five to pieces, but the sixth I misjudged by a fraction of an inch and instead of killing it the shot stunned it, and it soon recovered, but I can assure you it didn't get very far. What I did was to have my ·410 ready, immediately I saw a mole working in a run I crept down to within a few feet of the animal in my bare feet, and as you know a ·410 has practically no recoil, and I could therefore use it more like a pistol and place the barrel within an inch or two of where I knew the mole would be.

Having shot these six moles, and this was about 14 years ago, I have never seen a mole in the garden since. In my very early days when I was an apprentice on a dairy farm we used to catch them by the hundred with the old-fashioned mole trap, and in those days they were worth, I think, about 1s each, which to me as a youngster was quite a large sum of money.

Moles – Eradication of – 7

We recently paid seven pounds to a man who said he could clear our land of moles, and who spent the best part of a day running the exhaust from a portable engine down their holes. Is this a recognized way of dealing with moles?

The method you describe is sometimes used to get rid of moles. It can be quite effective if one attaches a hose-pipe to the exhaust of an ordinary motor mower. The drawback is that you can never be sure that you are pumping gas into all the moles' runs, and this is where the system depends on a measure of good luck.

Some local authorities have mole catchers, and you might care to contact them in case they can supply you with someone better.

Moles – Eradication of – 8

Many of your members I know are troubled with moles like I am, and have difficulty in getting rid of them.

I have recently found what I consider may be an answer to the problem when they are being a nuisance on a lawn at this time of the year.

For some weeks my lawn has been a mass of molehills. I have only managed to trap two, and in spite of trying various other means to get rid of them they have continued to work. About two weeks ago I put my Fly-mo over the whole lawn using it at full throttle. Since when there has been no sign of a mole.

It may be pure coincidence but on the other hand it may be that the downward pressure from the Fly-mo engine may stun a mole in a shallow run below the surface.

Molehills

I should be most grateful if you could kindly let me know what I can do with between sixty and seventy molehills on the lawn in front of the house. I have not been able to mow the ground since about October owing to floods.

I have only one gardener, and he has to be careful owing to a bad heart. I was told by someone to put poison down each hill, but having dogs I would not risk them getting some poison out of the ground or a dead mole. I should be grateful if you can tell me what to do, as soon as the ground dries after two feet of snow.

Either go to the local authority and see if they have a mole catcher or else go to your local chemist and buy strychnine, for which you must sign the poison book. Place the strychnine in a jam jar with a lid and add a quantity of live earthworms. Give a good shake so that they are well covered with the poison. Using gloves, put a worm down each molehill. This is supposed to deal with the moles. There is no great danger of other animals being affected because dogs and cats do not usually eat moles and they do not tend to come to the surface when affected by the strychnine, which acts almost instantaneously. The greatest care must be taken when handling the strychnine and on no account should it be put down a drain when no longer needed. The chemist who supplies you will advise you how to dispose of it in the safest way.

Mosquitoes

Please can you inform me what ought to be put on a pond, the quantity and when to kill mosquitoes and prevent breeding.

Crude kerosene (paraffin oil) will destroy mosquito larvae sprayed on to water at the rate of $\frac{1}{4}$ pt per 100 sq ft. The same result may be obtained by a much lighter dose of 2 per cent DDT in kerosene, preferably with a spreading agent. The aim is to obtain about 10 mgm of DDT per sq yd and a few puffs with a hand atomiser will apply about the right amount. Mosquitoes breeding in very small pools or water butts can be easily controlled by applying a spoonful of petrol to the surface. The oil treatment and the DDT, if the dose is exceeded, may sometimes be harmful to fish: but mosquito larvae are unlikely to occur in ponds containing fish.

Whatever treatment is adopted it should be repeated at fortnightly intervals throughout the summer starting in March or April.

Moss – Killing

The tarmac drive and paths of my house are becoming infested with moss. It has been suggested to me that the only remedy is an application of caustic soda in solution applied with a watering can. Can you advise me as to the minimum strength required to kill the moss without damaging the tarmac?

We are not certain of the long-term effect of this method and would suggest that you use Corrys Moss Killer.

Motorway Fencing

We have a client who has had part of his land taken for a motorway.
The Ministry (per the district valuer) wish our client to assume responsibility for boundary fencing erected by them (wooden uprights with four cross bars).
Have you any experience of the likely cost of maintenance for this type of fencing?

We duly spoke to our suppliers of fencing and they were surprised to hear that your client had been asked to be responsible for this type of fencing. They were under the impression that all motorway fencing was the responsibility of the Ministry of Transport.

It may be that the land taken was for a by-pass or some other new road, which was not a motorway, in which case it is possible that he would be asked to accept responsibility.

The upkeep of a timber fence is not expensive and if railings should be broken they are cheaply and easily repaired. In fact the main cost arising from this type of fencing would be of replacement in due course which might be any time after 10 to 12 years.

Mulching

I read an article somewhere on the subject of cane fruit refers to 'growing soft fruit on the new mulching principle ... no more hoeing or forking.' As I have recently planted raspberry canes and am about to plant gooseberries and currants, all to be in the same cage, I should be very grateful for further particulars.

The plan is first of all to see that there are no perennial weeds at all, and then when you are quite sure that they have been eliminated, the whole of the soil is covered with straw a foot deep. This is then sprinkled with a fish fertilizer containing a 5 per cent potash content. Each year a further dressing of straw (any straw will do) is given because the worms will have pulled some of it into the ground. The subsequent dressing need not be deeper than 3 in. Each year, too, the fish fertilizer is given twice a year, first of all in February and then again immediately the fruits have been picked, the dressing on each occasion being at 3 oz to the sq yd.

Straw Mulch

Having read and enthusiastically copied your suggestions of straw mulching on soft fruits there are still a few points that I am a bit concerned about, and would be most grateful for your answers. For the sake of convenience I set them out so that you can reply against each one. (1) Since the straw below the air-dried top gets very wet and ugly-looking, does it need to be turned over periodically? (2) Does one maintain the original supply of straw, merely topping up the mulch each year? (3) In dry weather does one need to water? If so, does one water at the base of canes only, or water over all the straw? (4) As I have five fruit trees against the wall of the raspberry cage (but not the currants) can one straw mulch them the same? They are cherry, plum and peach.

(1) The straw should never be disturbed. (2) Yes. (3) It is seldom necessary to

water because the straw keeps the moisture in the ground. (4) Yes, certainly.

Mushroom Growing

I own a twelve-acre property in Argyllshire. I have recently been giving some thought to possible small profitable ventures to which I might turn my hand when I retire from the Army. One of these is mushroom growing. Have you any information of a detailed nature on this subject?

Mushrooms would probably be a good idea, although you do not need much land for them, and in fact an acre would be enough. However, we suggest that you contact Mr W. R. Alderton of the Mushroom Growers Association, Agriculture House, Knightsbridge, London SW1, who would be able to give you details and advice.

There is a very good book published by Faber & Faber called *Mushroom Growing Today,* by Fred Alkins, which would tell you all you want to know, including where to get the necessary supplies, types of houses required, etc.

Mushrooms – Growing Wild Ones

In your excellent book 'A Guide to Country Living', you suggest 'putting down mushroom spawn'. Can you give me any advice about how to try and cultivate wild mushrooms on one's own land?

We would suggest you get into touch with The Mushroom Growers' Association at Agricultural House, Knightsbridge, London, S.W.1, they can supply spawn and also advise on the cultivation of mushrooms. It is best to put spawn down in a field where horses have been kept as horse manure seems to suit the mushrooms.

Netting Drips

I have recently planted out a strawberry bed and was intending to cover it with ½-in wire netting as a protection against birds. I have now been told that wire netting has an injurious effect on straw-berries. Is this so? The netting is not new, and I was intending to paint it over with bituminous paint.

The drips from galvanised wire netting certainly have an injurious effect on strawberries. If you painted the netting over with a bituminous paint you might prevent the 'galvanised' drips, but I have no idea how long this bituminous paint would last, neither do I know whether you could get a complete cover on netting. The better plan is to have wire netting sides and the cover made with fish netting, which can be put on at flowering time and taken off immediately after picking.

Nettles – 1

I have the use of about four acres of rather neglected grass lands for grazing a horse in the summer. Nettles are gaining a hold on it and I have found the advertised selective weed and brushwood killers enormously expensive and difficult to apply as recommended when the nettles are in full growth. Sodium chlorate has obvious drawbacks, but is still much cheaper. If I can check the nettles, do you think that the grass will grow over them and destroy them eventually?

We are afraid that there is nothing else we can recommend for the destruction of nettles, other than selective weedkillers, such as CGA Brushwood Killer or spot treatment with sodium chlorate. The last named would probably kill the nettles more thoroughly, but has, of course, the disadvantage that it also kills the grass and poisons the soil so that nothing will grow on the treated patches for up to six months after treatment. If there are large patches of nettles it will probably be necessary to re-sow these with grass after the nettles have been destroyed, although to a certain extent the existing grass would probably grow over them, particularly if you applied some fertilizer.

Nettles – 2

I have in the meadow in front of my house a quantity of nettles which I am most anxious to eradicate for good. They are chiefly along both sides of a ditch which runs along the side of the meadow. I understand that there is a chemical which I can sprinkle over them which completely kills nettles. I do not want to put down any poison here as cattle graze in their field. I should also be glad to know:

1. What quantity of chemical I should scatter over these nettles and whether one or more applications will be necessary, and also what is the best time of the year to put this chemical on?

2 Where the chemical is obtainable?

I should be glad of any further information you could give me with reference to the eradication of nettles in a field.

You could apply a 4 per cent solution of chlorate of soda. The chlorate of soda should be made into a solution using 4 lb of salt to 9 gallons of water and this should be sprinkled over the nettles, preferably on a sunny day. For the best results the nettles should be sprayed at an early stage of growth whilst the leaves are still tender.

Nettles – 3

May I amplify your reply concerning nettles? I have had considerable experience with an unadulterated form of sodium chlorate for nettles, and I much prefer to sprinkle it on dry. This is more expensive, but the danger of getting the liquid on the clothing is obviated. Further, if ordinary care is used, nettles growing through a fence can be killed without damage if it is applied to the leaves of the nettles only, preferably when they are damp. I should advise your enquirer to experiment on these lines with about 7 lb. of sodium chlorate. He will see the great possibilities of this chemical. It is non-poisonous to cattle and the results show that the grass recovers within a few months.

My fields, hedges and woodland which were all badly infested are now quite clean, and in my opinion it is an invaluable introduction.

Oyster Cultivation

I am thinking of starting up an oyster farm. Where can I get some basic information?

The Ministry of Agriculture and Fisheries have published a number of pamphlets on this subject. We would recommend you write to them direct either in London or at your local county town; their address should be in the telphone directory.

Pampas Grass

Would you be kind enough to give me your opinion with regard to two large clumps of pampas grass which I wish to move to another place. Is this the time of the year to transplant? Should the grass be cut to the ground before removing? I am asking your advice because some years ago I tried to remove clumps of pampas with disastrous effect – all the plants died.

We would advise you to delay the moving of the pampas grass until about the third week of April, and then only to do the moving if the soil is nice and dry. Do not cut down all the foliage, although you can, if you wish to reduce it by about half. It has been said that it is best to do the transplanting at night time, but we think that this may be carrying things rather too far. Get the transplanting, however, done within a few hours, plant very firmly indeed and be prepared to syringe the leaves over in the evening, should the weather prove dry in May and June. It would be better to wait until early May, should we have a rainy April and the soil be sticky.

Parrot – Companion for

We have a young West African grey parrot and although he (or she) is on the top of his cage all day we feel

that he requires a companion (not neces-
sarily a parrot). He longs to play with
our fox terrier but she is not to be relied
upon. We hope during the summer to
have an outside aviary adjoining the
house erected for him and consider that
this would be an opportune time to intro-
duce another bird. Our bird whistles a
great deal, is learning to talk and is
extremely tame, but we wonder whether
with the introduction of a mate he would
become silent, wild and lose his indivi-
duality and that there might be continual
friction between them. Is there any
method of sexing a parrot? We should
be most grateful for your advice.

Males of the African grey parrot have
a slightly larger head and bill than the
females, but it is not very easy to sex
these birds unless one has a number together for comparison. The bird might
not talk quite as much if it is kept with
another. Grey parrots have been bred
on one or two occasions in this country
in outdoor aviaries. They need to be
supplied ideally with a hollow tree trunk
in which to nest, the trunk being filled
to within about a foot of the entrance
hole with peat moss or leaf mould and
a layer of crumpled decayed wood put on
the top of this.

Talking of 'sexing' parrots, there was
a story of an owner who wanted to discover which was which of his two
parrots, and so he switched off the lights
and pretended to leave the room. When
fluttering was heard the lights went on
again and the male was identified easily.
The owner tied a white ribbon around its
neck, much to the bird's disgust. When
the vicar called shortly afterwards the
bird eyed him commiseratingly and said,
'So they caught you too!'

Parrots – Teaching to Talk – 1

I recently bought a young African grey parrot
and hoped to be able to teach it to say some
words. This was about three months ago and
I have so far had no success at all.

Can you or any of your readers suggest any
particular treatment to cure this situation?

We have consulted Harrods Pet Department, who are experienced in this sort of

problem, and they tell us that the only
method is to talk to the parrot as much as
possible and that this is the only way which
will encourage it to talk back. This, apparently, is particularly the case with a
younger bird.

To encourage, they tell us that they have
sold birds, which were said to talk, and that
sometimes they have not uttered for anything up to six months, then for no reason
they suddenly get chatty and talk their heads
off. But you must talk to it as much as
possible.

Parrots – Teaching to Talk – 2

I refer to the subject of grey West African
parrots, and in particular their ability to
talk. I do not claim to be an authority but
do believe that I have acquired a good deal
of practical and useful knowledge by continued contact with two (sometimes three)
of these birds, and with many long term
owners. As the *use* of the ability to imitate
depends primarily on the birds' disposition
and current *mood*, the handling is of considerable significance.

The grey parrot is possessive, rather
jealous, and can be ostentatiously affectionate. It enjoys attention from its owner,
or the immediate family but will normally
display an unfriendly attitude to others.

As you will know the parrot moves by
the use of legs and beak on the ground, and
many people tend to withdraw the hand as
the parrot stretches with its beak to reach a
finger (etc.) to make the first part of a forward movement. This withdrawal therefore
prevents the movement and disturbs the
parrot. It also affects adversely the parrot's
confidence in the individual.

The bird should be handled gently and as
frequently as possible. If this can be done at
regular intervals and times so much the
better. Wings of course can be clipped.

Regular bathing is good, and the bird
will come to enjoy it. No water at all on the
ears. This leads to trouble. Clean feathers
from presence of lice, fleas, etc. To keep a
parrot in good condition, therefore, one
must be able to handle it.

Parrots like to have head and neck
feathers ruffled, i.e., stroked forward
against the natural lay. They also like a
gentle stroking of the sides of the beak
between thumb and forefinger. They like

to be fed from the hand just as a dog or cat and will in fact 'beg' by pushing at the hand.

They will react in talking to a cue either in sound or sight. Often they will have play periods (equip the cage of course—swings, a chain etc.) and 'talk' periods, as well as sulky periods. They will, for example, start to talk when the meal is cooking, or when the interior lights are switched on.

I have seen a parrot which was inevitably unhappy if he could not go back into his cage at dusk. In imitating talking lessons use words or phrases which have distinctly different sounds. Parrots, I believe, will call a name or imitate a laugh because these are often distinct sounds among the many sounds they hear. The 'call' is an imitation, of course, and is a signal, and should be repeated to the parrot as a musical sequence. If father says 'Pretty Polly' in a baritone, and the rest of the family say the same words in different tones it will mean a series of different things to Mr Parrot. So, if you are all trying to teach, use different phrases and the parrot will learn all of them. Be careful what you pick because if your bird friend really feels on top of the world one day he's going to give you a recital—sometimes of the same phrases—for several hours and it can be tedious. If he does this do not cover him up to stop him because he will certainly sulk.

If you cannot claim his attention he will not learn anything, and the best way to have his attention is to have his confidence and affection. Just as you take a dog for a walk try to take the parrot out of his cage, or be close to him in his cage at the same time every day. I have seen parrots sulk and swear because they have not been visited and they know it is visiting time.

It is, incidentally, possible to go a long way in training a parrot that his droppings must not be on a dress or suit. The parrot in question would 'ask' to be moved, with the desired result.

You will, of course, be aware that a very young parrot will not talk. The emphasis on talking appears to be a product of good spirits, and noise is an expression of high spirits due to good health and contentment.

I trust that you will, over the years, have a talkative pet. I must not fail to warn you that you may at times wish you hadn't! You will know that the beak is extremely sensitive. Any damage, or mutilation is highly undesirable. Sometimes beaks are clipped if a parrot bites, and this rather naturally affects the bird.

Incidentally some birds are (commonly) long sighted and do not quickly identify near objects—a hand, food, etc. They (or he) may well wish to investigate with his beak, so don't assume that he is just going to bite you.

You will realise that I write from a real interest in these birds and because one sees so many unhappy ones, dull and lonely in small cages.

And again—

If your member could park the bird on my daughter's daily help for a few months, I think it would just have to learn something. She never stops talking.

The dottier the subject, the longer the letters we get on it!

Path Weeds

My parish council is much bothered by weeds in the gravel paths of our local cemetery. Could you advise on the best method of eradication? Chemicals appear to kill but leave unsightly brown herbage, and hoeing is impractical.

Weed killer is the best answer if manual labour is short. Gravel tends to 'set' if not raked fairly frequently, and constant raking would stop weeds gaining a foothold. Raking would also remove dead weed growth, once weed killer has been used. There really is no other way than using weed killer in the spring to prevent weed seeds germinating on the paths, unless you have a flame-gun. This is slower however.

Slippery Paving – 1

For years I have been trying to find a cure for slippery paving flagstones and have discovered the complete answer. I use a strong solution of Deosan Hypochlorate, as used in farm dairies for washing milking machines and utensils. This brings up the original colour of the flagstones, and one application has kept my flagstones completely free from slime for the whole winter, and they are not in the least slippery. In addition, it is non-poisonous and non-inflammable.

Slippery Paving – 2

Have you tried a strong solution of sodium chloride? Care must be taken not to get this on clothes because it is corrosive. If this does not serve your purpose, it should be possible to use a cold chisel on the stones, and using unskilled labour just to hammer little chips from the surfaces thereby roughening them up a bit. Another alternative would be to turn the stones right over, because the under surfaces should be rough.

Slippery Paving – 3

I have some paving flagstones laid outside my house, and when it is wet they become very slippery, just like walking on ice. I hope you will be able to tell me how to make them non-slippery.

The slime is formed by a very minute vegetable growth, and the best way to get rid of it is to sprinkle the stones with a fairly strong solution of sodium chlorate. However, be careful not to get this solution on your clothes because it is both corrosive and inflammable.

Peacocks – 1

We should like to consider keeping a pair of peacocks here, but we should need to know a good deal first about their care, habits, food, protection, etc. Can you very kindly put me in touch with any body or institution that might be able to give me information and advice?

A very good article on peacocks appeared in the *Field* magazine of November 17, 1966, and last month *The Country Gentlemen's Magazine* published an article on the subject. You could also try contacting the Gaybird Pheasant Farm, Great Missenden, Buckinghamshire, for further information, since they may have peacocks for sale or you could advertise for them.

Peacocks – 2

Can you give me some hints on keeping peafowl?

Peafowl of all varieties do much damage to young vegetables, though they do not damage flowers.

Peafowl roost on the lower branches of high trees. They go up to roost late.

They are polygamous. One cock can mate with any number up to five hens.

The adult Peacock loses his train in the autumn, but has assumed full plumage by about the middle of February. Peafowl do not mature until they are three years old, and the hens do not generally lay full clutches until they are four years old.

Peahens lay a small clutch during their second season.

The mating season in England is in May, June, and July. The period of incubation is 28–30 days.

A Peahen will lay as many as 15 eggs. They vary in colour from white to pale buff. The shell is strong and pitted all over.

Peahens make their nest on the ground ; a hollow scratched out, lined with leaves and grass, amongst thick grass or dense bushes.

Peafowl can be kept in pens, which should be large, the larger the better.

It is essential that there should be abundant cover and also sufficient perches for all birds.

Peafowl in the wild state live on land shells, insects of all kinds, worms and small lizards, but by choice they feed on grain and juicy shoots of grass and buds.

Peacocks – 3

On the question of peacocks doing damage in gardens, a garden hose is quite a good deterrent. But please never clip their wings. They then could not fly into trees for roosting—and would become easy prey to foxes, etc.

Peat

I wonder if you could let me know what quantities of peat you recommend for a

Kent clay soil? You might also be kind enough to recommend how best to apply the peat. In particular, I grow a variety of flowers, vegetables, and soft fruit. I presume that all would benefit from an application of peat. You might also be able to say whether you recommend granulated peat or vitapeat.

The aim should be to use sedge peat, medium grade, at the rate of two large bucketfuls to the sq yd. This can either be forked in lightly or of course you can use a Rotovator. For roses, flowering shrubs and soft fruits the sedge peat as a top dressing, an inch deep, and leave it there as a mulch.

Pigeons – Racing

If one should find a lost racing pigeon, what should one do?

You should give it a lot of rest and water, and a little food and let it go on the first sunny day. It should go home, if not, take the number and contact: The Royal National Homing Union, 22 Clarence Street, Cheltenham, Gloucester, Telephone Churchdown 3529, who can trace the owner.

Pigeons

I have just taken over an old barn adjacent to my house, one upper room of which is built as an inside pigeon-loft. There are about 200 nesting-places let into the inner walls of a room about 18 ft square and two outlet holes in the main wall. Could I start using them for keeping pigeons for domestic (eating) purposes. If I could do so, what type of pigeon should it be stocked with and what would the procedure be?

There is no doubt that there is a limited market for fast-growing squabs of the Silver King type. On the other hand it is doubtful if their conversion rate is any better than poultry broilers, and the labour is far greater for a relatively small output. The disadvantage of managing pigeons in the type of loft you describe is obvious. You can exercise practically no control over the matings at all, and there are problems like rats to contend with. Frankly, I should regard the proposal as a waste of time and money, although if you wanted to ornament your no-doubt charming old dovecote you could try a pair or two of ornamental pigeons; but you would have to be pretty quick on the use of Warfarin against rats. If an ornamental pigeon variety is chosen, then select a variety like the Pigmy Pouter, which is a wonderful sight when flying and does not do much damage to roofs or gardens, rather than a common White Fantail, which is a poor example of the real Fantail.

Pigeons – for Decorative Purposes

I would like to get some tame pigeons for decorative purposes to occupy a dovecote in my garden.

We suggest that the most decorative breeds are 'Nun', 'Pigmy Pouter', 'Dragoon', 'Archangel' and 'Modena', and for aerobatic purposes 'Tumblers' and 'Rollers'. There is, of course, the well-known 'Fantail', but opinions about this breed are rather mixed. Some people say that they are mischievous and cause a great deal of damage in the garden. All pigeons, however, will damage a garden unless they are properly fed. Before taking up pigeons we suggest that you write to the Feathered World, 9 Arundel Street, London, WC2, for a list of their publications on pigeon-keeping. The hardiness of pigeons depends entirely upon the stock from which they are bred. The average housing provided for pigeons, such as a small house on a pole, or a box about the size of a dog-kennel attached to a wall, is quite useless, unless the occupants are confined to a couple of birds or so. They are too small to be cleaned properly, and the birds will become infested with pests. It is far better to provide a proper aviary with the front facing south, something on the lines of a small portable shed, about 7 ft. long by 6 ft by 6 ft; this would do for half a dozen pairs or more. It should be raised above the ground to keep out rats and cats, and it also needs ventilating and properly fitting out inside with perches and nest-boxes. Pine or cedar sawdust is the best nest material. Upon arrival pigeons need to be kept shut in the darkness for at least a fortnight and then let out for a few days in a wire enclosure so that they may become accustomed to outside feeding and their surroundings. They should then stay in the area of their own accord when released.

Plastic Ponds – Painting

I have just had a small fibre-glass fish-pool installed, which was described as being 'stone' colour, but it does look very light and not very attractive (almost pinkish).

Although I appreciate that when the plants are installed it will look different, I would like to 'tone it down' if possible.

Personally I would not think that paint would be hard wearing enough or otherwise suitable for a pool that is to contain plants and fish, but I would be glad to have your opinion of this, or any other suggestion.

We would have thought that paint would not do as it will not adhere indefinitely to a plastic surface and might affect fish anyway.

We would suggest using a stain, such as are used for staining floors. You could experiment with the underside of the plastic to see whether this will work or not, but counsel caution as once stained this will be irremovable.

Plants – Scorched

Would you please give me some advice on plants in a greenhouse that have got very badly scorched such as geraniums, begonias, fuchsias, ferns?

There is not much you can do after scorching. If after watering the plants recover and put out new leaves you may be alright.

Poinsettias

My wife was recently given a Poinsettia in a pot. I would be grateful for information on how this should be treated when it has finished flowering and the method of re-potting and propagation.

When your Poinsettia has finished flowering keep it moderately watered. At the end of April prune back the shoots (or shoot if it has only one) to the second latent bud from the base. Turn the plant out of the pot, shake off the old soil and trim back any straggly roots. Re-pot into a pot just large enough to take the roots comfortably. An ideal potting medium is four parts fibrous loam, one part decayed cow manure and a half part potting sand, but the John Innes No. 2 Potting Compost is quite suitable. Keep the plant in a warm light position and when the pot becomes very full of roots re-pot into a larger one. During July and August the plant can be placed out of doors in a semi-shaded position. See it keeps moist. Syringing overhead in warm dry weather is helpful. Bring into the house (or greenhouse) in September and when the 'flowers' (which are really bracts) start to develop feed once a week with a balanced liquid fertilizer.

If you want to propagate the plant it should be cut hard back in April and the young shoots taken when two or three inches long. They should be rooted in a mixture of peat and coarse sand and they need a good deal of heat.

Pond Snails

I wonder whether you can give me any information about the introduction of Limnaea Stagnalis *or refer me to any standard authority about it. What I particularly want to know is: 1. Will it control tough growth like bulrushes or only soft weeds? 2. Is there not a danger of upsetting the balance of nature by introducing it, with unexpected results in other directions? 3. Do you know of the successful use of this snail in places where it has been artificially introduced and not found naturally? If so, can you tell me of any area where it has been used? I am interested in dealing with two ponds which are in danger of being taken over both by soft weeds and by bulrushes, having an area of 250 ft by 80 ft and 120 ft. by 80 ft.*

We have received the following in-

formation from our Biological Export:
1. *Limnaea stagnalis* will not control bulrushes and you are likely to be disappointed if you hope that it will control other rooted vegetation. These snails appear to feed mainly on the algae growing on the surface of weeds and also on plants such as bulrushes, when these are dead and decaying. 2. *Limnaea stagnalis* has remarkable powers of getting from one pond to another, though how it does remains something of a mystery. I foresee no great danger of upsetting the balance of nature. 3. We do not know of any example of the successful introduction of this snail for controlling vegetation. If the pond does not already harbour this species, it is quite likely that it is not suitable for it and therefore an introduction would be a waste of time. In this country *Limnaea stagnalis* is hardly ever found except in places where there are at least twenty parts per million of calcium. Generally we recommend introductions only into ponds which are very new or in which the fauna has been annihilated by some catastrophe.

Pond Slime

I am not clear whether preparation called GLBX can be used to kill the slimy green blanket on ponds without its killing fish, water lilies and other sorts of weed.

The makers of GLBX claim that it will not kill the fish, but we would suggest that if you do use it to get rid of the weed you follow the directions *closely*.

Pond Weed – 1

I wonder if you can help me get rid of an infestation of green weed, which suddenly appeared on my pond? The weed seems to consist of 3–4 or more petals twice the size of a pin head on thin filaments which intertwine. The whole surface is one green mat, and if some is skimmed off it appears to grow again within 24 hours. I have goldfish in the pond and I think they are still alive.

The green weed which has suddenly

appeared on your pond is probably duck weed (Lemna), and this will multiply until the late autumn when some seeds will sink to the bottom to rest for the winter. In the spring these will start a fresh infestation. The weed is harmless, and is eaten by goldfish when they have insufficient other foods. It is best removed by playing a hose on it from one side of the pond, gradually rolling it across the pond to one side. It will form into a deep mat-like roll which can be raked out of the pond and used as a mulch in the garden. After a few such treatments it will disappear. You may get a little after a time but it should not be difficult to keep the surface clear at this time of the year.

Pond Weed – 2

How can I clear chickweed from an ornamental garden pond in which there are no fish?

The only safe chemical that may be used in eradicating weeds from an ornamental pond is permanganate of potash, dissolving 1 teaspoonful in 1 gallon of water and spraying the offending weeds thoroughly with this. The alternative method is to drive the weed to one end of the pond with a hose-pipe, using a flattish spray, and then remove with a hand-net.

The safest method of all is to balance the pool properly with fish, underwater oxygenators and nymphaeas. It is almost inevitable that a pool planted only with plants will become weed-infected in time.

Posts – Apple Wood

I have an orchard which I intend to grub out, and I wonder if the apple tree trunks would be suitable for fencing posts. How does apple wood compare with oak and larch for the length of time it will last on the ground?

We have never heard of this wood being used for fencing posts. It is tough, however, and was sometimes used for beetles. If you use this wood we suggest that you have the posts creosoted with wood creosote. We do not think it will compare in longevity with oak or larch.

Posts in Concrete

Would you please tell me whether you recommend the practice of plunging gate and other posts in concrete when erecting same? I have always considered this good practice for two reasons: (1) the added stability, and (2) the longer life obtained, but now I have been advised by a practical man that (2) is not correct. He says that condensation, being confined, causes the post to rot sooner this way than when planted free. As I have more work of this nature to do, I should be very much obliged if you would give me your opinion.

So far as we know the setting of posts in concrete does not materially reduce or increase their life. It is true that in some soils the use of concrete would reduce the accessibility of air to the post, but if this were enough to have any effect at all it would reduce rather than increase the rate of decay, because a certain amount of oxygen is essential for the development of wood-rotting fungi. It is possible that the idea that absence of air would favour decay has arisen by associating absence of air with lack of ventilation. It is true, of course, that when wood is in a position where it may gradually become damp, e.g., a suspended floor, lack of ventilation can encourage decay, but this is because the flow of air is serving to remove the moisture and prevent the wood from becoming damp enough to decay; the mere presence of the air does not retard decay. Posts, however, are in contact with plenty of moisture, and the degree of ventilation in the soil or other medium surrounding them has no effect on decay except in controlling the level in the ground at which it occurs.

Forest Products Research
Department.

New Potatoes for Christmas

I am told that it is possible to have home-grown new potatoes for Christmas. One method suggested to me was to have a very late planting, harvest them young, and then put them in tins or bottles and bury them until wanted. Naturally the containers would have to be watertight and, I assume, airtight. Should they be put away by themselves or should I pack them in sand before sealing them?

The surest way of having new potatoes for Christmas is to get hold of a square biscuit tin with a tight-fitting lid. See that it is absolutely clean and dry, and then when you harvest your new potatoes in June, select those about the size of a hen's egg, or slightly smaller, and fill the biscuit tin with these. The tubers chosen should of course be quite free from disease and should not be damaged by the fork when harvesting. Put on the lid, seal the sides with a strip of Selotape, and bury the tin about 3 ft deep in a dry spot. It is most important that the drainage of the soil at this point should be perfect. Make certain that you have marked the spot with a stake or label, or otherwise a few days before Christmas you may fail to find your cache. Both May Queen and Ninetyfold have been stored quite successfully in this way, but we feel sure that other varieties like Home Guard or Arran Pilot will do equally well. May we underline, however, the importance of the tubers being free from disease?

Blue Primroses

Four years ago I raised from seed and then planted blue primroses in the borders of the herbaceous and rose beds. They have been flowering the whole year and this January they were the only colour in the garden. Is this unusual? I know of no other plant that flowers all the year round.

Although all varieties of primroses, including the blue kind, do throw the odd flower in mild weather in the autumn and winter it is certainly rather unusual for them to have flowered as continuously as yours have done. They must be a very floriferous strain, but we think that as they settle down they will probably revert to having the main flush of flowers in the spring with the occasional odd bloom at other seasons.

Prunus Tree

I have a well-formed prunus (pink-flowering) which has only had one or two blossoms this year and last year. It is exposed to west winds which are severe at times in winter, spring, and autumn, and as a result the tree leans over slightly. The soil is fairly heavy clay. The tree is 10 or 11 ft. high. Can you tell me why there are no flowers and suggest a remedy?

Unfortunately you do not state the age of the tree, and therefore it is difficult to know whether it is of the age when it should be flowering. Sometimes these prunuses take a number of years to settle down. You do not say how the tree has been fed, but I would advise the giving of a fish fertilizer with a 10 per cent potash content all over the soil as far as the branches spread at the rate of 4 oz. to the square yard. Do this in May and September. Have you had trouble with aphides ? If so the tree should be sprayed early in December with a tar oil wash such as Mortegg, using a 5 per cent solution.

Puff Balls

I am having trouble with puff balls that are appearing over quite large parts of my lawn. The lawn is an established one and I have never had this trouble before. Can you tell me how to get rid of these fungi?

I do not think you will have any trouble in getting rid of your puff balls if you water the lawn with a solution of copper sulphate in water. I think you will only need a dessertspoonful of powdered copper sulphate in a 2-gall can of water to do the trick. Do not put on more than about a pint per square yard, to start with at any rate, and give a second dose, if necessary, about three weeks later.

Rabbits – Breeding for the Pot – 1

Can you advise me where I can get information about breeding rabbits for the pot?

The Ministry of Agriculture do a booklet – 'Rabbit Meat Production' which is free, and a larger bulletin called 'Modern Rabbit Keeping' price 5s 7d including postage. These are obtainable from: Ministry of Agriculture, Publications Branch, Tolcarne Drive, Pinner, Middlesex.

For further information you could also write to the Secretary of the Commercial Rabbit Association – Mrs M. E. P. Netherway, Northlew, 70 Bilford Road, Worcester.

Rabbits – Breeding for the Pot – 2

I am seeking information about the prospects for commercial rabbit breeding, both for fur and meat, and would probably specialize in Havana Rex or Chinrex. I presume there will be no difficulty in selling the carcasses to local retailers, etc ; however, I have no detailed knowledge of markets for the skins. My inquiries have so far only received rather vague generalizations, but I naturally intend to have firm and definite markets before expanding. If you can supply me with the names of organizations or individuals who buy pelts of this kind, so that I may write to them, or any other information which will assist me, I shall be most grateful.

The best authority for the information you require is The British Rabbit Council, 273 Farnborough Road, Farnborough, Hants.

Racoons

I wish to buy a racoon for a friend of mine, and wondered if you could tell me where to get one, and how much they cost?

Racoons are obtainable from Harrods

Ltd, Knightsbridge, London SW1, and cost 45 gns each.

Rambler or Climber?

I have recently become the owner of a well-established, well-stocked garden with a number of roses on stone walls. I know very little about roses which climb – but have recognized Albertine, Paul and American Pillar amongst others here.

Can you tell me please how to distinguish between a rambler and a climber? Which are the above-named?

In very general terms ramblers only flower once each season and climbers tend to flower more often. Ramblers also generally do not flower from old wood and therefore the old wood should be cut out each season and the new shoots from the base should be tied in for their full length.

Climbers produce new shoots both from the base and higher up and all new shoots should be tied in and some old wood cut out to keep the general appearance of the rose tidy.

The three roses you mention, Albertine, Paul and American Pillar are all ramblers.

Raspberry Canes

Two or three years ago a correspondent in your magazine recommended putting down straw between the raspberry rows; I acted on this suggestion, which at first appeared very practical, for it kept the weeds down, kept the moisture in, and was dry and clean to walk on when the fruit was ripe for picking. However, the canes do not flourish as well as they did in former years, and it has been suggested to me that straw on the ground destroys the nitrogen. In your opinion is this the case? If so, should the straw be left on the ground for only a month or two? or in what form should nitrogen be added?

The raspberry canes must, of course, be fed through the straw. I give fish manure with a 10 per cent potash content to the rows of raspberries at 3 oz. to the square yard in February and again in August. This can trickle down in between the straw and has the desired effect. Straw might have a denitrifying effect on the soil.

Re-stocking a River

Can you advise us on re-stocking a fast-flowing Welsh river which rises in a lake? It has some brown trout, but except for sea trout and salmon the river is very poor.

This type of rapid river is always deficient in food. The best way to improve it is to put in a series of low weirs. These will form pools where silt will collect and on the silt snails and other bottom-living organisms will thrive. At first the pool will form about the weir, but after a few seasons this will silt up and a new pool will be formed below it by falling water. On both sides of the weir food will increase. You will have to experiment to find out what type of weir will stand best. You probably have heavy winter floods unless these can be regulated at the outlet, from the lake. There are other ways as well in which food can be increased, such as small side ponds which drain into the river.

Probably no stocking will be required. If it is, do not use rainbows; they have only proved successful in limestone streams. Ask the fish farm for slow-growing fish and stock with yearlings if necessary, though fry might be used in this type of stream. Make sure your fish cannot get into the lake or they will stop there.

Rhododendrons – Colour Loss

I have a number of rhododendrons which were planted many years ago. They have always had a bright pink flower but for some reason every one this year has produced pure white blooms. We are, of course, on the N.E. Coast quite near to the sea, but this fact does not seem to have affected them before. Could you give me some idea of the cause and what remedy might be used to get them back to the previous pink colour – some were deep crimson.

The Royal Horticultural Society tells us:

'This problem has been reported to us before on a number of occasions with different genera such as *Gladiolus* and *Iris* but we have not so far heard of this phenomenon with Rhododendrons. Enquiries made in the past to see if the cause can be determined have been negative and at the moment it is not possible to state definitely why plants which are known to produce coloured flowers normally should suddenly produce only white blooms. It is very probable that the change is due to a genetic variation within the plant but why this should occur in a number of Rhododendrons of different varieties at the same time is at present very difficult to explain.

'On occasions we have found on enquiry that changes in flower colour have been due to the stock becoming dominant but usually in the case of Rhododendrons this merely means that the normal purple *ponticus* stock takes over.

'There is no doubt, in my opinion, that these colour changes do occur but regrettably at the moment we cannot find a satisfactory explanation. It would be most interesting to know if the plants mentioned by your member remain white flowered next season or if some, or all of them, return to their original colours.'

Rhubarb

Most reference books warn that rhubarb should not be picked during its first year but none explain why. Could you please give me an explanation and indication of the perils that await one who ignores the warning?

The reason why it is advised not to pull the shoots of rhubarb during the first year is that, like all plants, it manufactures its food supply through its leaves. During the first year after planting the crowns should be allowed to have as many shoots (and therefore leaves) as possible in order to become healthy and well established.

Rhubarb is, however, a tough plant and it is probable that the pulling of a few shoots during the first year would do no great harm provided a number were left to develop leaves.

Riding School Surfacing

I wish to make a manege or riding school area out of an old walled garden. The area involved is some 120 ft by 90 ft and has been under cultivation as a vegetable garden and is in well kept condition. I presume as a start I should clear the area and plough it up but I require advice as to the type of surfacing I should have to consider. The manege would receive pretty hard work in that say five horse/ ponies would be using the track inside the perimeter and across the diagonals for some three hours about five days a week. Naturally I should like to get the manege in operation as soon as possible but the need would not be critical until the early spring. Of course the question of cost has to be borne in mind. There appears to be two alternatives, either grassing or turfing or covering with a mixture of sand and tan bark.

The first thing to do is to see that the ground is thoroughly drained. This is very important and if expense is a problem this should be the first item. If the land is badly drained you will have continuous trouble when it rains and afterwards. Then there should be a surface of about six inches of biggish stuff like clinker and hard core, this will also assist in the drainage and form a strong base. Lastly the ground should be surfaced, but not as you suggest with turf as the amount of wear you intend to get out of it will tear it to ribbons. Sand and tan bark will do but tan bark tends to consolidate. Wood shavings would be better and cinders are excellent, though they can be rather dusty in summer. This surface should also be about six inches. Blaise is also very good and can be obtained from the local shale mines near you. Coarse sand and shavings together make a good surface, but the main point is that if the drainage is good you can add whatever you are using to the top surface without having to start from the beginning again, every year or so.

Rookery

For some years we have been increasingly plagued by a colony of rooks which nest in some tall ash trees in our garden. Unfortunately our house is surrounded by houses on two sides and a road on a third side making it rather risky to shoot at them. We would be very much obliged if you could suggest some method of exterminating them, either a type of gun which would not be dangerous or else some other way.

The usual remedies, such as shooting or directing a hose against the nests to chill the eggs, are not applicable in your case. You could try using a series of poles or rods joined together, such as are sometimes used for drains, in order to knock holes in the bottom of the nests or dislodge them, but to do this someone will have to climb part way up the trees. If it did not disturb your neighbours too much, you might also try the effect of fairly cheap firework rockets used when the birds are trying to settle down for the night.

Poplar Roots

I would be grateful if you could advise me on how to deal effectively with the roots of poplar trees which are growing underneath my hard tennis court and raising up the surface.

We cannot really answer your question without knowing whether the poplars have been recently planted or not. Poplars are notorious for the length of their roots and the damage which these cause. If the trees are young then what has happened to your tennis court so far is mild compared with what will happen when they are full grown and you would do well to remove the trees at once, and sever the roots on the side of the tennis court.

Persistent Rushes – 1

We have rushes infesting a part of a field which seem to be spreading. Is there any way of preventing this.

On clay ground that is waterlogged rushes take a stronghold and they are difficult to get rid of, even when the land is ploughed and re-seeded. Indeed, cultivations seem at the start to bring on more rushes. What happens that rush seeds, which are often thick in the ground have a chance of germinating and unless a crop that the farmers sows get a quick and strong start rushes have no competition. The advice that I am given for an outlying paddock that has too many rushes in it is: plough carefully to bury the sod, then disc harrow, dress with lime and phosphate and finally give a heavy seeding of grasses and clovers. A neighbour tells me that he got rid of rushes by taking a mixture of Italian ryegrass, turnips and rape as a pioneer crop which he grazed carefully before seeding out with a permanent grass mixture. It is essential of course to get the drainage right as well as to raise the standard of fertility. Rushes are a sign of soil stagnation as well as poverty.

Persistent Rushes – 2

Rushes can be controlled by spraying provided there is good management. Any of the selective weed-killers can be used, but the 2.4-D types (16–24 ozs. per acre) are probably better than the M.C.P.A. types (32 ozs. per acre). If lime is needed it must be applied and heavy dressings of potash and phosphate are often required.

Sandstone Figures – Cleaning – 1

Can you tell me how to clean sandstone figures of moss?

Pour boiling water over the moss; this kills the roots, so that the moss can be gently brushed off in a few days without damage or staining of the stone.

Sandstone Figures – Cleaning – 2

We have in our garden a number of attractive small sandstone figures which are becoming moss-covered and beginning to flake and crumble. I wonder if you could kindly advise: (a) how the moss could be removed, and (b) with what solution we could paint the figures as a preservative. The age is probably 50 to 80 years. Our garden is surrounded by a stone wall and is between 150 and 200 yards from the sea.

These sandstone figures are almost certain to deteriorate owing to the softness of the stone. The moss can be removed with very careful strokes of a wire brush, or you could try a lawn moss removing preparation on a small section to see that the chemical does not make a stain. In any case, the figures should then be washed carefully with soap and water. The only preservation treatment afterwards might be to use a transparent sealing liquid such as that employed by builders for damp walls.

Seasoning Wood – 1

Can you tell me how long a felled beech tree must be allowed to " season" before it can be fashioned? Also, is beech a suitable wood for indoor panelling and furniture?

If beech is going to be used inside a house or building, the moisture content must be reduced; it must therefore be kiln dried. After this has been done, it would be suitable for indoor panelling and furniture.

Seasoning Wood – 2

With reference to your reply concerning the seasoning of beech, I do not agree with kiln drying. As a panelling and also high-class furniture is usually intended to last for many years it would be well worth while to season the timber by *air* drying, at the rate of 2 years per inch of thickness. This will considerably reduce the starch content on which the grub of the woodworm beetle feeds, so that the grub will starve before the timber is ready for use.

In kiln drying this is not so, but the worm may be still quite active after the timber is considered ready for use, so that the timber will be " worming " when the work is finished and in use.

To introduce such timber into a house is a certain way of infecting other woodwork. The extra delay, even for some years, is not too great a price to pay in order to avoid such a ruinous result.

The tree should be cut into planks of the required thickness and stored in a draughty place with a good current of fresh air circulating around it and left for the requisite period. If this is done the result will last for centuries, but no one knows how long kiln dried timber will last, probably less than a century.

Seasoning Wood – 3

I refer to two answers given on the subject of wood seasoning. It would appear that these two replies followed the commonly held misconceptions on the subject of wood seasoning and drying. Wood dried 'in the air' and in a wood kiln is seasoned in exactly the same way, that is to say, by warmth of the air, its humidity and its movement over the timber. In this respect kiln seasoning is every bit as much 'air drying' as any other method. It is true that the wood drying kiln has very often been abused by individuals who have no clear technical knowledge of the processes which are actually involved within the material itself. This occurs where it is desired to obtain results at high speed without rigorous control over the quality of material which is being produced. When the method of drying beech (or any other wood) has once been established to produce the best possible result, modern machinery will enable this result to be reproduced as often as is required. It is, of course, common knowledge that there is a very considerable difference between different batches of wood which has been subject to 'air seasoning' in the open. It is not possible to season sufficiently by storing wood outside in the UK if it is desired later to bring the wood into use in indoor conditions with heating, central or otherwise. In the case of the details to which you refer: (1) A slow starting temperature with beech will eliminate virtually all starches inside the material (this also applies when seasoning oak, where it is even more important). (2) All schedules for oak or beech should include a conditioning process in which no drying takes place, but by which all parasites within the temperature are automatically killed. (3) In respect of the excessive darkening of oak, this can be easily avoided in the wood kiln, provided the operating temperatures are kept reasonably low. Like most things, the wood seasoning kiln is a place where a little knowledge is a dangerous thing, although there is no doubt that in proper hands it can procure material of the highest class. Should any further information be required it is readily available from either the Forest Products Research Laboratories at Princes Risborough or the Timber Research and Development Association. Both these organisations have done much to make it possible for wood in its own right to be used in places that hitherto were impossible and have been able to prove time and again the versatility of the material when it is properly understood and handled.

Seasoning Wood – 4

I always read your replies with keen interest, and am not accustomed to writing to any publication lightly—indeed, I cannot recall the last time I felt strongly enough about anything to feel compelled to put pen to paper. However, some of the comments that have appeared both by correspondents and under your replies, on the subject of wood or timber, have been such that I cannot let them pass—much of it has been such utter nonsense. As I have been in the timber trade for some 25 years and am also a member of the Institute of Wood Science I think I can claim to have a basic knowledge of timber from both the practical and technical aspect. To come down to specific cases, there is a letter about difficulties experienced in getting satisfactory finish to preserve the appearance of an oak gate. Oak is one of the most difficult timbers to

use outside and maintain its original appearance. One thing is certain—linseed oil is quite useless in this regard. It is thick and sticky and only attracts dirt to stick to it. The problem of finding a really long term satisfactory clear external finish that will preserve the original natural appearance of the timber is one that still remains largely unsolved although a tremendous amount of research work has been put into it and at least there is a wealth of information available about the relative merits of the various finishes on the market, although none of them are 100 per cent without being re-applied every few years. First class information can be obtained on this subject from the Advisory Services Department Timber Research & Development Association, The Building Centre, Store Street, London, ask for their leaflet called " Maintaining Timber Exposed to the Weather." In your reply to the same letter you state that the fact that the oak may have gone almost black may be due to the original seasoning. I am sorry but this is just not so. You further state that kiln drying cannot compare with seasoned wood. Whether the timber has been air seasoned or kiln dried has no effect whatever on the colour the timber may ultimately assume after exposure to the weather. Furthermore your implied criticism of kiln-dried timber is misleading and certainly not in accord with the views of some of the highest class manufacturers of joinery, furniture etc. in the country. The essential thing to remember is that by and large seasoning and kiln drying are different ways of achieving the same end—namely to dry the timber, ie, to reduce its moisture content. There's nothing mystical about the age-old term " seasoning "—it just means drying. It is true that because it is a much slower and longer process than kiln drying it tends to reduce the starch content of the timber more than kiln drying does. This means the timber may —only may mark you—it depends on which timber and a number of other factors—be less likely to attack by woodworm. But this risk has been greatly over-exaggerated in recent years, mainly by the makers of various preservatives etc. It is far more important to use timber at the right moisture content for the job concerned than it is to start worrying about risk of worm because you may be using kiln-dried timber instead of seasoned or more correctly " air-dried timber." If timber is air-dried, or seasoned if you insist, by natural means in the open air, it will hardly ever reach a moisture content below 14 per cent—if that—16 per cent is a far more likely figure. For furniture or high class joinery or fitments in a modern home, shop or office etc. this is far too high. Because of central heating etc. the wood will ultimately settle down at around 12 per cent moisture content, possibly less in certain situations. If you put timber into the job that has only been air-dried or so called seasoned to say 14–16 per cent moisture content, one thing is absolutely certain—sooner or later it will shrink and that means trouble. By kiln-drying the timber can be reduced to the moisture content appropriate for the job in hand whether it be 12 per cent, 10 per cent or even 8 per cent—certain Government Departments have specified all their timber to be 8 per cent for some uses for many years. When the House of Commons was rebuilt after damage in the last war, large quantities of English oak were used for panelling, joinery, fitments etc. some of it up to 4 in. thick—it was all kiln dried before use. I have not heard of any criticism of the finished result then or since. Many of my comments are also applicable to the letter headed " Wood Seasoning." This letter again is full of misconceptions and quite misleading statements. I will not trespass on your time further by replying to that letter in detail, but one point I must make. It is true that kiln drying will not definitely preclude the possibility of attack by woodworm at some future date—although as already stated the risks have been much exaggerated. However, it should be clearly understood that kiln-drying definitely does kill any worms or grubs alive in the timber before kilning. Therefore when the timber is considered fit for use after kilning you can be sure it does not contain any live worm. Finally, may I enter a plea that when asked for information on any aspect of the use of treatment of timber please get up to date scientific

and reliable information and do not " repeat old wives' tale " such as have appeared both in letters from you correspondents and in your replies. The Timber Research & Development Association will be only too pleased to help you in any way they can as will also the Forest Products Research Laboratory.

Share-farming

Would you be good enough to give me an outline for a working arrangement for a share-farming proposition for a dairy farm? The proposer will buy the cattle I house, work them, supply all hay and pasture and he shares the meal bill and also pays for half turnips and mangolds. The milk cheque to be shared between us. Should this be evenly distributed?

I do not think this sounds a very satisfactory proposition. In any case there are so many contingencies that it is not really very satisfactory to attempt to offer an opinion. The scheme is not clear, but assuming that costs work out per cow something like as stated below:

Cost per cow	£
Purchased food ...	16 (50–50 shared)
Home-grown food	16 (inquirer)
Grazing	4 (inquirer)
Labour	20 (inquirer)
Herd depreciation	5 (proposer)
Miscellaneous ...	12 (50–50 shared)
	73

It looks to us as if you were going to contribute the value of £54 to your proposer's £18. Therefore, the cheque for milk should be shared something like five-sevenths to you, and two-sevenths to the proposer.

Share Farming in New Zealand

On a farm with 90 cows, the total income of which is £3,000, the "share-milker", with no capital in the business may get 40 per cent of this sum, plus a rent-free house with electric light and possibly a car. He has to pay a boy from £2 18s. 6d. to £5 18s. according to age. As there may be readers who would like to experiment with the system, I asked a friend to give me more details. He writes "The share-milker arrangement is widespread and represents the best way for a practical young farmer to assemble capital he requires to take a farm on his own. The milker pays income-tax on his share after deducting the wages of the boy. The owner, who receives 60 per cent of the farmer's income will have credit on his tax assessment for any mortgage interest paid by him, although most places are clear of debt. He can also claim the usual deductions for herd culling and replacements (he owns the herd), for repairs, renewals and maintenance, for fertilisers, etc. This type of investment is very lucrative and so popular."

Shares for Sheep Keeping

Farmer A owns some ewes and rams, and these are kept by Farmer B. B provides all the keep and hand feed, medicines, dip, etc., and pays vet fees. For shearing and dippings, and dagging, each farmer provides one or two men. What do you think would be a fair distribution of the proceeds of wool and lamb sales at the end of twelve months?

In our opinion a fair distribution would be 2/7 to 5/7; i.e., 2/7 to A, 5/7 to B or $\frac{1}{3}$ to A, $\frac{2}{3}$ to B.

Blind Sheep – Superstitions on

We have a neighbouring sheep farmer, who operates on a highly commercial basis, but has two incredibly ancient ewes, which are blind, and which, plainly for humanitarian reasons alone, ought to be put down. On mentioning this to a friend the other day, he remarked that no sheep farmer will sell or destroy a blind sheep. It is considered terribly bad luck. This appears to me to be the only possible explanation, but I wondered if any of your readers have other comments to make about this.

One sheep-farming member said his old shepherd would never destroy a blind sheep.

Sheep

I have about 6 acres of reasonably good grazing, about to be cut for hay. A neighbouring farmer has suggested that I might do worse than keep a few sheep: he rather pooh-poohed my protests that sheep took time and specialist knowledge. I wonder if you could advise me: (a) is it worth keeping and fattening a few lambs or hoggets? Can this be done on a week-end/evening attention basis? (b) What age should I look for? (c) Must I dip them even if I don't keep them a full year? (d) How many can I run to the acre?

We think that you may find a little more difficulty than anticipated in keeping sheep, and the best thing you can do would be to let your farmer graze his own sheep on your land at a rental, making sure, however, that no tenancy agreement is involved and limiting the time to less than a year. Alternatively, the simplest way, of course, is to keep a few lambs weaned at 14 weeks, or hoggets for fattening, and you might be able to do this on a week-end/evening attention basis. The age for your hoggets should be about 15 months onwards. You may still find it necessary to dip them, because they are almost bound to be struck with fly. The number you run depends on the quality of the feed available, and for this you should get local advice.

Jacob's Sheep – I

Where can I buy Jacob's Sheep? Can you give me any information about them?

1. There is no Breed Society.
2. Mrs. Griffiths, the Woodland, Forden, Welshpool, is one of the few people who might have any and might sell some. We believe that the Duke of Devonshire is another breeder.
3. They have horns but this should not be a disadvantage except possibly where indoor housing is practised.
4. We should imagine they are not nearly as good as Scotch half-breeds but

". . . Crept to within a few feet in my bare feet . . ."

(See page 107)

might be more prolific.

5. They will almost certainly be crossed with a Suffolk or Dorset Down for early fat lamb production. The best lambs appear to be Scotch half-breed crossed with Suffolk and the ewe lamb crossed again with a Dorset Down to produce these quick maturing high quality lambs.

Jacob's Sheep – II

Your correspondent may like to know that a flock of these sheep are kept in Chideock Manor Park, near Bridport, Dorset. The owner, Lt. Col. H. J. Weld, is an authority on the history of the breed, and various articles on the subject have been printed in the *Bridport News* and the *Western Gazette* of recent years.

Jacob's Sheep – III

The Jacob's ewe is found here and there through all Great Britain. It has a mottled coat which does not sell well, but this is its only disadvantage. It needs no feed whatsoever, and lambs twins without assistance and without extra feed; nor does it need 'steaming up'. Price is about £7 for 4-year-old ewes. It has the advantage of lambing successfully until 12 years old, which is a great length as compared with any breed. The best ram to use is a Shropshire or a Suffolk.

Jacob's Sheep – IV

A considerable amount of tommy-rot has been recently talked about Jacob's Sheep. As I have had 43 years' experience of keeping these sheep from time to time, may I be permitted to put this breed before your readers in its proper perspective ? The breed is little known because it has no flock book and has never been publicised. It suffers from bad wool at 3s 6d per lb, and will produce all black cross lambs unless crossed with a Dorset Horn or Polled Dorset Ram (then it produces few black lambs).

These are its *only* disadvantages. It has 300 small flocks spread between Inverness and Land's End – also in Wales. Its ewes are sold in early autumn at Marlborough (Wilts) yearly. Major Purefroy has a big flock, over 100 years old, at Shalstone Manor, Buckingham, and knows all breeders of same. (His farm is on A422 between Brackley and Buckingham.) Lord Bradford, Shifnal Park, Shropshire, has biggest flock. *Its advantages.* The hardiest breed in all Britain and needing the least food. Takes ram at all seasons and will produce lambs twice yearly. Extreme prolificacy (ie, over 2 per cent per ewe) and successfully milks for these lambs. Will do on any soil from lightest to heaviest. Can stand intense changes of soil, climate and height. I recently took ewes from heavy clay 400 ft. Dorset farm to a 1,250 ft Welsh border farm of lightest soil. They throve and fed excellent – 14 week fat lambs there (by Clun ram). Very quiet indeed, and needs no dog to control them, needs merely small fence or two low lines barbed wire, and don't try to break fences. Prices about £6 or £7 for three-year-old ewes, so the breed can be absolutely recommended to persons without shepherds. N.B. Buy two or three horned ewes if possible.

Jacob's Sheep – V

I was in Bury St. Edmunds Sheep Market recently and there were several pens of these sheep entered in the sale: indeed I have seen them on a number of occasions. If your correspondent were to write to Messrs Lacy Scott & Sons, the auctioneers, he would soon find out who the sellers were. As for the wool, in the years before the war it did have a market; for some friends of mine in Wiltshire used to cross the Jacob's with a Hampshire Down ram, and this got them a black lamb every time, this black wool was sought after by some of the specialist makers of quality tweeds in Scotland – whether this is still the case I do not know. As for their name, if you want to know why they are so called read Genesis XXX, verses 37 to 41 – or if that great work is not to hand read Shylock's account of it in the *Merchant of Venice,* the speech beginning, 'When Jacob kept his Uncle Laban's flock.' I believe these sheep are native of Spain, and I rather suspect they came into England in the wake of the Peninsular war, as did the Wellingtonia. I have heard another tradition that they were imported from the Cape in the early days of settlement there, in exchange for a piano, but it is too long a story to give to you chapter and verse.

Jacob's Sheep – VI

About two years ago you published some very good and informative letters about Jacob's Sheep. After some difficulty I was lucky enough to obtain three ewes and an unrelated ram, and now I am the proud possessor of six newborn lambs. I feel sure that many of your members are in the same circumstances as myself, with two or three small paddocks and not knowing what to do with them and how to keep them in good order if ponies are kept for the children. My neighbouring farmer was not prepared to bother with fields of only one or two acres. Ducks were a lot of trouble, very smelly and eat me out of house and home. Strawberries proved to be a very heavy burden and required much casual labour. For me Jacob's Sheep have proved to be the perfect answer. I have a shepherd who visits me twice a year to attend to feet and tails and to administer a dose. Our butcher is keen to buy any fat lambs which we cannot winter, and their skins are dressed for only 30s and make very nice bedside rugs. I hope this information may be of some use to your members.

Jacob's Sheep – VII

Ralph Whitlock contributed an article in our Magazine on Jacob's Sheep which brought forth some interesting ripostes . . .

Ralph Whitlock writes:

Well, well, seldom have I been so properly ticked off as I have been over my mention of Jacob sheep (in the May issue of the magazine). My facts are all wrong, say the critics; my management of my Jacob sheep must have been equally faulty; the poor animals were probably half-starved; I do a splendid breed a grave injustice. Indeed, so dramatic have been the assertions that I checked on my files from the time when I was keeping Jacobs, just to see whether my memory had been playing me false or whether indeed we were thinking of the same animals.

Miss K. M. A. Clark, of Dundrennan, Kirkcudbrightshire, writes:

'. . . *The article may, like the curate's egg, have been good in parts, but certainly the part about the Jacobs was not one of the good parts. I have now kept Jacob sheep for some seven or eight years and can say nothing but good about them. From Mr. Whitlock's remarks he seems to have started off with some very poor quality stock—the type of animal I simply don't possess, and their being such poor lambers and so wild, I would say, only showed bad stockmanship on Mr. Whitlock's part.*

I never keep dark-fleeced hoggs nor a thin, light-boned, leggy type. Like any breed, one has to be most selective in both foundation stock and replacements; and surely Mr. Whitlock put all his lambs, irrespective of what breed, on good pasture to finish. You cannot expect to finish any breed on fresh air and good pasture.

I am a member of the newly-formed Jacob Sheep Society and also on the Committee and feel it is very sad when any breed is tried and then given up through no fault of the breed.

If Mr. Whitlock is ever up in this part of the country I would be only too pleased to let him or anyone else interested see my flock. It is four-score strong and is kept on strictly commercial lines, and my markets for both mutton and wool are excellent.'

Then we have Miss H. B. Hamilton, of Inverleithen, Perthshire:

' *"Low productivity" and "the ewes had a job to average 100 per cent lambs in a season"; you must be joking, when they are renowned for their fecundity, many of the ewes lambing twice a year. I have a small* flock of two-score, and my main worry is what to do with the odd ones out, among triplets, as with no ewes having singles, one is left with numerous "bottle" babies. Either you tup or your management, or both, must have been sorely at fault.

You go on to say that "the lambs were slow to come to maturity and to put on weight", hardly surprising if they had to thrive "on poor pastures". Personally I usually manage to sell the majority of my lambs fat off their mothers, when they fill out at around 40 lb. without any extra feed. Mine are extremely amenable, but they do not work well for a dog, preferring to follow rather than being driven. . . . It is not uncommon for lambs to have lambs themselves before reaching more than a year.

No, I am afraid I consider you have done the Jacob sheep an injustice in more ways than one, as you also infer that they are mainly ornamental, being easily sold to zoos and country mansion parks. Whilst this may have been true in the past, it is now a very different story, and I feel sure that the formation of the Jacob Sheep Society will prove that they are very much a commercial proposition, not only in their own right but also for producing ewes for crossing with a Down breed for out-of-season fat lambs and tups for crossing with a hill ewe for greater productivity.'

Mrs. G. Rodwell, of Oxhill Manor, Warwickshire, takes me gently to task.

'Somehow I cannot help feeling there must have been a certain lack of rapport between Mr. Whitlock and his Jacobs, or they just did not have enough to eat.

They certainly have a fearful reputation for leaping about the countryside, but that is because so many people have just a few to keep their tiny nettle- and dock-infested orchards in trim, and after they have grazed every edible leaf they just do feel forced to hip over the fence to better pasture. . . .'

And Mr. G. L. H. Anderson, of Devizes, comments:

'Mr. Whitlock quotes the results obtained from his small Jacob flock—100 per cent lambing, late maturity and slow growth. I would make two comments. It is very dangerous to judge a whole breed on the basis of the performance of a handful of sheep. Secondly, the level of production achieved by Mr. Whitlock's flock was probably as much a reflection of his methods of management as of the true ability of the sheep. The results

achieved by Jacobs under good management conditions show them to be extremely prolific —some flocks average 200 per cent lambing and individual ewes more over a long breeding life. Crossed with a Down ram, as is normal practice for most ewes, they produce very acceptable fat lamb which is neither slow-growing nor late maturing. I have also seen them paddock-grazed very successfully.

Mr. Whitlock writes that present-day Jacobs are mostly black. This is not so. Black specimens are the result of crossing Jacobs with another breed.'

Those are samples of letters I have received on the subject, and it seems as though I ought to be hanging my head in shame. But I plead guilty on only one count. That is, that I did not know there is now a Jacob Sheep Society.

And I think I have an excuse for my ignorance, for the Society must be of very recent formation. For soon after I acquired my own sheep, early in the 1960s, I first enquired whether there was a breed society for the Jacobs and then I wrote to various people whom I knew had flocks to learn whether they would be interested in forming one. These enquiries followed some articles I wrote in various papers about that time, but I encountered a massive lack of interest. I am glad that someone else has been luckier. No one has thought to tell me just when the Society was formed or to give me its address, but one lady whose letter is postmarked 'London' tells me it now has 124 members and that there are over 3,000 sheep registered with it.

For the rest, my Jacobs were sold in 1965, after having lived on the farm for several years. When I advertised them, prior to dispersal, enquiries came chiefly from zoos, parks and people who, as Mrs. Rodwell says, wanted to use them to keep a paddock tidy. I could find no one at that time who was keeping a sizeable flock commercially.

My own Jacobs were kept with a much larger flock of Devon Closewools. At least, they were kept on the same pastures and given the same food, but they held themselves strictly aloof from the others. The Devon Closewools were placid and contented; the Jacobs active and wild. The Devon Closewools never attempted to get out, even after the Jacobs had shown them the way; the Jacobs would jump a fence four feet high and push their way through a hedge that would have held an ox. The

Devon Closewools grew fat on the pasture provided; the Jacobs did not.

I am sorry I had no one's experiences other than my own to draw on. Readers can now see the testimony of others who have been luckier than I, and it is good to know that the Jacob has not only become a breed but has so vastly improved, almost beyond recognition, in the last five years.

It seems, though, that there may be still points to be settled before this paragon of breeds supersedes all the others. Colour, for instance. Mr. Anderson takes me to task for saying that present-day Jacobs are mostly black. As has been noted, he categorically denies this and states that 'black specimens are the result of crossing Jacobs with another breed'. But another reader has sent me a coloured postcard of Jacob sheep. It bears a publicity paragraph for the breed and is inscribed 'By courtesy of Jacob Sheep Society'. Of the four animals shown, two are more black than white and a third is almost entirely black.

Shire Horse Society

I believe there is a Shire Horse Society; do you know who the Secretary is?

Yes: R. W. Bird, Esq., 12 Priestgate, Peterborough.

Shooting – For Youth

Could you tell me if there is any scheme which could offer a sixteen year old boy social shooting during the Christmas holidays?

The boy is a good shot and used to handling guns. He shoots for his school.

It does not matter in what locality the shoot is providing it made provision for board and lodging.

In reply to your inquiry regarding shooting for a 16-year-old boy during the Christmas holidays, there is no scheme, or organisation which makes such provision, that is of course assuming you are referring to small game shooting. Arranging shooting of this kind is really entirely a matter for private enterprise, and the way most likely to succeed is for you to approach some local land-owner, or shooting man with whom you are either acquainted or to whom you can obtain an introduction, with a view to obtaining his help.

As target rifle shooting is such a completely different sport from game shooting, it is felt your boy's chances of obtaining some shooting would be greatly improved if he first attended and received lessons at a shooting school, that is if he has not already done so. In our opinion Messrs. Holland & Holland's shooting school at Northwood is one of the finest in the country, and Mr. Norman Clarke, who is one of their shooting coaches, could not be unfairly described as the best instructor in the world. However if you felt Northwood was too far to go, Messrs. Grudgington, gunmakers of Bath, have a perfectly adequate shooting ground there, where the instruction is sound.

Shrubs for a North Border

What shrubs do you recommend for a north border for foliage effect?

The following shrubs should do reasonably well in a north border:

Berberis thunbergii atropurpurea—purple leaves all summer.

Berberis thunbergii atropurpurea nana—a dwarf form of the above.

Cornus alba elegantissima—silver variegated leaves, red stems.

Cornus alba spaethii—gold variegated leaves, red stems.

Cotoneaster horizontalis—very good autumn colour and red berries—if grown as an open-ground plant and not trained up a wall will 'carpet' a considerable area.

Euonymous radicans argentea—silver variegated evergreen leaves, low-growing and spreading.

Mahonia japonica bealei—decorative pinnate evergreen leaves and scented yellow flowers in late winter or early spring.

Sambucus plumosa areus—a golden-leaved elder with very bright leaves.

Vinca variegata—the gold variegated-leaved Periwinkle.

Weigela florida variegata—yellow variegated foliage and pink flowers.

Variegated hollies (Ilex) would also do well.

Camelias too do best on a north-facing border.

Slugs and Snails

I was appalled by part of Mr. Watson's article on " Slugs and Snails." He uses and recommends metaldehyde, and as regards its effects on the beneficial birds such as thrushes which prey on slugs and snails, he merely says that he does not know this effect; he " hopes it is not serious."

So do I and, I am sure, you. But what if the effect is in fact serious—and fatal? He will then not only be denuding England of one of its joys, but will be slaying (nastily) the very predator which preys consistently on the enemy.

This is the sort of thing which makes the civilized onlooker despair—the glib using of a dope, because it produces a quick answer, without first ascertaining the full nature and ecological result of its use.

I think the RSPB or the BTO (Sand Lodge, Sandy, Bedfordshire) will give Mr. Watson the information he lacks. But can you not comment yourself?

Firstly, I wish to reassure you that I neither use, nor recommend any pest control products, such as metaldehyde, without first seeking all the information I can get on their side effects. In this instance I have been unable to get any information on the effects of slugs " doped " with metaldehyde on birds like thrushes. I was very sincere when I said I hoped the effect was not serious. As far as I know metaldehyde has been used for over 30 years without anyone looking at the side effects. Most people treat it as non-poisonous, but I know of a case locally of a dog eating slug pellets and dying, hence my healthy respect for it as a poison.

Secondly, I wish to point out that one purpose of my article was to try and bring out how little we really know about slug control and the need for much more research on the whole subject. The losses to farmers, growers and private gardeners through slug attack amounts to a very large sum of money each year. I recently

had a letter from a farmer who lost half the potatoes from 50 acres as a result of slug attack. I have seen complete lettuce crops wiped out by slug attack. This is the reason why people use metaldehyde, even though it is an indifferent control.

Thirdly, I would point out that we still have a great deal to learn about the side effects of many products in everyday use. The build up of DDT, aldrin and dieldrin residues in wild life food chains is now well known. However, we are still importing food from countries where these pesticides are widely used. Detailed analytical surveys on pesticide residues in foodstuffs have only recently started. The side-effects of many contaminants are not fully known, eg, diesel fumes, the organic lead compounds used as anti-knock agents in petrol, food preservatives, food dyes, many drugs and industrial effluents. If you have not already done so I recommend you to read Elspeth Huxley's *Brave New Victuals*—this gives a very good account of this whole problem.   E. B. Watson.

I was interested in E. B. Watson's article on slugs and snails, having been troubled by extensive slug damage to my potatoes—particularly Golden Wonders and Redstains. I tried the various forms of metaldehyde without success. In the 1965–1966 seasons, both of which were wet here, I greatly reduced slug damage by scattering wood ashes from the bonfire along the drills before planting. This has the incidental advantage of supplementing the potash supply. I have also grown the variety Orion and find it almost immune to slug damage.

Snails

I was interested in a recent article in a popular periodical concerning snails, edible variety, and the fact that some two and a half million were imported into this country last year. It appears to me that although not an over popular dish at present, the demand could conceivably grow considerably. Could any member please tell me where I may find information on the breeding, environment, etc., of these creatures?

Snails have been eaten from the earliest days. They were even reared and fattened by the Romans, at the cost of fabulous sums of money.

Helix Pomatia, which is the edible snail, is of a large family. They would all be edible if they did not feed on poisonous herbs. The large sized snail, the vinery and apple orchard snail, is eaten in France, those that have fattened themselves in the vineyards of Bourgoyne are a speciality, and these are actually imported into this country.

Their food value is not as great as is often imagined, and poisoning can result from the fact that they have been eating non-edible foods before being caught for human consumption. Only when they can be brought straight from the vineyards may their value to the Englishman be assured.

During winter snails fast, and it is therefore the moment to catch them. They are cleansed of noxious matter and can be fed up in the spring on sweet herbs.

For preparation, they must be cleaned by immersing them in boiling water with some wood ashes. Leave them for about quarter of an hour, until they have rid themselves of their cover, then they must be picked out carefully of their shells. Leave them in a basin of warm water for three hours, rub them between your hands, and wash well in cold water. The shells are scrubbed and dried.

Baked Snails: Mix 2 oz. butter with 1 tablespoon chopped parsley, and add salt, pepper, and a little grated nutmeg. Prepare 2 doz. shells, and place a piece of the butter mixture in each. Put a snail in each and cover with some more butter. Put these on a cast iron pan, mouths upwards, make the pan air-tight, and bake in moderate oven till the parsley darkens. Serve them in their shells, hot.

Snails a la Bourguignonne: Prepare some Bourgoyne snails, and having salted them for a few days, and washed thoroughly, strain and put them in a stewpan. Add sufficient water to cover them, and put some sweet herbs, cloves, whole pepper, and salt, and cook till they leave their shells. Clip off their tails. Prepare some ' butter, parsley, shallots, chervil, all chopped, add sifted breadcrumbs, and some white wine, season and knead well. Clean the shells then fill partly with the butter mixture. Put back the snails, and sandwich them with more mixture ; cover with breadcrumbs and bake in an oven for four minutes.

Soil-less Gardens

Would you please let me know if there are books on soil-less gardening? I read an article about this way of gardening in a paper.

The following books on soil-less gardening can probably be obtained from the Landsmans Bookshop Ltd, Buckenhill, Bromyard, Herefordshire. We would advise writing direct to them for prices and availability: *Hydroponics — the Bengal System* by J Sholto Douglass, *Profitable Growing without Soil* by H F Hollis, *Soil-less Culture* by T Saundy, *Soil-less Gardening for Flat and Home* by M Bentley (published in South Africa).

Sparrow Deterrent

Do you know of any means of deterring sparrows from roosting on the ledges and beams of an open-fronted garden shelter? Until we boarded in the eaves of the house they roosted and nested in the eaves and roof, making the roof space filthy. Since then they have transferred themselves to the shelter with the result that the walls and floor of it are covered with droppings. I have seen a spray advertised, Morkit, a Baywood product, which is intended to deter birds from eating flower and fruit buds, and I believe some London Boroughs use a sticky substance to stop the starlings and pigeons roosting on the ledges of buildings. What we need is something that would keep the birds away and yet not be offensive to anyone sitting in the shelter. It would be possible to enclose the space by wire but it would be very unsightly.

We assume that you have already tried the effect of black cotton string above the beams about one or two inches in height. Alternatively, you could try using some crinkly substance such as cellophane paper or mirror wrap which would, of course, have to be secured to the beams with string. Once the sparrows find their perch inaccessible they will not return for quite a while.

The sticky substance you have in mind is a product of Rentokill Laboratories Ltd. This firm will supply an estimate for the work entailed, and organise the whole undertaking.

Sparrows

How can I prevent sparrows from roosting in my garage in the rafters, other than shutting the doors every time I take the car out. I have tried placing a few moth balls on the rafters without much effect.

Whenever sparrows make up their minds to roost somewhere it seems that there is very little to prevent them from doing so. Thousands of pounds and scores of ideas have been tried to prevent birds roosting on or in public buildings, and all have been to no avail. This may sound very discouraging, but it is possible that with a little ingenuity you may effect a cure, particularly if something is done before the birds get into the habit of roosting in a strange place. You might find it helps to try and obtain an old stuffed cat or contrive something of this nature and either hang it from the rafters where it will swing a little, or tie it to a rafter changing the position from time to time. We cannot suggest the use of an obnoxious deterrent such as the Foxorine because you may find this unpleasant also. If you have an electric fence near to hand you might run wire along the rafters or conduct some similar experiment with a wire connected to a battery. Do not use the household current for this purpose. Ordinary bird scarers such as the Chase Glitterbang Scarer may help and you can also try the effect of black cotton strung from rafter to rafter or put it about 2 in. above

and parallel to the rafters which will hinder their landing when trying to roost.

Sparrows – Disposing of

Can you tell me if sparrows are listed as protected birds?

This last year or two we have been troubled with swarms of these species, and would like to bring them under control if possible.

Sparrows are not protected. You could buy a sparrow trap, but I am afraid you will have to dispatch them by hand when they are caught.

Otherwise take them in the boot of your car and release them from the trap as far away as possible. Personally I do not think this works because I think they will get home effectively in due course.

To reduce the population I knew an old gardener once who used to 'blow' the eggs where the sparrows nested and replace them. They would sit for the whole summer according to him and not lay again that year.

Spaying Bitches

I should be very grateful for any information you can give me on the subject of spaying (if that is the word) bitches. I recently read a book that inferred that it was a common practice in Australia though I do not think I have ever heard of it being done in this country. In particular I should like to know if there are any special disadvantages and what effect it is likely to have on the physical and mental characteristics of a bitch which has had a litter of puppies.

Spaying is an internal operation involving the removal of the uterus and ovaries, preventing further heats and breeding. Obviously, this is a fairly severe surgical operation and it would need to be carried out by a vet specializing in dogs and with theatre facilities if 100 per cent recovery was to be assured. Physically a spayed bitch tends towards obesity, but one that had bred before the operation would remain mentally the same. Spayed maiden bitches are inclined to be retarded and puppyish. On the whole, unless it is essential for health reasons, the spaying and castration of dogs is not recommended.

Squirrels – Grey

Can you suggest anyone who will give me advice on exterminating grey squirrel?

The Secretary of the Forestry Commission at 25 Savile Row, London, W.1, will supply a free pamphlet on the problems of grey squirrels and their extermination.

(*See also* page 41.)

Squirrels – Proof

All attempts to prevent the grey squirrel from eating my strawberries have so far failed. They have bitten holes in new nylon nets and burrowed under wire netting. Their cunning and persistence is remarkable but at the same time most irritating. Can you suggest how to make a strawberry bed squirrel-proof?

The only way to prevent squirrels from entering a fruit cage is to bury the wire at the foot for at least 12 in below the ground. This could be added to any cage already erected.

Squirrels – Trapping of

Can you give me some advice on trapping grey squirrels?

Fortunately the grey squirrel is, in some respects, very stupid. It cannot resist running through tunnel-set traps – if they are set where it likes to run. To make these tunnels you only require some pieces of old board, 18 ins. to a foot long, and about 6 ins. to 8 ins. wide, and a loose board laid on the top. The two side boards require two pegs of wood driven in soil near the ends of each board to keep the side boards upright, and one peg on the outside in the middle of each board – top pegs to be level with top edge of boards, and lay a top piece of board on the top of side ones – to complete tunnel. (Any old board answers best.) This board is not fastened down so put a brick on top if you like. At each end set an un-

covered 4 ins. gin trap with the tail outwards and placed so that the plate of trap is about 3 ins. inside end of tunnel. Set the plate of trap lightly. I use two traps – because if one watches, a grey squirrel goes through in leaps and may miss the plate on one trap and get caught at the other end. Old traps are better than new ones for choice as long as they are strong. Drive a good strong peg in the ground through the ring of trap chain. No one knows which tunnel the grey squirrel will prefer or why. I have five tunnel traps set all around one area (size of a tennis court) and two tunnels catch all the grey squirrels – never the other three. The total there this year is 39. If you have a flat-top garden wall it is possible to make a tunnel of old bricks set up longways on edges and halfway along one side leave a space of about 2 in. and set one trap the plate inside and tail of trap projecting out of wall – put a bit of rough board on the top longways on the bricks. Once a grey squirrel has been caught you will probably find that more grey squirrels use that tunnel. If you get a female it is a good idea to rub the tail end of her body well on the outside ends of the tunnel – it attracts others. Small rat gins are not good as the plate of these is too small – and the grey squirrel misses it.

Stack – Estimating Volume of Grain in a

Most of us know that a near approximation to the weight of a hayrick can be got as a result of measurements. In the same way, the volume of grain in a corn stack can be fairly well estimated, though less near to exactitude than with hay.

One well-known agricultural reference book gives the following figures: wheat stacks 27 cubic feet to one bushel grain; oats, 18 cubic feet to one bushel; barley, 22 cubic feet to one bushel.

Obviously, however, something depends on the season, and this season the grain yield per cubic foot of stack volume will commonly be rather less than usual.

To get the cubic contents of the body

of a square or oblong stack, you multiply the average length by the average width, and then multiply the product by the height to the eaves.

For the roof, multiply the length at the eaves by the breadth and the product by half the vertical height from eaves to ridge. Add the two resulting figures together and you have the total volume.

Starlings – 1

One of the woods on my shoot, approximately 1½–2 acres, has suddenly, since the end of the shooting season, been invaded and virtually taken over by starlings. Not only have they disturbed the game, but they have practically killed the scrub, quite apart from the terrible smell they are causing. I am wondering whether you could give me any advice on how to get rid of these starlings.

We can only commend to you the words of the Duke of Wellington to Queen Victoria when faced with this similar problem at the Crystal Palace: 'sparrow-hawks' – the difficulty is to get rid of the starlings without getting rid of all the game. Bird scarers would certainly affect both in our opinion. Members may have suggestions to make on the subject.

Starlings – 2

Collect old oil drums and make two rings of holes near the bottom of each drum. Set these on two bricks throughout the wood, fill with small dry branches and some coal coom on top to make as much smoke as possible and a lid or sheet of tin placed on the top. A quiet still night is best as the fumes will then filter slowly through the wood. Light the fires and when the tins are well heated a large handful of sulphur placed on each lid. The men should then withdraw. This should be done each night until the starlings disappear.

Starlings – 3

About a month ago I asked your advice as to how to dislodge roosting starlings from a covert. You suggested that I should try rockets, combined with mixed sawdust and creosote burning in a tin. It may interest you – and perhaps help others – to know that I have tried this combined method and it has been successful. We had tried shooting by itself, but it did no good. The success has to be slightly qualified. The wood contains about 300 acres. The starlings have not been driven completely from it, but they have left the valuable young plantation on which they had settled and have moved to some big trees at the other end of the wood, where they will not do much harm. This good result was probably due more to the rockets than to the flares as the latter usually went out.

Statuary Preservation

I have a pleasant piece of statuary made of a white marble which some experts say is not suitable for outdoors. Is there any way of giving it some weather protection—a silicon preparation or something of that sort? I shall be grateful for advice, especially based on experience.

Your own suggestion of a silicon preparation should serve the purpose. Unfortunately these silicons are fairly modern and we have not yet gained any information as to their effectiveness. However, we can publish your letter to see if any of our readers have experimented successfully.

Statue Cleaning – Lead

I have a number of lead ornamental garden statues which have gone green and generally need cleaning. Can you advise me of the best method to do this.

Your query concerning the cleaning of statues is a little bit puzzling. In the first instance, lead should not turn green. Its natural colour is grey or white and any green would suggest that there was an alloy of copper or brass. If, in fact, the statues are copper or brass they will turn green unless they are waxed, but people generally prefer the green colour.

The best way to clean lead statues is by gentle brushing with a soft brass wire brush which will not leave scratches. If the statues have been painted this will have to be removed first. If the green colouring is in streaks as a result of copper nails the brushing will also remove this staining.

War Memorial Stone

We have a small problem here with the War Memorial. It is made of rather soft stone and has become dirty, mostly from water of nearby trees, and badly needs cleaning. The stone being soft easily flakes, and would not bear such things as a scrubbing brush or steel wire. Can you recommend anything to do the job? I wonder if there is anything in the nature of a soft soap which would do if used with a sponge. I shall be very glad of your advice.

We have consulted the Ministry of Works, who suggest that you hose it down with clean water. If really necessary, you could use a weak soap solution and a soft brush.

Strawberries

I suffer badly from field mice and shrews, which attack my strawberries, nibbling them long before they are ripe. As a result I have to pick every berry which shows the slightest sign of colour. They take several days to ripen, in trays indoors. Is there any method of dealing with the mice, apart from complete net-ting with, say, ¼-in mesh wire? The strawberries toughen up when ripened indoors. Is there any method of retain-ing their freshness?

As far as we know wiring is the only method. Strawberries picked early and ripened on a tray usually go hard and tend to dry out, and we do not know of any method of getting round this. Readers may be able to help. Polythene cloches which rattle in the wind might act as a deterrent too.

Tree Stump Removal – 1

I have seen an advertisement which shows what appears to be a satisfactory stump killer, that operates by decom-posing the wood fibres right down to the roots. I should like your advice as to its possible efficiency, or maybe you can recommend some way of disposing of tree stumps.

We were ourselves interested in the advertisement and wrote to the firm asking them to let us know what chemi-cal the stump destroyer was based on. In spite of enclosing a stamped addressed envelope we received no reply. To the best of our knowledge the only chemical that will actually rot away tree stumps is saltpetre. Holes are drilled in the stumps fairly close together and at least nine inches deep, and these are filled and refilled with saltpetre over a period of three weeks. The holes are then plugged and the stumps will gradually rot away but it is a very long process. It can be hastened if at the end of three weeks' treatment with the saltpetre the stumps are covered against the rain and left approximately three months. At the end of this time, choosing a dry day, uncover them and expose as much of the roots as possible and play a blow lamp on them. Being impregnated with the salt-petre they should smoulder away, but it may be necessary to rekindle once or twice.

Tree Stump Removal – 2

I would be grateful for some advice on the subject of tree stump destruction. Briefly, my problem is the elimination of three or four stumps of mature Scots fir and chestnut which have either to be dug out or removed in some other way. I have heard that it is possible to inject quantities of a highly toxic or corrosive chemical which after a period reduces the roots to dust. This method, if prac-ticable, would obviously be much less laborious than digging, though I suspect some earth moving may have to be done in the end in order to obtain a com-pletely flat surface.

We would suggest that you burn the stumps out. This is done by saturating the wood with a chemical – either Potassium Nitrate or Sodium Chlorate – and then igniting it and leaving it to smoulder away, which might take some time. Bore holes 1 in. in diameter, 9 in. apart and 6 in. deep, sloping downwards towards the centre of the tree. One ounce of the chemical in its crystalline form is placed in each hole, which is then filled with water and plugged with clay. After three months the chemical should be well absorbed, and you can then ignite the stumps – you may have to use a little paraffin to start them off.

Agricultural Subsidy

I own about fifty acres, mostly of woodland, but have recently formed two paddocks for my daughters' ponies. Can you tell me whether I am eligible for obtaining any grant for fertilizers for these paddocks, and if so, how do I set about obtaining it?

You may be eligible for a subsidy. You should contact the Ministry of Agriculture, Government Buildings, Marston Road, New Marston, Oxford. They will confirm whether you are eligible.

Sundial – 1

I wish to obtain a sundial, and shall be grateful if you could put me in touch with a maker of these. Before the last war there was a firm, H. Baker & Son Ltd., 12 Clerkenwell Road, E.C., but a letter sent to that address recently was returned marked 'not known'. If this firm is still in existence, they may have moved years ago to another address.

We have a sundial specialist on our files called A A Holt Esq, Burton Holt Ltd, Goudhurst, Kent.

He makes them and erects them, but this was two years ago, and we hope he is still in business. If not, Carter's Tested Seeds sell ordinary garden sundials, but possibly these are purely ornamental and by no means accurate. They have a shop at Victoria Street, London SW1.

I know sundials are a very specialized thing, and the making and setting up of them varies on different latitudes.

Sundial – 2

Can you advise me on the basic rules when setting up a garden sundial (a) with the sun, and (b) when the sun is not out?

It is really quite simple to set up a sundial—when the sun is out, look at your watch at midday and move the dial so that the shadow falls on the twelve. Of course it is not possible to set up a sundial when the sun is not out—or at night!

Sundial – 3

I expect that Sir Alan Herbert will add to your note on sundials (February) that your watch should read G.M.T.—and you should be at Greenwich. What, as you suggest, is even more vital, is some sun. You may know the lines by Sir Bede Clifford,

I am a sundial,
And in this English clime,
Once in a while
I measure time.

I would not wish to discourage you by adding Hilaire Belloc's comment,

I am a sundial, and I make a botch,
Of what is done far better by a watch.

Sunflowers

Could you please give me some advice on the growing of sunflower seeds? There seems to be a demand at present for sunflower seed oil, and I have been wondering about the possibilities of growing sunflowers commercially for this purpose.

Sunflowers do best in rich, deeply cultivated soil. The seeds should be sown in rows 2½ ft. apart, the aim being to have the seeds 9 in. apart in the rows. If the crop has to be grown in a windy situation some earthing up has to be done as if for potatoes. 4 lb. of seed is needed to sow an acre. Where seed is to be saved the heads are cut off as they mature and laid in an airy shed to dry before being harvested. Mice and rats are very fond of the seeds unfortunately, and so they have to be kept at bay. Do not attempt to grow sunflower seeds unless you can get a contract from the buyers at the beginning of the season.

Swans – Pinioning

How can one pinion swans?

Pinioning should be done during the winter and a veterinary surgeon could easily do it. The method is to remove the first nine flight feathers of one wing only, amputating that part of the wing tip on which these nine feathers grow. The reason for doing this operation in winter is that in the summer there is a risk of flies laying eggs on the wound and it is practically impossible to put any kind of dressing on this wound as the bird will tear it off.

The usual method is to do the pinioning when the cygnets are not more than a few days old, when they do not suffer the slightest pain or loss of blood. It is of no use to pull out the end feathers but better to cut them to within three inches of the root, and then there is no risk that the feathers will be replaced before the next moult whereas if they are pulled out they will grow again within about six weeks.

Swans – Supplier

We have a lake in our grounds and would like to put some swans on it. Can one buy swans from a riverboard, or what is the source?

A pair of swans can be obtained quite easily by making application to the Lord Chamberlain, St. James's Palace, SW1. Every year at the swan upping the young birds are marked by the Royal Swan master (who lives at Cookham) and the other two companies that own swans. If the Lord Chamberlain (or in practice his secretary) agrees, he will instruct the Royal Swanmaster to catch up and send a pair of swans to the applicant, who should satisfy the Lord Chamberlain that he has adequate water on which to keep them. The swans will arrive in due course by passenger train in a crate after material arrangements have been agreed with the Swanmaster. They will be pinioned – that is, in the case of swans the under wing on one side will be severed so that they will not be sufficient support to the main wing to lift the birds off the water. The birds will be a gift, but the cost of transport and catching up will be sent to the applicant by the Royal Swanmaster, and this will probably amount to about £5 if he lives in England.

If the swans are not pinioned, and also if they are not a true pair (cob and pen), as sometimes happens if obtained from friends, they are apt to wander, especially the cob which may walk a long way off in autumn in search of a proper mate. Swans do not start nesting until they are three years old, so that one should not imagine they are wrong sexes when no nesting occurs in the second year. The pen is easily recognizable after a while as it always follows the cob, does more " titivating " to her plumage, and is the shier bird of the two.

Sweet Pea Supports

It occurred to me that you might be interested in the problem of sweet pea supports (applicable to runner beans, etc., as well) which I have solved in my own way, and tried out over two years exposure to all weathers. It does not require one cane per plant, it is very stable and does the job well. So once up, the erection is good for two years, the trench being made on one side the first year and the other the next. If one is prepared to use the same trench two years running, the structure would be good for four years, I am sure.

Briefly, I make a series of three-legged 'pylons' of 10 in. bamboo, using the gyn lashing. I space these along the trench at roughly 6 ft. intervals, then I connect the tops with more bamboos laid horizontally and square lashed. Roughly at mid height I square lash another horizontal layer of bamboos to two legs of each gyn or pylon.

The third leg either straddles the trench or points away from it as the case may be, and two legs are parallel with the trench. The feet of the legs are pushed into the soil about a foot. Then I hang my polypropylene net over the structure, tied as necessary. The plants, as they grow, are woven in and out of the netting and the result is splendid, the only trouble being when the plants are pulled down in autumn and even that is not difficult. I get a firm structure about 8 ft. high. Of course if you want to slope it by straddling the legs more you can get 8 ft. of growing space at the cost of more ground area, and you can reach the top of the plant without steps. Incidentally, if you do not straddle too much you can use a curved trench rather than a straight one, as I did the first time.

Some of your members will not be old Sappers as I am, or old sailors, and the gyn and square lashings will baffle them. If members are interested enough I could produce a pamphlet. Alternatively, it would be easy but more costly to produce a simple 'meccano' structure on which to hang the net. The essence is that any such structure be permanent yet movable, rigid yet light.

Tape Worms

Can a heifer pick up and develop a human tape worm? If it can, the value of the animal is seriously reduced and a herd and the land becomes suspect. Some of my fields adjoin roads used by motorists, hikers, etc, who could easily climb the gates and trespass on the land.

The tape worm's life cycle is somewhat involved. The adult tape worm inhabits the intestinal tract of man and is passed out in the faeces as a proglottid which contains eggs. If an animal ingests a proglottid or eggs when grazing, the immature form of the tape worm may penetrate into the body and reach the musculature; here the immature form develops into a small cyst. If such a cyst is ingested by a human being it will develop into an adult tape worm in the intestines. Naturally adequate cooking of meat will break the cycle.

Generally there is no effect on the animal's health whatever unless the tape worm cyst develops in some important site, such as the heart muscles, and even then unless the infestation is extremely high they are unlikely to cause any damage. The most usual muscle affected is the jaw muscle and this in many abattoirs is routinely inspected at slaughter. The incidence in cattle in this country is estimated on abattoir figures to be between 0.23 and 1.2 per cent.

The incidence of human tape worm is extremely rare in this country and we would think it unlikely that chance infestation might occur as suggested by you unless infested picknickers actually defaecated on land to which your cattle have access; and even then it is unlikely that the full cycle would be achieved. It is of some interest to note that it has been claimed that cattle may become infected from mature proglottid carried by seagulls from sewage outfalls into rivers or seas where the sewage has not been treated adequately. Thus you will see that we consider the chance of infestation occurring as you suggest as being extremely remote.

Home-grown Tobacco

I believe it is legal to grow tobacco for one's own personal use only. Also that you can join a society to whom you send it for curing. What sort of conditions do tobacco plants require – and since we live in Inverness and it is cold, would it have to grow in a greenhouse?

We suggest that you contact David Chalmers of 39 Milton Road, Kirkcaldy, Fife, who runs the Scottish Amateur Tobacco Growers' Association. He will provide you with the plants themselves, give you advice on growing it, and I believe has a curing centre where you can send the tobacco leaves for curing.

One is allowed to send 25 lb per person for curing, and the tobacco must only be for your own use – it is illegal to sell it, give it or even throw it away.

Tomato Disease

I wonder if you could put a name to a mysterious trouble I have with tomato plants under glass? The lower leaves of the plant turn yellow, starting from the tip, not from the stem. Only the lower leaves turn and the quantity of fruit does not seem to be materially affected. I should be glad to know if this trouble has a name, and if anything can be done about it?

Without seeing a specimen leaf from your tomatoes it is not possible to be absolutely sure what is wrong with them. These plants do suffer from a bewildering number of virus and fungus diseases, but from your description we would suspect that no disease is involved and that the yellowing of the leaves is due to the ageing of the plant and some small mistake in culture. It may be that at some time the tomatoes have been either under- or over-watered or the atmosphere in the house has been either very dry or else too humid, or the plants have been exposed to too bright sunlight. Provided the quality and weight of fruit borne is not affected we do not think that you need to worry.

Town Garden – Planting of

We have a small town garden about 20 yd by 8 yd and the borders are largely planted with herbaceous plants.

Last year we had a wonderful show from about late July onwards, but this year I want us to enjoy a little colour as soon as possible and for as long as possible.

We have a fair selection of bulbs from croci to tulips, but I should like to have your advice on a series of annuals – cheap, colourful and flowering successively from April–May onwards.

It will not be very easy to get annuals to flower as early as April/May because you cannot sow them out of doors much before the second or third week in March – with any hope of their germinating – and this does not give them a long enough season of growth to produce flowers in April or May.

We would suggest that you sow pansies (the winter flowering varieties) in late July; these should then flower as soon as the weather warms up in the spring and they have the advantage that once they are established they seed themselves freely. Biennials such as wallflowers, Canterbury bells and Sweet Williams will flower in April, May and June, but these need to be sown in May of the previous year and we appreciate that with your small garden it is not really possible to spare room for a seed bed. However, if you could spare a corner to sow a few of these and then thin them to 4 in apart and put them in their flowering positions in September or October they would give you a lovely display next year.

Tree Bleeding

What can I do to stop an elm tree 'bleeding' continuously from an area approximately 6 in by 6 in upwards from ground level. The bark at this point and on other parts was extensively bitten off by ponies about two years ago. Further biting was prevented by 'bark protector' and the tree has survived this and is healthy in every other way, but I fear that it will die if this bleeding is left to continue.

In reply to your query concerning tree bleeding, we advise as follows: The bark should be cut away to where it is sound, the wood treated with Arbrex Pruning Compound and the whole bound up with moss, covered with sacking until callous has formed from the margins of the wounds.

Trees – Debarked

I have half a dozen young Cox's apple trees which were planted two years ago. I had intended to guard the stems with wire netting but unfortunately never got around to it, with the result that rabbits or hares have de-barked them up to about 18in. from the ground.

Is there anything that can be done or will the trees just die off?

In theory they should die if they are completely ringed. Ringed trees have been saved by bandaging with black electricians' tape, but usually when very young. It might be worth experimenting with this.

Trees – Ginkgo

I wonder if you could tell me anything of the necessity to grow two Ginkgo trees, and not just one alone. I have one which at the moment is doing very well, but the other day I was told that it is necessary to have a male and female plant, as one on its own will not grow well. Could you please tell me if this information is correct?

We have not been able to find any authority to verify the necessity of male and female Ginkgo trees flourishing together. The Ginkgo has the oldest ancestry of any known tree. Its other name is maidenhair tree.

Tree Lopping

I have an avenue of fine old lime trees. One or two of the trees appear to be withering at the top. I have asked timber merchants whether it would be advisable to lop off the tops. They tell me that if this were done the limes would soon die. I should be grateful for your advice on the best method of preserving the trees.

We are advised by the Men of the Trees Organization that there is no reason why the tops of the limes, which appear to be withering, should not be lopped off carefully, and that the timber merchants are quite wrong in suggesting that by doing so it would kill the trees. Lime avenues at Hampton Court Palace have been pollarded back for many years and are still flourishing – probably the timber merchants wanted the job of felling the trees. We strongly advise you to remove the branches that are withering with very great care, dressing the wounds with Stockholm Tar, and we think that you will find the trees will be all right.

Tree Measurement

Am I right in thinking that the following formula gives one a fairly accurate assessment of the cubic content in cubic feet of mature timber in an oak tree? (Cordwood omitted.) Girth in yards, five feet above ground by the height of the trunk from the ground to the highest point which will provide 'sawing timber'. Please correct me if I am wrong.

To find the timber content of a tree: (1) Measure the height of the tree up to the 'stop'. The 'stop' is the place where the first sudden break in the uniform size of the trunk takes place. (2) Measure the girth of the tree at a height of 6 ft from the ground, and take off the allowance for the thickness of the bark as follows: For thick bark allow 1 in per foot (nearest) or girth=nett girth. For thin bark allow $\frac{1}{2}$ in per foot (nearest) of girth=nett girth. (3) Find quarter nett girth. (4) To find the cubic contents: square the quarter nett girth, and multiply by the length of the bole to the 'stop'.

Protecting Young Trees

How can one protect young trees against rabbits or hares without extensive wiring?

The following precautions have proved successful against rabbits, but we have no experience with hares. If the lowest branch is about 18 in from the ground wrap a newspaper around the stem of the tree. If the branches are nearer the ground make a ring of fairly straight sticks around the tree a few inches clear of the branches, spacing them about 2 in apart and leaving 15 in to 18 in of each stick above ground. If the stem is already ring barked bind insulating tape around the barked portion and remove it about six to nine months later.

Trees – Pruning Oak

I have recently bought a property with

about an acre of woodland containing a number of old oak trees on which there are quite a few dead branches. These branches must obviously be sawn off but I am wondering whether there is any particular action I should take or if there is a special time of the year when the work should be done. Your advice would be appreciated.

The best time of the year to do this is when the sap has stopped flowing in late autumn or winter. The branches should be cut at an angle so that no rain water can lodge in the severed portions. They should also be painted with tree cement. We suggest Arbrex Pruning Compound.

Trees – Yew – 1

I have heard that yew trees are poisonous to farm animals, yet they grow in large numbers around the countryside.

Can you please tell me whether this is so, and if it applies equally to all varieties of yew and to all animals – also what the poison is?

All varieties of the British yew trees are poisonous, but owing to its more frequent cultivation, the common yew is most often responsible for outbreaks of poisoning among animals. The Irish yew and the Yellow yew appear to contain less of the poisonous principle, which is called Taxine and is an alkaloid. The bark, leaves, and seeds all contain the active toxic principle, the leaves usually being the parts eaten. The older dark green leaves, especially if these have been cut off and left to wither for some hours, are more dangerous than the fresh green young shoots, which cattle have been known to eat in small amounts without harm. Cases of poisoning have been noted among horses, asses, cattle, sheep, goats and pigs. The majority of cases occur in cattle.

Trees – Yew – 2

I note that in a reply to a question you suggest that yew is only dangerous when it is wilting. I think this oversimplifies the case. I have always understood that yew is always poisonous but that the fresh foliage is also bitter and is thus not often eaten by stock. I feel that where stock are confined and there is much yew, as in the case mentioned, there is considerable danger. I have always understood that the same is true of Ragweed – when fresh it is not eaten because of the bitter taste but that if cut or pulled and allowed to wilt without being cleared from the land, it can cause poisoning. I have known cases of horses poisoned in this way.

Trout – Breeding and Stocking – 1

Where can I obtain information about breeding trout? Also on re-stocking?

There are various addresses that might be able to help you:
Salmon and Trout Association, Ltd, Fishmongers Hall, London Bridge, EC4.
Berkshire Trout Farm, Hungerford, Berks.
D F Leney, Surrey Trout Farm, Shottermill, Haslemere, Surrey.
P H Wilson, P M Wilson, Bibury Trout Farm Ltd, Hinderclay Hall, near Diss, Norfolk.
Fishery Management Services, The Rise, Brandon Village, near Coventry, Warwickshire.

Trout – Breeding and Stocking – 2

I wish to put trout into a small lake of about 1½ acres. There are no fish in it at present.
The relevant facts are:
(1) Average depth 4 ft.
(2) Acid water from the bogs on the mountains.
I want to put in shrimps and snails to increase the feed. Do they require certain weeds to maintain them?
Should I put in lime (easily available)

to reduce acidity?

Where can shrimps and snails be obtained, also necessary weed?

It would be very unusual if the lake in question did not already contain many forms of under-water plants and various forms of life in the shape of insect larvae and other aquatic subjects. Fresh water shrimps (Gammarus pulex) and the water louse (Asellus aquaticus) could be caught by dragging dome water plants from a pond or river and shaking them onto a sheet of paper. Many oxygenating plants could be obtained from ponds, etc, in the neighbourhood, and they would soon spread in the new lake. The acidity of the water would not harm the trout. Water snails could also be collected as above or they could be obtained from one of the dealers who advertise in the Aquarist and Pondkeeper magazine.

Suitable plants would be: Elodea Canadensis; Egéria densa; Ceratophyllum demersum; Myriophyllum proserpinacoddes.

Cleaning Garden Urns

I have recently acquired a fine pair of cast-iron garden urns about 2 ft 6 in high with bowls of approximately 20 in diameter. Over the years they appear to have been successively coated with thick layers of what appears to be a cement based paint and the very fine exterior design is almost obscured. Short of the laborious task of chipping the coating off, can you please suggest how it can most easily be removed and subsequently what is the best type of paint with which to treat the urns.

If the substance *is* cement based paint, chipping may be the only method for removal. Immersion in water may soften the cement mixture. A very stiff wire brush or wire pad may do the job and will also leave a rust-free surface. There are several good brands of rustproof paint on the market or a galvanized paint could be used as an undercoating first of all.

Vineyards – British Wine Growing

I seek information about British Viticulture and advice about growing grapes for wine making in this country. Can you help?

We think that your best course would be to write to the Viticultural Research Station, Rockfield Road, Oxted, Surrey. They offer reports containing advice and instructions on the cultivation of grapes for wine as well as suitable varieties of vines for this purpose.

As, with R. Barrington Brock, one of the two pioneers of the reintroduction of viticulture to Britain, I hope that your forecast of commercial vineyard expansion in this country (September number) will be realised. But I was a little surprised at some of the figures and facts which you published. In fairness to those people who may be encouraged by them to invest money in a vineyard, I believe that they should be qualified.

From 15 years' experience and from my knowledge of the Hambledon, Beaulieu and above all the Oxted vineyards, I should have thought that an acre of established vineyard ought to be considered as producing an average much nearer 2,000 bottles of wine a year than 4,000; that the figure of £1.25 per bottle retail price does not give a very good idea of the real return on the investment; that although a vineyard will indeed bear fruit in its second year it should not be allowed to; and that, when it comes to the mini-vineyard, 100 vines can certainly not be 'expected' to produce an average of 200 bottles a year for 25 years.

It may do so; just as the four-acre vineyard may produce 16,000 bottles. But to obtain such results one must have the right varieties, in exactly the right conditions cultivated with skill and knowledge. And even then there is the factor of irregularity—a number of varieties which in other respects are right for British conditions, are irregular in their cropping behaviour. There is another phenomenon to be watched for: encouragingly heavy crops in the first few years with a serious falling-off thereafter. Moreover, again in my own personal experience, there is a very considerable difference in yield from one part of Britain to another and I do not think that the impression should be allowed to become established that all parts even of southern England are equally suitable for vines.

This letter is not intended to be discouraging: on the contrary, for I believe that southern and eastern England could be one of the wine-producing countries. But I cannot help recalling, as will many other members of the Association, how the remarkable success which the late Justin Brooke had with peaches and apricots in Suffolk, and his infectious enthusiasm for their cultivation in orchards, led too many people to believe that it would be easy to emulate him. It is surely desirable that the risks as well as the promise of growing wine in Britain should be understood.

Yours faithfully,
EDWARD HYAMS.

Voles

I should be glad to learn if any member of the CGA has successfully dealt with a plague of voles and for details of the method employed.

Mole fuses have proved ineffective. Our local pest control officer has no suggestion to offer other than pouring Jeyes Fluid around the remaining fruit trees and rose bushes in the hope that these rodents will be deterred from eating the roots, and being thus deprived of their natural food, will move on to pastures new.

The only effective deterrent for voles is a large cat, preferably not too well fed. The cat scoops the voles out of their runs and in time should deplete the population for you.

Walking-Sticks – Curing Warp

I have a blackthorn walking-stick which is still covered with the bark. This I have had for four years. Now the straight portion is becoming slightly out of straight and the crook is straightening out. I should be pleased if you could tell me what I can do to correct these conditions, bearing in mind that I do not wish to strip off the bark.

We contacted James Smith & Sons of 53 New Oxford Street, W1, who are specialists in walking-sticks and umbrellas. They advised that you should keep the walking-stick out of all extremities of heat and cold as these do tend to affect its shape. To get it back into shape you should put it into hot water and bend it back.

Wall Paint

I have a cottage in Surrey built of pleasant rose brick, and about 70 years old. Unfortunately, the previous owner had it pebble-dashed, in what I consider is a very dreary brown. I want to whiten the walls with Snowcem or some such treatment. However, I am doubtful whether the rather large and shiny pebbles will take Snowcem, and in any case the surface is so deep that it would probably be very wasteful and expensive to Snowcem it, as it stands. To strip the whole pebble and cement surface off down to the brick, would be even more expensive, and I doubt whether it would be practicable. Can you, please, make any suggestions to me? Is it possible to pull or scrape the pebbles off without making it a major operation?

You might experiment with a small section of your wall by using a thicker solution of Snowcem than is recommended by the makers, i.e., less dilution with water. If the pebbles can be roughened in any way the Snowcem would certainly adhere to the surface. You may damage the wall if you attempt to strip off the rough cast.

Wall Plants

In my garden I have two turf terracing walls, about 150 ft in all, which are at present covered only with grass and weeds.

Can you advise me what plants I may use to cover the vertical faces of these walls to keep down the weeds and grass and prevent soil erosion, especially by frost? I feel the plants must be evergreen and not too bulky as there is a pathway at the bottom of these walls. Also they must not be too expensive as there is a large area to cover. Each wall is about three feet high.

With regard to the turf walls, we think that you would probably be best to plant trailing shrubs on the top of these and then allow them to trail down the walls. In most cases the shrubs we recommend will root into the walls.

Cotoneaster dammeri – bright red berries – will spread over a wide area.

Any of the variegated leaved ivies – these are very decorative and will again cover a wide space.

Winter Jasmine – this is not evergreen but the green shoots are pleasant even when it is not in leaf.

Cotoneaster mycrophyllus – similar to dammeri but larger berries.

If you would prefer to plant actually into the walls we would suggest any of the following: the trailing saxifrages, sempervirums (house leeks), sedums (stonecrops), thymes, the creeping campanulas.

A good general nursery where you could obtain any of the above is Messrs. Notcutts, The Nursery, Woodbridge, Suffolk.

Walnut Tree

I have a large walnut tree of an age of between 200 and 300 years in my garden, and it is showing signs of going back – i.e., a number of small branches at the extremities are dying. All the main and principal branches are still sound, but each year more of the little branches appear to die, starting from their extremities. It has been suggested to me that one must be very careful pruning walnut trees or they 'bleed' to death. Is this really so? My feeling is to cut back all the dead wood. If this is so, would it be better to wait till the autumn, or could I start now, as the leaves are already beginning to turn?

A walnut tree is always somewhat tender, the young foliage being frequently affected by late frosts and particularly vulnerable to any disease when mature. It may be that your tree is now long past its prime and is gradually dying back, in which case there is very little you can do about it. We have not heard of walnut trees bleeding to death, particularly from pruning, in fact the old adage: 'A woman, a dog, and a walnut tree, the more you beat them the better they be,' applies to the time when the nuts were gathered by thrashing the tree with long sticks, which must have damaged its extremities quite severely, but no countryman would have continued to do so if the effect was really harmful. If you decide to prune the tree, this can be done after the middle of October.

Irish Terrier – Wandering

I have had an Irish terrier since puppyhood. He is now a year old and has taken to wandering. He always comes back but has been away up to four days. I think he wants canine friends but if I got another dog I fear they would both go off. Would a bitch be similarly corrupted or is there any cure?

The problem of the wandering dog seems to be a growing one. Apart from the natural urge to pay court to bitches in season (when a dog may besiege the lady's house for days on end), the reason may be boredom. Nowadays the tendency is to keep working breeds as house pets, not allowing for their inborn "instinct" to be up and doing; in the case of a gundog, walking miles at the heels of a keeper on his daily round, and with a terrier the rough and tumble of ratting in the rickyard or a day's rabbiting. The wandering habit is hard to cure once it is established, and the main thing is to make the dog a *personal* companion, letting him join in the daily chores and go out in the car. Routine, too, is a help. Two meals a day at set hours and a daily walk. Animals like routine and soon learn to expect certain things at certain hours, and this, in the case of the dog, gives him a feeling of belonging which is essential to the intelligent companion dog. In the case of male dogs, enforced celibacy can also make them wander, and if it is possible to find some stud work for him (as it should be with a pure bred terrier) then this may do a lot towards settling him at home. A canine companion in the house, preferably a bitch, will make a difference to a dog, but will not in itself cure the wandering habit.

Warts – (On Horses)

Can you suggest a cure for warts on horses?

A member cured them on his horse by using a solution of formaldehyde. 1 in 10 of water is effective without being too painful. Applied twice a day, they disappear in a week or two. It is advisable to make a ring of zinc and castor oil ointment around the wart first to prevent the formaldehyde getting on the bare skin.

See cures under Horses.

Wasps' Nests – Destroying

Most disappointing! 'A Guide to Country Living' does not appear to tell me how to destroy a wasps' nest in the garden under veronica.

Insert a cloth or rag to bung the hole well after nightfall. Shove home with a stick. Pour on a gallon of paraffin, which will soak through the cloth and into the nest. Light. A few wasps may escape, but the nest will be destroyed.

I have done this dozens of times and have never been stung.

A non-inflammable method is to fill a beer or lemonade bottle with petrol and insert it in the hole—again well after dark to let the wasps settle. The bottle's shoulders block the hole and the petrol fumes kill the wasps. Do *not* light or the whole thing will go off like a bomb with you too.

Water Cress – 1

Can you tell me how to establish water cress beds?

To cultivate Water Cress in a running stream is difficult unless the stream is exceptionally shallow with but one or two inches of water. On the other hand it is comparatively easy to establish water cress on the banks of a running stream, with steady temperature of 50 to 52 degrees F. all the year round.

The method usually adopted in this case is to take out trenches running from the sides of the stream, sufficiently deep to allow up to 6 inches of water to run through them. The series of trenches are so arranged to allow the water to run in at one end of a trench and flow out at the other end into the next trench and so on. The most convenient width for each trench is 5 feet, whilst the length of each trench may be arranged to meet local conditions and requirements.

After the trenches have been prepared, small tufts of water cress roots, or failing this, strong cuttings should be planted with a dibber about 1 foot apart and in rows about 1 foot apart they should then be trodden or rolled down with the object of inducing the plants to establish themselves quickly.

Water may now be allowed to flow into the trenches to a depth of about $1\frac{1}{2}$ inches, and when it is observed that the plants have become established and are growing freely, the depth of water should be increased to 3 inches. During the winter there should be at least 6 inches of water in the trenches in order to protect the plants during severe weather. It is usually best to replant each year, either in April or early in September. The plants or cuttings should, if possible, be obtained from a local source, but at the same time, quite satisfactory results may be expected from imported plants or plants obtained from another locality.

There are two distinct varieties of cress, the green variety which comes into use during the summer, and the brown or hardy variety during the winter. Plants of the green variety will be ready for transplanting during April or early May according to weather conditions, whilst plants of the brown variety should be transplanted in September.

Water Cress – 2

Would you please give me all the information available for growing watercress on a commercial scale?

We suggest that you get in touch with the National Watercress Growers Association, 45 Bedford Square, London, WC1.

The Ministry of Agriculture have issued a leaflet "The Cultivation of Watercress" Bulletin No. 136, obtainable from HMSO, York House, Kingsway, London, WC2.

The leading authority on watercress in England is Mr. C. H. Sansom, Croxley Hall, Rickmansworth, and we feel sure that he will be able to give you some advice.

Water Cress –3

In the absence of running water. Water cress may be grown with a reasonable amount of success in trenches. Although shade is not essential a shady site will usually be moister than one subject to direct sun, moreover, it will reduce the amount of labour needed to water the plants during dry weather.

Prepare the site by taking out about 12 inches of soil to a width of 15 inches. In this excavation, place about 6 inches of farmyard manure then fill in trenches with the excavated soil until the surface is about three inches below the original level. Subsequently, and before planting, give a good dressing of old soot, this will act as a fertiliser for the watercress, and as an effective deterrent to the slugs and snails which seem to be very partial to the crop under terrestrial conditions.

The usual method of procuring watercress plants for garden culture is to raise them from seeds, sowing these during late March or early April. The resulting seedlings should be pricked out about three inches apart each way, in boxes that have a layer of manure over the drainage holes, and are then filled with sifted loam. Water the seedlings, and never allow them to become dry. Place them on a moist base and shade from direct sunlight until well established; then keep them under thin shading until they are hardened off.

Early in June the plants will be ready for transference to the shallow trenches; stagger them at six inches apart. If the prevailing weather is showery, no watering will be necessary, but otherwise a thorough soaking should be given. On no occasion must the plants become dry, and it should be a routine operation to make sure the plants are adequately supplied with moisture. After they are well re-established, a weekly application of weak soot water, or liquid manure, will prove very beneficial. During the heat of the summer the plants will probably want to flower, but this should be prevented by removing all the tips of potential flowering growths, so soon as embryo buds are seen. In the second year the plants will flower, but they should by then have well served their purpose and may be discarded. The trenches should then be replanted.

The crop is marketed in a standard non-returnable package known as the 12 lb. chip which holds 36 bunches or 7 lbs. of cress.

Profit from proper commercial water bearing beds of greensand or chalk may be as much as £1 per square yard.

Water-divining

See Dowsers.

Waterfowl

Can you suggest anyone who will be able to advise me about waterfowl?

We suggest you contact: Lt Col Johnston, Ixworth, Bury St. Edmunds, Suffolk. (Pakenham 16.)

Water Lilies

I am particularly anxious to find some method other than dredging or rather tedious defoliation, by which water lilies can be controlled. I would be interested to learn if any spray or systemic weed killer has yet been produced which affects these plants, but which is innocuous to fish.

I know of no method of destroying water lilies by chemical means. Anything put into the water strong enough to kill them would certainly kill all other water plants in the pond as well as the fish. Copper sulphate is one of the chemicals used to control algae, but as copper is deadly to fish, a fifth part to a million of water is enough, it can be realized how careful one must be. The best way to destroy many of the lilies will be to have a grapnel hook on a rope and drag out as many of the rootstocks as possible.

Water Lilies

Do you know of a nursery that will supply water lilies and give me some information about them?

We suggest you contact: L. Haig & Co., Beam Brook, Newdigate, Surrey. They supply water lilies and will also give information on suitable types, spread and effect on duck.

Waxwings Birds

I wonder if you would be kind enough to help me identify some rather unusual birds which appeared in my garden early this year. I have certainly never seen them before in Germany or anywhere else. There were nine in all and I first noticed them feeding on some berries or shrubs in the garden. They seemed hungry and comparatively tame and I watched them for some time through glasses and would describe them as follows: Size, rather bigger than a common starling but smaller than a thrush; colour, dove-grey head and breast with darker grey back; distinctive markings, crest on head, red flash half way along wing. Yellow and black marking around tail feathers. My house is on the outskirts of Munchen Gladbach near Dusseldorf. I would describe the flight of these birds as being similar to that of a common starling.

The birds described were Waxwings, a large number of which also entered this country just after Christmas. Periodically they invade Western Europe from cone forests further east, either when the population gets very large, or there is a failure of their winter food supply. The colour is more brown than grey but their other points in the description leave no doubt of their identification.

Weed Killer – Ivy

I am troubled by ivy growing on a cob garden wall, which seems to be rooted in the cob so that I cannot uproot it without damaging the wall. In these circumstances the only way to deal with it would seem to be by using a weed killer which acts on the leaves. Would you agree with this, and if so what weed killer would you recommend for the purpose?

The only alternative to digging out the ivy is to spray with brushwood killer. You may find that several applications are necessary and it is sometimes difficult to prevent re-growth from the root.

Weeping Trees

David Paton's article anent the weeping beech, Fagus Sylvatica, car. pendula, growing beside the church in the village of Horsehouse, leads one to wonder how these weeping varieties of trees originate. It was common practice years ago to plant Grevillea Robusta ('Silver Oak') as shade trees in Coffee Plantations in South India. When these shade trees had developed on my plantation I noticed a single weeping variety; the only one over an area of about 350 acres. The Grevillea Robusta seed had been procured from well-known seedsmen, and they had never heard of the weeping variety. The Agricultural Department expressed ignorance of the weeping variety of this well-known shade and ornamental tree and, on receiving my photos and description, tacked the term 'pendens' to the variety (i.e. Grevillea Rubusta, var. pendens). The tree bore no seed, and my efforts to propagate this rarety by layering were unsuccessful. One drawback of the Grevillea Robusta as a shade tree was that it was deciduous, and the coffee bushes were matted with the fallen leaves. On the same plantation, however, grown from the same seed stock, there appeared fifteen Grevillea Robusta of another variety, which were not deciduous and the coffee bushes under them were fairly free of the fallen leaves. The growth was also noticeably different from that of the ordinary 'Silver Oak', being much more of the fir tree type, the branches being closer together and more regular; an ideal shade tree. But the trees bore very little blossom,, and I failed to collect seed. Again the Agricultural Dept. was mystified, as also were the seed suppliers!

Well-Cleaning

Can you or your readers suggest an easy and cheap way of cleaning the walls of a 20 ft. well. It has been pumped dry and following continued drought has not refilled. The brick is honeycomb and the surrounding earth is clay. The well may be on a spring but normally seems to fill adequately from seepage. Being a rediscovered well it was foul before pumping. It would be needed for drinking water.

Since the use of any chemical or soap mixture will taint the water, it seems you may have to resort to hand scrubbing with plain water and a stiff brush and then mopping out the residue at the bottom of the well before it refills. It might be simpler to use some sort of plastic lining at the bottom of the well to collect the residue. One wonders whether the use of a blow lamp on the brickwork would sterilize the fungi or other growth.

Well-Digging

I should be much obliged if you could give me any information or put me on to any literature on the subject of well digging. All the wells in this village have been filled in many years ago and the people who sunk them also departed.

There are two principal methods of constructing wells – excavation and boring – and although the latter is the more specialized operation and one only to be entrusted to firms whose particular business it is, it is much the best to have any well work done by a thoroughly experienced man, although the sinking of a shallow well by a process of excavation proceeds mainly on the lines of sinking any other vertical shaft, such as a tunnel or mining shaft. A frame of four walling timbers joined at their ends, forming a rectangle, is laid out on the ground. Outside are driven vertical polings or sheeting, then inside as the sheeting is being driven, the earth is excavated to a little above or a little below its lower end, depending upon whether the ground is hard or soft. When the excavation is some 4 ft below one frame, a new frame is placed, and so on to the depth of the length of the sheeting. If the shaft is to be shallow, it may be started large enough at the top, so that the sheeting may be vertical and the shaft reduced in size by the thickness of the timbering at the bottom of each set of sheeting, which may be from 10 to 20 ft long. The main thing to be avoided in shaft-sinking is to do anything that may start a general movement of the earth, which is apt to be started by cavities at the back of the timbering which, causing it to deflect, set in motion a progressive movement of the earth. The main point, therefore, is to avoid the formation of such cavities by driving and placing the timbers carefully and wedging tight. The excavation is 2 ft 6 in larger than the intended finished internal diameter of the well. This allows for 9 in lining and 6 in of clay puddle backing. The wallings are formed flat on the face, and they are curved on the back to fit the poling boards set upright around the circumference. They must be at least 4 in deep and they are set in pairs opposite each other, one pair being a few inches below the other so that the struts may cross. At the base is a sump about 12 in deep for any silt to settle in, while above this open-jointed brickwork permits the infiltration of the water, while the remainder is brick in cement and backed by clay puddle as indicated. A hole is sunk as deep as may be safe without any timbering and then the curb is laid. This is formed of oak or elm, 9 in wide and of the same internal diameter as the well. It is built up of small sections of timber cut out from planks which are screwed together in two layers breaking joint. Upon this curb a length of the well lining is built up, and as further excavation proceeds below it, the weight of the finished section is supported by struts and footblocks, as indicated. Of alternative methods of construction one might mention the use of fireclay or stoneware pipes in place of the brickwork, suitably perforated ones being sold for the lower portion, while large wells, principally those in connection with public water supplies, are often sunk by means of a steel curb with a cutting edge on which cast iron segments are built up to form the shaft as the curb sinks by excavation within it. Sometimes concrete sections are used in place of cast iron or brick; they are relatively inexpensive and are obtainable from firms who make a speciality of concrete sewer pipes cast by the centrifugal process.

Willow

I have two water meadows of 2¼ acres each which become flooded some four or five times each winter. They are down to grass but of poor quality, and near-by farmers are not interested enough to cut and bale it for the gift of the hay. This is a pretty poor return for grassland and I want to try something different. Having cut down parts of a much overgrown box hedge (not on ground subject to flooding) I was much impressed by the quality of the wood. It is dense, uniform in texture, and machines perfectly. Surely there is a market for 'box' if properly grown! Can I use my meadows to grow a boxwood plantation for cutting, say in 15 years' time? Would the flooding be detrimental to the growth?

We do not think that your boxwood plantation would be very successful in such meadows, nor does there appear to be a regular market for boxwood. In actual fact it sells best to flowershops for its leaves. We suggest that you consider planting your meadows with bat willow, since this will make a fairly quick return, and in this connection we would advise you to contact either the Forest Product Research Association, Princes Risborough, Bucks, or the Forestry Society of England and Wales, 49 Russell Square, W.C.1, for further particulars.

Willows – Pollarding

I am concerned over the fact that I have got 150 Willow Trees, all of which have not been pollarded for over twenty years and require being dealt with right away.

In the past these were normally pollarded by cutting the branches with an axe and I believe it was the theory that in order that they should grow properly they should not be pollarded with a saw, but only with an axe.

I am obtaining an estimate from a small firm, who are of course going to use power saws.

Can you let me know if the branches in fact are sawn off, whether or not any harm will be done?

I have checked in several Forestry books, but can find no reference to the necessity to cut willow branches with an axe rather than a saw. I have also consulted a Tree Surgeon, who considers that either tool can be used.

Fungi diseases and tree pests can become more easily established on a sawn surface rather than on the smoother cut of an axe. A power saw is more usually used to reduce labour costs and a fine-toothed saw is preferable. The cut should be made as close to the bole as possible and with a downward slope to throw off water. The surface of the cut is best painted over with Arbrex to seal it off from infection.

Wireworm

Every autumn I sweep up a lot of leaves, mainly beech and sycamore, and put them in a heap to rot down. They make very good leaf mould, but my impression is that whenever I use this either as a mulch or dig it in I suffer from an infestation of wireworms, which appear to breed in the leaf pit. How, please, can I treat the leaf mould?

It is unlikely that the use of leafmould encourages wireworm, as this pest breeds mostly in grassland. We think it is probable that the pest you mention may be some saprophytic eel worm, which feeds on decaying vegetable matter, and which are harmless to growing plants. These are not unlike wireworm in appearance. If you wish to take precautions against wireworm, then we suggest that Aldrin dust is applied to the soil just before planting, about four days normally, and worked into the soil to a depth of 3 to 4 in. Usually Aldrin dust is used at the rate of 1–2 oz to the sq yd.

Woodpeckers

I have been approached by one of the churchwardens of our ancient village church in connection with damage done by woodpeckers. I understand that these birds are attacking the shingle of the fabric spire, and defy all efforts to remove them, I believe that the woodpecker is a protected bird, and, therefore, it would not be possible to shoot them. There may, however, be some permit that one can get to prevent damage to historic monuments, and I should be grateful for your advice and suggestions.

Woodpeckers are protected birds in most areas, so they cannot be shot. The best thing to do is to remove the source of the trouble, which we think will be caused by wood insects upon which the woodpeckers are feeding. The shingle, therefore, should be treated with creosote or some other protective, which will have the doubly beneficial effect of preserving the shingle and keeping away the woodpeckers.

Wood Wasps

I have recently read that one type of wasp has been known to eat a cedar shingle roof, and as I am proposing to apply Cuprinol preservative next summer I would be glad to know if this, or some other additive, will protect against this risk.

Current attacks of this nature have not come to the attention of the writer, but it is highly likely that wasps were attacking the roof for the sole purpose of obtaining wood to macerate when building their nests. Western red cedar which is of a very soft nature would prove highly desirable to the insect for this purpose. The application of Cuprinol wood preservative would tend to render the timber obnoxious, and should consequently prevent any further damage from this source.

Wounded Game – Killing

I wonder if you could recommend the best way of killing wounded game?

The best way of killing wounded game, such as mallard or goose, is by hitting it sharply at the back of the head with a sharp stick. A shooting stick can also be used for this purpose, and this is the best method of killing hares, pheasants, etc. It is also possible to wring the necks of smaller birds.

Rabbits and hares if held by the legs can be despatched quickly and humanely with a blow to the base of the skull with the side of one's hand.

Wrought Iron Gates – To Avoid Rust

Can you give me any advice on how to protect my wrought iron gates from becoming rusty?

We have found that, once the rust and scale have been removed and the gates painted, the best thing is to paint over thinly two or three times a year with RAW (*not* boiled) linseed oil. This sets into a hard film and protects the paint and thus the metal. It is best not to apply in dusty conditions, but the gates seem to remain clean and shiny and if one wants to make them look specially neat one can put on another coat at any time. The oil normally dries in 24/48 hours. Boiled linseed oil is not suitable because it takes a very long time indeed to dry.

LEGAL AND PROFESSIONAL

This section comprises questions on legal points,
and those which can usually be answered by
Accountants, Chartered Surveyors, Tax Specialists
aud Solicitors

Right of Access

I have a three acre field of Christmas trees with an entrance from the main road. To prevent thieving I have boarded up this entrance and it has not been used for a year and may not be for another two. It has been suggested to me that I may be prejudicing my right of this entrance if it is not used for a time. Can you please say how long this time can be?

You have under planning law, an existing right of access to the public highway and this can only be extinguished by certain regulated procedures for the closure of an access, or where an owner abandons the access over a period of time. In our opinion it would seem advisable for you to fit an unclimbable gate with heavy duty padlock so that you cannot be accused of abandoning your right of access by boarding it up. We believe this suggestion is by far the most practical and sound way of overcoming your difficulty, as otherwise in years to come you may find the Planning Authority will take the view, that having blocked the entrance up, you had shown an intention to abandon its use.

Disputed Account – Settlement of

I rendered an account for work done. Because he considered I had over-charged, the customer sent me a cheque for less than the amount. I handed the cheque back pointing out that I would not accept less than a full settlement. He then got his solicitor to send me the cheque with a request that I should accept it as it was reasonable for the work done. Previously, I had told him I intended to sue for a full settlement. Would it be wise to cash the cheque and sue for the balance, or would it be wiser to return it and sue for the lot?

Three courses are possible in respect of your disputed account:

(1) Cash the cheque and reconcile yourself to the loss of the unpaid balance;

(2) Cash the cheque and sue for the balance;

(3) Return the cheque and sue for the whole amount.

From the practical point of view and unless the balance is really substantial No. (1) is your best course. Many just claims are abandoned solely because of legal costs.

The possibility exists, too, that your issuing a writ in courses (2) and (3), payment would be promptly forthcoming without litigation. In these matters it is all a bit of a gamble; and you may well be content to gamble.

Agents Commission

I own a farm which is let on a full agricultural tenancy, and is administered for me by chartered land agents and surveyors. Some while ago on my agent's recommendation I applied for planning permission on some white land considered ripe for development, and this was turned down. Again, on my agent's recommendation, I went to appeal with him, and the appeal was turned down, all of which involved me in some considerable expense for no return. I have now been approached by a developer wishing to purchase this land on the basis that they would stand the cost of a further appeal, and, subject to the appeal being granted, they would purchase the land from me.

As these prospective purchasers have not been introduced by my agent, would I be under any obligation to pay him agent's commission should the sale ensue, in view of the fact that he has been in no way instrumental in introducing the purchase, or the proposition?

In broad terms, where an agent plays no part in the introduction of a purchaser, no commission is due to him. However, we would be a little more careful in an instance where a firm of land agents is engaged in a managerial function, in case there is any contract between yourself and the firm, with a clause applying to ultimate sale of part or the whole.

We would at any rate advise you to inform the firm of land agents that you are negotiating direct with a developer in order to clear up beforehand any claim which they might make for commission.

Agents' Deposit – Interest on

We have recently sold our house through an estate agent. Due to legal complications the transition was not completed for four months, during which time we allowed the purchasers to occupy the place.

We have now been paid the purchase price, less legal fees and deposit and plus interest for four months at 9 %. This was paid through our solicitors. However, the deposit, which has been held by the estate agents for four months, has been paid, less fees and without interest. As the agents sold the house to the first and only viewer on the day that it came on the market—and at my suggested price, which was £1,000 above theirs—I feel that they are being somewhat grasping.

Have I any legal grounds for demanding interest on the deposit?

This is a question which we understand has been under discussion recently among the professional bodies concerned. It is a vexed question and we understand there are no hard and fast rules and no legal position on deposit interest has been established. Estate agents tend to regard interest on deposit of this nature as a 'perk'. If the estate agent was holding the money as 'stakeholder' then you have no grounds for demanding the interest on the stake, but if he was acting as your agent, you could approach him and ask for the interest in view of the circumstances. But the only pressure you can bring to bear is moral pressure.

Amenities – Protection of

One street in the village in which I live has become infested with lorries, which in some cases would not appear to belong to the people who live there. The lorries are ruining the road verges, mounting and destroying the footways and generally making the carriageways very dirty. Furthermore, some leave between 3 and 5 a.m. making a great noise.

Four or five lorries with trailers are kept in a farmyard. The lorries are registered in the name of a farmer living 10 miles away, although I think the owners of the farmyard have a financial interest in the lorries, beside driving.

Further up the road is a property which is registered as a smallholding. As far as is known, father and mother own the property, but are now away a lot. The son runs the smallholding and his wife looks after a few cows and horses. He now has two lorries which are parked in the yard and in a make-shift garage on the property. It is doubtful if the lorries are owned by the owner of the smallholding and his family.

Further up is a small cottage which used to be a smallholding which has a narrow concrete drive up to some old buildings. A lorry with trailer is being kept there overnight and leaving early in the morning, driven by the occupant of the cottage.

One has no wish to deprive these people of making their living, but they are ruining the amenities of our village and the roads are simply not wide enough to take heavy lorries. I am meeting the district surveyor after Easter, but without major widening operations it appears little can be done to improve the road.

Can anyone start up a lorry business, when and where they wish, park and keep the lorries in any convenient yard or drive which does not belong to them and for which they are not paying rates?

We greatly hope that your interview with the district surveyor will help you in your efforts to restore and guard the amenities of your area. Our comments, for which you ask on specific points, are:

(1) Intrusion of business premises into residential area: a primary purpose of the Town and Country Planning Acts is to preserve the amenities of a residential area. You may find, upon enquiry of your area planning officer, that the coal business and the other enterprises calling for the use of heavy lorries are without the requisite planning permission.

(2) Parking of lorries on public roads: lorries can be parked on a public highway in the same circumstances as any other motor vehicle. There are no specific regulations governing lorries at the moment.

Ancient Lights

My problem concerns my greenhouse. I use it for growing crops for market on a part time basis although it is not my livelihood. The house property is in an urban area.

Planning permission is being sought to build on the land to the south of the greenhouse. Have I any rights which would restrict the height of buildings to be erected within a certain distance of it? The crops depend on direct sunlight, particularly in the early part of the year. Can I claim that the light and distance of buildings should be such as not to obstruct direct sunlight with the sun at its maximum elevation? Say early in February.

If I have no rights over the height and distance from the greenhouse of the proposed building, have I any rights over the spacing between the buildings?

We think that you may well have valid objections over interference to your rights to light. Under the Prescription Act, a right to the use of light for a dwelling house or other building is obtained by the enjoyment of it for twenty years without interruption. You are entitled to such an amount of light as is necessary for the beneficial use of the property in question and any obstruction of your light, to justify the grant of an injunction, must be of such a degree as to constitute a nuisance.

There was a case for instance between the Attorney General and Queen Anne's Mansions, where buildings which had been erected in close proximity to a building used for religious services were of such a height as sensibly to diminish the light available for religious services and for viewing the decorations of the chapel. This was held to be an interference with access of light under the Prescription Act and an injunction to restrain such an interference was granted.

We would advise you to go to the Planning Officer of your local Council and if you can obtain no satisfaction:

(a) Approach your local Councillor personally, and

(b) Consult a solicitor with a view to obtaining an injunction against buildings being erected which will deprive you of light and injure the marketing of crops from your greenhouse.

Animals Act (1971)

The Animals Act 1971 came into effect on 1 October 1971. It removes some of the contradictions which seemed to exist in the Law as it was applied to animals. I must confess to considerable difficulties in dealing in *The Guide to Country Living* with trespass and damage by animals due to apparently contradictory rules.

Henceforward, until the Law is changed, the rule is that when livestock stray on to someone else's land, the owner of the livestock is liable for any damage due to the trespass.

If the livestock are detained, again the owner is liable for the expense incurred. The ancient remedy is abolished and livestock can only be detained for 48 hours unless notice is given to the Police and the owner (if known). The right of detention ceases when compensation is offered for expenses or damage. If no one claims after 14 days the livestock may be sold. The detainer may deduct from the proceeds any costs or expenses arising, but anyone detaining stock must look after them properly.

Whilst there is no Common Law liability to erect fences it is generally agreed that the owner of livestock has a duty to keep them in. Putting up fences is plainly the best way and where a landowner has a contractual duty to maintain fences then the owner of livestock would not be liable for damage if his livestock strayed under such circumstances.

One of the difficult points under previous legislation was dealing with cases where livestock trespassed from a highway.

The new Act removes the anomalies by laying down that livestock straying, provided they are lawfully on the highway, do not render their owners liable to damage or expenses arising out of their trespassing. Where negligence by those in charge of the livestock can be proved the owner is again liable. If the livestock stray from their own pastures or from their owner's land on to the highway and then on to your land, the owner is liable because they were on the highway unlawfully.

Previously there was a notable case (*Searle v Wallbank*) where an animal escaped on to the Highway and injured a cyclist. Because there is no Common Law liability to fence land it was held that the owner of the horse was not liable.

The Animals Act abolishes this judgment and places the liability firmly on the owner of the livestock straying on to the highway and applies the ordinary rules of negligence, which must be proved.

There is therefore added need to ensure owners of livestock and animals are insured against claims for damages due to the change in the Law here.

One exception applies to livestock grazing lawfully on Common or traditionally unfenced land. Plainly it would be unreasonable to expect owners of livestock in such circumstances to accept the same liability as applies to livestock on enclosed land.

The spread of Safari and Wild Game Parks throughout the United Kingdom has necessitated some tighter regulations which are also contained in the Animals Act. Dangerous species are defined as those not usually domesticated in the British Isles and which, when fully grown, require restraint.

The keepers of such animals are liable for damage as a rule. This can mean the father of a child under 16 years of age, who has a tame elephant.

Trespassers who enter and are injured by a dangerous animal, i.e. one of the specified dangerous species, cannot claim damage if the animal was not kept there for protective purposes or if it was, it was not unreasonable to have kept it there for that purpose. Where animals are not specified as coming from a dangerous species but even so can be dangerous, their keeper will only be liable if its keeper knew that it could cause severe damage unless restrained. For instance, bulls, horses and dogs can be dangerous and the only defence will be to plead that the injured party was at fault, or that the owner did not know the animal was dangerous.

An interesting point is that a guard dog may be held to be unreasonably employed as such if it was known by its keeper to be savage.

The Act clears up uncertainties too about dogs which attack livestock. The keeper of a dog which damages livestock or kills them is liable for damage as a rule.

An exception is where the livestock were themselves trespassing on the dog's owner's land, or where the fault lies in the owner of the livestock.

For those confused by the contradictory rules of the past the Animals Act 1971 should be welcome as clearing up points of doubt.

Animals – Legal Liabilities for – Book

Can you recommend a simple book on an owner's legal liabilities for various animals acts?

There is an excellent book called Animals and the Law by T. G. Field-Fisher published by the Universities Federation for Animal Welfare, 7a Lamb's Conduit Passage, London, W.C.1.

Architects and Landscape Gardeners – Responsibility of – 1

I bought the land on which the house was built in 1968. Construction started as soon as contracts were exchanged. I employed an architect and a landscape gardener. When I first owned the property there stood on it a beech tree, an elm, an ash, an old walnut and a young walnut tree. The property was subject to a tree preservation order. The elm and an old walnut were considered dangerous and permission was obtained for their removal. The house was built and the garden landscaped on the understanding that the remaining trees would stand.

The beech, which is enormous, started showing signs of distress this summer. I called in Southern Tree Surgeons Ltd., Crawley Down, Sussex, for advice on how to save it. They tell me it is dying and no measures can save it. It was killed, they say, because we dug trenches near it for water and electricity, and we made a drive near it, which must have damaged the root structure. Felling, with my house and my neighbour's built, will cost £180 or thereabouts. Had the tree been felled before building started the cost would have been about £30.

The water and the electricity could have been brought in without going near the tree. The drive could have been sited to avoid proximity to the tree.

Is it too much to expect that between the architect and the landscape gardener this fatal damage to the tree could have been avoided or at least that I should have been warned of the risks I was running by allowing them to carry out their plans?

These sort of questions are most difficult to deal with because no doubt the architect and the landscape gardener will deny that the cause of this tree's demise is anything to do with their operations. It would probably be very difficult to prove that, in fact, this was the case, however great one suspected that the firm you called in from Crawley were correct. We suggest that you write to the architect and landscape gardener and put it to them that you have suffered damages from their negligence and see whether they would be prepared to foot the bill for the removal of this tree. This is not as disastrous from their point of view as it may sound as most professional firms carry professional indemnity policies, which protect them from claims for professional negligence. We do not think that it will pay you to pursue the matter into the courts, however, if they resist your claims.

Architects and Landscape Gardeners – Responsibility of – 2

When I employ an architect to draw up plans for the alterations to my house, how long should I expect it to take from his engagement to the commencement of the work?

Much will depend upon the size and complexity of the job. The longer you are able to give the architect for the preliminary work the better. Our architect's experience is that some members make their approach in the early spring in the hope that the work might start during the first period of settled weather. It would be more satisfactory if the architect could be engaged at least two or three months previous to this. Preliminary work often takes longer than is usually allowed for by a client. In addition, delays can be met with at the tendering stage, and in finding suitable builders who could start the work within a reasonable time should their estimate be successful.

Arbitration – Comprehensive Policy on House

The Comprehensive Policy covering my house contains a clause saying that differences should be referred to an Arbitrator or perhaps two who would in turn appoint an umpire. I might wish to invoke this procedure. Are you able to tell me anything about it?

The Arbitration was designed to give parties unable to agree a means, less cumbersome and much less expensive of reaching a settlement. When the arbitration clause in an insurance policy is invoked the decision reached by the arbitrators (or by the umpire in the event of the two appointed arbitrators being unable to agree) is normally accepted; it is only when a point of law is in doubt that an appeal to the Courts is made. Then one of the parties, either the insurers or insured asks the arbitrator to state a case for the opinion of the Court.

The arbitrator is not necessarily a lawyer. There is an official Panel of Arbitrators and a Panel of Referees, where the arbitrators and referees are officers of the High Court; and the Institute of Arbitrators (10 Norfolk Street, London, W.C.2) has its register of Fellows and Associates. You would receive guidance from the Clerk if you cared to ask.

Attorney – Power of

Last year I went abroad for two months and an Attorney was appointed on my behalf to act as a Trustee. This year I am going overseas again and wish to repeat this process. Must I draw up a fresh Deed?

Section 25 (3) of the Trustee Act, 1925, provides that the power of attorney giving authority to act on behalf of a Trustee going abroad for more than one month, is revoked by his return to the U.K. A new Deed is therefore necessary.

Author – Registration as

As a retired officer, and for National Insurance purposes, "unemployed," I am doing a good deal of writing—short stories, articles, and so on. I was told rather vaguely the other day that I ought to register as an author. Can you tell me anything about this, how to go about it, and what are the advantages with regard to taxation? Presumably one would then become self-employed and have to contribute a larger amount to National Insurance.

We suggest that you write to the Society of Authors, 84 Drayton Gardens, London, S.W.10, giving, if possible, details of your writing to date, and they will send you a brochure on the function of the Society and advise you whether it would be to your advantage to join. They have recently advertised their scheme for Retirements Benefits for Authors and it has had wide publicity; the friends who advised you to register as an author may have had this in mind.

Badgers – Gassing of

Apart from the control of the occasional 'rogue' badger with a taste for poultry, which is best shot, the damage caused by these attractive animals is slight and is outweighed by the pleasure they give with their families to those of us who spend happy evenings badger watching.

I have heard recently of cases of gassing of badgers, and your magazine could help to dispel the illusion that gassing of badgers is legal. It is *not* legal, and I am informed at the local Police Station that under the Agriculture Act 1947 (England and Wales), and the Agriculture Scotland Act 1948, it is open to most people to prosecute if gassing of badgers is found to be practised.

Under the above Acts poisonous gas may be placed in any hole, burrow or earth for the purpose of killing foxes and moles, and it is illegal to use gas to kill any other wild mammal except rabbits and rodents in their holes or burrows. (Vide Predatory Mammals in Britain, Council for Nature, 1967.)

Bailee – Involuntary

An old, derelict motor-cycle has been left on my property by a young fellow who was living here in his caravan. He promised when he left to fetch it away, but has not done so. I have informed him by registered letter that unless he removes it by the end of the month I shall dispose of it. Am I entitled by law to do this? I do not want to run the risk of him coming along at some future date and claiming some ridiculous sum for the wreck.

You have been placed in what is often a disagreeable position; against your will you have been given possession of another person's property. The law imposes upon you, being a bailee against your wish, this duty only: you may not wilfully damage or destroy the cycle. But you are not bound to warehouse it. You may not dispose of it as your own; that may give rise to an action for conversion against you. Perhaps you should allow the cycle to remain a little longer. If it really becomes an eyesore to you, we suggest that you tell the owner that (unless he authorises you to do with it what you think fit) you will instruct a carrier of the Railway Commission or another, to deliver the cycle to him " carriage forward." We add this, though it only remotely bears upon your problem. You are in the position of one to whom a pushing tradesman has sent unsolicited goods for trial. You incur no liability for the goods thrust upon you; but if you do use them you are assumed to have bought them and must pay their price.

Bank Interest – Calculation of

I understand that interest on deposit accounts is worked out by one's bank on what is known as the 'product system'. I want an explanation of the method used. Please give as an example, if necessary, a fairly complicated case where balance is changing from month to month, etc.

The bank we spoke to had not heard the term 'product system'. They tell us that bank interest is worked out on a daily basis and credited to the principal every six months. You then start again. Because it is worked on a daily basis it covers the fluctuations. Frankly, if you want examples worked we would suggest you approach your own bank manager for an explanation and examples. If you have a deposit account no doubt he will be glad to do so.

Barbed Wire

Can you please tell me whether it is legally permissible to use barbed wire in a fence adjacent to a public highway?

Whilst it is not illegal to use barbed wire along a road or highway, there is good reason for exercising great care in so doing. If barbed wire must be used it is advisable to run the barb on the inside of the fence away from the highway. The Barbed Wire Act, 1893 (Section 3) enables the local authority to serve a notice on the occupier of any land adjoining a highway, on which barbed wire has been placed in a position or manner where it may be dangerous to persons or animals lawfully using the highway. The notice will require the occupier to abate the nuisance within a certain period, not less than a month, and should this not be complied with, the authority may obtain an abatement order, carry out the work itself, and recover summarily the expenses incurred.

A highway includes a footpath so that damages would be payable if, for instance, a gust of wind blew a pedestrian's coat against the barbed wire fence at the side of a public footpath and the coat got torn.

Bees Close to Boundary

Can you give me information on the placing of beehives against a boundary fence? My neighbour is very worried, as new occupants of the house next to her's keeps bees and have placed the hives against the division fence, which is only wire netting and a clipped hedge. They are Italian bees which I believe are not very fierce; but her old gardener was badly stung some years ago and is naturally nervous. Is there any ruling on the subject? They own about ¾ acre of land. A very big Devon wall to the south divides them from the downs. The public road and footpath is on the north side.

The law relevant to this can be put as follows. An occupier is entitled to use his land to the utmost, even up to his neighbour's border, the one restriction being that the use chosen by him must not subject his neighbour to so great a degree of annoyance as no reasonable man would expect his neighbour to tolerate with equanimity. In this give-and-take world we are all required to put up with some irritation from one another's activities; and bee-keeping is a permissible and desirable use of land.

There is, indeed, a recorded case – an Irish one – where damages were awarded to one severely injured as a sequel to the escape of bees from his neighbour's land. But the circumstances were quite exceptional: an outrageous number of hives stood close to the fence, loss had previously occurred to the plaintiff, and complaints had been ignored, and the harvesting of his honey by the bee-keeper had sent the infuriated bees across the fence.

There is, you see, no ruling on the matter. It is always, as with other forms of nuisance, a question of degree. The bee-keeper might well have been more considerate in his siting of the hives; but, on the facts put by you (and we are assuming that no very unusual number of hives is there) we are quite certain that no legal remedy exists for the annoyance.

Birds – Nuisance from

Recently my neighbours have started keeping white pigeons. These began with six birds and are now increasing. We are in a very much built-up area within the town boundary. Some months ago the pigeons very much enjoyed my newly planted Brassica, which I replaced. Now last week we planted 40 young chrysanthemums which were at once set on, breaking them off at the roots and also pecking the foliage quite extensively.

My gardener has, with a small gun, hit two, causing the feathers to fly with no great effect. I am informed by their owner that no one else has suffered any damage, and that carrier pigeons never eat greenstuff. I should be grateful if you could tell me if this is correct. I can hardly believe it, and what the legal position is if the pigeons are not controlled.

The law does have its remedies when a neighbour entertains such an inordinate number of birds as amounts to a nuisance; you can sue him for the damage done and can ask for the issue of an injunction restricting the number to be kept. And, whether or not the number is unreasonably great, you have an action for trespass when the pigeons injure your plants; for the statement of your neighbour 'that pigeons do not eat greenstuff' is absurd. Your are obliged to tolerate some amount of annoyance from a neighbour's lawful activities, but there is not to be such a demand upon your tolerance as no reasonable man would ask of you.

It is reasonable to assume that you will shrink from legal action against your neighbour. Still, his becoming aware that such action is possible may inspire him to moderate his number of pigeons.

Bird Scarers – Legal

I wonder whether you can give me any information about bird scarers? I am referring to the ones which sound like a gun firing and go off at regular intervals.

We are surrounded by fruit farms and orchards so that there is a good deal of use for these bird scarers, and I realise the necessity for them. However, I would like to know if there is any rule covering the times when they may be used. Last year for several nights these bird scarers were going off throughout the hours of darkness. I checked with the local police, who informed me that there was no limit to the times. I thought that somewhere I had read that there was.

We have been in touch with the Noise Abatement Society who have written to us as follows:

'Explosive bird scarers are a constant source of complaint, and most local authorities have a by-law prohibiting their use during the hours of darkness. The Ministry of Housing and Local Government sent round a circular to all local authorities on the subject. This states that, 'It is recommended that the existing model by-law prohibiting the use of explosive bird scarers during the hours of darkness should be varied to apply to all types of audible bird scarers. The Ministers understand that the Home Secretary is prepared to consider any proposals that local authorities desire to make for by-laws differing from the model on the lines recommended.'

'Farmers usually argue that explosive scarers are the only method of protecting their crops, and naturally local authorities are consequently somewhat chary of taking strong action. You could perhaps suggest to your member that she brings to the notice of the Council's Public Health Department that a silent scarer which has been found very effective in certain conditions exists. It was developed by a firm of commercial fruit growers.'

Bonfires

I live in a thatched timber cottage, and have on many occasions had to remonstrate, as on three sides bonfires are lit in high winds and without consideration of the direction of the wind. I still have a neighbour who burns his garden refuse piled on a bedstead supported some four feet from the ground – using paraffin – and although he has a wind vane spurts high ashes only thirty yards from my cottage.

If damage is done I am of course insured for damage to the cottage, but this does not cover living expenses while repairs are being done. Could you let me know the law on such damages, and is anyone causing damage from bonfires liable?

These are the points of law in respect of the lighting of bonfires that might menace your cottage:

1. If your neighbour allows the escape of fire from his bonfire so that it damages your cottage he incurs the liability to compensate you. This liability would extend to such loss as is not covered by your insurance; and your insurers would be able to claim against him for what they paid you.

2. To prevent such happening, you could, in the event of your being unable to persuade your neighbour to move the apparatus, ask the County Court Judge to make a Declaratory Judgment that the proximity to your cottage of the menace constituted a nuisance and should cease.

As to this, however, your letter

indicates your awareness of the fact that the law requires a good deal of toleration for one another's activities.

Boundaries – 1

Do I have to fence my property or maintain its boundaries?

No ; except along the highway or in order to keep *in* your own livestock. You are not obliged to keep anyone or anything out.

Boundaries – 2

Can you tell me how one can establish where a boundary is by existing hedges and ditches, post and rails or walls?

If the Deeds of the property do not establish this there are some rough rules which are normally accepted.

(a) *Hedge and ditch**
   The far side of the ditch from the hedge is the boundary.

(b) *Hedge without ditch*
   If both owners have kept their sides of the hedge in trim, then the boundary is the half-way mark. If one owner has kept the hedge in order then the furthest side is the boundary.

(c) *Post and rails or wire*
   The boundary runs along the far side of the rails or wire from the posts.

(d) *Walls*
   The owner of a wall is the person who erected it or his assignees and the outer surface is the boundary. Buttresses will generally be found on the owner's side when doubts exist.

* The NFU think differently as will be seen by the item on p. 140. They are not necessarily right but giving the farmer's point of view.

Boundary Controversy – Arbitration

Unfortunately I am having a boundary controversy with a neighbour and should like some advice.
I wish to avoid if at all possible going to law, and I am considering arbitration if the other party will agree.
(1) Can you suggest to whom to apply?
(2) How will costs be based, and on whom would they fall—i.e., both parties or the loser?
(3) Would the arbiter's decision be both binding and final for both parties?

(1) You need apply to no one except the other party in order to initiate the arbitration. You ask him to agree to arbitration: you and he sign an agreement to submit the matter in controversy to an arbitrator; you state in your agreement that each of you will consider the arbitrator's decision to be binding upon you both, and you make such agreement as to costs as you think fit. (If you make no stipulation about costs these are at the discretion of the arbitrator; he may think it well that each party bears his own costs and pays half the arbitrator's fee.)

(2) You may decide to have a solicitor or counsel to put your case; if so, he will expect a fee. Apart from that there will only be the costs of preparing documents. The arbitrator is entitled to a 'reasonable remuneration,' and unless you and the other party agree upon the amount, and state it in your agreement, the arbitrator himself is entitled to fix it.

(3) It is well to agree that there should be finality. You may agree upon whomsoever you please as an arbitrator, judging him to be competent to judge the matter, to be ready to hear whatever is relevant to the question and to be without favour to either party.

Boundary Disputes

How to settle.
Shows of hostility or aggressiveness are fatal in such circumstances. Country-dwellers should read *The Territorial Imperative* by Robert Ardrey.

If a dispute arises invite the other party for a glass of sherry and discuss the difficulty in a civilised way. It is very difficult for one's opponent to be unfriendly under such circumstances. This manœuvre seldom fails even with the most lunatic neighbours.

Boundary – Ditch Ownership

The National Farmers' Union considers that there are misconceptions in the minds of many people as to the relationship of hedges and ditches in respect to farm boundaries. This is unfortunate, as important points such as who is responsible for cleaning and maintaining a ditch depend upon ownership. In every case the question of who owns a ditch depends primarily on what the deeds to the land say.

Moreover, in modern practice the conveyance terms of agricultural land usually refer to the Ordnance maps, or carry plans extracted from such maps. In Ordnance maps the boundary line of a field is almost always taken to be the centre of the fences or hedges and areas are calculated accordingly. It is obvious, then, that in all such cases the ditch is taken into the field on the ditch side of the hedge. It is only when there is no other way of ascertaining the ownership that an ancient presumption comes into play.

This presumption originally arose as it was assumed that when digging a ditch a man dug it on the extremity of his own land and threw the spoil back on to his land, thus forming a mound on which a hedge was planted. Unfortunately this (which is only a presumption applicable where no other evidence as to ownership exists) has been assumed to be a custom applicable to every case. No greater error could exist and the consequences of this error are often serious.

Boundary – Fence

I would be very glad if you could advise me on a point in connection with fencing. I have been told that where the fence is a post and wire one dividing two properties the burden of upkeep lies with the owner on whose side the posts are, not with him on whose side the wire is attached. Will you please say if that is the law, or if not, what the law is in the matter?

The law for a boundary fence is as you state, namely that the occupier of land erects posts on the very edge of his boundary and nails fencing on the far side. Unless there is any evidence to the contrary, it seems that the burden of upkeep for the wire lies with the owner on whose side the posts are.

Boundary-Limits

A short drive leading to one of my cottages runs alongside the wall of a neighbour's house. I recently put up a gate across the drive and put one of the gate-posts within one inch of the neighbour s wall. The neighbour now requests me to move the post six inches away from his wall, as he says it damages the foundation of his wall, and he also states that there is a law that the posts may not be put up within six inches of his wall. Is he correct?

You have a legal right to use the whole width of the drive for your structure if the drive belongs to you. You may not, by excavating or other activity on your own land, harm your neighbour's property, but he cannot complain unless he can prove harm. There is no law, such as your neighbour asserts, prohibiting the erection of a post close to the boundary.

Boundary – Rebuilding Wall – 1

I have a cottage that adjoins another person's garden—the boundary is a wall belonging to me. Recently this wall has got in a bad condition and I have pulled part of it down and marked the boundary by a post and rails. The owner of the adjoining garden says that the wall is a boundary wall and that I must rebuild it. As the wall is mine, it seems to me that I am under no obligation to rebuild it.

Since the wall is yours, erected as it is on your land, and since there can be no covenant by you to maintain the wall for the benefit of your neighbour, you have an unfettered discretion concerning it. You may remove it wholly and leave your land unfenced, you may replace it by such other boundary structure as you think fit, or you may leave it without troubling about its deterioration by wind and weather.

In short, your neighbour exceeds his right by dictating what you shall do.

Boundary – Rebuilding Wall – 2

I have a walled garden, the wall being probably 140 years old.

It is very important from an amenity point of view. It also forms the boundary between my land and farmland belonging to a neighbouring farmer.

The farmer ploughs to within about one yard of my wall, and through constant ploughing over the years the level of his field appears to have dropped slightly.

There is some suggestion by a surveyor I have engaged that this difference in level is causing the soil to dry out at the base of my wall (the soil is clay), so that the wall is beginning to lean out in places and is having to be buttressed to prevent it falling.

Can you tell me what rights I have, if any:

(1) to build buttresses on my neighbour's side of the wall to protect it.

(2) to stop him ploughing too close in, say to not less than two yards, in order to protect the wall?

The best approach in such circumstances is to reach agreement by an amicable arrangement with your neighbour farmer, and without contention over legal rights.

For your guidance the relevant legal rules are:

1. Entry upon the farmer's land, even for such a purpose as the buttressing of your wall, is lawful only with his consent, expressed or implied: lacking that consent, entry is trespass.

2. The farmer must not by operations on his own land so detract from the natural support given by his land to yours as to endanger your wall. His restriction of ploughing to within a yard of the wall indicates his knowledge of this; and you have no legal right to dictate what the intervening distance shall be.

The suggestion by your surveyor, that some loss of support is evidenced, may be doubted: it would be a burden to convince a Court that the conjecture is fact.

Boundaries – Overhanging Trees

My neighbour's trees increasingly overhang our boundary and are a nuisance. Can I lop the branches overhanging my land? My neighbour refuses to cut them back himself and says I can't do so either. He also says they have established a right to be there as they have been overhanging for 20 years or more.

The owner of the tree has no right to prevent you, lawfully in possession of your land into or over which its roots or branches have grown, from cutting away as much of them as project over or under your land. Notice need only be given if you must enter his land to do the cutting. But the branches so cut belong to him.

As for the overhanging branches establishing a prescriptive right, there was a case in 1895 in the House of Lords which established that no such right can be gained either by the Statute of Limitations or under the ordinary law of prescription.

Boundary – Roadside Hedges and Ditches

The local authority are demanding that I clean out a ditch along my boundary and cut back the hedges—i.e., setting up, as they call it. Must I do so?

Yes. Under the Land Drainage Act 1930 you must cleanse a water course as owner of the land through which it passes. As far as the hedges are concerned, either you will have to cut them back, usually to avoid obstructing the highway, or the local authority will do it and send you the bill.

Boundary – Roots and Fences

A housing estate is being built on land adjoining my orchard which is fenced with posts and wire and has a privet hedge on my side of the fence – the walls of the first house, now occupied, are within 5 ft. and a path and small border has been cut so that the earth into which the posts are driven has been dug away thus making the post no longer rigid. I think that the roots of the hedge will have been cut.

Could you please tell me the legal position and advise me how to proceed? The matter is urgent and we have two newly weaned foals in the field.

Could you also inform me as to how near the fence I can plant trees which I have ready to fill in the gaps in the hedge? They are some form of Macrocarpa.

We are in some difficulty because you do not say to whom the post-and-wire fence belongs. Are we right in assuming that these are the housing estate's? If on the other hand the fence is yours then you should approach the housing estate manager and point out to him that his excavations have undermined the fence. As far as the Macrocarpa are concerned it is usually assumed that the roots will extend to the height of the tree. What you must watch out for is (a) that the roots cannot damage your neighbour's premises by spreading under the boundary and (b) that if you plant close to the boundary and your neighbour cuts off the rots trespassing on his land (which he is quite entitled to do) the trees may die.

Bridle Way – Dedication of

I own a cottage lying with two or three more on an unmetalled lane leading up a steep hill, on top of which the land becomes a field path. Just before it does so the rural district council built, some ten years ago, two council houses. As the lane is the only access for me and them, and must take cars and tradesmen's vans, etc., I wrote to the R.D.C. suggesting we should join in making it up and dedicating it. Their reply is that the lane is a bridle path and that they have " no authority to participate in a scheme for making up this right of way." Is this correct?

The lane to your cottage is, quite clearly, an easement giving a right of way to reach the cottage from the highway; it is not a highway repairable by the inhabitants at large, and the local authority therefore has no power at all over it. If, as is stated by your R.D.C., probably correct, the lane is a bridle path only, the taking of wheeled vehicles along it is a trespass against which the landowners could take legal action. With the additional building, however, the lane is going through the usual course whereby a right of way restricted to a few becomes a public highway available for all, and for all manner of traffic. When the trespassing traffic becomes greater by the building of more houses, the local authority will be constrained to take over the way. But you cannot at the moment put any pressure upon the authority.

Bridle Ways – Alteration to

The parish council of a parish, where there are a number of registered bridle-ways, propose that these should be upgraded (to use their words) by making them available to all kinds of traffic (vehicular and otherwise), in fact, almost making them a public road and apparently the county council agree.

Can they legally do this and, if so, would a landowner be able to get compensation for the change?

The answer to your question concerning the power of a parish council over a registered bridleway is this: The Parish Council Act 1957 gives power to provide certain amenities—seats and shelters on roads, lights on roads, and parking places for bicycles and motor cycles. It gives no power to convert a bridleway into a highway available for vehicular traffic. The parish council can make representations to the county council as highway authority that such conversion is socially desirable; but it is for the county council to decide whether it should take place. As always when a landowner is required to relinquish part of his land for public service, adequate compensation is payable. You may not be too late to protest to the county council that the conversion is unnecessary.

Bridle Path – Width and Use of

Could you tell me the approximate width of a bridle path? I understand this to be a right of way for people to walk along, ride or lead a horse along, but I would not like to say ride two abreast. Would you say a light car could be driven along it? Surely the answer to this last question is No, as a bicycle must not be ridden along a footpath although one can push it.

There is no definite width unless specified in some document. The width of the way is usually that which has always existed. It is fair inference to state that a bridle path is for single horse traffic only as a convenience to riders in much the same way as a right of way or footpath across a field is a single track for pedestrian use. It would be an abuse for horsemen to use a bridle path four abreast. A bridle way is a horse way, on which horses may be led or ridden. It includes a footway. It does not include a carriage-way, over which vehicles may be taken, nor does it include a driftway, which is a way for driving cattle.

The Bull in the Field to Which the Public have Access

My father owns a field which he lets to me (part of the home farm of a larger estate). There is a right of way seldom used through the field, and I am in the habit of running a bull in the field with some heifers. What happens if the bull attacks a pedestrian? I might say that the bull has always been absolutely quiet.

The legal position is this: the Common Law of England regards the bull as coming into the same category as cows and sheep. No general law, therefore, is against having an untethered bull in a field to which the public have access. But most county councils have a bye-law of which the type is: 'No person, being the occupier of any field or enclosure through which there is a public path, may permit any bull exceeding the age of twelve months to be at large.' An enquiry at the county hall would bring

you the precise wording of the bye-law.

The liability created by the bye-law is, you note, a criminal liability. The owner of a bull can be under a civil liability only when a person injured by the bull can establish that the owner knew, or should have known, of a vicious propensity in the bull—when that is, scienter is shown. And, even when there is scienter, no civil liability to a trespasser —and one diverging from the path is a trespasser—exists.

This result emerges: (1) in no circumstance could your father, owner of the field, or you, the lessee of the field, be under any liability, civil or criminal; (2) the owner of the bull might be under a criminal liability under the bye-laws; he would be under civil liability only if he knew his bull to be vicious.

Bulls – More About

I understand in Herefordshire that a bull may be run loose in a field where a public right of way exists provided that there are cows with the bull.

It has always been my idea that a bull is not a domestic animal but one known to be dangerous and, at Common Law, one would be in serious trouble if it attacked a person using the right of way. Can you kindly explain the present law on this point, taking into account the apparent Herefordshire bye-law?

It is, contrary to what you have supposed, as assumption under the Common Law that a bull is a gentle domestic animal, so that keeping a bull loose in a field over which a right of way exists is not an offence, nor, in the absence of a knowledge by the owner of the bull's propensity to attack persons, does it expose the owner to civil liability. It is to counter this common law rule that, under the powers given by the Local Government Act 1933, most county councils and many borough councils have made bye-laws regarding bulls. The type is: 'No person, being the occupier of any field or enclosure through which there is a public path, permit any bull exceeding the age of twelve months to be at large.' There are variants, and in some counties (Hereford being one) is the proviso: 'This bye-law shall not apply to any bull which is at large in any field or enclosure in which cows or heifers are also at large.' Female society and discipline banish truculence. (See also Trespass – p. 188.)

By-way

Can you please give me some information regarding opening a long-neglected by-way (it is marked on the map). It runs from this cottage to the road leading to local woods and would make a very pleasant walk, as well as saving quite a long distance.

We suggest that you contact the Footpaths Preservation Society, 166 Shaftesbury Avenue, London WC2 as they are particularly interested in this sort of inquiry and will be able to supply all the information you require.

Capital Gains Tax

Can you give me any advice about the Capital Gains tax and its effect on the sale of property?

I am faced at the moment with the question of whether to sell or relet a house which has been rent-controlled but of which I now have vacant possession.

In connection with a possible liability to Capital Gains tax in the event of your selling the property, two factors to which consideration should be given are the length of time for which you have owned the house, and the date on which it became vacant. If you have owned the property for a number of years, and if it did not become vacant until after April 6, 1965, then it seems to us that, in the event of your selling, it would almost certainly pay you to elect to have the chargeable gain calculated on the time apportionment basis rather than to opt for the gain to be computed on the actual increase in the value between April 6 1965 and the date of sale. We say this because if the house was let at a controlled rent on April 6 1965, then any valuation as at that day would obviously reflect this fact and be considerably lower than the value today with vacant possession.

On the time apportionment basis the chargeable gain would be calculated by firstly arriving at the actual gain over the whole period of ownership, and then taking that proportion of the total gain that the period from April 6, 1965, to the date of sale bears to the whole period of ownership (if, however, the property was acquired prior to April 6, 1945, it will for the time apportionment basis be treated as having been acquired on that date). The proportionate basis would, in effect, have the result of spreading back part of the gain to the period before April 6, 1965, where it would not be assessable to tax.

Caravan as Residence

I own the house in which I live; it stands in about 1 acre of garden in a small community of houses on the main Oxford-Banbury Road. The field which edges my property on three sides is owned by a neighbour and has been let to a farmer to graze his cattle.

This farmer has recently moved a caravan into this field and is now living in the caravan which is parked about 100 yards from the front of my house.

There is every sign that this caravan is being turned into a permanent residence, its surround is gradually being cluttered up with all manner of unsightly items. In general it is an eyesore.

Have I any legal right to request that this man moves himself and his caravan or alternatively is there not some rule or bye-law which forbids the like of this man from setting up a caravan site in full view of my house?

It can hardly be that the farmer has obtained the permission requisite under the Town and Country Planning Acts of the area Planning Authority to use the caravan as a residence. You should, therefore, get into touch with your area Planning Officer, who will take steps to end a development not sanctioned by the Authority.

Perhaps we should add, however, that our law gives no right to an occupier to have a pleasing prospect preserved and it may be that an objection to the

ugliness of the development would not
be supported by the Planning Authority.

Caravan Sites

*Can one establish a caravan site in a
field on one's farm without permission?*

No. You must obtain a licence from
the Planning Authorities, probably your
local R.D.C.

Payment to Casual Labour

*May I have your advice as to whether
I ought to pay (1) for Bank Holidays
and (2) for Saturday afternoons, a man
who only does odd days work in my
garden which is not run for profit?*

The answer to your question is No:
you pay a casual worker for the hours
he works; he is not entitled to more in
respect of holidays. Any additional payment you make to him is a matter of
grace.

It is the "Wages Councils Act, 1945"
that governs this matter. This stipulates
for minimum rates of wages and for
holidays with pay for workers; and
Section 23 (1) of the Act defines
"worker" in this way: 'Worker' means
any person who has entered into or
works under a contract with an employer
. . . except that it does not include any
person who is employed casually and
otherwise than for the purposes of the
employer's business." Payments to such
casual workers are determined by agreement between employers and employed.

Cats – Protection Under the Law

*Is there a special association for the
protection of cats, other than the
R.S.P.C.A.?*

There is the Cats Protection League,
of Prestbury Lodge, 29 Church Street,
Slough.

Cattle Grids – Liability for Injury

*Am I liable if someone injures himself
on one of my cattle-grids?*

There is a common duty of care
towards persons lawfully on any land.
Trespassers for instance are not protected.
A warning notice should therefore suffice
to protect you from any liability.

Commons Registration

*I shall be grateful for your advice upon
the following points which have arisen
hereunder, viz.:*

*1. I am the freeholder of certain lands
let and used agriculturally and including
cliffs used for grazing both by sheep and
beasts, which abut upon National Trust
foreshore.*

*2. These lands are within an area of
outstanding natural beauty, and the
Gower Society, an unofficial local
amenity organisation, has filed an application to have a large portion of the
lands scheduled as common although
they are well aware of their being my
freehold.*

*3. I hold the freehold deeds by con-
veyance from the Penrice Castle Estate
and apart from this have absolute title
by possession over the statutory term of
years.*

*4. It appears that the Gower Society
have included certain other properties in
their application, but the Glamorgan
County Council refuse to let the Society
withdraw or amend its application,
stating that there is no machinery that
permits this to be done.*

*5. The Gower R.D.C. (in connection
with an irrelevant proposed sewerage
scheme) have acknowledged that the
lands in question are my freehold.*

*Are you of the opinion that the
County Council are correct in stating
that the Gower Society cannot withdraw
their application and, if so, under what
section of the Act?*

'Yes' is the answer to your question
whether your County Council is correct
in stating that the Gower Society can-

not withdraw their application. The machinery set up by the Act for registration of commons makes withdrawal impossible. For the registration authority – in this instance the Glamorgan County Council – is required, upon receipt of the application, to enter the lands listed on a provisional register. This is subject to objections ; and, doubtless, you will have already lodged your objection. That being so you can be quite sure that no land in respect of which you can produce title will appear in the final and conclusive register. This will be compiled when objections have been dealt with and the time, limited by the Act, for making objections has passed.

These items of information may be desirable:

1. The forms of registers required are prescribed in the Commons Registration (General) Regulations, 1966.

2. Applications for registration will not be accepted after January 2, 1970.

3. Objections may be made from October 1, 1968, and for a period ending not less than two years after the date of registration.

4. If, after January 2, 1970, land that could have been registered has not been registered, that land ceases to be common land or a town or village green, and any rights of common over such land as have not been registered will lapse.

Company – Transfer of

I see you have an office in Jersey – will you please inform me what are the requirements of becoming resident there?

Is it possible to move a private investment company there?   Kindly give me any information you can.

Section 482 of the Taxes Act 1970 specifically provides that it shall be unlawful, unless carried out with the consent of the Treasury, for a company resident in the United Kingdom to cease to be so resident; or for the trade or business (which would include the holding of investments) of a company resident in the United Kingdom to be transferred from that company to a person not so resident.

There are severe penalties laid down for offences under the Section, the maximum being two years' imprisonment or a fine of £10,000, or both.

It is of course possible that if you were to take up permanent residence in Jersey the Treasury would, upon formal application being made to it, grant permission for a private investment company that you control also to become resident in Jersey. We would not, however, recommend that you should attempt to transfer the residence of an existing company; our advice to you would be to liquidate the English company and to form a new investment company in Jersey after you have become resident there.

Care should be taken about the timing of the liquidation of the existing company in order to minimize the liability to capital gains tax. The liquidation should be deferred until after you have become resident in Jersey and cease to be resident and ordinarily resident in the U.K. for tax purposes.

Apart from income tax and capital gains tax there are important estate duty considerations involved in your contemplated removal to Jersey, and we think that you ought to be professionally advised, in detail, before any transactions are undertaken. The Association has had considerable experience in all these matters, and we should, of course, be very pleased to act for you on a normal professional basis if you so wish.

Contract – Uncompleted

On August 27, 1969, two electricians came to my house, by my invitation, to install a television aerial. They fixed a three channel mast to the chimney but when the television set arrived it was found that it would not receive one channel at all and the other two have reception so poor that at times we cannot see a picture.

I have telephoned the electricians several times and have written once. They replied to the effect that they would try to get another aerial and would return to install it but to date have not done so.

I would like to know if I am legally able to have the aerial corrected by another firm and to deduct its charges from the electricians

Boundary Disputes
Invite the Other Party for a Glass of Sherry

(See page 163)

account when I receive it.

You have no legal right to call in a second contractor to complete satisfactorily a contract undertaken by the first contractor unless you have a right to assume that the first contractor has abandoned the unfinished contract. You should, therefore, write to the electricians to this effect:

This is to notify you that, at the expiration of . . . . days, I shall assume that you have abandoned the contract you undertook on the 27th of August. I shall then call in other electricians to complete the contract, satisfactorily and at your expense.

It may add to the compelling power of your letter to tell them that their defective work has made them liable for professional negligence.

Conveyancing Charges

I shall be most grateful for your advice. I am in process of selling my house for £5,997 and all legal and conveyance charges to be paid by the purchaser. I have an idea that solicitors vary their charges somewhat. I shall be glad if you can inform me as to what these charges should be

(a) Conveyance charge.
(b) Vendor's legal costs.
(c) Purchaser's legal costs.
There is, of course, stamp duty. I may add that one solicitor will act for both sides. Surely charges of this nature should be standardised.

We advise you that solicitors' fees are in fact standardised, the scale being approved by the Lord Chancellor. Your purchaser will pay to the solicitor, if as we assume the land is unregistered, one sum of £75 'for deducing the vendor's title' and one sum of £75 'for investigating the vendor's title'; and the stamp duty, the consideration being below £6,000, is 75p. (The double £75 would be a double £47.50 for registered land.) Your purchaser would pay at least £150.75; and the solicitor might think fit to add something for 'disbursements'. Apart from an agreement similar to yours the vendor would pay the first £75.

Copyright – 1

I shall be grateful for any information that you can supply on the following situation. I have conceived a children's game, rather after the style of scrabble, but of course not so good, and before marketing it, I feel I ought to patent it or procure some form of copyright. How do I set about doing so?

To procure a copyright of your game you must go to a patent agent. If you do not know of one there is a large number of agents listed in the London Classified Telephone Directory.

Copyright – 2

Please may I have answers to the following questions:
(1) For ordinary literary works, how long does copyright hold—so far as their texts is concerned?
(2) Does the same period exist for illustrations in such books?
(3) How long does copyright hold for oil paintings—e.g., portraits?
(4) If an engraving is made of a portrait and pressings are made from the former, who holds the copyright?
(5) If a portrait is reproduced in a book, being a copy of an original painting, who holds the copyright of the illustration in the book?
(6) Does the same law apply to sales catalogues—for example: if a portrait, put up for an auction sale, is illustrated in the sale catalogue, whose is the copyright?
(7) What is the position in the case of a portrait which has been sold and passed overseas?

1. Copyright in literary, dramatic and musical works 'shall continue to subsist until the end of the period of fifty years from the end of the calendar year in which the author died' (Section 2 of Copyright Act, 1956).

2 and 3. Yes: Section 3 provides for the same period of copyright in 'artistic works', meaning 'irrespective of artistic quality, paintings, sculptures, drawings, engravings and photographs'.

4. The engraver holds the copyright, and

a pressing, being unauthorised by him, is an infringement.

5. The taker of a portrait, or his employer for the purpose of taking, holds the copyright; he it is that should be asked to authorise reproduction.

6. Answer (5) applies, but it would probably be assumed that copying had been tacitly authorised.

7. Part V of the Act has elaborate provisions whereby the copyrights of authors receive protection in all such countries as enjoy reciprocal rights for their own subjects.

Copyright – Music

Can you give me some information about music copyright ?

We suggest you contact: The Performing Right Society Ltd., 29 Berners Street, London, W.1 (01-580 7137).

Costs in Lands Tribunal Proceedings

If one personally fights or disputes a case brought against one by the Agricultural Land Tribunal does one become liable for costs if the ruling of the Tribunal is against one ? I intend to dispute a case being brought before the Tribunal by a neighbour who is trying to compel me to open a ditch in one of my fields which I have deliberately left closed for years to stop him flooding my field. Unfortunately some of the roadmen who come under the District Surveyor entered my property without permission and opened this culvert in June last. They had no right to do this. I intend to contest the case if it goes to the Tribunal myself as I have known this field, etc., for more than 40 years. It is not a recent acquisition. I do not want to risk heavy costs, however, if the decision goes against me. I shall be glad of any advice you can give me re costs.

We have to say that in general – and your contention with your neighbour over the ditch is one instance – the costs of proceedings before the Lands Tribunal are in the discretion of the Tribunal. (See Section 3 (5) of the Lands Tribunal Act, 1949). The tendency seems to be to award costs to the successful party only when his opponent's case is frivolous and vexatious parties are left to bear their own costs.

The Act, however (in Schedule I, Part II) lays this down about the award of costs when the dispute concerns the compensating price: when the acquiring authority has made an unconditional offer in writing and the sum awarded by the Tribunal does not exceed the offer, the claimant will be ordered, apart from any special reason why he should not, to pay the authority's costs in so far as they were incurred after making the offer.

Derelict Cottages – Repair of

I own one of a row of three thatched cottages on a main road, the other two have not been lived in for some years and are now derelict. The owner has carried out no repairs or alterations for a number of years. The doors and windows are open and the roof is leaking. The condition detracts from the value and general look of my cottage, and there is a risk of youths or a tramp starting a fire.

Have I any right to demand that the owner at least repairs the roof and keeps his property locked or boarded up so that access is denied to undesirables ?

Has the local authority any power or interest in this direction ?

We would have thought that the first thing you had better do is to approach your local authority, i.e. the rural district council, and have a word with the public health authorities. It may be that they could put pressure on the owners to take some action, but private ownership does imply a right to allow a house to fall down if one so desires. One should, therefore, approach the problem with this in mind.

Cottage Improvements

A relative of mine, who is over ninety, has a small property, including a cottage in the village. Her gardener lives in it and pays her seven shillings a week rent. He is forty-six and has been employed for twenty-five years.

She is leaving the property to me but

is allowing her gardener to go on living in the cottage rent free for the rest of his life.

The cottage will need a bathroom put in when main drainage is completed in 1970 and also will require routine maintenance and repair. Could you tell me how I stand in this matter, as it may be an expensive item to inherit?

If the tenant of your relative's cottage is working for her then this is a service tenancy and under the Contract of Employment Act the gardener should have written conditions of employment which should also set out the terms under which he occupies the cottage.

The C.G.A. has standard forms of agreement for this set of circumstances, and only where a written agreement exists can either party be certain as to their obligations. We would say, however, structural repairs and alterations are generally a landlord's liability although rentals can be adjusted to take into account such expenditure. It is probable, therefore, that you would be liable for the expenditure of putting in a bathroom in due course, although it is possible to obtain grants from the local authority for this type of improvement.

Cottage – Tied

What is the legal definition of a 'tied cottage' and how can a 'tied cottage' become 'untied' and vice versa?

A tied cottage is a cottage occupied by an employee who is required to occupy the cottage as an essential condition of his employment, but who is not a tenant. A tied cottage can become untied, when it becomes vacant, by letting the cottage to a person so that he becomes a tenant, and vice versa.

Covenants

Search inquiries before purchase of this cottage revealed a covenant binding all the future occupants to have two windows fitted with frosted glass on the side overlooked by my nextdoor neighbours. My nextdoor neighbours have given me a letter nullifying this covenant. My

lawyer says this is not enough, but to be permanently effective I must take legal action involving legal, stamp duty and land registry charges. Having satisfied my neighbour, is there no simpler and less expensive way of removing the covenant?

Covenants are a nuisance because very often the reason for them disappears and the occupiers of a house may be bound indefinitely to maintain conditions which no longer apply.

We think you should ask your lawyer what will happen if you ignore the covenant. If no one is likely to object we would then have thought that the simplest course is to have the frosted glass removed if this is what you wish to do, on the basis that it is unlikely that anyone will insist that the covenant is carried out.

As far as we know there is no other way of removing a covenant, and if you were to ask us for a strictly legal opinion, our answer would be the same as that given to you by your solicitor.

Covenant in Lease

A tenant farmer has occupied our home farm (some 98 acres) for 23 years and although the lease is still in his name, it is virtually run by his sons.

Owing to the way they now manage the place we are not on the best of terms and our agents have not been successful in terminating the lease in our favour.

Now the only cottage let to the farm has been condemned and scheduled for demolition by the local council and the cowman given a council house. We have no other cottage available to offer the tenant farmer, but it states in the lease we must provide one during his tenancy of the farm and he is sticking to this. I might add, we are not anxious to build another as we would not require it ourselves upon the lease being given up.

I should very much appreciate your opinion as to how we stand, especially if we do nothing.

We advise you that you are bound by the express covenant in the lease in respect of this cottage. Nor does the

Agricultural Holdings Act, 1948, authorise modification of the tenancy agreement by way of arbitration. Your agents will be constrained to make such arrangement as they can with the nominal lessee; if nothing is done the lessee has his action for breach of covenant.

Discharge of Restrictive Covenant

I wish to have discharged the Restrictive Covenant on a 4-acre site recently acquired. The land was originally part of a large garden of a big house.

The Covenant, which dates from about 1921, states that the land may not be used except for horticulture or as a garden, and occupants of the house were to have the right of way on it for walks, etc.

The land is never used by the present occupiers, and is overgrown and neglected. Houses have already been built alongside it. The persons the Covenant was originally designed to protect have long since departed, and housing development would not apparently prejudice anyone's amenities. It looks as if the right of way has not been used for very many years.

Can you tell me:

1. To what official body I should apply?

2. What is the procedure?

3. Is it necessary to have planning permission before applying to discharge the Covenant?

It will be necessary, if you propose building on the restricted ground, to seek development permission from your Area Planning Authority. You would then be told whether or not you should apply to the Lands Tribunal for a formal discharge of the restrictions; you may be told to ignore them. For the position is this:

1. The law regards a restriction as extinct if the character of the neighbourhood in which the protected property lies is so altered that it would be inequitable and senseless to insist upon the rigorous observance of a covenant no longer of any value: that is the law, apart from the Law of Property Act, 1925, which provides the following method for the formal discharge or modification of restrictive covenants.

2. Section 84 of the Law of Property Act, 1925, provides for an application to the Lands Tribunal to have the restriction wholly or partially discharged or modified on the ground " that by reason of changes in the character of the property of the neighbourhood . . . the restriction ought to be deemed obsolete, or that the continued existence thereof would impede the reasonable usage of the land for public or private purposes without securing practical benefits to other persons."

Covenant – Construction of Stock-proof Fence

This property is bounded on two sides by a rather sparse thorn hedge. The Deeds require that I shall 'maintain a stock-proof fence' and I am therefore erecting a wire fence all round. Will you please let me know if I am correct in my belief that the wire fence should be outside the hedge?

It is obviously impossible especially in the case of a thorn hedge, to dig post holes in the centre of the hedge or even in line with the outer edge of the stems. Is there any specified clearance allowed?

The strict legal position in respect of your covenant to maintain a stock-proof fence is this: it must stand, unless the owner of the land for the benefit of which the fence is to be maintained gives his express or tacit permission to utilise part of his land, wholly on your ground. There is not, as you suppose, any specified clearance beyond the existing thorn hedge. It comes to this, therefore: you must either find a way, in spite of the thorn hedge, of fixing your posts on your border; or you must reconcile yourself to a sacrifice of a tiny strip of your land by having the posts within the hedge. That is the strict law; but, for ourselves, we should assume a permission to place the posts beyond the hedge and on the adjoining land.

Crest

I have recently inherited various posses-

sions on the death of my father, and am trying to piece together details of my family from the odd documents. I have a seal with a crest which is supposed to have been used by my great-grandfather. Could you please advise me who I should approach to find details of this crest, to whom it was granted and when? Do I have to register before I am entitled to also use this crest? I know the family lived around Leicester from 1600 onwards, and presumably are included in Parish rolls, etc. Can you advise me who I can write to in Leicestershire so I can consult such records or otherwise try and trace the entries?

The best thing for you to do would be to get in touch with the College of Arms, Queen Victoria Street, London E.C.4, and ask one of their experts to trace this crest for you. If you knew the district or village where your great-grandfather lived you could contact the parish clerk, who would certainly have records and could refer you to other parishes which the family married into in the area.

Crops – Damage Caused by Spraying

A neighbouring farmer has been spraying his crops. The spray is drifting and I am worried about damage to my strawberries and fruit trees. I would like to know what legal action, if any, I can take. Can I sue for damages, if damage is caused, and is it possible to restrain the farmer from damaging my fruit trees and strawberries?

Further to your enquiry concerning damage by spraying of crops, we advise you that the farmer is wholly responsible, quite independently of any negligence on his part, for damage done to neighbouring property by the escape of noxious chemicals from his farm land. That escape, when it harms a neighbour's property, constitutes a nuisance. For such nuisance the neighbour can (1) sue for whatver loss he has sustained, (2) ask for an injunction ordering that there shall be a cessation of the nuisance.

In practice, a friendly settlement with the farmer nearly always (and very wisely) takes the place of litigation.

Crowing Cockerels

Our client, who is a member of your Association, is experiencing some trouble due to the crowing of cockerels near his house.

The house in which he lives is in a semi-rural, semi-residential area, and there is reason to believe that the crowing of the cockerels constitutes a private nuisance on the part of the adjoining occupier.

Your member has asked us if we would write to you to see whether you have any particular information as to this sort of problem.

The relevant points for consideration in respect of the interference with comfort and convenience through the crowing of cockerels are:

Injunction is the appropriate and drastic remedy; but it would be granted only if the petitioner's enjoyment of his house has been seriously diminished over a substantial period of time. The annoyance, that is, goes far beyond what neighbours are expected to tolerate from the lawful activities of one another. An occasional dawn chorus of cockerels would not be grounds for an action for nuisance. In *Leeman v. Montagu* (1936), where injunction was granted the similar annoyance, in a partly residential area, had lasted for weeks.

Injunction is not granted where an alternative remedy is available; and a judge might well consider on the evidence tendered that the annoyance would end if he made a declaratory judgment that the untimely crowing did amount to a private nuisance. For normally a man will cease doing what he learns to be unlawful. And, as you well know, the county court has jurisdiction in the matter.

You will gather, therefore, that in our opinion the possibility of your client's getting an injunction is remote, though he might get a declaratory judgment. Moreover, an intimation by you to the owner of the cockerels that you are seeking an injunction is likely to be adequate, without the need for litigation.

'With reference to the problem of crowing cockerels you might be interested to

hear that a similar nuisance afflicted the Brigadier Commanding the garrison in Camp Razmak on the North-West Frontier of India when I was there in 1928. He solved the problem by issuing a brigade order that 'all cocks will be covered with blankets before reveille.'

Damage Caused by Over-flowing Burn – Owner's Liability

A small burn runs through a part of my property. At times of very heavy rain it sometimes overflows on to the adjoining unclassified road making it impassable for a short time. Debris and silt and fallen trees have caused 'blocks. Some years ago you gave a similar case in which the Court held the owner not to blame as he could not control the elements. How do I stand?

The legal position in respect of the facts related by you is this:
(a) The flooding of your own land, in so far as it is caused by the activities of higher riparian owners, is a private nuisance: if you thought fit you could take legal action to restrain it and to claim damages.
(b) The flooding of the highway by the escape from your land of water reaching your land by natural causes and without your intervention imposes no liability upon you: in *Neath R.D.C. v Williams* (1951 this was said: 'The common law of England has never imposed liabilities upon landowners which happen to their land in the natural course of affairs', and the law of Scotland does not differ upon that point.
(c) The authority answerable for the upkeep of the road could seek compensation from the creators of the blockages now appearing; but you have not contributed to the creation, and need not concern yourself about this possibility.

Damage to Roses by Escaping Spray

A neighbouring farmer has been spraying his crops adjacent to our boundary and a bed of roses close to the hedge shows signs of having been affected.

That the escape of spray from the farmer's field constitutes a private nuisance to your ground admits of no doubt; and you are entitled to compensation in full measure for the damage directly caused by the nuisance. Your trouble is that at the moment the amount of damage is a matter for conjecture.

You will, we assume, already have told the farmer what has happened and that you will make a claim against him; and, we greatly hope, the farmer being a sensible man has admitted his liability and is only concerned in having a just measure of the damage. Our suggestion is that you and he agree upon a competent arbiter to make an assessment; a member of your CAEC appointed by the Chairman would probably be acceptable to both you and the farmer. It is possible that the farmer may have an insurance indemnifying him against such claims as yours; if so, his insurers will need to be consulted about the arbiter.

Death Duties

I shall be obliged for information on Death Duties and methods of paying the duty in instalments.

There is no pamphlet published on Death Duties, as of course this is a vast subject covered by a number of textbooks which are, to say the least voluminous, the leading book being probably *Dymond's Death Duties* which is published by the Solicitors Law Stationery Society. The following summarizes the position regarding paying duty by instalments:
1. Realty – by eight yearly or 16 half-yearly instalments, but if property is sold during the eight-year period, the unpaid instalments are immediately payable, together with interest.
2. In the case of an annuity provided by the deceased, then duty is payable on the capitalized value of that annuity and can be paid by four equal yearly instalments. The same conditions apply to a continuing annuity, such as to a surviving spouse. This arises when either the husband or wife purchases a joint annuity.
In all cases the first instalment is due one year after the date of death.

3. (*a*) Shares or securities of a company valued on an assets basis; (*b*) Shares or securities of an unquoted company not valued on an assets basis where at least 20% of the total duty payable arises on these shares or other assets that qualify for an instalment basis; (*c*) The net value of a business.

4. The above are the only cases where duty can be paid by instalments and it should be particularly noted that where an annuity ceases on death so that a slice of the property on which it is charged becomes subject to duty, the provisions regarding the payment by instalment do not apply.

Death Duties – Life interests

A friend of mine left a will in which many things which it was desired to keep in the family were left to his sister for life, then to a nephew for life and finally to the nephew's baby son.

Am I correct in thinking that there would be no more death duty to pay as long as any one of the three was alive?

On the death of the sister of the deceased they will attract duty in the ordinary way unless they are objects of national, scientific, historic or artistic interest that are certified by the Treasury as such, in which case they are free of duty until sold. Duty will again be payable on the death of the nephew unless the same position is applied regarding the nature of the objects, and death duty will also be paid on the nephew's son at the time he dies. All this, of course, is in accordance with present legislation which may be changed by the time the nephew and his son inherit the articles.

Deer Damage – Legal Position – 1

It is Section 14 of the Agricultural Holdings Act, 1945, that gives to a tenant the right to compensate for damage by game; and 'game' for this purpose is 'deer, pheasants, partridge, grouse and black game.' The Section runs: 'where the tenant of an agricultural holding has sustained damage to his crops from game, the right to kill and take which is vested neither in him nor in anyone

claiming under him, other than the landlord, being game which the tenant has not permission in writing to kill, he shall be entitled to compensation from his landlord for the damage if it exceeds in amount, the sum of one shilling per acre of the area over which it extends.'

The tenant can recover damages only when: (*a*) he has given notice in writing to the landlord before the expiration of one month after the tenant first became, or ought reasonably to have become, aware of the occurrence of the damage, and a reasonable opportunity was given to the landlord to inspect the damage; (*b*) he has given notice in writing of his claim within one month after the calendar year.

In default of an agreement about the amount of compensation the amount is to be settled in arbitration.

Whatever happens a tenant has no right, without sanction, of entry into woods, whether for the shooting of the deer or anything else.

Deer Damage – Legal Position – 2

We have a garden adjoining St. Leonard's Forest and numbers of deer appear to take early morning walks through the garden, taking the choicest shoots from the roses, azaleas, etc., for their breakfast.

What can be done about these deer? They are multiplying rapidly both in and around the forest.

What says the law? Apparently, the deer belongs to no one.

Protection of your property against the incursion of deer is for the most part a matter of self-help; in Goodwood Park, for instance, are stretches of electrified fence designed to keep sheep in and the larger possible intruders out. The self-help extends to the shooting, even in the statutory close season, of trespassing deer on enclosed land. Section 10 of the Deer Act, 1963, which makes it a criminal offence to kill deer in the close season, makes an exception of 'the killing by means of shooting of any deer on any cultivated land if the shooter proves that his action was necessary to prevent serious damage to crops on that land'.

You will be aware, too, that under Section 98 of the Agriculture Act, 1947, the Minister of Agriculture may serve notice in writing requiring steps to be taken for the destruction of pests (deer being among them). If the deer in St. Leonard's Forest arc in fact a menace to crops, the Minister could be invoked and asked to tell the Forest Authorities to take appropriate action. Are not the farmers adjacent to the Forest concerned?

Deer Damage – Legal Position – 3

With reference to the above letter, clearly control of the deer is the best way of minimising damage. I cannot imagine fencing other than proper deer-fencing, electrified or not, keeping deer out, and substances to paint around the garden to deter deer by smell or taste do not seem very effective. Control should always be done with a rifle used by an experienced person, and I think you are wrong to encourage garden owners to 'self-help' themselves by shooting. If they were fully experienced they would presumably do this anyway. If not they are likely to lean out of the window and pepper the deer with a shotgun, almost certainly wounding it in a most nasty manner. I suggest that you refer such complaints, which I have read in the CGA magazine before, to the British Deer Society, who can put the person concerned in touch with the local Deer Control Society.

Deer Damage – Legal Position – 4

I would like to draw your attention to the above Control Society which was formed and is affiliated to the British Deer Society and is operating in your area. We are already controlling the deer on various farms in the St. Leonards area, and would be quite willing to assist you in any way we can. This is a completely voluntary organisation, and as such free of charge to landowners.

L. Preston, Hon. Sec., Surrey-Sussex Border Deer Control Society, Norwood Hill Orchards, Norwood Hill, nr. Horley, Surrey. Tel. Norwood Hill 439.

Defaulting on Small Debts

I possess a small cottage which I let during the summer and in 1961 one tenant never paid his rent, neither did he reply to any requests for payment nor to a solicitor's letter threatening action. My solicitor advised me that it would not be worth while going to Court over the matter of £20.

However, one of last year's tenants, a well-to-do businessman who paid a £10 deposit, has also failed to pay the rent. What do you advise in these cases? Are there Debt Collecting Agencies? Is it economical to employ them for bills to the order of £15–£25? Or can anyone obtain a free holiday simply by not paying rent?

We do not agree with your solicitor that a £20 debt is not worth while suing for in the County Court: unless he charges a quite unreasonably large fee for his appearing, you should be able to recover a substantial amount of the £20. The probability is that the debtor will allow judgment to be signed in default of appearance, and the debtor will pay his judgment debt promptly out of fear for other disagreeable results. At all events your debtor should not be permitted to rejoice in a successful bilking of his creditors: if your solicitor is reluctant to issue a writ, put your debt with a debt collector. His commission will leave you a worthwhile residue.

Dog Control – Barking

The people in an adjoining detached house are newcomers and have two dogs, one of which is constantly barking. I asked a member of the family some time ago to keep the dog under better control and some improvement has been evident since but the dog still barks with a high pitched yap at intervals of approximately 15 miniutes. The breed is I believe known as 'Kerry Blue'.

What I would like to know is this, is there any legal way of enforcing on these people stricter control of the dog?

Interference for a substantial length of time with the enjoyment of neighbouring property constitutes a nuisance; and against this nuisance the sufferer can ask the High Court, or indeed the County

Court, to issue an injunction forbidding its continuance. The trouble is that the degree of interference determines whether or not an injunction shall be granted. For a reasonable amount of toleration of a neighbour's lawful activities is expected in this give-and-take society of ours; and what is reasonable can seldom be precisely defined.

Unless the dog's barking is really what its owner cannot expect his neighbour to put up with, if for instance the barking constantly disturbs the hours of rest, it would be hopeless to seek help from the Courts. You will be obliged to depend upon the considerate efforts of your neighbour, who cannot himself be wholly reconciled to the recurrent noise.

Dogs – Damage by

I see you advise that dogs may enter completely open, unfenced gardens without involving their owners in any legal liability.

In my case my garden is surrounded by hedges and where the hedging is weak fenced with wire netting. Has any dog the right to break down my fences and to make holes in my hedges without my having any legal redress from the owner of the dog?

Apart from an encouragement by its owner to enter upon another's premises, you have no legal remedy for the loss caused to you by your neighbour's dog. Our law gives a peculiar immunity to dogs and cats in respect of their roaming propensity; you cannot sue the owner for damage caused by their unauthorised intrusion into your garden, as you could sue a farmer for the trespass of his cattle. The criminal law requires the owner of a dog to keep it under proper control; but a criminal prosecution would afford you no consolation.

Dogs – Hunting – Legal Position

I would like the advice of your legal department on the following problem: This part of Hampshire is entirely given over to pheasant shooting and we are

surrounded by large, well-keepered shoots. I have two terriers and have recently had a complaint from a keeper over their hunting hedgerow rabbits, while out for a walk with me.

Could you tell me the legal position over dogs (1) Hunting in hedgerows of a public road. (2) Ditto in a grass lane which is also a right of way.

I would emphasise that I have never had a complaint from a farmer. The dogs in question are absolutely steady to a feather (we have a chicken farm ourselves) and also with sheep.

I would also like to know the legal position over dogs straying alone on land over which one has not the shooting rights – though of course one makes every effort to prevent this happening.

The answers to the two questions put by you are:

(1) No court would impute any liability upon the owner of a terrier that, being on a highway or on a lane that is a right of way, indulged in its natural propensity and hunted rabbits in the verges of the way. The keeper's complaint is ill-founded.

(2) The Dogs (Amendment) Act, 1928, and Dogs (Protection of Livestock) Act, 1953, contain the statutory rules relating to the owners of dogs trespassing on 'agricultural land,' the owner is both liable to damages and to a penalty when his dog worries livestock. (See these Acts) and, under the common law, it would appear that an occupier has a right to shoot a trespassing dog, when shooting is the one way of preventing killing or maiming of animals on the land. But 'to justify the shooting it is necessary to prove that, when the dog was shot, he was in the very act of killing the fowl and could not be prevented by any other means.'

Dogs – Legal Liabilities of Owners

What are one's legal liabilities as a dog-owner?

An owner's responsibility for what his dog does is, briefly, this: (a) For the dog's fleeting visits to the land of others the owner is *not* liable to an action for trespass; for dogs are outside the category of the 'cattle' for which an owner is liable in an action for cattle trespass, damage feasant. Nor is he liable for what his dog does in obedience to his ordinary instincts; and to worry a cat seems to be one of those instincts.

(b) If, however, he knows or should know, that his dog has a propensity to do mischief beyond what is to be expected of all dogs, he is under obligation to guard against its doing that particular mischief. (Thus in *Read v Edwards*, 1964, the defendant was held liable in a Scienter action; the Court recognised that dogs do chase birds; but here it was proved that the defendant's dog was of a 'peculiarly mischievous disposition' in this respect.)

(c) Before the Dogs Act 1906, a dog was 'allowed to have one worry' in this sense that, unless and until it had worried cattle on at least one previous occasion, knowledge (scienter) could not be imputed to the owner as to the dog's vices in this respect. The obligation to prove knowledge was a heavy burden upon the owner of cattle; and the Act makes the owner of a dog liable for any injury to cattle; without the need for showing either a previous mischievous propensity of the dog or the owner's knowledge of it, or that the injury was due to the owner's neglect to exercise control. And 'cattle' in the 1906 Act means 'horses, mules, asses, sheep, goats and swine,' and the Dogs (Amendment) Act, 1928 added 'poultry' (domestic fowls, turkeys, geese, ducks, guinea fowls and pigeons) but cats (and human beings) are outside the protective Act.

(*See also* Animals Act – 1971, page 157.)

Dogs – Licences

Do I need a licence for a sheepdog?

It is not necessary to take out a licence for a sheepdog provided that exemption has been granted at a Petty Sessional Court; the total number of exempted dogs in one ownership may not exceed eight, and the number of dogs a man may keep will be related to the sizes of his flocks.

Daily Domestic Help – Holidays

Would you kindly let me know if a domestic help employed throughout the year is entitled to a week's holiday with pay, or a fortnight's holiday with pay?

She comes daily, mornings only, five days a week, sometimes four days. Is there a legal, or moral, liability in this case?

We advise you that no statute or statutory instrument makes provision for a holiday, whether with pay or not, for such a worker as you describe. It is wholly at your option to decide upon the matter. Part-time workers are not affected in the various Acts and Regulations (as, for instance, the Contracts of Employment Act, 1963, and the Selective Employment Tax) unless they are normally employed more than 21 hours in a week.

Land Drainage Law

Adjoining and below my property is a plot of what has been waste land for over forty years. It has been covered in trees, bushes and scrub. Now the local council have given planning permission for a dwelling to be built on it, and have written to me telling me to stop my drains seeping on to this ground.

There is a sheer drop from my property to this plot, and it is correct that water from the drains does seep down the slope although my drainage system is on my own property. This has been going on for over forty years with no objection from anybody, and I am wondering if I have any rights from long usage, as the re-routing of the drainage system is going to be a costly job.

The request that you should divert drains seeping from your land on to the proposed building site is in the category of 'try-on'; you could resist a claim to be responsible for what is the consequence of the natural lie of the land. However, the two points for your consideration are:

1. There would be difficulty in applying the rule that twenty years' continuance will, by prescription, legalise a private nuisance such as a right to dis-

charge rain-water from your eaves on to your neighbour's land. For a plaintiff may as in *Sturges v. Bridgman,* 1869) have come to the nuisance.

2. If, however, the flow is no more than would occur independently of your drainage system, you are not under legal obligation to control it.

Perhaps, nevertheless, you may think it desirable to offer co-operation ; you could write and say that you cannot be responsible for the natural flow of drainage due to the lie of the land, which obviously cannot be avoided. You could then offer to co-operate provided you are not involved in any undue expense and say you are willing to meet their surveyor and discuss the matter without obligation.

Drains – Access and Liability for

I am a leaseholder with 30 acres of agricultural land and my neighbour is also a leaseholder with about the same area. The house drainage (through a septic tank) and much of the field drainage in an open drain into which the septic tank effluent empties itself, flows through the neighbour's land, through open-ended field drain pipes I believe, and I am not sure whether any other drainage from his land flows into that pipe which carries my waters, possibly not.

Over the period of years the drain on his land becomes blocked and has to be opened up. My neighbour and I are unfortunately not on speaking terms. When recently approached he said: 'You can open up your drain which carries your waters although it is on my land.'

Can you tell me the legal position?

You will appreciate that, in the absence of evidence as to the ownership of the blocked drains, it would be hazardous as well as most costly to enter upon a legal fight concerning it. The probability is that you have an easement over your neighbours filed for the purpose of drainage; and such an easement would imply a right of access – which apparently your neighbour does not dispute – in order to maintain the drain in efficiency.

Our suggestion, therefore, is that you reconcile yourself to accepting the permission offered and to do the work yourself.

Driving – Liability for Accidents

I should be glad if you would advise me on the following: if a driver of a motor car, coming out on to a busy road asks his passenger to look out for the traffic from the left and tell him when it is safe from that side – acts on what he says, what is the legal position? Is the driver wholly responsible or can the passenger be proceeded against if there is an accident?

The driver, not his passenger, is wholly responsible for his driving; he cannot delegate to another the reasonable care imposed upon him to keep adequate outlook upon other road traffic. It would be no defence, in the event of an accident caused by him, that he was misled by his passenger. Nor could he sue his passenger (unless in the very unlikely possibility that he could prove wilful misinformation by the passenger) for negligence. If he chooses to depend upon a careless or unobservant passenger, he identifies himself with the passenger.

Electricity Cable – Damage by

My house stands some 100 yards from the roadway and the electricity supply comes to the house by an over-head cable, in one long line and fastened to a chimney stack. The chimney stack was sound, well pointed and in apparent good condition. Last Friday the whole stack gave way and slewed round at a complete right angle to its footing. I have had to have the Eastern Electricity Board take down the cable, and the builders are at present dismantling this perfectly good chimney stack and will have to replace it.

Have I any claim on the Eastern Electricity Board for this very expensive repair?

You will doubtless find that, before the Electricity Board affixed their cable to the chimney stack, a licence was obtained from your predecessor in title; and this licence will we are pretty sure, contain stipulation in respect of remedy for possible damage. Your inquiry will elicit what the agreement contains; and with your inquiry you should seek an assurance that you will be indemnified against the loss you have suffered.

Electricity Cables – Way-leave for

The Electricity Authority wish to run an underground electricity cable through the garden of a property in which I am interested. What rights has the owner got in such circumstances? The authority must have access but what should the owner insist on in any agreement with the authority in order to protect his position?

The Electricity Board cannot use privately owned land except with the owner's permission or, when such permission is not given, by an exercise of the power given by Parliament for the fulfilling of their statutory duty. The Board will have its standard form of agreement – you will probably have a copy by this time; and this will stipulate for the payment of a small annual sum in respect of the licence for a way-leave and of the incidental right of access for repair. The payment of this is a necessary acknowledgement of your ownership and your proprietary rights are thereby adequately guarded.

Electricity Act 1947 – Powers

I should be very grateful for your advice on a legal matter I have today been asked (verbally) by a representative of the Electricity Board, if I would agree to three high voltage cables crossing my land. The pylons on either side would be on adjacent land. The cables would be about 20 ft above my garden, and cut right across the view from my living room window (which is a feature of the property), at a distance of about 60 yards.

Apart from spoiling the view, and the attractiveness of the garden for me, I am

certain that this will reduce the value of the property, should I wish to sell at any future date.

I have therefore declined to give my agreement, but I imagine that this will not be the end of the matter.

I should like to know the legal position, and what the procedure is in a case of this nature.

In reply to your letter. We advise you that the Electricity Act 1947 gives powers of compulsory purchase to the Electricity Board: 'Section 9(1) is: "The Minister may authorise an Electricity Board to purchase compulsorily any land, which they require for any purpose connected with the discharge of their functions, as if the Board were a local authority. (2) In this section the expression "land" includes easements and other rights over land, and an Electricity Board may be authorised under this section to purchase compulsorily a right to place an electric line across land, whether above or below ground, and to repair and maintain the line, without purchasing any other interest in the land.'

If, therefore, your Board get the requisite authority from the Minister, you may expect a compulsory purchase notice, and, assuming that the passage of the cables, across your garden is the one practicable route, a protest by you will be unavailing.

You will be entitled to compensation: if you and the Board's Valuer fail to agree upon the amount, the Lands Tribunal will decide what must be paid.

Estate Agents – Selling a House

As a member of the Association I would be so very grateful for your advice and help regarding the best and most economical way of selling our cottage in Devon. We wish to get its true market value and sold if possible without high estate agents' fees, which added to any capital gains tax makes things terribly hard after many years of interior and exterior expenses.

We have always thought that it is a false

economy to try and sell a house without using an estate agent, unless, of course, one has the time and patience to test the market by advertising the property very fully and dealing with the consequential influx of viewers, or one has someone whom one knows is interested and one can approach direct. The competition aroused by placing the house in an estate agent's hands will usually guarantee you the highest price even when commission is deducted.

What for instance really is the commission involved? Say your house is worth £6,000:

5% on the first £500 ...	...	...	£25	0	0
2½% on the next £4,500	...	...	£112	10	0
1¼% on the residue i.e. £1,000	...	£15	0	0
	Total £6,000	...	£152	0	0

By the time you have advertised the property yourself probably, for several months, even if you were to obtain exactly the same price, this would not really give you much advantage to warrant selling privately.

As far as capital gains tax is concerned, you do not pay capital gains tax on your own principal private dwelling house. If you have more than one house then you have to decide which is your principal dwelling. If you have a more valuable house elsewhere which you might sell within the foreseeable future one should not consider declaring the house you are proposing to sell now as your principal house to avoid the tax. This is only a rough answer however and an over-simplification.

Estate Terrier

I would be grateful for information as to what is meant by 'Estate Terrier', and where I can obtain a copy if it so happens that it is a form of ledger.

An Estate Terrier is simply a concise record of all the property of an estate, whether let or in hand. We do not know of a published copy, but many estates get a local printer to print loose-leaf sheets to insert in a binder. Some people have a hand-written pocket terrier to take with them on estate visits. Suitable details for inclusion in the terrier are: (a) names of premises or holding and tenant; (b) ordnance survey numbers and acreages; (c) rent and rent per acre; (d) date of entry and term; (e) repair responsibilities of landlord and tenant; (f) schedule of buildings and services; (g) tithe, insurances, etc.

Executor's Duties

I have agreed to act for a friend as executor to execute his will. It is a small estate consisting of a bungalow, industrial shares and savings. Could you kindly inform me of the first and important things I have to do on his death?

The first duties of an executor are: (1) To ensure that the funeral arrangements have been properly carried out and any express wish included in the will in connection with cremation, etc, put into effect. (2) Ensure that the widow of the deceased has sufficient income or other funds so that she can carry on financially until probate is available. (3) Collect particulars of the estate both as to assets and liabilities, and arrange for valuation as at the date of death, where necessary.

In order to obtain this information it will be necessary to examine the effects of the deceased and to get in touch with his bank and taxation accountants as the latter will be able to supply details of any income tax repayment that is due to the estate or any surtax or capital gains tax liabilities that are outstanding.

The above only briefly summarizes the main points to be dealt with, but of course there may be a number of other matters to be taken into account depending on the circumstances of the deceased. If you have had no experience of acting as an executor, then we would recommend you to read a recent publication, namely *Wills and Executors*, by Edward F. George (published by Methuen & Co at 27s 6d).

Farming – Small Acreages – 1

I wonder if I may seek your advice on a somewhat personal problem.

I recently bought a small farmhouse in the Cotswolds, near Stroud, together with 48 acres of land, including about five acres of orchard and woodland and the rest well-watered pasture. For the previous 18 years at least there has been a dairy herd on the land, and it has good outbuildings.

My question in its broadest form is whether your experts consider a farm of this size a commercial proposition and, if so, for what type of farming. If I let the land to a neighbouring farmer what sort of price could I ask, and what are the legal snags about letting farmland?

Perhaps it might be possible for you to enlarge your answer to cover the tax and other legal advantages and disadvantages of farming as against letting the land together with anything else you might think would help me make up my mind.

If it is your intention to keep a dairy herd on your property, and this appears to have been the practice over a great number of years and the farm is obviously geared to this type of farming, then there is no doubt in my mind that it would be extremely difficult for you to obtain a living of other than a bare subsistence standard on such a small acreage.

If you are keen on pursuing the idea of farming, then I would suggest that there are two avenues open to you:

1. To acquire further land in order to bring your grazing acreage up to about 100 acres upon which you could run a dairy herd of 70 upwards.
2. To concentrate on intensification on the existing acreage of creating non-land-using enterprises such as pigs or barley beef.

In both cases, this would require considerable additional capital investment, and unfortunately you have given me no indication of whether such capital would be available.

If you are to consider letting the land, I would anticipate you could expect to receive a rent of about £10 per acre per annum, although this figure can fluctuate considerably according to the quality of the land and the relative supply and demand in your area. Unless the land is let on an annual grazing tenancy, renewable every 364 days, any tenant would gain security under the provisions of the Agricultural Holdings Act, 1948, which would make it virtually impossible for you, or any successive owner, to regain occupation of the land while the tenant is alive. Creation of such a tenancy would have the effect of reducing the market value of your property by approximately 20 per cent.

There are undoubtedly considerable taxation advantages which could accrue to you by farming the property yourself as opposed to letting it, but it is first essential that you satisfy yourself you can obtain a reasonable return both from the point of view of your own standard of living and as a return on capital before the taxation situation is investigated in detail.

I am afraid that, at this stage, it is only possible for me to give you general lines of advice as I would need considerably more information about your affairs before being able to express a detailed opinion.

Farming – Small Acreages – 2

I own a total of 7½ acres adjoining my house —there are three paddocks adjoining each other, two of them being separated by a stream with cattle watering places available from both paddocks. On these paddocks there are two 'shelters', both with hay stores. For the past 30 years these paddocks have been let for grazing and the local farmer has decided that he will no longer wish to graze. All fencing is in first-class order—the grazier having been responsible for it as well as cutting the grass two or three times yearly and also liming. I have already had offers of around £7 to £10 per acre for similar grazing rights.

I feel, however, that I can put this land to better use. I have, however, my own business commitments and could only devote a few hours a week to any project—however, reliable labour is available if necessary.

The grazier has usually had six to eight bullocks and a couple of mares on the land. The bullocks usually arrive each Spring and are taken off in the Autumn.

If I decided to rear bullocks myself—what time (and capital) would I need? I also have some outbuildings which comprise three large stores (each about 12' × 10') and a similar size cow (milking) shed with three separate boxes. These outbuildings are a very solid construction and well roofed.

No doubt many of your members have similar problems and you might wish to publish this letter with any recommendations or ideas for their benefit as well.

In my opinion it would be quite impossible for you to use this land in any better fashion than to let it for grazing. The amount of capital required and the uncertainty of the enterprise combined with (with respect) lack of management expertise, would mean that there is absolutely no way in which you could make better financial use of this land, particularly if you can obtain £10 per acre.

I would emphasise, however, that it is essential for you to ensure that this land is only let on a less than one-year grazing basis. Under no circumstances must you let it for one year or more because in so doing you will lose all right to subsequent vacant possession. That is to say, your tenant can easily establish that he has the land on an agricultural tenancy and is thus protected by the 1947 Agricultural Act which gives virtually complete security to tenancy.

I would advise that you consult your solicitor to draw up the agreement or use one of the C.G.A.'s standard Grazing Agreements.

Fenn Traps

The statement in our May issue that the Minister of Agriculture had, under the Pests Act, 1954, approved the use of Fenn traps, should have been attended by a statement of the restricting conditions. These are:

The traps shall be used only
(a) for the purpose of killing or taking grey squirrels and stoats, weasels, rats, mice or other small ground vermin, and set in artificial tunnels for this purpose,
or
(b) for the purpose of killing or taking rats or mice, and set in the open on their runs.

It does not seem that 'rabbits' are 'vermin' and included; but it is hard to see how the trapping of rabbits is to be effectively guarded against. (See page 225.)

Field – Points on Letting for Grazing

Can you tell me what to look out for
when letting a field for grazing. Who is liable for damage if the person taking the grazing's cattle escape and trespass?

1 The first necessity is to avoid the person taking the land establishing an Agricultural Tenancy. This means you can never get them out unless they farm the land so badly that the Lands Tribunal will endorse a notice to quit.
2 To avoid a tenancy you enter into a Sale of Keep Agreement which should be for a period of less than one year. Bear in mind you are selling the grass in the field and this is all.
3 There must be no implication that one such agreement will be followed by another. In other words, each period of letting must be separate and no mention of renewal must be made.
4 Liability for cutting weeds, keeping the grass properly cropped, maintaining hedges and fences should be placed squarely upon the tenant.
5 Sale of Keep arrangements can be effected by the use of C.G.A. Sale of Keep Agreements, (price 3s 6d each) or by an exchange of letters. This latter arrangement involves your writing out the terms of the Sale of Keep, and the purchaser of the Keep accepting in writing.
6 The owner of the animals is liable for any damage done by them if they get out.
7 It is prudent on the part of the Landlord to take out a public liability policy to cover such eventualities as trees falling upon tenants and passers-by or the tenant's animals. We use the term 'tenant' here loosely because in fact the purchaser of keep never becomes a tenant and should never be referred to in this way.

Field – Possession of

I bought a two-acre field at a property sale in June; the auctioneer stating at the time that the tenant was agreeable to vacate the field at quarter day.

Shortly after that the tenant herself told me she would give me possession in November and I did not serve her with a written notice thinking her word would be sufficient.

I have bought ewes to stock the field and it now seems likely that the tenant does not intend to vacate the field; her relative has sheep and wishes to use the land himself.

Have I any grounds on which to obtain possession? And if not must I allow her relative to graze his sheep there? In view of the fact that she is the tenant.

The position in respect of the field is this:

(1) You were entitled to rely upon the auctioneer's statement, that the field would be vacated at quarter day;

(2) The tenant's statement, that she would give you possession in November has no legal effect; for it was made, we assume, without her receiving any consideration for her promise. She is, therefore, entitled to the twelve months' notice as provided for in the Agricultural Holdings Act, 1948, and, on your giving notice, may as provided in the Act serve on you a counter-notice. Nor can you object to her purposed use of the field.

Your legal remedy is against the vendor (whose agent was the auctioneer); he would have the vendor's authority to make the statement inducing you to purchase.

Fishing Rights

I am proposing to sell off part of my estate which will include one bank of river for about two miles. I propose to retain the fishing rights and not to include them in the sale. As neither my solicitor nor my agent are able to advise me I should be most grateful if you could assist. The problem I am having difficulty in resolving is whether I should sell to the centre of the river or whether I should retain the whole of the river bed to ensure the preservation of the fishing. From the point of view of the best interest of the fishing, it appears to me to be desirable to retain ownership of the whole of the river and retain right of access to the banks, but this may result in my being responsible for the whole of the charge which might be made by the River Board should they carry out some improvement scheme.

As I understand the position, any works carried out by the River Board are apportioned between the adjoining owners thus if I own the river bed I should be held responsible for both banks instead of my usual half if I sell to the centre of the river.

Could you please advise, therefore (a) From the point of view of the fishing, is it necessary or desirable to retain ownership of the whole of the river bed? (b) If it is desirable to retain the whole of the river bed, is this likely to result in the whole of any charges made by the Severn River Board falling upon myself and not being shared by the purchaser of the adjoining land?

To take question (b) first: if she retains ownership of the whole river, she must clearly retain the legal responsibilities attendant theron.

As regards question (a): ownership is not necessary if the tenant of the fishing rights has a properly drawn lease to enable him or her to do whatever may be necessary to keep the river in good order from the point of view of the fishing.

My advice, therefore, would be for this member to sell the bank of the river, and the river up to the half-way mark as is usual, and thereafter to lease back the fishing rights on that bank. This will give her the fishing rights of the whole river, as I understand the position, and actual ownership of half the river, as she will be the lessee of the other half, and if, as already indicated· the lease is properly drawn to give her the access and facilities she requires to keep the fishing in good order, all that is required will have been achieved.

In conclusion it should be stressed that, to try and expropriate the fishing rights, land, or the river from the sale is only storing up trouble for the future. If, however, she is determined on such a course, she should ensure legal access over the land to the river bank, or in the event of dispute she might well find access across land, not her own, quite properly denied her, and this is only one cause of possible friction!

Fishing Rights – Book on Law of

Can you recommend a book on angling law?

Angling and the Law, published by Charles Knight, of 11–12 Bury Street, St. Mary Avenue, London, EC3. It is by Michael Gregory.

Footpath – Closing a

I wish to close a public footpath which cuts across my land, hindering cultivations and increasing their cost. The path is hardly ever used, as an adjacent bridleway gives the same access across the land and does not interfere with my farming operations. Can you tell me what I should do to have the footpath closed?

You seem to have good grounds on which to obtain either an extinguishment or a diversion order.

Under Section 110 of the Highways Act 1959, you can apply to the highway authority for an extinguishment order. This would have to be confirmed by the Minister of Housing and Local Government, who must be satisfied that it is shorter or more commodious path, it is expedient to do so· having regard to the extent (if any) to which it appears to him that the path would, apart from the Order, be likely to be used by the public.

Alternatively, the highway authority may consider it more appropriate to issue a diversion order, under Section 111 of the Act. To obtain such an order, the owner of the land concerned must satisfy the authority that for securing the efficient use of the land, or producing a shorter or more comodious path, it is expedient that the line of the path should be diverted. The order will be confirmed by the Minister of Housing, providing he is satisfied that the public will not be inconvenienced by the diversion. A notice of the intended change must be published, and should any objection be made by the local people, the Minister may order a local inquiry.

Should the highway authority refuse to make an order for extinguishment or diversion of the path, you may apply direct to the Minister of Housing, but he will certainly consult the County Council and the R.D.C. before taking any action.

Footpath

I would be most grateful for your advice concerning the use of a footpath between a field which I own – it passes along one boundary of it – and the land surrounding my own house and a wood. A portion of 200 yards of the footpath joining my field and my garden passes between the boundaries of two farms. The path is marked as a footpath on the Ordnance map. I was told that the parochial council intended to approach me to ask me not to move a pony between my two pieces of land by this path. I have done so for the past 13 years without hindrance. I am quite willing to give a modest undertaking that the pony will be led and not ridden on this footpath.

You will know that the Highways Act, 1959, reiterates the duty of public authorities to prevent whatever diminishes the right of the public to the dedicated use of a public way; and you will agree that it can be urged that the riding even of a pony on a way dedicated as a footway goes beyond the use contemplated in the dedication.

It is, however, reasonable to assume that the leading of the pony along the particular stretch, instead of riding it, would meet no objection. Technically it would be an excessive use; but we anticipate that your undertaking of no riding will settle the matter.

Footpaths – Trespassing and Misuse of

I would much appreciate your views as to the following: (1) Has one a right to walk on another party's land to pick up game shot on his own land or is it a matter of custom that so many do it and may be wrong? (2) Has one the right to walk along a public footpath on private land carrying a gun? (3) Does the existence of a footpath entitle one to take a dog on leash or at heel? I have a number of footpaths on my land and have noticed people wandering all over the place, i.e. not sticking to the footpath.

(1) A person trespasses when, without permission, he goes upon another's land to retrieve game shot on his own land: where the custom exists of so doing, it is assumed that the owner of the land entered upon has impliedly given his permission. When it is clear that he has not, there is trespass.

(2) The paths dedicated for the purpose of passage: it is a trespass to use them for a purpose quite remote from passage. In *Philpot v Bugler* (1890) the Judge said that the defendant had a right of way over a footpath, but he was there with his dog and a gun for the purpose of sporting and he should have been convicted of trespass.

(3) There can be no valid objection to taking a dog on leash or at heel along a footpath, provided that the footpath is being used for passage only.

Footpath

How wide is a footpath?

There is no rule of law specifying a standard width for public paths. The width of a public path is, broadly speaking dependant upon the circumstances under which the path came into being.

If the path was created by some explicit legal instrument, e.g. a deed of dedication, an inclosure award or a statutory order – then it is very likely that the legal instrument will have specified the width of the path to be created. The widths vary greatly under these circumstances: some deeds of dedication provide for paths only two feet wide; some inclosure awards provide for paths as much as twenty feet wide.

If, as is more commonly the case, the path came into being as the result of implied dedication, and therefore without any explicit legal instrument, the common law has two general rules. Firstly, the minimum width of a path is determined by the amount of room needed for two normal persons to pass one another (say, three feet). Secondly, the maximum width of a path may be determined by the physical boundaries, if any on either side of it, provided that the whole of the intervening space is used by the public.

In other words, where a public path runs between two hedges or fences the law presumes that the whole of the space between the hedges or fences is subject to a public right of way, unless the physical character of the ground ran counter to the presumption. It follows from this that the wider the space is between the hedges or fences the more difficult it is to show that public use extends over the whole of the space.

How is the layman to know whether the width of the path has ever been defined in an explicitly legal instrument? His best plan is to consult the Map and statement prepared by the County (or County Borough) Council in the course of the Survey of public rights of way. He can identify the path on the Map; and the accompanying Statement usually indicates the width of the path, if the width is definitely known.

Do bridleways differ from footpaths in this question of width? They differ in one very important respect. Although the law does not specify the universal width of a bridleway, it does impose upon the highway authority the duty of ensuring that every bridleway shall be maintained at a width of at least eight feet. There is one exception to this rule; where a gate crosses a bridleway there need be a space of only five feet between the posts.

Foreshore Rights

We own a house and plot of land in Anglesey on the shore, and in consequence have rights to the same width of foreshore above the high water mark.

Would you please be good enough to tell me what are the rights in this connection because without permission a number of people are parking sailing dinghies on the foreshore and adjoining our sea wall, and it is becoming a bit of a nuisance, and has only happened recently.

I presume the public have the right to walk across the foreshore, but have we any right to enclose it?

There can be no question concerning the rights over the foreshore adjoining your land; it is yours and a use of it by others, even for walking across it, is a trespass unless you have, expressly or by implication, given permission for such use. An implication for the necessary permission may well be assumed by people for walking over it; but the parking of sailing dinghies is a quite different matter. You have, when the parking is without your express sanction, power to order the trespass off; and you can take action against him if the order is not promptly obeyed.

Ground Ivy

I own a wood which is covered with ground ivy, which grows into and under the boundary hedge between my land and my neighbour's garden. What is the legal position when ground ivy spreads on to a neighbour's land? Am I under any liability to prevent it spreading?

You are not entitled to allow the plants growing on your ground so far to indulge in their roving propensity as to encroach into or above your neighbour's ground. The neighbour whose ground is invaded is entitled, if he chooses to take the trouble, to cut back to his own border such parts – roots or branches – of the plants as do intrude. If, however, he is unwilling to be ever vigilant to prevent intrusion and possible damage, he may apply to the court for an injunction that would constrain you to end the continuing nuisance; and in its discretion the Court may, judging an injunction to be equitable, issue it. The answer to your question is, therefore, Yes: you are under risk of liability.

Hares and Rabbits Damage – Legal Position

Section 14 of the Agricultural Holdings Act, 1948 (the Section that gives a tenant a right to compensation for damage by game) restricts the meaning of 'game' to deer, pheasants, partridge, grouse and black game; it does not include hares and rabbits. The reason for the exclusion is that, whatever the lease says, the tenant cannot divest himself wholly of the right of taking 'ground game' (i.e., hares and rabbits). The tenant has that right as incident to and inseparable from his occupation of the land by the Ground Game Act, 1880. He has the right though his landlord may have reserved shooting rights. The tenant can claim no compensation from his landlord in respect of the damage; but he can account for the damagers.

Hedge – Height of

Could you advise me as to the height of hedge or fencing a householder is permitted to have, by law?

The owner of a house bordering my drive persuaded my predecessor to cut the hedge down from 7 to under 5 ft. and is trying to insist—by clipping it himself—that it remains at this latter height.

There is no legal maximum height of hedge or fence—it would obviously be quite impracticable for there to be one.

A number of other factors, however, do arise. For instance one must be certain before getting too involved in a dispute of this nature as to who is the owner of the hedge. One wonders what are the objections of your neighbour to having the hedge 2 ft. higher than it is at present. Plainly it will be better to reach a compromise, as otherwise this sort of dispute can become a bone of contention lasting for years. On the other hand if the hedge is entirely your property and you could prove that this is so then you are entitled really to do what you like with it including cutting it down and replacing it with anything else if you so desire.

Highways – Repair of

Our village of Barnsley situated on the Trunk Road A433, between Burford and Cirencester, is suffering severely from the increasing heavy lorry traffic which is not only damaging adjoining walls and buildings, but by mounting the Footways in order to pass one another, has almost entirely removed the kerbs, and these Footways are now unsafe to walk on.

We were assured early this year that the Footways would be repaired or reconstructed this spring, but we have now heard from the

Yes, It is Illegal to Shoot Game on Sundays

(See page 214)

Gloucestershire County Council Surveyor, that this work has been deferred for at least a year, due to lack of money.

Under Section 67 of The Highways Act 1957, it makes it clear that it is the duty of the highway authority to provide a proper and sufficient footway, and, under the Highways (Miscellaneous Provisions) Act 1961, and which came into force in August 1964, action can be taken against a Highway Authority in respect of damage resulting from their failure to maintain the Highway, and which includes the Footway, and they can no longer disclaim civil liabilities for injuries arising from non-repair of Roads, Footways, etc.

I am informed that under the Act of 1961 the ancient defence of nonfeasance has been abolished.

Our Parish Meeting would value your advice as to the Legal position, and what steps they should now take to compel the County Council to comply with their liabilities under these Acts.

You have stated precisely and with clarity the statutory obligation of the County Council under the Highways Act, 1957, to maintain reasonable safe footways; the former defence, when injury resulted from a failure to repair, of nonfeasance was in fact abolished by the 1961 Act.

As to the legal action available to you, it is this—the continuing condition of disrepair constitutes a public nuisance, since it affects Queen's subjects in general. The proper plaintiff to the Court, in search of an injunction ordering the cessation of the nuisance, is the Attorney-General. He can act on information by a private relator as well as by your Parish Meeting.

Perhaps, if you told the County Surveyor that you had in mind the laying of information with the Attorney-General, this itself would bring you prompt relief.

Horse Leasing

Do your professional services extend to the drawing up of a simple form of agreement for the lease of a horse, a registered show-jumper, for the coming show-jumping season?

We, the lessors, wish to have certain safeguards, and so does the lessee – he does not want the horse sold under him and so forth.

We do not have an agreement for lending horses, but apparently if you write to the BSJA, National Equestrian Centre, Kenilworth, Warwickshire, giving the name of your registered show-jumper they will send you a form for this. The charge is £1. When you write you must give them the name of the owner and the name of the person to whom you are leasing the horse.

Fox Hunting

We would be very much obliged if you would kindly let us know what are the legal rights and liabilities of a fox hunt and/or its members hunting over farm land, and whether you recommend the farm owner to take any action to protect his position. Last year the hunt came through our farm one week before lambing and scattered the flock over the neighbouring moors. We believe we lost a number of lambs as a direct result. We would appreciate your advice.

Hunting exists by the courtesy and permission of the occupier (or if the sporting rights have been reserved by the landowner) by the permission of the landowner of the land over which the hunt passes. To follow hounds over land where the occupier has warned off the hunt is a trespass and any person doing so is liable to a civil action. The Master is responsible for his own trespass and that of the hunt servants. He is not liable for the trespass of other followers if he has warned them not to go on the land. Persons following hounds, even over forbidden lands, are not guilty of poaching even though the quarry is a hare, which is game. Where hounds go on to forbidden land and are not followed by the Master or hunt servants, the Master is not guilty of trespass if he has attempted to whip the hounds off. If he or any of the hunt servants go on to the land to attempt to stop the hounds they are guilty of a technical trespass but probably no Court would award anything but nominal damage against them.

Prohibition of Hounds

I have the shooting over land that for

*years belonged to my family. The farm
was sold a year or so ago, but the shooting rights were retained. There is one
covert on the shoot. The owner farmer
has banned the hounds over his land,
padlocked some of his gates, and last
season threatened the Hunt with legal
proceedings. I read somewhere that it
was the shooting tenant who could give
permission or not, for the hounds to
come over the land. Is this correct?*

The retention of shooting rights over
land sold does not include a right to
decide whether or not fox-hunting over
the land shall be permitted. That decision
rests with the owner of the land: the
farmer is wholly within his rights in
what he has already done; and his
threat to bring action for trespass is not
an empty one. In the case of *Paul v.
Summerhayes* (1878), where fox-hunters
persisted in riding over land of a farmer
in spite of his express prohibition, the
hunters were held to be liable for trespass.

Ill-Health and Income Protection

It is not generally realised that a chronically
sick person, who is drawing National Health
Sickness Benefit, one of the few tax free
sources of income, need not transfer to
National Retirement Benefit at the age of
65, with its subsequent drop in income due
to the Income Tax payable on the latter
benefit.

It is of great advantage to defer 'retirement' until 70, at which age sickness benefit
is no longer payable and one must officially
'retire'.

To quote our own case, my husband has
been an invalid for some eight years with a
progressively disabling illness, and our sickness benefit is currently £8.70 per week including allowance for wife and one child,
income tax free. My husband has just passed
his 65th birthday and had he 'retired' his
national retirement pension would be the
same but less 42p. in the £ income tax (£186
per year) as, due to other income, tax is paid
at the standard rate in our case.

With the expense of an invalid needing
extra heating day and night, help in large
garden and in house, telephone and car as
necessities due to living three miles from a
village and ten miles from a town, having to

get in outside help for all repairs to house,
and electrical equipment usually done by an
active husband, and the expense of a teenage
daughter only 13 years of age, this saving of
£186 per year for five years is a very important item.

Other members, similarly placed, with
'65' looming in the near future, may be very
glad to learn that they may take this further
five years of sickness benefit.

It is important not to sign the form agreeing to retirement when it arrives a few
months before the 65th birthday, but to
state that you will defer this until the age of
70, in the space provided. There is no
pressure put on anyone to 'retire' before 70,
even though he has not actually worked for
years due to chronic illness, and it is perfectly legal.

Improvements – Grant Aid

*I intend having some disused accom-
modation in a farmhouse turned into a
flat so that a worker on the farm may
be housed. I shall be obliged if you will
inform me whether an agricultural grant
can be obtained, and if planning permission must be sought.*

If the accommodation you are referring to is in an existing house, we would
have thought it necessary to obtain
planning permission. Grants can be obtained both from local authorities and
the Ministry of Agriculture in certain
circumstances for improvements such as
the installation of sanitation, baths, lar-
ders, etc. We suggest you contact both
authorities and discuss the position with
them. If you do establish a flat in an
existing farmhouse, you will of course
have rates levied on it. Incidentally, you
should be able to claim income tax relief on
the net cost to you (i.e. after deducting any
grant) over a ten-year period under the provisions of Section 68, Capital Allowances
Act, 1968.

Intestacy

*My father recently died and I am the next of
kin, his wife and daughter pre-deceased him,
and he left a house which has been sold.*

*I have been informed by his solicitors that
when the house is sold the money raised is to*

be divided as follows: half to myself and the other half to my deceased sister's children. I understand as he left no will and as I am his only surviving child, that whatever he left should be mine. I fail to see where my niece and nephew come into this as my daughter does not seem to be included. Can you tell me if his solicitor is acting rightly?

All children are treated equally, so that you are entitled to one-half of the estate and the other half passes to the issue of your deceased sister. If you yourself had predeceased your father then your daughter would have taken your share, and the ruling given by your solicitor is quite correct.

Insurance Liabilities – Thieves Bill

I have a small house at Lydd which was recently broken into by two men who clearly stayed there for a few days. The thefts and damage in all will probably be in the region of £600.

These two put on the central heating gas boiler and turned it up to 200° F. and left it. I had just paid the quarterly gas bill but there is now a bill of £205.90.

Can you tell me if I am legally liable for this bill?

I have not encountered this situation before. However, it is unlikely that there is any cover for a loss of this nature under his policy. We have in the past had the odd claim where someone has lost a vast quantity of water following a fractured water pipe and the companies do not normally meet the Water Board's bill under these circumstances.

It appears that this is a secondary residence left unoccupied for weeks at a time and the insurance company may have imposed certain conditions as a result (one of these being that it should be visited at least once a week). They may on the other hand have insisted that the central heating be left on. It really depends on the conditions of the insurance cover but we would normally expect to persuade *our* companies to take a sympathetic view and share the bill fifty/fifty on an ex gratia basis. Manager: C.G.A. (Insurance Brokers) Ltd.

Joint Liability – Driveway

I wondered if you could give me any help with the following problem: The drive and yard to this house is our property but it is the only means of access to the adjoining farm, and the farmer has a 'right of way' over it. We have two problems in connection with this matter.

1. Although it states in our deeds that the drive and yard is to be maintained in good condition jointly by the farmer and us, the farmer always states that nothing needs doing to it and therefore does not pay for any repairs. Have you any suggestions as to how we can make him pay for repairs to the condition which we consider necessary, but which he is quite happy to either tolerate or not pay for?

2. In haymaking season a good deal of hay is scattered on the drive and in the yard, and this the farmer refuses to sweep up or pay for it to be swept up.

The farmer is, quite clearly, a person that will fulfil his obligations only under the threat or actuality of legal proceedings. Our suggestion, therefore, is this: (a) There is here a joint liability to maintain the drive and yard in good condition; and the law will imply an agreement that each of the persons liable will do his share in the maintaining. If the farmer does not contribute you could sue him, preferably in the County Court in a quasi-contract action. The rationale of such an action is this: if you alone maintain the way the farmer gets an unjust and undeserved benefit; a fictitious contract obliges him to pay for the benefit.

(b) The farmer is under covenant to contribute equally towards the upkeep; and you, as a person aggrieved by his failure to contribute, even to the extent of clearing up his own hay, could seek a mandatory injunction.

Jointly Owned Chimney

The house I live in is a rented one, and it joins another house. Our back chimney is a joint one. It is in bad repair and the landlady is not willing to spend money on repairing it. My back bedroom is very damp on walls and ceilings. The house that is joining mine is self-owned. Could you please let me know what ways or means I can have to get it repaired. One builder who has seen it says it ought to come down. It is a stone chimney

The legal position is this:

1. Unless your tenancy agreement makes you liable for structural repairs, your landlady is under an implied obligation to maintain her premises in the state to command the rent; that is, she should effect repairs. The pressure that you can exert upon her to fulfil her obligation is the possibility of bringing against her an action for breach of contract.

2. By its defects the chimney for which your neighbour is jointly liable, has caused and is causing damage, it is also a danger. The chimney, therefore, constitutes a nuisance. Your neighbour should realise that you are able to sue him in respect of the damage caused by the nuisance, and are also able to ask the Court for an injunction ordering the cessation of the nuisance.

Land Drainage Law

Adjoining and below my property is a plot of what has been waste land for over forty years. It has been covered in trees, bushes and scrub. Now the local council have given planning permission for a dwelling to be built on it, and have written to me telling me to stop my drains seeping on to this ground.

There is a sheer drop from my property to this plot, and it is correct that water from the drains does seep down the slope although my drainage system is on my own property. This has been going on for over forty years with no objection from anybody, and I am wondering if I have any rights from long usage, as the re-routing of the drainage system is going to be a costly job.

The request that you should divert drains seeping from your land on to the proposed building site is in the category of 'try-on'; you could resist a claim to be responsible for what is the consequence of the natural lie of the land. However, the two points for your consideration are:

1. There would be difficulty in applying the rule that twenty years' continuance will, by prescription, legalise a private nuisance such as a right to discharge rain-water from your eaves on to your neighbour's land. For a plaintiff may (as in *Sturgis v. Bridgman*, Ch. 1869) have come to the nuisance.

2. If, however, the flow is no more than would occur independently of your drainage system, you are not under legal obligation to control it.

You could offer to co-operate provided you are not involved in any undue expense and say you are willing to meet their surveyor and discuss the matter without obligation.

Land Owner's Liability

This property of about 30 acres consists of cliff land on the edge of the sea, the sea-side boundary being entirely rocks on the south side. Two public rights of way traverse the land roughly east to west.

Will you please advise me whether I am under any obligation to persons if they should have an accident on the land or falling from my rocks and possibly drowning?

If I am under any obligation is it affected by whether the accident happens to a person:

(a) on a public right of way;

(b) on a pathway that I allow the public to use but have not dedicated (and so close on one day a year); or

(c) to people trespassing over any part of my property?

You owe a duty of care towards the lawful visitors to your property (these being such as have your expressed or implied sanction to enter). This duty is now defined in the 'Occupiers Act, 1957'; it is 'a duty to take such care as in all the circumstances of the case is reasonable to see that the visitor will be reasonably safe in using the premises for the purposes for which he is invited or permitted to be there'. It applies to all your land, including the public ways, and it means that you must give adequate warning of possible dangers. You are not expected to be an insurer, bound to make your premises safe or to pay for failure to do so; nor are you liable when injury comes as a result of the ignoring of your warning. (The duty does not extend to a visitor injured by going where he was warned not to go: in Anderson v. Coutts, 1894, where the injured man fell over a cliff through getting on the wrong side of railings erected by the proprietor, who had also put up a notice of danger, the occupier was held to be free from liability.) You fulfil your duty by warnings reasonably to be thought effective.

Your slight, probably negligible, liability to trespassers is still that of the common law, expounded by one Lord Chancellor in this way: 'Towards the trespasser the occupier has no duty to take reasonable care for his protection or even to protect him from concealed danger. The trespasser comes into the premises at his own risk. An occupier in such a case, is liable only when the injury is due to some wilful act done with the deliberate intention of doing harm to the trespasser, or at least some act done with reckless disregard of the presence of the trespasser.'

There has recently been a case where damages were awarded against British Railways, I believe, for injuries a boy received whilst trespassing on the railway line. The Rail Board had not looked to its fencing.

We allow a farmer to graze cattle, horses, ponies and sheep and/or take hay off two fields (about 10 acres) surrounding this house sometimes with a grazing agreement, for a period of less than a year, and sometimes without.

Would we be liable for any claim arising from:

(a) any damage caused to the farmer's animals whilst on our land;

(b) any damage caused to third parties or their property by the farmer's animals whilst on our land (there is a right of way through both our fields).

If there is a potential liability involved in the circumstances described could you advise me on what, if any, insurance cover might be effected. As far as I can gather the farmer is covered against third party risks involving his animals but would the fact that they are using our land involve us in any way too?

Any liability upon you arising from the permitted presence of the farmer's animals in your fields is well-nigh negligible. You would, upon enquiry of your insurers, probably learn that the remote liability is coverable by a nominal premium.

1. There is no duty upon you as occupier of the fields to keep the animals safe while they are there; they have not been delivered into your custody and the farmer keeps them there at his own risk. You could only be answerable for injury directly due to yourself or one for whom you were answerable (as if your dog worried a sheep or a guest injured a pony by a stolen ride).

2. Any liability for injury to third parties arises from the right of way (particularly if this is a public right for the safety of which your local authority is responsible). You would run a risk, for instance, if you tolerated the presence of an untethered bull in your fields. But that, obviously, is quite imaginary.

Legal Charges – Dispute

Eighteen months ago my neighbour and I agreed to exchange a small piece of land in order to facilitate access to our respective properties. The area of land was only four square yards and no monetary transaction was involved.

I instructed my solicitor to deal with the legal aspects and asked for an approximate cost.

I cannot remember the exact figures quoted but it was certainly less than £20.

I have just received a demand for the sum of £84.37½ and a letter explaining that the transaction was more involved than was anticipated.

I feel that this fee is much too high and would like to know if there is any way I can effectively challenge it.

Is there anything to prevent an unscrupulous solicitor charging any fee he likes and should I have obtained a written estimate?

The reason that the transaction has taken so long is the slowness of my neighbour's solicitor.

We cannot conceive justification for the payment asked from you. Our suggestion, therefore, is that you defer all payment until you have the written reasons why it so greatly exceeds the ordinary. When you have these you can inquire of the Law Society whether they amount to justification.

Solicitors' charges are governed by statutory orders; they are either scale fees or under Schedule II, 'such charges as may be fair and reasonable having regard to all the circumstances of the matter'. But a solicitor may elect in writing, before undertaking a business, to charge under Schedule II where a scale fee would otherwise apply. It does not appear that your solicitor did so elect; he must, accordingly, charge under the statutory scale, which is the '£20 or so' of his estimate.

As to your question, whether you should have had a written estimate, the one advantage of a written estimate is that evidence of its existence is stronger than the evidence of an oral estimate. But you get the estimate, written or oral alike, in order to decide whether you will or will not commission the work for the stated price. Presumably the solicitor will not deny his '£20 or so'; and a Court could reasonably support your contention that you were entitled to rely upon it. Because a contract has proved more difficult than the contractor expected is no justification for asking more than the contract price.

We should value a note telling us what you ultimately pay. If your solicitor had told you that the transfer of ownership would be so expensive, you and your neighbour need not have bothered about a transfer at the moment. You could have given gratuitous licence to one another to use the plots concerned; and, after the prescriptive period (one year on the licence and twelve years of adverse possession), the transfer would have been effected without the intervention of lawyers and without the payment of lawyers' fees.

Lessee's Installation of Bath

If a tenant with a three years lease puts in a bath without letting the landlord know anything about it, can the tenant remove the bath at the end of his tenancy when he leaves the house?

The answer to your question is: 'Yes, provided that the tenant has no intention of affixing the bath for the permanent benefit and equipment of the property.' The bath, though attached to the water-pipes remains the tenant's personal chattel and does not become his landlord's fixture; and this is so whether or not the landlord is aware of the installation. The landlord can require the tenant to make good such damage to the property as is caused by the installation and removal of the bath, but cannot claim it as a fixture.

Collapse of Building on Highway – Public Liability

Our Local Churchyard is separated from quite a busy road by a wall about 6 ft high. This wall is now showing a considerable bulge on the side towards the road. Should part of this brickwork give way and either land on a pedestrian or fall into the roadway causing an obstruction who would be liable? I had an idea that if the Parochial Church Council consider it a possible danger it would be up to them to take action, but I am not sure of this and the Council appear to be disregarding it.

The answer to your question is, in such a contingency as you have imagined your Parochial Church Council would be under liability to compensate a sufferer.

Television Licences

I have a licence for my radio and television set. Does my resident housekeeper require one for her set, which at present she rents from a local dealer?

The radio and television licence which you have covers your whole household, which means that your housekeeper does not need another licence for her hired set even if the set is hired in her name. You could have as many sets in the house as you like on the one licence. If your housekeeper lived in a self-contained flat in the house, then she would require another licence.

Lord of the Manor

Could you tell me how it is possible to find out who is the Lord of a specified manor?

The authority you require is the Manorial Register, Historical Manuscripts Commission, Quality House, Quality Court, Chancery Lane, London W.C.2.

Lords of the Manor

What is the origin of Lords of the Manorships?

Manors were lands granted to tenants, generally known as Lords of the Manor, before the Statute, *Quia emptores* (1290). A Manor usually included the lord's demesne with his residence and the waste lands of the manor. It also included lands held of the lord by his freehold tenants who did suit at the court baron of the lord. A manor might include lands held of the manor by copy of court roll, but these were not necessarily part of a manor. If there were not at least two freehold tenants the manor ceased to have a living existence, but it could be a manor by repute – Law of Land, Theobald (St. Catherine's Press, 1929). The customs and law relating to manors and manorial rights are residual survivals for the most part of an older order of society, but they are nonetheless operative at the present day. They relate mostly to the use and preservation of the waste land or common of the manor and touch upon many matters of sporting interest, relating to hunting, shooting, fishing, fowling, etc.

Manor Boundaries

Although most of the rights and incidents of a manor were swept away by the legislation of 1925 a few advantages still remain. In this connection could you tell me please if the geographical boundaries of a manor are conterminous with those of (a) the civil parish or (b) the ecclesiastical parish or, for lack of evidence, is there any prima facie presumption as to the boundaries?

We have contacted the Secretary of the Historical Manuscripts Commission who has replied to your query as follows:

'The boundaries of a Manor are not conterminous with those of either the civil or the ecclesiastical parish, and no prima facie presumption can be made, as the boundaries are dependent upon local conditions.'

Motor Mowing Machine – Licensing

My enquiry concerns the definition of an agricultural or mowing machine for the purposes of registration.

I have a self-propelled pedestrian-controlled Hayter mowing machine. The drive to the cutting blades is by V-belt. I have an electric generator which can be mounted on the machine, and is used to provide electricity for a hedge trimmer and chain saw. When the generator is in use the grass cutter cannot be used and vice versa.

My land is crossed by a public road, and during the winter months the machine is used for hedge trimming, etc, and not for grass cutting; furthermore, the grass verges of the road are cut by the council, and so my only interest in taking the machine off my land is when it is not a mowing machine. It is not used for any haulage.

My man is worried because the machine is unregistered and unlicensed. I cannot decide from Form VE5 whether it is in fact necessary for the machine to be licensed. If a licence be required, is it because the road has to be crossed, or because the machine is used on the verge? Could I, for instance, drive the machine over the road in a van, and then unload it on to the verge in order to trim the hedges?

The machine has no brakes and no reverse gear.

This fulfils one condition only of the two conditions requisite to make necessary its registration and licensing under the Vehicles (Excise) Act, 1962: being propelled by its own power it is, though pedestrian controlled, a 'mechanically propelled vehicle'. Being used, however, solely for purposes on your private estate and, when occasion requires it, transferred in a van and not on its own wheels along the public path, it does not fulfil the second condition: it is not 'used on public roads in Great Britain'.

Used in the way described in your letter, therefore, no need exists to register and license the machine.

Picking Wild Mushrooms

Can I take any action against villagers coming onto my land to mushroom?

If I find someone with picked mushrooms on. my land can I confiscate them?

What happens if my son goes onto my land which is let to a tenant for the pur-

pose of picking mushrooms?

The law in respect of picking wild (as distinct from cultivated) mushrooms was thus stated in the Queen's Bench case of 1887 (*Gardner v Mansbridge*): 'it is no offence to take mushrooms, blackberries, primroses, or wild plants of any kind, or to trespass to find them.' It is, however a civil wrong to trespass and actual damages can be recovered either in the County Court or the High Court by a civil as distinct from a criminal action.

Applying this to your specific questions: (1) the only action (which is in practice worthless) that you can take against a person picking uncultivated mushrooms in a meadow is a civil action for trespass; you cannot take the mushrooms from him, since they become his property when he severed them from the realty, and you could in the absence of malicious damage get only a nominal award on account of trespass. (2) Your tenant farmer would have the same right of action; for an entry unsanctioned by him, of your son into his meadow would be trespass.

One way of protecting your rights. is to put down mushroom spawn, whereupon you can claim that they are cultivated. Notices to this effect can then be erected.

Name – Changes of – 1

When a person succeeds to an Estate, he (or she) has often to change one's surname; many wills stipulate that the heir must do this. How is it done? Has the change to be registered or advertised?

Have one's title deeds, share certificates, and birth and marriage particulars with Somerset House, etc., to be changed? Has a solicitor to be employed?

Yes: a gift by will may be subject to a condition that the intended donee shall change his or her surname. Ordinarily, one may change his name without any formality; it is enough for legal purposes that evidence of identity (as by advertisement in a local newspaper) is available. When, however, the change is in order to make the gift by will effective, formality is requisite.

The acceptable formality is a deed poll executed by the donee, and this serves for all purposes, no change being needed in other legal documents relating to the donee (though to save trouble of reference an endorsement on a document of the change is made).

The deed poll is your announcement to this effect: 'Know all by this deed signed, sealed and delivered by me on this 27th day of March, 1971, that I hitherto known as John Smith have changed my name to Tom Jones and desire so to be called henceforth.' The signing is in both new and old names, 'signed in my old name John Smith and in my new name Tom Jones'. The sealing can be taken for granted. The delivery will be to the Filing Department of the Supreme Court in the Strand, where your cost will be £2, and you will also advertise the change in the *London Gazette*.

You can do all this yourself.

Name – Changes of – 2

I would refer to your reply to member's letter, published in the May, 1971, issue of our magazine, which is misleading in respect of change of name by deed poll.

The conditions of enrolment laid down in the Enrolment of Deeds Poll (Change of Name) Regulations, 1949, made by the M.R. under the J.A., S.218, as amended from 20 March, 1951, and on the 27 October, 1969, must be complied with.

Briefly as follows: The applicant must be a British subject and the manner of citizenship described. A woman must be described by the status she has. An applicant must produce, as proof of British Nationality or of citizenship of the U.K. and Colonies, documentary evidence to that effect, and in the case of a woman, her certificate of marriage with, if necessary, the written consent of her husband witnessed by a solicitor upon the Deed Poll. A widow must produce her certificate of marriage and certificate of death of her deceased husband. A divorcee (feme-sole) must produce her certificate of marriage to her former husband and the decree absolute of divorce.

The deed poll and the required certificates above must be exhibited to a statutory declaration by a British subject who is a householder resident in U.K. who has known the applicant for not less than 10 years. The declaration must cover and include these two points: Subsequently after enrolment, the deed poll must be advertised in the *London Gazette* and a copy of the *Gazette* containing the advertisement must be produced when the deed is taken up.

The case of minors is more deeply involved!

The enrolment of a duly executed deed poll is effected by the Chief Clerk, Filing and Record Department, Room 81, Royal Court of Justice, London, W.C.2.

The cost at present is approximately £4.00 in addition to the revenue fee of 50p and solicitor's charges.

A solicitor must be employed, or consulted as to the form and preparation of a deed poll suitable to the requirements of the individual.

I have written with the object of being helpful as I tried to use the information given by your legal adviser in all good faith without success.

National Insurance – Employer's Contribution

When one employs a part-time gardener who also works for others, who pays the NH stamps?

The responsibility for paying the contribution in respect of a part-time worker is as follows, the worker being employed by more than one during the week:

(*a*) The employer having the services for the longest period is responsible for the full contribution.

(*b*) Where there is equality in the periods the employer during the first period in the week is responsible for the full contributions.

In either alternative he makes his own arrangements for collecting a due proportion from the other employers.

Nationality of Child

Can you tell me of what nationality is a child born of foreign parents working in this country and domiciled here for over two years? The child of course was born in this country. I have been told it is of dual nationality and that the parents can 'opt' for it to be either their own nationality or British.

You are quite right in assuming that it has dual nationality. It is the place of birth which counts for Britain. The child however must declare itself one way or the other when it comes of age.

Nuisance from – Agricultural Buildings

About 2–3 years ago two large buildings for battery hens were erected next door to the house adjoining mine, these buildings are roughly 50 yds. from my house, and I now notice foundations are being prepared for a further battery hen 'factory'. I have taken the matter up with the Local Council to endeavour to stop the erection of the buildings, but they assure me that as they are agricultural buildings they are powerless to act.

The nuisance from these 'factories' is becoming quite unbearable, what with polluted air coming from 'the buildings, the attraction of rats and flies, and the continual noise night and day, from, I presume, an electric ventilating fan, it is like living near a factory.

I understand that Civil Action is the only method one can take to remedy this nuisance. Can you advise me about this?

This is indeed a problem which many people are now facing but cases have been fought about it. Sometimes when the nuisance is extreme, steps have been taken, but the Courts are always most reluctant to interfere with a person's lawful activities and the keeping of a chicken farm is one such activity. The law does expect that neighbours by their mutual forbearance will lessen this discomfort as much as possible. Would it not be best to tell the factory owner that you are thinking of going to Court unless he does something to mitigate the smell etc. There is a new substance on the market called 'Allamask' which is an odour control compound manufactured by May & Baker Ltd, Dagenham, Essex. He might be prepared to try it.

Your action would be, not in the Bench of magistrates, but either in the High Court or the County Court; and to succeed you would have the heavy task of satisfying the Court:

(a) that the 'factory' activity was conducted in a manner that showed not the least consideration for his neighbours ;

(b) that the foul smell escaping could be mitigated and that other chicken farms were conducted without such an escape, and

(c) that the 'factory' was making upon the neighbours a wholly unreasonable demand for their tolerance. You might, at considerable cost to yourself, succeed in doing this.

At the least indication of your rights in these matters being prejudiced you should notify the offenders that, failing a cessation of the nuisance to your ground, you will apply to the Court for an injunction to restrain the nuisance.

Nuisance – Cars

We live in a private close (5 bungalows). One owner appears to have a catering business, combined with guests; which involves an average six cars a day including delivery vans. This business has grown out of proportion as there is no parking space.

Could you advise on the legal position?

The remedy for you and the other residents aggrieved by this is given by the Town and Country Planning Act, 1962. To develop a private residence into a guest-house is a 'material change of use': this being so planning permission is needed for the change and your letter suggests that no such permission has been given. You should call the attention of the area Planning Office to what is taking place.

Nuisance – Noise of Tractors

I should be most grateful if you could tell me if there are any steps I can take to stop a local farmer from using his tractor full out all day. The noise here when the wind is this way is abominable and when he had it going night and day it was impossible to sleep. I complained to him and he now turns it off from 10.30 p.m. to 7 a.m.

The law does provide its remedy when noise, arising from activities on adjoining land, is such as interferes with the comfort and convenience of the house.

The degree of interference must, however, be greater than is reasonable to expect the sufferer to tolerate. The remedy is to obtain, either from the County Court or the High Court, an injunction requiring the creator of the nuisance either to end or to mitigate it.

An injunction is not lightly granted: when the noise arises from lawful activities, the law expects toleration in the absence of aggravated and unnecessary incidents, such incidents would indicate the indifference of the farmer to the effect of the noise on his neighbours. The fact that the farmer has now stopped his tractor from 10.30 to 7 a.m. may be enough for the Court but if he should start it again at night you might well have a case.

Possibly if you mention to the farmer that you are seeking an Injunction he might be willing to do something further to stop the noise being such a nuisance.

Nuisance – Noise

I shall be obliged if you will kindly advise me regarding the law concerning the use near residential property of:

(1) Automatic firing bird-scaring guns used for crop protection, and (2) unsilenced tractors.

In each case what level of noise is legal and what would constitute a nuisance?

The Noise Abatement Act, 1960, now gives help to a resident aggrieved by the distressing noise of bird-scaring guns and other agricultural implements used nearby. The Act does not alter the definition of 'nuisance': that is still an interference with the comfort and convenience of your home as you cannot reasonably be required to tolerate. The Act makes your procedure easier and less expensive. If you and at least two other residents, suffering as you do by the serious detraction from your comfort, can satisfy the local authority that the noise amounts to a nuisance, the Act says that the 'nuisance' is a 'statutory nuisance' in respect of which the local authority will serve an 'abatement notice' upon the creator of the nuisance; and, if the 'abatement notice' is not complied with, the justices will issue a 'nuisance order' to be obeyed under penalty.

We add that the Act makes it a good

defence in that the user of the obnoxious implement 'has taken the best practical means for preventing and for counteracting the effect of his use. The burden of proof would be heavy for the tractor without a silencer.

We hope that you will be able to prompt your local authority to action.

Nuisance – from Damage in Respect of Private Quarry

There is a large quarry established some 12 years ago adjacent to my land and the vibrations from the underground blasting are causing damage to my house and buildings. Cracks have appeared and are gradually becoming wider in the walls of my house, shippon and my employee's cottage.

As the damage has affected the value of my property and will cost a considerable sum to remedy am I entitled to compensation and if so should I consult a Land Agent or a Solicitor to make my claim?

Escape of vibrations from an occupier's land is a nuisance when the escape occasions damage to adjoining property beyond what reasonable people can be expected to tolerate ; and it is quite clear that such nuisance exists here. Most likely the quarry operators will be well aware of their legal liability for the damage incident to their working of the quarry. You may, therefore, avoid a good deal of trouble by going yourself to the managing director in order to put your claim ; if he is sensible he will accept liability without obliging you to go to law, or to bring in outsiders.

If there is hesitation about accepting liability, instruct your solicitor.

Nuisance – Affecting Water Supply

A very old property exists at a higher level, across the main road, from the land on which my house is built.

At a point along the road-side boundary, a continuous trickle of clear water flows over the land from a drain which passes under the road—this flow of water has been used to construct an ornamental water garden as it flows through my property. While usually this water is quite clear, an occasional trace of soap suds has been noticed—presumably from the kitchen sink of the above mentioned house.

Never during the last 20 years, has there been any trace of sewage effluent in either watercourse.

There is now a possibility of the old house being renovated and a problem of sewage disposal therefrom arises. It is not unlikely that they will desire to turn the sewage effluent into the brook course with very objectionable results for me.

Please advise me if I could—and how —effectively protest and should such be either contemplated or attempted.

Concerning the creation of a nuisance, we advise you that the law gives you ample protection against the possibilities incident to the renovation of the house at the higher level.

You are entitled to protection from any activities, whether of the highway authority or of the owners of the house, whereby more water is precipitated upon your ground than would flow upon it apart from those activities. And, in particular, you are entitled to have the water, used by you in the garden, reach you unpolluted.

Party Fence

I wonder if you could advise on the following problem please.
1 As shown in the deeds, the dividing fence belongs to our neighbour. The neighbour and ourselves are discussing taking down the present fence and replacing it with a party fence.
2 Can you please suggest what documentary action is necessary to avoid complications should the present neighbour or ourselves move elsewhere?
3 For example, would it be necessary to alter the deeds or would a receipt suffice?

To replace the fence by a party fence does not involve any transfer of ownership of land. A note, therefore, to this effect would express your intention and provide evidence in the event of future questioning:

The under-signed, by an agreement dated as below, have agreed that the fence owned by the first signatory shall be replaced by a party fence maintainable at their joint expense.

Signed this day.........A. B.
    ,,   ,,   ,, ...D. C.

A copy of the note attached to each deed of conveyance would preserve the evidence of ownership.

Motoring Pheasants – 1

We have been asked a question as to the position should a motor-car hit a pheasant on a public highway, kill it, the driver pick it up, put it into the boot of his car and drive away, or what happens if a following car driver picks up the bird.

From general practice we think that this in one case would, and in the other would not, be a question of larceny, but the writer has in mind that within the last few years he has seen a report of some case, presumably in the Magistrates Courts, which would not be reported in the usual Law Reports, dealing with this particular subject rather fully, and we shall be obliged if you can let us know whether you have any information on this particular subject or could refer us to any publication where this report might appear.

We are unable to trace a report that lends any support to the suggestion that, in either of the two suppositions posed by you, a conviction for larceny is possible. For the statutory definition of larceny is 'without the consent of the owner, fraudulently and without a claim of right made in good faith, taking and carrying away anything capable of being stolen with intent, at the time of such taking, permanently to deprive the owner therof' (Larceny Act, 1916).

A pheasant on the public highway is no one's property until reduced into possession; until so reduced it is not 'capable of being stolen,' since it has no owner entitled to make a charge of larceny. He that picks up the pheasant

killed by the car, whether by the driver of the killing car or another, becomes its owner by 'finding.'

Motoring Pheasants – 2

I submit that your legal adviser has misstated the law, and that his statement could have mischievous results. I am not myself a legal authority, but have much trouble from poachers as a landowner; and I am advised that the courts have held that where a road is ' classified' it does not belong to the owner of the land even if he owns both sides; but that where the road is 'unclassified' an owner who owns the land on both sides of the road also owns the land under the road. The public only have the right of way at all times on or over the road for lawful purposes, whether the public authority maintains it or not.

Thus the owner retains the sporting rights on and over the road with its hedges, and a pheasant on the road, whether alive or dead, remains technically on his property and is his to 'take.'

Similarly, pheasants' nests along the roadside belong to the owner of the sporting, if he owns the hedge.

In any case under Section 23 of the 1831 Act a person commits an offence if he 'takes' or 'kills' game without a licence—apart from shooting it—so the onus would be on the person in possession to show why he had killed it. If he did not have a licence he would not be entitled to 'take' it away.

The restriction on discharging firearms on, or near a road, is an important ancillary point.

A wild bird, when alive and free, is no one's property, wherever it is; its body, when killed by a car on the public road, is the property of him that takes possession.

Pheasant Ownership

I am rearing pheasants, and before putting them to cover they are ringed on the leg. What is the law about them wandering on to my neighbour's land and being shot? Can I stop him shooting them? Can I claim the bird after it is shot? Can I go on his land to drive them home?

The answer to your query is 'No' in every case. The fact that you have ringed your pheasants makes no difference: it still remains a wild bird and the property of whosoever's land it is on.

Photographic Rights

The house from which I write is scheduled as one of historical interest because a well-known Cornish painter was born here. Frequently passers-by ask permission to photograph it. One such person photographed it last year with her daughter standing in the doorway. I now find that the "Western Morning News" has reproduced this in colour on its 1969 Calendar. I had no notification or request for permission that they would do this, nor did I greatly object. I wrote and asked them if I could buy a dozen copies at a discount. They replied briefly that they did not supply private buyers, and I should place my order at the full price with a stationer.

Rather incensed at this attitude, I reminded them that they had made use of my house for their profit without my permission, and that I had to explain to my friends who the strange woman on my doorstep was. They ignored this letter. Have I any legal remedy?

I understand your resentment at the churlish manner in which the publishers of the photograph answered your request for copies. You were entitled, at the least, to a courteous explanation, and you have my sympathy, the more so since you have no legal redress in the matter.

The position is this: the scheduling of the house as of historic interest has added to its popularity as a subject for photography. In respect of that the one control you have is that, if you choose to do so, you can forbid access to your land for the purpose of taking a photograph or for posing to be taken. You could, for instance, have told the girl

not to pose in your doorway. Once taken, however, the copyright in the photograph belongs to the taker or to his employer for taking. He it is that can sell copies, and he may adopt such system as he thinks best for the selling; the newspaper, doubtless, has agreements with retailers not to sell by retail itself. It is a little surprising that no exception was made in selling it to you as owner of the house; but, evidently, adherence to the agreement seemed to be the preferable course. You have no redress at law against any of the parties, photographer or publishers; nor, I am sorry to add, have you any redress at law for being now and then quizzed about the girl, posing with something of a proprietary air in the doorway.

Fish Poachers – Legal Powers Against

What am I entitled to do legally about poaching of my private waters?

(1) The powers are given, by Sections 24 and 25 of the Larceny Act, 1916, and may be exercised by the owner (i.e., of the fishery) or his servant or other person authorised by him: no difference is made. They may 'demand from the offender (i.e., the unauthorised fisher in private water) any rod, line, hook, net or other implement for taking or destroying fish which are then in his possession, and on his refusal to deliver them may seize and take them from him for the use of the owner.'

The taking or delivering of the implements, however, exempts the offender (i.e., the poacher) if angling between the first hour before daylight and the last hour after daylight from being sued for damages and from having to pay a penalty for poaching.

(2) For night poaching there is this difference: anyone, not alone those enumerated above, may arrest without warrant and forthwith take him before a neighbouring justice of the peace.

(3) The powers remain the same though the poacher is on a public highway or on a bridge over the private fishing while angling: he that uses the public highway for a purpose wholly alien to the right of passage is a trespasser.

(4) The cessation of actual angling on the approach of a bailiff or other authorised person will not prevent the exercise of the powers.

(5) One thing that the protectors of the fishing may not do is to take from the poacher any fish that he has caught. The fish in a running stream belong to no one; they become the property of the first that catches them.

Possession – Rights of

A friend has been allowed to occupy the old groom's quarters in the stables, has improved them structurally, and has now resided there for some 19 years—at no time has anything been put in writing, nor has money changed hands. The rates have been covered in the rates on the house, as also water and electricity consumed.

Do you consider the friend has, or has not, a legal right to retain possession—and if so under what legal provision?

If so, how can this be established?

If not, what action should be taken to regain possession?

The status of your friend, as occupier free from rent of the premises, has throughout the period been that of licensee: the fact that the licensor continued to pay the rates upon the premises indicates that control still rested with him. There could, therefore, be no accord to your friend of a squatter's right of ownership. The licence, therefore, may, despite its length, be revoked by the licensor or his successor.

The answer to your question is, therefore, this: your friend is in equity probably entitled to a reasonable notice, possibly also to compensation for improvements: but, if such reasonable notice is given of revocation of the licence, his further occupation will be a trespass.

Pylon – Siting

Could you advise me on a matter of a notice I have received (verbally) from CEGB? They intend to take HT electricity lines on pylons across a corner of my forestry land. This may involve destruction of a planted area and loss of amenity. I do not think I can resist the proposal but wish to get best terms, including siting of pylons so that they are not in my view from my house. I am away in Wales until end of next week, but following my return the CEGB representative intends to ask me for an appointment to meet on my land.

You will know that the Area Electricity Board is one of the swarm of administrative bodies recently created in order to execute Parliament's policy with the least curtailment of the individual's freedom to deal as he please with himself and his property. That is why the Electricity Act 1959 enjoins, when it is necessary to place pylons on an owner's land, in Section 28 enjoins the giving of 28 days' notice of entry upon the land for the purpose of exploration and survey. The meeting that the Board's representative seeks is to ascertain your views and, if at all possible, to arrange the site of the pylons as you would have it. You cannot effectively resist the Board's proposals; but you may with confidence expect that your wishes will be satisfied if reasonably practicable. We think that the interview will leave you well satisfied.

Rating – Agreement on

A tenant farmer entered into an agreement with the local council under section 11 (2) and 11 (3) of the Rating Act, 1925, whereby he paid rates on his cottages whether empty or not and obtained a 10% discount on them. The farmer died in August 1966 and his executors paid the rates under the agreement up to March 1967 and the farm was then taken over by another farmer. The Council says that the new farmer must carry on with the agreement until such time as he gives notice to terminate it given before the end of the rating period. Unfortunately the new farmer did not know of the agreement until after the end of a rating period, and the Council will require nearly two years' notice to terminate. I replied informing the Council that there were various law cases which have decided that the death of a person automatically cancels an agreement, except where the executors are liable.

Can I object to the Council's proposals?

Section 11 of the Rating Act, 1925, has

now been codified under the General Rate Act, 1967, section 56, sub-section 3. This states, as you are probably aware, that notwithstanding a change of ownership, an agreement shall continue in force until determined by notice and shall continue to be binding upon the new owner. Whilst the Act does not specifically mention a change of ownership through death, a contract is not necessarily dissolved by death of either of the parties of it.

We doubt whether you will therefore succeed in your objections but it is worth trying. If the Council stick to their guns, notice should be given to the Council in due time.

Agricultural Rating

Some months ago after buying this house I was able to buy the adjoining field of 6¾ acres. I have started a small spinney in about ¼ acre taken off the field. The field is recorded by the Agricultural Census branch as No 45/33/47 on the parish list and I make agricultural returns. I also sell a little produce from my garden. I feel this house should therefore be rated as agricultural. May I please have your observation on this?

I do not think you can claim that the house should be rated as an agricultural hereditament because the adjoining land is agricultural. My own house is not rated as an agricultural dwelling although the four acres that go with it are agricultural and I make returns to the Ministry on them. To be classed as agricultural you must be farming or market gardening more fully to get the designation changed.

Rating Assessment – 1

I have recently sold a portion of land which was part of the garden belonging to a cottage let to a tenant. The frontage of the part sold was 80 ft. and fetched £3,500.

I applied to the District Valuer for a reduction in the R.V.

His reply was: 'The garden land taken

from this cottage to which you refer did not, in my view, add anything to the value and was not reflected in the assessment so that, now it has gone, nothing can be deducted.'

I have always understood that road frontage was taken into account in assessing the R.V. of a property. Must I accept as fact that the original frontage was not so reflected?

The basis for assessment is the rental for which you could let the property. The question, therefore, is has the sale of part of the frontage increased or decreased the hypothetical rent which could be obtained? If you think the rent for your property would be decreased then you should go back to the Valuation Officer and say so (frontage really doesn't come into it).

Rating Assessment – 2

The rates on my house have been increased. The amount is small and unimportant but, at the same time, I feel it quite unjustified on the grounds that I have only improved the property from the standpoint of it being below standard originally, ie, I have brought it up to the standard which it should have been in the first place. Could you advise me: (a) Whether I have a case? (b) If so, are these the sort of grounds on which I have any hope of succeeding?

The contention is easily understandable, that one is not expected by his own exertions to add to the impositions thrust upon him by way of tax, and that it is inequitable to require it of him. The law in respect of rating assessment, however, does so without the least compunction: if (whether by your own work or by paying another) you have brought your house into line with more highly rated houses in your area, the valuation officer is correct in bringing your rating assessment in line. Your chance of success in an appeal to your local valuation court is negligible, and you would avoid futile trouble by withdrawing your objection. Certainly, if you did achieve a temporary success, it would vanish when the valuation officer, under S.72 of the General Rates Act 1967 took the appeal to the Lands Tribunal.

For the one thing that matters is that you have added to the measuring rod of rateability: you have added to 'the rent at which the hereditament might reasonably be expected to let'.

Rebuilding in the Green Belt – Rights

I have heard rumours that if there is a cottage or house in the Green Belt, which has the mains water supply, it largely or entirely entitles the owner to alter or pull down and rebuild a new house. Is this correct please?

What you have heard is correct: there is no need to seek permission, under the Town and Country Planning Acts, to alter or rebuild an existing house in the Green Belt.

The position is this:

(1) Under the Acts permission is requisite for 'development,' and there is no development unless the land concerned is to be used for a purpose different from the existing purpose.

(2) Under the Town and Country Planning (General Development) Order, 1963, you have this specified right in respect of the house; 'The enlargement, improvement or other alteration of a dwelling-house so long as the cubic content of the original dwellinghouse (as ascertained by external measurement) is not exceeded by more than 1,750 cubic ft. or 1·10th, whichever is the greater, subject to a maximum of 40,000 cubic ft.' The right is independent of water supply.

Reburial

My son was killed whilst serving in the army and buried at Weston-super-Mare which was his wife's home town. She has now remarried and moved elsewhere and we would like to move my son's body to our own village grave-yard where there is a family grave. The widow has given her permission I might say. How can we accomplish this?

The Secretary of State at the Home Office is the authority to whom you must apply.

Removal of Refuse etc.

We have been told that our dustbins will not be emptied unless put outside the gates when the refuse van comes each week to our village. This is very inconvenient. Can we make the Council change their minds?

We are sorry to tell you that you will be obliged to reconcile yourself to a compliance with the Council's request. For Section 72 of the Public Health Act, 1936, has this among other provisions: 'A local authority who . . . have undertaken the removal of house refuse may make bye-laws (a) imposing on the occupiers of premises duties in connection with the removal in order to facilitate the work which the authority have undertaken.' Placing the rubbish on the main road comes within the scope of this provision.

Rent Book – Where got

Could you please let me have a form of agreement to cover a six-month furnished tenancy of a flat and garage? I should be grateful to know where an approved rent book may be obtained and whether the tenant requires any receipt for his payments of rent other than an entry in the rent book.

We suggest that you buy a rent book from the Solicitors' Law Stationery Society Ltd., Publishing Department, Oyez House, Breams Buildings, London, E.C.4 and we think this should be sufficient. I am afraid we do not have standard forms of agreement for letting a furnished flat. Our agreement for a country cottage is not suitable, but the Solicitors' Law Stationery Society sell what you need.

Repairs – Claim for Expense of

I recently sold my house, which is over 100 years old. The purchaser after he had occupied it a week or two, found woodworm in the floor-boards of several rooms and is claiming from me—though his solicitor the expense of repair—£105.

He bought the house with borrowed money, probably through a building society and the house was surveyed prior to the sale and appeared satisfactory although the valuation of the house following this examination was £2,000 less than that of the estate agent. I was not asked if there was any woodworm in the house as I had seen no evidence of this, possibly because it was found underneath carpet and linoleum that had been down some years. The purchaser had ample opportunity to take up lino and carpets to see for himself prior to the sale.

My own solicitor takes the view that I am liable to pay the expense on the ground that this is a latent and not a patent defect.

If this is correct I see no end to this kind of blackmail as further investigation may continue to find latent defects indefinitely.

We ask you to dismiss from your mind any anxiety over the claim made against you, and to decline payment. There is, indeed, a duty upon the vendor of a house to disclose latent material defects *in his tithe* and also latent defects *so far as known to him in the physical state of the house.* But *caveat emptor* applies in full force to the buyer of a house; and, after completion, he cannot sustain a claim for defects that should have come to light on a competent survey by himself or his professional surveyor; and one imperative question that a competent surveyor puts to himself is whether woodworm is present. It is *not,* as your solicitor says, a latent defect; for removal of the floor covering to a reasonable extent would have revealed it, and *Yandall v Sutton* (1922) would apply. That is the defect would be visible to the eye; it comes into the category of protest defects.

Nor would your knowledge of the presence have imposed a duty of disclosure upon you, unless you had (as put in one case) 'industriously concealed' it. Thus in *Kenyon v Lord Cadogan,* (1851), it was held that no action would lie against B who had let A an unfurnished house without disclosing that it was in a ruinous state.

Reservoirs

You recently published an article on reservoirs for trout fishing. I would like to mention one important point not correct in the article, and that concerns the Reservoirs (Safety Provisions) Act, 1930. This Act states that any reservoir designed to hold more than 5,000,000 gallons of water above the natural ground level, must be designed and the construction supervised, only by an engineer appointed to a panel of engineers, by the Home Secretary. Also, any such reservoir above this capacity has to be inspected by an engineer at least every ten years.

Riding Road Sense

When riding one horse and leading another it is, I think, customary to ride on the right side of the road, when the lead horse is on your off side, and on the left when the lead horse is on your near side.

It is correct that the led horse should be on the near side and that the rider should be on the left of the road.
British Horse Society.

Rights of Way

What is the legal position over a Right of Way?

A right of way is a right of passage only. It may either be enjoyed by the public at large or be restricted to private individuals: and the right varies in extent. That famous legal writer of ancient days, Sir E. Coke, classified 'way' as being of three kinds—and the classification still holds good—thus: 'There are three kinds of wayes whereof you shall reade in our ancient bookes; First a footway . . . and this was the first packe and prime way, because it is both a footway, which was the first or prime way, and a pack or drift way also. The third is via aditus, which contains the other two, and also a cartway" . . . which he explains may include a way for cattle and may either be the King's highway for all men or between neighbours and neighbours. (As to the creation of private and public rights of way, see 'Law of Highways.')

It is generally presumed that a right of carriageway or cartway includes a right of footway, driftway and bridleway, and that a right of driftway or bridleway alone, covers a right of footway but not a carriageway or cartway. Sometimes a right of way is granted for light carts only or for cattle only: and a right of cartway does not necessarily include a way for cattle. All these distinctions have to be maintained by evidence as to grant or user.

Ownership of land adjoining a highway carries with it the right of the owner to access to the highway from any part of his land adjoining it. This is a private right, wholly distinct from his right as a member of the public to use the highway.

One tenant cannot acquire a right of way by user over the holding of another tenant under the same landlord, however long he may have been permitted to use such way; and where a man has a right of way to reach one particular piece of land, this does not give him the right to use it to reach other pieces.

Though a right of way may be acquired by evidence of use the claim may be defeated by proof that the user was not of right but by permission of the owner, or that the owner resisted and interrupted such user. The privilege of using a path can be controlled by the grantor requiring from the grantee a written acknowledgement clearly stating the extent of the grant and agreeing to a normal periodical payment therefore.

There is no common law liability on the grantor's part either to construct or repair the roadway where a right of way exists: but the person entitled to use it has the right to enter upon the grantor's land and make the roadway effective in such a manner as is reasonably necessary to enable him to enjoy it to the extent to which he is entitled and to repair it from time to time. On the other hand, there may be an express obligation to repair, resting either upon the grantor or upon the grantee.

Wrongful interference with a right of way is an actionable nuisance. (See 'Law of Nuisance.')

Right of way acquired by user may be lost by non-users but the law prescribes no length of time by which loss can be brought about: it being a matter of evidence of intention and possible also of discontinuance in fact of dispute.

Right of Way – Excessive User of

I would be grateful if you would inform me as to what Agricultural Rights mean in relation to a drive that gives access to a neighbour's field.

In my particular case the mode of access to my neighbour's field passes along my drive and in front of my house. In the past the rights have only been invoked to permit the passage of cattle and the occasional tractor concerned in the maintenance of the field. Now I find that the field has been let to the owner of a riding school, and this involves the passage twice daily in front of my house of two horses and the assistant pupils who come to collect them and later in the day return them to the field.

This means, in effect, that people who are complete strangers to us pass through our garden twice daily, and we have been disturbed in the late evening by the arrival of the horses' owner in his van.

Do the above facts in your opinion constitute a fair interpretation of Agricultural Rights? Would I be justified in asking my neighbour to have the horses removed?

The rights about which you inquire are not agricultural rights but rights arising out of the existence along your drive of a 'right of way.' Your predecessor in the ownership of your property is deemed to have granted a limited power of passage to the owner of the field; and in your instance the limitation, whether expressed or implied, would certainly be 'in order to use the field for farming purposes.'

You have a right, therefore, to object to the different and more extensive right of passage 'in order to use the field as a riding school.' And—as *Milner's Safe Co. Ltd. v. Great Northern and City Railway Co., 1907*, Chancery, illustrates —he that makes an excessive use of a right of way is a trespasser and may be restrained by injunction from the excessive use.

Probably you will be able to make an arrangement satisfactory to yourself without having recourse to the cumbersome and expensive machinery of a legal action.

Rights of Way – Paths to Sea

I have recently purchased a property on the Isle of Skye through which runs a road to the sea. This is described in my title deeds as a path which can only be made use of by my neighbour, a farmer, for moving his cattle through my property to his fields or for driving a tractor and farm produce, e.g., hay, grain, etc., over.

The public have, however, found this path and now regularly use it to drive cars to the beach. They are not discouraged by the farmer from camping in his field so reached next to the beach. How can I protect myself from the public using this path which passes by my back door and across the stable yard as I do not wish a 'regular user' to be set up? There is no specific agreement concerning the upkeep of the road.

In Scotland the matter of rights of way are always difficult as the Public Rights are always difficult to determine. However, legally, it is quite clear that no right of way exists unless the public have enjoyed 40 years of uninterrupted use. It is however unlikely that this is so in your particular case, and from a practical point of view, it would seem that the solution for you would be to put a gate on the path and provide the farmer with a key for the padlock. The public would then have to prove that the 'right of way' was in existence, and our adviser feels that this would then make it almost impossible for them to prove. There is a Right of Way Society who are meant to have an up-to-date list of 'rights of way,' but if there is nothing in your title which states this, it would seem that the 'right of way' is not established, and therefore, you have nothing to fear.

A new 'right of way' can, of course, be dedicated at any time by the owner of land in question, but this would probably appear in the titles. Where a way has been enjoyed as of right and without interruption for forty years, such way shall be deemed exclusively to have been dedicated, unless there is evidence that there was no intention during that period to dedicate the way. A notice by the owner of the land over which the way passes, inconsistent with dedication, placed in such a manner as to be visible to those using the road, is sufficient evidence to negative any intention. If the notice is torn down or defaced, the landowner can protect his interest by giving written notice to the local atuhority that the way is not dedicated to the public.

Rights of Way – Ploughing Up

I would be very pleased if you could help me. I have a small spinney, and to get to this I have a 12 ft. right of way (this is shown on my deeds) over land owned by a number of other people. One of these has ploughed up the right of way making it very difficult to get over with a motor vehicle.

Could you please answer the following questions?

1 Can the owner of the land plough up the right of way?
2 Can I fence the right of way?
3 What would be the position should I drive over and damage any crops planted on the right of way?

You will know that Section 119 of the Highways Act, 1959, gives to the occupier of agricultural land over which a public way crosses a right to plough the way together with the rest of the land. To exercise that right he must give the highway authority not less than seven days notice of his intention, and after the ploughing he must as soon as may be make good the surface of the path so as to make it reasonably convenient for the exercise of the public right of way. An easement such as yours of a private right of way cannot, unless there is some specific and very unusual provision in your deed of conveyance, be in a more privileged position than a public right of way.

The answer, therefore, to your questions are:

1 Yes: the occupier has a right to plough;
2 No: if you fenced so as to hinder ploughing, you would be trespassing; the occu-

pier would have a right to throw down your fences and could sue you for damages;

3 The occupier would be obliged to put up with any unavoidable damage to the crop as a result of the exercise of your right of way.

Riparian Rights – 1

Could you tell me the exact meaning of the term 'Riparian Rights'? Does it mean that those claiming these rights can fish in waters that do not belong to them?

Riparian Rights are the rights recognized by law of a landowner in respect of a natural stream flowing either through or alongside his land. When 'alongside' applies, he has the rights up to mid-stream. These natural rights include the exclusive right of fishing in the waters, and this enables him to licence others, whether members of an angling association or specified individuals, to fish in the waters. The right given by the licence carries with it a right of reasonable access to the waters.

The answers to your two questions are: (i) Apart from a licence, a riparian owner has no right to encroach upon another riparian owner's fishing right. (ii) With such licence he, as your letter puts it, 'can fish in waters that do not belong to him'.

It is not, you are probably aware, strictly accurate to speak of 'ownership' of waters; the riparian rights over the stream are enjoyed by both upper and lower riparian owners. A riparian owner has no property in the waters.

Riparian Rights – 2

Some time ago you printed an article by Lord Meston entitled 'Riparian Owners'. It is, perhaps, a tribute to the practical value of the CGA Magazine that I appear to be in precisely a situation dealt with in the article.

I own a cottage whose ground extends to the high water medium tide level of a tidal river. Soon after I bought the house I discovered that British Railways, whose ferry service runs from a pier near by, wanted to fill in the whole of the creek on which my land abutted for an extension to their then existing car park, to the extent of six acres. Strenuous local opposition reduced the extension to two acres, and it did not shut off my land from the main estuary.

In conveying the news of the reduced area to me, the local authority said that in granting the permission for the extension they had laid down numerous conditions . . . 'inter alia, that no further extension of the site will be permitted.'

Now, almost two years later to a day, the same authority will not confirm that they have no intention of permitting further extension—I have lost an opportunity to sell the house at a good price, since a would-be purchaser has withdrawn for this reason. The authority has answered my request for an explanation of this complete volte face, by saying, amongst other things:

'I confirm the content of my letter dated the 22 July 1969 which you have quoted as being correct and indeed at that time presented an accurate appraisal of the situation.

'You will, of course, appreciate that over a period of time situations can and indeed do, change. Circumstances show that a greater need for certain development may be established after an earlier permission has been granted restricting development to a certain area.

'Consequently, I must state that if an application to increase the size of the car park was received by this council, it would be considered upon its merits and the established need at the time the matter was under consideration but I do assure you that when the council's planning committee was considering any application which might be received for an extension of the car park, they would be advised of the content of my letter to you dated the 22 July 1969 and this would be taken into consideration when a decision was being given upon an application.'

I am endeavouring to find out if I have any remedy on this score.

You have, we are sorry to tell you, no remedy against the changed attitude of your area planning authority. For the condition imposed, when permission was given to British Railways to acquire the acres—the condition 'that no further extension of the site will be permitted'—is inept: the planning authority now realises that it means nothing and should not have been imposed. It purports to bind the successors of the authority and Parliament itself cannot limit the power of its successors. The Planning Act makes provision for change. The development plan of the area is to be reconsidered every five years. It is a prophesy of permissions likely to be granted and the permissions likely to be repressed; but the prophesy now and again is like the prophesies of the witches to Macbeth.

The letter you have now from the authority explains the position. If it should, at some remote period, be thought imperative to deprive you of access over your land to the river, you will be told that individual rights must be subordinate to public needs, but that you are entitled to full compensation for the deprivation. Perhaps your last purchaser was too diffident. The fact that compensation would be payable could point to an alternative site.

Our article on 'Riparian Rights' makes consultation with an 'expert' unnecessary: he would tell you that your consultation fee would be unproductive.

Riparian Right – Proposed Transfer of

There is a stream at the end of my garden and the adjoining owner has proven it is his stream. As he intends to develop his land he has offered the stream to me plus 1 ft. for £1 providing I am responsible for piping it if the local authority insists when my neighbour develops. Two questions:

(1) Am I reasonably entitled to ask for more than 1 ft. for care and maintenance?

(2) Will I become a riparian owner and therefore no authority can insist on piping?

The answer depends on which side of the stream is the foot of land you are being offered. If your garden is contiguous to the stream then you are already a riparian owner, with such owner's rights to draw water. There can be no proving by the adjoining owner that he owns the stream, for no one owns running water until it is impounded.

If the foot of land is on the other side of the stream, the transfer of that foot

to you ends any riparian rights of its former owner. He would, however, if he developed his remaining land as a housing estate, have saddled you with what might be a heavy liability in respect of the stream. For Section 262 of the Public Health Act, 1936, gives much power to local authorities to require culverting and other work when building operations are in progress.

The offer made to you, we are quite sure, calls for circumspection before accepting

Road Charges

The council are proposing to make up our rough lane and charge the various property owners, including myself, accordingly to their frontage. One of my neighbours has a large house on a corner site whose main and only entrance faces the road which lies along the top of our lane—his garden has a long frontage down the lane but no entrance, and therefore he never uses it, though, of course, it is a public highway.

The question is, is he liable to pay his share of the road charges? I understand the work is being held up because he refuses to pay.

We advise you that the owner of the corner house is unable to hold up the road-making beyond a limited period; he can within a month object to the proposed works on the ground (among others) that 'the provisional apportionment of charges is incorrect.' Then the authority applies to a magistrates court for the hearing and determination of the objection (Sections 7 and 8 of the Private Street Works Act, 1892). He will probably be held liable as a 'frontager' notwithstanding that no access from his 'front' exists to the road; though there may be some modification in that 'the greater or lesser degree of benefit to be derived by any premises from such works' may be taken into account. But frontage is the overriding consideration (e.g., expenses on one side of the street may be apportioned on owners of both sides. See *Clacton Local Board v. Young and Sons*, (1895).

Royal Warrant

In a talk I had the other day, a friend asked me if I knew how a firm—say of caterers or other such suppliers—had the right to put on their paper words such as 'Suppliers to Her Majesty the Queen.' I wonder if you have any general idea as to this among all your information.

In reply to your query concerning the right to put on a letter heading 'Suppliers to Her Majesty the Queen,' the only way in which it is possible for this to be done in a proper manner is to possess a Royal Warrant which is issued by the Lord Chamberlain together with the right to print the Royal Coat of Arms it is only logical for someone who has supplied the Royal Household to be able to state that he has done so. The correct procedure, however, is to obtain a Royal Warrant through the proper channels.

Scheduled Buildings

Would you please provide me with information concerning Scheduled Buildings viz:
  (a) What constitutes a Scheduled building?
  (b) How does a building become designated as Scheduled?
  (c) What are the advantages or disadvantages to an owner of possession of a Scheduled building?
  (d) What are the owner's responsibilities in owning a Scheduled building?

A Buildings Preservation Order may be made under Section 30 of the Town and Country Planning Act, 1962, or under the Historic Buildings Act, 1953, in respect of buildings of special architectural or historic interest, whether or not the building has been listed. This restricts the demolition, alteration or extension of the building without the authority giving prior consent. Enforcement notices can be served for preservation works and the expense of such works should be recoverable. Appeals against such Notices can be lodged. Execution of works, other than those approved, may lead to a fine of up to £100. The local Planning Authority will supply details of any listed building in their area.

Service Contract

I should be glad of your advice regarding private domestic service employment.
  (1) Is a contract of service necessary under the Contracts of Employment Act 1963 for a married couple, the man working full time as gardener-handyman, paid weekly, the wife cooking occasionally as required and paid separately, self-contained detached accommodation being available rent free?
  (2) Whether or not (1) is necessary is a written contract advisable and how should it be worded?
  (3) Should a couple prove to be unsatisfactory what difficulties are there in obtaining possession of the accommodation after termination of employment, if they refuse to leave?
  (4) Does the inclusion of some furniture in the accommodation afford any protection and how much might be required? At the moment there are some curtains and a three piece suit only, apart from night storage heaters, electric cooker and refrigerator.

A Contract of Service should be entered into for the man who is working for you full time as a gardener-handyman, but it does not seem likely that his wife works sufficient hours for you to warrant a contract.

The CGA have a Domestic Service Agreement which will safeguard you as far as possible where you have a gardener in occupation of your cottage, and we can let you have one of these at a cost of 52½p.

If the tenants prove unsatisfactory, you are entitled to recover the accommodation, but you cannot evict the tenants without application to the Court. The inclusion of furniture does not affect the issue one way or another where a service tenancy is involved.

Sheep Killed by Motorist

I have a seven-year grazing lease of approximately 500 acres from the Ministry of Public Building & Works (Holyrood Park, Edinburgh), now the Department of the Environment.

Occasionally, I have sheep injured or killed by motor vehicles, private cars being allowed to use the Park roads. In a recent case two sheep were killed outright and I asked my solicitor to make a claim. He tells me that the motorist's insurers have replied denying negligence and claiming damages for the car.

I feel that with a 30 m.p.h. speed limit and in an open area to hit two sheep so hard as to kill them argues a considerable degree of negligence even if they cross the road unexpectedly.

The terms of the lease protect the Ministry from becoming involved or liable in any way.

(1) In Searle v. Wallbank (1947), where the House of Lords rejected a claim by a cyclist injured through colliding with a straying horse, one Law Lord said, 'There must be mutual respect and forbearance; the motorist must put up with the farmer's cattle; the farmer must put up with the motorist.' The motorist is under a duty of care to other users of the roads, and animals are among these users; his killing them by his speed can hardly be other than negligence. This is especially so where there are warning signs.

(2) The denial of negligence with its counterclaim of damages by the motorist's insurers is, as your solicitor knows, a recognised routine to stave off a valid claim: it succeeds at times. Our opinion, however, is that your insistence on your claim will not result in litigation but in an offer to settle. If you are obliged to sue the odds are heavily in your favour.

We add that our sympathy is wholly with you, and that we shall be glad to learn that you have had some compensation for your loss.

Shooting at Night

Is it legal for a tenant farmer to shoot rabbits at night with the use of the lights of a tractor, and also is the shooting of pheasants allowed after sunset?

A tenant farmer is not entitled to shoot rabbits between the expiration of the first hour after sunset and the commencement of the last hour before sunrise. The lawful shooting of pheasants is allowed after sunset, but it is an offence to destroy any game unlawfully at night upon any land under the Night Poaching Act.

Shooting – Unauthorised

I should be obliged if you would let me know the legal situation with regard to unauthorised persons shooting or carrying a gun on my property. Would you please answer the queries below:

1. If unauthorised persons are caught on my land with shotguns, can the weapons be confiscated (a) by day, (b) by night?

2. Is it correct that if unauthorised shooters are caught on my land, the police have no law under which to prosecute unless dead game is found on them?

3. Most poachers say they are shooting pigeons. They have had some shots but no pigeons are found on them; what can I do about it?

4. Boys with airguns say they are shooting blackbirds. These are protected birds. If no dead blackbirds, what can I do about it?

5. Sunday shooting – is it illegal to shoot on Sundays?

6. If the police cannot do anything, can I do something with regard to trespass, and, if so, what is the law of trespass?

The answers to your questions are as follows:

1. Yes; the guns of trespassers in pursuit of game may be seized at any time, and, if a court of summary jurisdiction orders it, they may be forfeited. (The position is explained in the Game Laws (Amendment) Act, 1960.)

2. No: it is incorrect to say that a prosecution cannot be instituted unless dead game is found on the trespassers; other relevant evidence is available.

3. Again, in regard to the 'pigeon shooters,' it is a question of evidence; would a court believe the excuse?

4. The answer to (3) applies to boys with airguns.

5. Yes: it is unlawful to shoot game on Sundays.

6. You can sue a trespasser in a civil court and obtain damages; you can also prosecute a trespasser in pursuit of game in a criminal court.

. . . Liable to Shed Branches at any Time

(See page 227)

Shooting over Another's Land

I own and live on a small nursery which is completely surrounded by land owned and shot by a neighbouring large estate. My property is bounded by three hedges, two of which are my responsibility and the third the estate's.

I am being caused continual anxiety by the fact that not only do these shooting parties shoot across the main road, but also across my private garden, where there are nearly always young children playing.

This morning, after several shots across my garden, a pheasant was eventually brought down in it. A gamekeeper and the gentlemen responsible for the shot forced their way through the hedge saying that any damage was not our concern as this was the estate's hedge. The keeper then crossed my lawn, sent a large dog through my herbaceous border to locate the bird and walked through another flower bed himself. When I protested he merely said he was doing no harm and had every right to do so.

I would like to make it clear that I am not trying to claim their bird, but I would like very much to know:

1. If they are entitled to shoot across my garden and nursery?

2. If they have a right to enter either at will without first requesting permission to do so?

3. If permission is refused, what is the position regarding the bird?

4. What are the regulations regarding shooting close to our garden across a public highway?

We advise you that such behaviour as you report is an actionable matter and that unless you are assured that it will cease you should seek the protection of the court. The answers to your specific questions are:

1. They are not entitled to shoot across your garden and nursery: in *Cliften v. Viscount Burg* (1887), Hawkins, J., held that bullets, traversing the plaintiff's land at a height of 75 ft. on their way to their military target gave rise to an action for nuisance. It would probably too, be held to be a trespass.

2. The gamekeeper was wrong, and probably knew he was wrong, in his stupid statement that he had, without your sanction, a right to enter your land. You could bring an action for damages in respect of trespass against the keeper, the shooter, and also against the keeper in respect of the dog's trespass.

3. To go upon the land of another, without permission, to pick up dead game (though legitimately shot) is a trespass for which a civil remedy lies. Such game, however, is not the property of the person on whose land it is found; an action for conversion would be maintainable against him if he declined to give it up.

4. Under Section 72 of the Highway Act, 1835, it is an offence (punishable by a fine of 40s. and the damage done in addition) to fire a gun or pistol within *50 feet* of the centre of any carriageway or cartway.

Shotguns – Licence for Visitor

I understand that you now have to have a firearms certificate for a gun in England. I hope to come over for a few days shooting in the autumn, probably less than a week at a time. How do I arrange for the gun to pass the Customs in the time available and to which police authority do I apply if necessary? I bring the gun with me.

You will not require a shotgun certificate as the law now states:

'As from May 1, 1968, anyone who wishes to possess, purchase, or acquire a shotgun will be required to hold a valid shotgun certificate issued by the police. The only people exempted will be:

(a) Visitors to Great Britain staying less than thirty days in twelve months.

(b) Persons using someone else's shotgun to shoot at artificial targets at a place and time approved by the local chief constable.

(c) Persons who borrow a shotgun from the occupier of private land and use it thereon while he is present.

(d) Persons exempt from holding a firearm certificate under Part I of the Firearms Act 1937.'

You will be covered by part (a).

Shoot – Valuation Appeal

My shoot was first sprayed with poison

by plane in 1959. Since then I have had practically no partridge and much reduced pheasants. Before this spraying I averaged about 200 partridges and 200 pheasants yearly.

Attempts to get the shoot's valuation reduced have got nowhere, and I informed the authorities I wished a date for the appeal to be fixed; but we have not been able to get a date and the 'officer' has informed my agent that 'very definitely no reduction can be made.' I am certainly not going to appear before a man who has already made up his partial mind almost without hearing my side of the case.

The diminished yield of the shoot, whatever the cause of the diminution, must be taken into account when assessing the valuation. If the valuation officer himself considers the valuation fair, he is nevertheless not entitled to assert 'very definitely no reduction can be made,' for it's his valuation that is subject to appeal. Your local committee, after you state your case for a reduction, would ask for his comments, and you need fear no bias in favour of the officer. Our suggestion is that you yourself conduct your case before the local committee. You are more likely to have a favourable hearing than is given to a solicitor or counsel. The proceedings are pleasantly informal and you will lose nothing by being without legal attendant.

It might be desirable to have your solicitor in the event of your being aggrieved by the decision of your local committee, and deciding to make a further appeal to the Lands Tribunal, for proceedings there are more formal. Even so, our experience seems to suggest that an appellant in person does not jeopardise his chance of success.

Your appeal is not, as appears to be what you think 'before another valuation officer,' and it is before a tribunal quite independent of the valuation officers.

Sparrow-Hawks

Is it true that sparrow-hawks are now protected? My keeper says they are vermin.

Sparrow-hawks are protected under the Protection of Birds Acts 1954–1967. Anyone attempting to shoot them are liable to a £25 fine if convicted in a Magistrate's Court; the second offence carries a prison sentence.

'Squatters' Right'

'Squatters' Right' is the term applied to the acquisition of an indisputable title —a " possessory title," it is called—by the unlicensed occupation of a plot of land and the exclusive use of it over a period of 12 years. Provided that the occupier, the 'squatter,' can prove that his occupation (a trespass, in fact) was during that period open, peaceable, and as of right, no person can, after the 12 years, effectively challenge his title. The title does not need registering or other formality: the adverse possession over 12 years establishes it. For one reason or another, however, it may be desirable to obtain from the Land Registry a land certificate in respect of it.

Stamp Duty for Conveyances – 1

On the subject of charges for conveying property, some confusion has occurred on the current rates of Stamp Duty. The scale is:

Up to £5,500: nil.
Between £5,500 and £7,000: 25p for each £50; £7,000 and over: 50p for each £50.

Stamp Duty for Conveyances – 2

I refer you to the letters on page 88 of the February issue of the Estate Magazine under the heading of Stamp Duty for Conveyances.

What you have to say is rather ambiguous and could be taken several ways. In order to clarify the matter, would you be good enough to tell me what the Stamp Duty would be on the following amounts for conveyancing of land?

£4,500
£9,250
£13,650.

Since August 1963 the Stamp Duty payable on conveyances of land is normally £1 per £50 or any fraction of £50. If, however, *the deed of conveyance contains a statement that the transaction does not form part of a larger transaction or series of transactions,* on conveyances where the consideration does not exceed £6,000 the rate per £50 is:

1. Where the deed is certified as £3,500: Nil.
2. Where the deed is certified as £4,500: 25p.
3. Where the deed is certified as £5,250: 50p.
4. Where the deed is certified as £6,000: 75p.

The answer to your question, therefore, on the assumption that the transactions are separate, is:

1. On £4,500 the Stamp Duty is £22.50p.
2. On £9,250 the Stamp Duty is £185.
3. On £13,650 the Stamp Duty is £273.

If the £4,500 transaction formed one of a series the full rate of £90 would be payable.

Stamping Leases

The counterpart of a lease can be stamped with a 5s. stamp even if the lease itself is not stamped.

The liability to stamp the lease rests with the tenant and he is liable for a penalty of £10 for not stamping the same. He is also liable for a penalty of £10 and double duty if he wishes to stamp it and does so after the expiration of 30 days from the date thereof.

If it is desired by the landlord to stamp the counterpart with a 5s. stamp only, it must not be signed by the landlord but only by the tenant and should be endorsed 'Counterpart of a Lease.' (See Section 72 of Stamp Act, 1891.) If signed by the landlord it becomes a duplicate and is liable to the same stamp duty as the lease.

If the landlord signs the lease only it is desirable to call the tenant's attention to the fact that he is liable for stamping it. He can, of course, please himself whether he does so or not.

A denoting stamp showing the stamp with which the lease is stamped is not necessary on the counterpart of a lease.

The stamping of an agreement and the counterpart is identical with that of a lease and counterpart. An agreement can be signed by a duly authorised agent, whereas a lease, which is a deed, must be executed by the landlord or by some-one acting for him under a power of attorney.

Stiles – Upkeep of Public Footpath

Through our property we have a private accommodation lane over which there is a dedicated public footpath with a gate and stile at each end. Would yo be good enough to say who should bear the cost of the upkeep of the stiles—the council or me?

A gate or stile is a curb upon the public freedom to pass; and, though the owner of land has a right to maintain gates or stiles across the way, the Highway Act, 1959, gives each local authority the statutory duty of seeing that stiles do not reasonably hinder freedom of passage.

The answer to your question, therefore, is that you and not the local authority are to maintain the gates and stiles so as not to be a menace to passers using the footpath. Remove them you may, but, if they remain, they are not to become troublesome impediments to passage.

Tax – Capital Gains – 1

I am writing to ask your advice about my selling property, a new Colt house and flat in London, which is my permanent home and more valuable than the bungalow. If I sell the bungalow before selling the flat, would I then be obliged to pay the special taxes when I sell the flat, which could be sold with a profit?

The tax to which a sale of your real property may give rise is Capital Gains Tax.

The position with regard to Capital Gains Tax could, however, be more complicated. A capital gain arising on the sale of a property which has been owned for more than a year will be assessable to Capital Gains Tax unless that property was the vendor's only or main residence throughout the period of ownership, or for the period from April 6, 1965, to the date of sale if this is shorter. Where a person owns more than one private residence, Section 29(7) of the Finance Act, 1965, gives the owner an option, within certain limits, to choose which property shall be treated as his main residence for the purpose of securing relief from Capital Gains Tax on a disposal of that property. If you envisage selling both properties within the foreseeable future, and you consider that the greater capital gain is likely to arise on the sale of the flat, then obviously it would pay you to treat the flat as your main residence, and we would recommend that an early notification to this effect should be given to your Inspector of Taxes.

Provided the Inland Revenue accept the nomination of your London flat as your main residence—and there could be some doubt about this if at the time of your nomination of it you had had the use of both the flat and the bungalow as a residence for more than two years —there would be no liability to Captial Gains Tax on the sale of the flat, whether this took place after or before the sale of the bungalow.

Alternatively, provided you yourself had used the bungalow as a private residence—e.g., as a week-end cottage, —you could nominate this as your main residence with a view to obtaining relief from Capital Gains Tax when it is sold. Following the sale of your London flat the bungalow would then become your private residence, and on a sale of the flat you would get some relief from Capital Gains Tax, but only in respect of that part of any gain attributable to the period or periods during which it was treated as your main residence. That part of any gain from the flat attributable to a period after April 6, 1965, for which the bungalow was nominated as your principal residence would remain chargeable to tax.

Tax – Capital Gains – 2

In 1954 my father bought a house for about £2,000 and lived there until his death in January 1964, when it became my mother's property, and she now occupies it. I think it was valued at rather over £4,000 for probate. It is likely it would now fetch £6,000. One day it will become my property. Will it be liable to capital gains tax and what would this amount to? Can you give me an idea of the cost of living now, compared with 30 years ago, i.e. the late 1930s?

If the property is your mother's only or main residence, then if she sells it or it passes to you on her death, under the provisions of the current Finance Acts it will be free of capital gains tax. If your mother owns more than one house and she occupies both then she can decide which is her main residence, as only one of them will be free of capital gains tax. This exemption from capital gains tax is in addition to the exemption of the first £5,000 of capital gains on her death.

With reference to your second point re the cost of living taking 1938, according to the Treasury the £ was then worth 64 and is now worth 18·3. Thus you take the calculation: $100p \times \dfrac{18·3}{64}$ which works out at 28p, which is the value of the £ today. Well done, our friends at the Treasury, you may feel inclined to say!

Tax – Development

I have building permission for one dwelling on part of my property, and propose to build a house for my retirement. When I vacate my present residence would it be subject to capital gains tax? Should it be sold, or would it be advantageous to let this furnished, from the point of view of saving income tax?

The figures you quote did apply for some years but as a result of recent changes in legislation the exemption limits are now £5,635 for earned income only, and £2,500 for unearned income only. We confirm that both types of income are aggregated in arriving at the overall surtax liability.

The effect of aggregation is to make the starting point for surtax vary between £2,500 and £5,635, according to the respective amounts of the two types of income and the personal reliefs and other deductions to which the taxpayer is entitled.

The matter is complex but the starting point for surtax can be arrived at by the application of the following rules:
(1) From your unearned income deduct all allowable charges on income, e.g. mortgage interest, bank interest, etc, and also the amount by which the total of your personal allowances (but excluding life assurance relief) exceeds the single person's allowance—£325 for 1971/72. Call

the resultant figure the 'net investment income';

(2) If your earned income is less than £2,573 deduct from it the earned income relief, add in your net investment income, and if the resultant figure is:

  a. Not more than £2,500—there is no liability to surtax;

  b. Between £2,501 and £2,681—you pay on 40% of the excess over £2,500;

  c. Over £2,681—you pay at normal rates on the excess over £2,000;

(3) If your earned income is between £2,573 and £5,046 you pay surtax only if your net investment income exceeds £500;

(4) If your earned income is between £5,046 and £5,635 you pay surtax if 85% of your earned income in excess of £5,046 plus your net investment income exceeds £500;

(5) If your earned income exceeds £5,635 you pay surtax on your net investment income plus 85% of the excess of earned income over £5,046, subject to marginal relief if your net income chargeable to surtax does not exceed £2,681.

The foregoing rules presuppose that the investment income will be sufficient to absorb the deductions for charges on income and for the allowable personal reliefs. If the investment income is insufficient to cover these deductions the rules would require modification to fit the actual circumstances of each particular case.

From the above you may well conclude that anyone subject to surtax should seek professional advice. The C.G.A. Tax Department is always pleased to help.

Tax Relief on Improvements

I would like to inquire if it is possible to offset money spent on improving rented property against the rent, for tax purposes, and if so for how long after the expenditure of each capital unit?

Income tax relief for capital expenditure incurred on improving rented property is only available where the property concerned is used for agricultural purposes, including the occupation of dwelling houses by agricultural workers. Where such income tax relief is due it is granted on one-tenth of the qualifying expenditure for each of the 10 income tax years of assessment following

that in which the expenditure is incurred. The relevant statutory authority for claiming this relief is Section 68 of the Capital Allowances Act, 1968.

We regret to say that no income tax relief is due for the actual cost of improving non-agricultural property, whether rented or not.

Where money is borrowed expressly for the purpose of improving property owned by the borrower in either the United Kingdom or Eire, income tax relief can be claimed for the interest payable on the loan. If the loan takes the form of a bank overdraft, this relief is limited to a period of three years unless the property concerned is (*a*) farmland or market garden land, or (*b*) woodlands managed on a commercial basis and with a view to the realisation of profits, in which case there is no overall time limit for the granting of the relief.

Finally, we would remind you that expenditure on the improvement of let property should be carefully recorded, because it will normally be deductible in computing any capital gain arising on a future sale of the property.

Tax – Surtax

Will you kindly put me right concerning the following: I understand that surtax is not chargeable on the first £5,000 on earned income and on the first £2,000 on unearned income. Can earned and unearned income be joined for the surtax charge?

The figures you quote as the surtax exemption limits for earned and unearned income are respectively correct, and we confirm that both types of income are aggregated in arriving at the overall surtax liability.

The effect of aggregation is to make the starting point for surtax vary between £2,000 and £5,000, according to the respective amounts of the two types of income and the personal reliefs and other deductions to which the taxpayer is entitled. The actual starting point for surtax can be arrived at by the application of the following rules:

(1) From your unearned income deduct all allowable charges on income, i.e. mortgage interest, bank interest, etc., and also the amount by which the total

of your personal allowances (but excluding life assurance relief) exceeds the single person's allowance—£220 for 1965/66. Call the resultant figure the 'net investment income';

(2) If your earned income is less than £2,571, you pay surtax on the amount by which your earned income, less income allowance, plus net investment income exceeds £2,000;

(3 If your earned income is between £2,571 and £5,000 you pay surtax on your net investment income only ;

(4) If the amount of earned income is between £5,000 and £9,945 you pay surtax on your net investment income plus 8/9ths of the excess of earned income over £5,000;

(5) If your earned income exceeds £9,945 surtax is payable on your net investment income plus £4,395 plus the excess of earned income over £9,945.

The foregoing rules presuppose that the investment income will be sufficient to absorb the deductions for charges on income and for the allowable personal reliefs. If, however, the investment income is insufficient to cover these deductions the rules would require modification to fit the actual circumstances of each particular case under consideration.

Agricultural Tenancy

I shall be grateful for your advice on a matter arising under the Agricultural Holdings Acts. I have a small farm which is let on a lease which expires later this year, and will be renewed.

The original lease was executed in the tenant's own name, but he now trades as a limited company and pays his rent in the name of that company. What would be the advantages or disadvantages of renewing the lease in the name of the company ? Would the company enjoy any greater, or less, protection under the Acts than an individual ? The tenant owns the house in which he lives, there being no house on the farm.

We assume from your letter that the assignment of the lease by your original lessee was by deed, was registered with you or your solicitor or your agent

within six months, a fee of one guinea paid, and that you have been acquiescent. That being so your tenant is now a limited liability company, a quite distinct legal person from the shareholders that own it.

If, therefore, you renew the lease it cannot but be with the limited liability company. A lease to your original lessee would be a fresh lease ; and you might meet difficulty about its acceptance.

So far as security of tenure of the farm comes into consideration, it is quite certain that under both alternatives your tenant will have the protection given by sections 22–29 of the Agricultural Holdings Act, 1958. For, if questions about notice to quit should arise, the committee to answer them will regard the reality of the tenancy and not its name.

The one possible drawback to a landlord in having a limited liability company as his tenant is the fact that its assets are limited and inadequate to meet the landlord's claims, the landlord's selected individual probably not.

Tenant Farmer – Death of

In the case of a tenant-farmer who takes his son into partnership (the tenancy of course remaining in his own name), can you inform me whether under current legislation the son has any security of tenure on his father's death?

The statutory provision in respect of the effect upon the tenancy of an agricultural holding when the tenant dies is in the Agricultural Holdings Act, 1948, Section 24 (1) (which enables a tenant to whom notice to quit has been given to serve a counter-notice) and in the exception in proviso Section 24 (2) (f).

'The tenant with whom the contract of tenancy was made has died within three months before the giving of the notice to quit, and it is stated in the notice that it is given by reason of the matter aforesaid.' The notice will be served on the personal representative of the deceased tenant.

The landlord, that is, assuming that he acts with reasonable promptitude, is able to give an effective notice to quit; if he delays beyond the statutory three months he will be deemed to have accepted the surviving partner as tenant. The machinery of the Act for giving security of tenure will then be operative.

Apart from this constructive acceptance of a son as tenant, no statutory security of tenure exists.

Tenant Defaults on Rent – Furnished Tenancies

Could you be so kind as to clarify the position with regard to furnished tenancies.

We have a pair of cottages, at present used as one dwelling and which is let furnished.

Our present tenants signed an agreement for one year from last May.

Despite references etc., we are now having extreme difficulty in getting any rent out of the tenants at all, and are wondering whether the Rent Act provides any protection for landlords. One can hardly believe its functions should be so one-sided that tenants may pursue peaceful and rent-free existences indefinitely.

We very much regret to say that the Rent Act makes it impossible for you to evict your tenants without first obtaining from the County Court Judge an Order for Possession.

You can take him to Court for failing to pay the rent but you cannot evict him. Your agreement with him was perfectly valid but the Rent Act does not take this into account. As the Minister said, during the Third Reading of the Bill, even an occupier under a mere licence would be protected from being deprived of occupation except in compliance to the Order of a County Court Judge.

Further, Section 2 of the Act says that: 'If in proceedings by the owner against the occupier of any premises, the Court makes or has before the commencement of this Act made an Order for Possession the Court may suspend the execution of the Order for such period, not exceeding 12 months from the date of the Order, as the Court thinks fit.'

Possibly your tenants will pay their rent under the threat of Court proceedings.

Tenancy of Council House

A friend of mine has a mortgage on his property with the local council. However, due to ill health and unable to follow his occupation he has fallen into arrears with payments. The council have now written to him saying that unless arrears are paid by December 31 they will take possession. This has caused my friend a lot of worry and we should like to be advised of the true legal position in the matter, and his best line of action in the circumstances. As far as I can gather his arrears are not more than 6 months.

Section 5 of the Rent Act, 1968, is thus:

(1) A tenancy shall not be a protected tenancy at any time when the interest of the landlord under that tenancy belongs to any of the bodies specified in subsection (2) below. . . .

(2) The bodies referred to are (a) the council of a county or county borough. . . .

The implication is that the council, as trustee of the ratepayers' money, has unrestricted power to manage council houses including full power to enforce payment of rent. The one possible way of your friend's retention of the house is, therefore, his making an acceptable offer to pay off arrears; he can expect sympathetic consideration of a reasonable offer.

Tenancy – Gentleman's Agreement – 1

I have a cottage that I wish to let furnished as a 'weekend' cottage. Can you suggest any method by which I can do this without the following risks: (a) Not being able to get rid of the tenant if unsatisfactory, (b) The tenant appealing against the rent agreed to and/or demanding improvements, (c) Having to pay at least half the rent in income tax.

I have in mind a 'gentleman's' agreement by which the value of the agreed rent is met by the tenant paying for bills incurred by me. I appreciate that such an agreement has no legal binding on either side.

Gentlemen's agreements never work—what is more, if you enter into an arrangement outside the law you are inviting your prospective tenant to take advantage of you should you fall out. You could not take him to court or obtain restitution because he could give away your tax avoidance manoeuvres.

We would suggest you use one of the C.G.A.'s furnished cottage tenancy agreements because this will give you protection against a tenant who will not go, for the simple reason that the occupier never becomes a tenant legally speaking. In addition if the 'rent' is in fact in consideration of the furnishings which you provide, then it is to be doubted whether you are liable to tax because of the depreciation of the furniture.

If you would like one of our furnished letting agreements they are two guineas each.

Gentleman's Agreement – 2

Part of the answer published above was somewhat misleading. Although the Inland Revenue will make an allowance for the wear and tear of furnishings, and the cost of any actual repairs to furniture and fittings may also be claimed, these allowances would not normally be sufficient to result in the rent being free of tax.

There are, however, many other allowances that it may be possible to claim in arriving at the net tax liability under a furnished letting. These include the following if ultimately borne by the landlord: Advertising expenses, cost of tenancy agreement, cost of inventory, insurance of property and contents, general and water rates, repairs and redecoration to the property, externally and internally, commission on rent collection, cost of telephone, cost of lighting and heating, cost of cleaning between lets, taxation agents' charges for preparing computations for the Inland Revenue.

Tenancy – Furnished Service Cottage

The Rent Act makes it very difficult to get a gardener out of a service cottage except with a court order. Does the Act still apply if the cottage is furnished, and if so, what is the minimum of furniture which would be required to be considered as a 'furnished' cottage? No rent is charged of course, whether furnished or unfurnished, rates and water rates are paid by me.

We are sorry to tell you that Section 32 of this Act (which prohibits eviction without due process of law) has this, bringing your gardener within the scope of this protection given: 'A person who, under the terms of his employment, has exclusive possession of any premises otherwise than as a tenant shall be deemed to have been a tenant.'

Whether his tied cottage was or was not furnished, and whether or not he paid rent, are both irrelevant facts: if he declines to give up occupation when his employment has ended, he becomes what the Act calls a 'residential occupier'; and the owner of the cottage can get possession lawfully only by way of an Order for Possession granted by the County Court Judge. Your gardener was a licensee, occupying the cottage by a permission that could be withdrawn. The Act converted him into a tenant.

Sitting Tenancy and Ownership of Property

Some years ago a relation with two small girls became homeless, so I bought a small house and put her in it. At first she paid a nominal rent, but this stopped. She has lived in the house for more than eight years, and I have been told that if I allow her to live in it for 12 years rent-free she could claim it. Please, what is the legal position? I intended leaving the house to her for life and then to go on to the girls.

The information given to you, that your tenant can claim the house after twelve years' rent-free occupation, is erroneous: your tenant does not acquire the 'adverse possession' (whereby she becomes a squatter whose occupation may develop by lapse of time into ownership) until you give her a valid notice to quit. Till then she occupies by your licence.

She is in fact acting as though what you contemplate is already accomplished, and that you have given her a settlement for life. But she cannot, by selling the house, defeat your intention that the house on her death shall devolve into the joint ownership of the two girls.

Tenancy – 364 Day

What are the conditions of a 364 day tenancy. Who is responsible for hedges and ditches?

A letting of land for 364 days certainly does not come within the provisions of the Agricultural Holdings Act 1948. Such a tenancy automatically terminates at the end of 364 days, when the landlord can resume possession without having to give any notice to quit. No ingoing or outgoing valuation or disturbance compensation is payable except by express agreement. The tenant would be liable to keep the hedges and ditches in reasonable condition in the absence of express agreement to the contrary.

Tenant's Shooting Rights

I would appreciate your advice on the following—I have authority from the Landlord to shoot over three farms, whatever I like in the way of game, vermin, etc.

As I understand it, under the 1906 Act the farmers themselves have the right despite the Landlord reserving shooting rights himself (which I have from him) to shoot vermin, including pigeons. I believe the farmer and/or perhaps his son?—and one other named person, in writing, can shoot ground-game including vermin and pigeons only. In other words—the tenant farmer can authorise two people (one being himself or son) to shoot pigeons etc. Would you kindly confirm that that is so?

Under the Armed Trespass Act I believe that policemen must, or may, walk over the field to ask the person with the gun what authority he has to shoot there, and so reduce poachers. Is it a policeman's duty to find such people? It is obviously the gamekeeper's duty to do so, but I have no gamekeeper, so is it the duty of the police to catch these poachers, I of course helping when I am able?

The Ground Game Act, 1880, gives to every occupier of land, as an inseparable incident of his occupation, the right to kill and take 'ground game'—hares and rabbits only. His right to destroy wild pigeons and other pests is given by section 90 of the Agricultural Holdings Act, 1948.

The farmer may authorise in writing any number of persons to take ground game; but only the farmer himself and *one* other person authorised in writing may kill with firearms, and that one person is to be a member of his household resident with him, or be in his employment. Any other person, having like you a concurrent right, is entitled to see the written authority.

As to the police officer's power and duty in respect of poaching with or without firearms, the Game Laws (Amendment) Act, 1960, in section 1 (1) provides 'A police constable may arrest a person on any land . . . trespassing in pursuit of game by night'. Section 2 authorises the officer to enter on land; and section 3 empowers the seizure of guns and cartridges.

The Acts have no peremptory must to the police constable; may is the word consistently used, but whenever he has 'reasonable grounds for suspecting', his power to require removable of the suspicion arises by implication.

Titles – Hereditary

I shall be glad to receive information on the following: The son of a baron died and subsequently the baron died and was succeeded by his grandson. The brother and sister have assumed the courtesy title of honourable. I am under the impression that this is not correct, as I believe that, in such a case, the widow should obtain permission from the reigning monarch to adopt those titles which she would have been entitled to if her husband had lived and succeeded to the title, she becoming a peeress and her children honourable.

Your assumption that the brothers and sisters of a peer who directly succeeds his grandfather in that peerage dignity do not automatically become entitled to use the appropriate courtesy styles is correct. A Royal Warrant of precedence authorizing such use must be obtained. As a general rule, although complicated cases sometimes arise, the peer himself (unless a minor) must petition for the warrant in favour of his brothers and sisters; in other words, no one can obtain a royal licence or precedence unless his or her brother is the holder of the peerage in question.

Trade – Permission to

Our village shop and P.O. is almost certainly closing in the near future, and I intend to apply in due course for the sub-P.O. and would also like to open a village shop. The premises I intend to use require no external alterations. Is any trading licence required by law, and is planning permission required from the local council?

You should take up this matter with your local R.D.C. forthwith. It seems likely that you will require a ' change of user' and that planning permission will be necessary, and you must, therefore, go to your local planning authority. We are sure that you will find them helpful and they will explain the various requirements to you.

You may require to register the business name with the Registrar of Business Names under the Registration of Business Names Act, 1916. You should apply, within 14 days of commencing business, to: The Registration of Business Names, Companies House, 55/71 City Road, London E.C.1.

Trade Descriptions Act

Can you tell me whether the Trade Descriptions Act covers date of delivery? The situation is that I ordered some greenhouse equipment through a firm who when they confirmed the order wrote that delivery would be in two to three weeks. It is now 11 weeks and no delivery. I am unable to cancel the order as I have already paid with the order to obtain discount.

The Trade Descriptions Act, 1968, does not in the list of false trade descriptions given in Section 2 include a false statement about term of delivery. This is so though, in some cases on the sale of goods, 'time of delivery' is referred to as part of the description. Nor would a successful prosecution be of any real benefit to you: all you would get out of it would be such satis-

faction as you might entertain from the penalising of the defaulters.

Your means to getting a remedy is to write:

'This is to notify you that I cancel my order for equipment given to you on. . . . You undertook to deliver in two to three weeks, and eleven weeks have already elapsed. I do not propose suing you for breach of your contract; but I require the return of the payment made to you.'

The firm will know that their contract to supply the equipment comes into the category of the mercantile contracts considered in Reuter v. Sala (1879 C.F.D.), when Lord Justice Colton condemned as 'dangerous and unreasonable' the attempt to apply this rule of equity that time is not of the essence of a contract. You will, I think, get your money back all right.

Traps – Fenn

I am writing to enquire whether it is illegal to put Fenn traps out (similar to the old gin traps), I gather to catch rabbits?

Fenn traps have been approved by the Minister of Agriculture under Section 8 of the Pests' Act, 1954. This applies to England and Wales *but not to Scotland*. The answer to your question is, therefore, that it is *not* illegal to put Fenn traps out. (But see also page 186.)

Trees on Adjoining Land

Some trees on land adjoining mine are unsafe, and are liable to shed branches at any time, what should I do to have these trees removed?

You should make the owner of the trees aware that they are dangerous for – when the owner of a tree knows, or as a prudent owner should have known, that the tree is a potential danger ; unless he does take reasonable precautions, he is answerable for damage caused if the risk should become a reality. A warning by you of this likelihood will fix the owner with the knowledge, assuming that he does not already have it, that demands precautions. He should, at the least, lop and top the trees.

Trees – Apprehended Danger

On my boundary I have some Lombardy poplars, planted about 60 years ago and making a very attractive sight from the house. After the last war a bungalow was built on the adjoining land and the owner is asking for the poplars to be felled, as he is afraid of them blowing down. Between my land and his is a sunken footpath, about 5 foot below the land level, so I hope the roots are contained. Anyway he hasn't mentioned them.

While sympathising with his point of view, he knew the trees were there when he built and I would be grateful if you would let me know what the legal position is.

The position, in respect of the danger dreaded by your neighbour from the proximity of your poplars to his bungalow, was explained in the House of Lords case, *Caminer v Northern and London Investment Trust Ltd* (1951); and the decision is that case has received statutory approval in the Occupier's Liability Act, 1957. The legal rule in brief is that the owner of a tree is liable for such damage as it causes in falling provided that he knew or, as a reasonably prudent manager of his estate should have known of the danger of its falling.

It follows, therefore, that, in the unhappy event of the fall of one of your poplars, such fall causing damage to your neighbour's property or inflicting injury, you could not (in view of your neighbour's warning that he thought danger existed) be able to plead, lack of knowledge as a defence to an action for compensation. You would have been put upon inquiry as to the condition of the trees.

The point upon which you lay stress in your letter, that the poplars were there long before the bungalow was built, is no defence. (See *Bliss v. Hall*, 1838, in which it was held that a tallow-chandlery was a nuisance to a householder who came within smell of it only after some years.)

This, too, is relevant: if the poplar roots, which have a roving propensity more than most trees, undermine the

foundations of the bungalow, you would be held liable to compensate whether or not you were aware of the danger.

Trees – Destruction of

The owner of a property adjacent to mine is cutting down and clearing a wood. I believe that this is with a view to development for which permission has not yet been granted.

I understand that one was not allowed to cut down a tree of more than 4in in diameter without permission. I have mentioned this to a member of the parish council, who states that he has been advised that only trees with a preservation order are immune.

If I am correct in my thinking I wonder if your legal representative could give chapter and verse for such restriction on all trees above a certain size.

You are correct in thinking that, with specified exceptions, the felling of trees without a licence from the Forestry Commissions is a crime punishable by fine (up to £50 by the Forestry Act 1961 but increased by the Civic Amenities Act 1957 to £250 or twice the value of the tree felled).

The exceptions to the requiring of a licence include:
(a) the felling of trees with trunk diameter not exceeding 3 in., or, being in a coppice or underwood, not exceeding 6 in.;
(b) the felling of fruit trees or trees in a garden, orchard, churchyard or open public place.

Moreover, the owner of a woodland may without a licence, and in order to improve the growth of other trees, fell trees with diameter not exceeding 4 in. He may also, in any quarter of the year, fell up to 325 cu. ft. (Forestry Act 1961).

But there can be no indiscriminate clearing of a woodland unless in order to carry out a development authorised by planning permission granted under the Town and Country Planning Act 1962 or the Town and Country Planning (Scotland) Act 1947.

Trees and Electricity Wires – 1

I have a belt of trees which run along the side of a main road between the road and my house. In 1948 the Kent Electricity Power Co put up poles and wires along the road and I had to give them a wayleave for the purpose.

A few of these trees are dangerous now, leaning over the road and should be taken down for safety, but it is not now possible to cut them down unless the wires are temporarily removed.

The Electricity Board want to charge me £90 for doing this.

I feel that the trees were there long before the wires and that the work is for the benefit of the Electricity Board as well as road users and that the charge is unreasonable.

What rights have I in this matter? If the Board would take all responsibility for any future damage that might be done if the trees fell, then as far as I am concerned they could stay.

On looking up the wayleave I find that if at any time I intend to use the land for anything other than agriculture they will remove the poles and wires on being given six months' notice. I don't know if this is of any help to me.

In the House of Lords case, *Caminer v. Northern and London Investment Trust Ltd.* (1951), a tree from the defendant's land fell on the plaintiff's car being driven along the highway. The ground upon which the House relieved the defendants of liability was that they neither knew nor ought to have known that the tree was dangerous.

That defence obviously would not be available for you if one of your trees fell doing damage. We suggest, therefore, your writing to the Electricity Board to this effect:

'I return to the topic of trees in danger of falling upon the highway.

'My study of the Caminer case points to my liability if they fall and do damage, whether to users of the highway or to your wires. I ask you, therefore, to remove the wires so that the trees may be felled without harming them.

'I demur, though, to the payment of £90 to you for doing so. The wires are yours, not mine, that I wish to be put in safety; and I point out that you chose to have the wayleave where it was easily foreseeable that the trees would be a menace. It is inequitable to charge me for correcting your error of judgment.

'Will you then reconsider this question of charge? I shall be glad of an early answer in order that I may decide whether or not to consult my M.P. Your wayleave, as you know, does contemplate removal.'

Trees and Electricity Wires – 2

I was surprised at the tone of the letter you suggested your Member should send to his Electricity Board. Relationships between the Boards and their consumers are not improved by this kind of letter or approach.

There obviously are other facts to be considered before judgment can be made in this case.

The appropriate Ministry is the Ministry of Power and it has machinery for dealing with cases like this.

If the Member will write to the Secretary of his Consultative Council whose name and address can be obtained at any of the Board's offices or Service Centres, he will put the case before the Members of the Council (local men or women appointed by the Minister) who will consider it together with the Board's arguments and make a recommendation.

Trees – Encroaching

I have the following problem about trees:

My neighbour owns three very large trees which stand as close as they can be to our mutual boundary. The branches of these trees overhang my garden by more than 20 ft., and are proving a serious nuisance. I have requested my neighbour to cut the offending branches but he refuses to do this, although he, of course, accepts the fact that he cannot stop me from doing so. He says, however, that if by cutting the branches I do any permanent damage to the trees, he will hold me liable.

The branches in question are so large and the trees themselves so old that I can appreciate that cutting off these branches may well have a detrimental effect upon the trees. Apart from anything else, removing the branches at the boundary fence will so upset the natural balance of the trees that I think it is quite possible that they could be blown down in a strong gale, of which we have plenty.

I would be very grateful if you could advise me as to my legal position with regard to liability for damage (or even destruction) of the trees if I cut the overhanging branches, as I wish to do.

No reason, legal or moral, exists why you should not, in this absence of co-operation by your neighbour, cut back such branches of his trees as have come into the air-space over your ground. Moreover, you may also saw off project-ing roots. This right of self-help to abate a nuisance is fully explained and upheld in *Lemmon v. Webb* (1895 Appeal Court) and *Butler v. Standard Telephone* (1940, King's Bench). The fact that the cutting may disfigure, harm, even destroy the tree does not affect your right. The neigh-bour's threat that if damage results he will hold you liable matters not at all; what does matter is that the law will not hold you liable.

Assuming that the cutting does increase the risk of the trees falling, your neigh-bour is, under the Occupiers' Liability Act, 1957, liable for any damage caused by a fall provided that, as an ordinary careful manager of his estate, knew or ought to have known the tree to be dangerous. (See *Noble v. Harrison*, 1926).

Tree Felling – Legalities of

Can you explain the general position over felling trees, licences and preservation orders, etc.?

Confusion arises because two distinct authorities are involved with felling and preservation of trees.

Preservation

Local Authorities can make Tree Preservation Orders and this generally happens where an estate is acquired by a developer who may well reap a rich harvest by cutting down every tree in sight and ruin the amenities of a con-siderable area. Anyone can apply to the Local Authority for trees to have Preservation Orders made.

Felling

Broadly speaking a licence is required to fell trees from the Forestry commis-sion. When in doubt it is best to apply because you may be contravening the Forestry Act, 1967.

There are numerous exceptions outside the Act, the most pertinent one from a private householder's point of view is that trees in private gardens can be cut down without a licence.

General Information

For general information on felling and preservation orders we recommend a booklet entitled *Tree Preservation Orders* published by the Arboricultural Associa-tion, 38 Blythewood Gardens, Stansted, Essex.

Tree – Elm – Legal Liability

I believe there has been a case on owner's of elm trees being liable for damages should they suddenly fall or should a branch fall. Can you enlighten me please?

This question was debated at great length in *Caminer v. Northern and Lon-don Investment Trust*, 1950, a case that was ultimately decided in the House of Lords. If you have easy access to the House of Lords report of the judgments, it makes most interesting reading.

An elm growing near the highway crashed upon a passing motor-car, injur-ing a man and his wife travelling in it, and compensation was claimed from the owners of the elm. In the High Court the Lord Chief Justice allowed the claim, holding that a prudent landowner should have known that the tree needed atten-tion and should have acted on his know-ledge. But neither the Court of Appeal nor the House of Lords followed the Lord Chief Justice in imposing upon a landowner the duty of constant and expert vigilance: if the landowner is 'reasonably prudent' he is exonerated from liability. Unless you know or ought to know that the elms are in fact a menace, you need not worry.

Lord Porter put the point this way: 'If it is the duty of every owner of an elm tree to lop and top that tree as soon as it has reached an early middle age, however sound it is found to be on exter-nal examination, then the respondents were negligent. Short of that they appear to me to be free from blame. For my-self, I do not regard the evidence as estab-lishing that elm trees are so plainly a danger as to require their being lopped and topped lest they fall, though to all external appearance they are sound and no inspection would raise a doubt as to their general condition. If such a duty existed there would be, I imagine, a vast number of negligent persons who are only saved from liability owing to the chance that their elm trees have resisted the forces tending to make them fall.'

Tree – Neighbour's

Could you advise with regard to a large lime tree in my neighbour's garden which is damaging the foundations of my house? Friendly approaches to the neighbour have failed.

The owner of the tree whose roots damage a neighbour's property is liable for the expense incurred in making good the damage. You are entitled to cut through any roots trespassing on your land. Lime trees are not usually associated with this type of complaint, and the offending tree must stand very close to the boundary concerned.

Tree Overhanging – Rights

I wonder if you can advise me on the old problem of trees overhanging a neighbour's fence?

Most people understand that a branch overhanging a boundary fence may be cut back to the boundary. However, can—

(1) The neighbour lop the branches without giving warning of his intention?

(2) Enter on to my land, or climb the tree to carry out the work, without prior permission?

(3) Cut back in some cases as much as 6–7 ft. inside the fence?

(4) Leave the debris where it has fallen, thereby creating a nuisance and in some cases damaging shrubs underneath?

(5) Is there any redress in law?

The answers to your questions are as follows:

(1) when the nuisance can be removed by the abator without entry upon the wrongdoer's land, no notice is requisite. (In practice, however, courtesy and a desire to give the neighbour his chance of abating the nuisance in his own manner suggest notice.)

(2) Without the permission of the owner of the tree it is a trespass that he can restrain to enter upon his land or climb his tree to abate the nuisance.

(3) Any, even the shortest cutting back within the neighbour's land without that neighbour's sanction, justifies the neighbour in suing for damages.

(4) Similarly, any consequent damages due, by falling branches or otherwise, is ground for claim by the owner of the tree.

Perhaps we should add that self-help to abate a nuisance is a perilous remedy in that the sufferer from the nuisance can so easily exceed the right that the law gives him.

Trees – Ownership on Boundary

Could you give me any advice on the ownership of a growing tree on a public highway.

The tree in question is a fig tree which has its roots in the road and rests against a farm building wall owned by a woman who sells the fruit locally. She did not plant the tree. She lets the building to a farmer.

The farm buildings used to belong to a relation of mine and I know there was no question of a fig tree mentioned in the agreement.

Would you know if there is a legal distance from a wall which an owner can rightfully call their own?

Firstly, the boundary is a boundary and if the wall you are referring to is the boundary that is the end of the matter. It would plainly be impracticable if boundary walls were able to claim ownership over land beyond them. This brings us to the second point, which is a tree belongs to the owner of the land on which it stands. Its roots and branches and fruit belong to the same owner. If any of these parts of a tree protrude into the property of anyone else, whilst the trespass, they do not become the property of the person who owns the other land. Presumably, therefore, the trees growing upon a public highway belong to the highway authority.

Trees – Preservation of

Land adjoining my own ground has just been purchased for building development. A belt of fir and other trees about 25 ft.

in width on purchaser's ground divides us. Is it possible to secure the retention of this belt, which will in no way impede the erection of houses as they will be at the rear of the property? I would have the support of neighbours who are in the same situation.

The Town and Country Planning Acts give power to the area planning authority to make a Tree Preservation Order; and, where the amenity of an area would be harmed by the removal and no substantial loss to the owner of the trees would accrue, such an order would be made.

We therefore suggest that you have a talk with the area planning officer at your town hall on the matter; he will probably be anxious to help in the preservation.

Trees – Threat by Neighbour

My garden is ringed by tall elm trees. New houses have crept up on one side and our neighbour finds that the sun is kept from his garden. He asks for permission to take two trees down—so spoiling our ring. He suggests—very amiably—that he could dig a trench on his ground and fill it with quick lime—killing the trees.

What would the legal position be if he did this?

My trees are about 2 ft. from his boundary.

We advise you as follows in respect of your trees:

1 Provided that the trees are wholly (root and branch) within your land you have the right to let them grow as high as you choose—and this is so however greatly they obscure the sunlight upon adjoining land;

2 If roots or branches do stray into adjoining land, the owner of the land invaded has the right to sever the intruders up to his boundary; and this is the full extent of his right;

3 If he should carry out his threat to cut a trench in order to destroy the trees by quick lime, he commits a crime under Section 20 of the Malicious Damage Act, 1861, punishable by imprisonment up to five years. The Section is:

Destroying . . . Trees in value of more than £1 in gardens: 'Whosoever shall unlawfully and maliciously . . . destroy or damage the whole or any part of any tree growing in . . . a garden, in case the injury done shall exceed one pound.'

It is entirely at your option whether or not to have the trees cut down.

Trespass – to Gain Access for Maintenance

My house is situated right at the edge of my property so that two walls actually form the boundary with a neighbour's garden. There is only one small window overlooking the other garden. The house walls are extended as normal garden walls and these, apart from one section, appear to belong to me.

Although nothing is specified in my deeds I have no difficulty at present in obtaining access to the neighbouring garden in order to undertake maintenance on my house. The house has been standing for a long time, and at least ten years in its present modernised form.

Is there any customary right or legal ruling that would guarantee me free access even though the neighbouring property should change hands?

The law of trespass is stringent: any unjustifiable interference with another's occupation of land is a trespass that the law, being invoked, will restrain. This means, among other things, that your entry upon your neighbour's land, even for such a purpose as the trimming of a hedge or the repair of a wall, needs his expressed or reasonably assumed permission in order to turn a trespass into a lawful entry. Lacking the requisite expressed or tacit permission, the propping of a ladder against a neighbour's wall is trespass (see *Gregory v. Piper*, 1829).

Certainly, denial of permission is a rarity, and you most likely have not the least cause to anticipate it. But denial can come when, unluckily, neighbours are at loggerheads; and 'No' is the answer to the specific question you ask. There is no 'customary' right or legal ruling that would guarantee free access even though the neighbouring property should change hands. Entry, without permission or other lawful excuse such as the wish to help in saving your neighbour's house from being burnt down, is trespass.

Trespass – Bull

Will you please tell me if there are laws

dealing specifically with the control of bulls?

(1) If a bull breaks out on to neighbour's land and damages a boundary fence between the two farms, is the bull's owner responsible for the damage?

(2) If a bull which has so broken out serves a neighbour's heifer which is too young, and the bull is of an unwanted breed, can the bull's owner be sued?

In reply to your query concerning damage done by a bull, this is a clear case of trespass.

The owner of the bull is liable for the damage done by the trespass of his animals. This liability is strict; he has no defence in an action in showing that he took every reasonable precaution to keep his bull in. The liability is independent of the owner's negligence. It is also independent of whether or not the owner of the land invaded had a cattle-proof fence, or indeed any fence at all. The obligation to keep his cattle in is upon the owner, no obligation lies upon the owner of private land to keep them out.

The owner of the land invaded can claim against the owner of the bull for the damage done by previous trespass— i.e., the serving of his heifer, and should also state that in the event of further trespass he will seek an injunction ordering steps as will be effective in keeping the bull from entering his land.

Trespass – Cat

Can you tell me the legal position with regard to a Siamese cat belonging to an immediate neighbour.

It comes into the garden, digs in the newly planted rockery, enters the house if windows are left open, and has twice savaged an elderly doctored cat, which has needed veterinary attention.

Co-operation from the neighbour is unlikely, and in any case I cannot see how control can be enforced. Am I entitled to shoot the cat on my premises, or what other remedy have I?

There is unfortunately no legal obligation for the owners of a cat to keep it under control because a cat is a natural strayer. As you say, the owners of the cat are unlikely to be able to enforce

such control even if they desired to do so.

You are not entitled to shoot a cat on your premises, and if you injure it in driving it off, other than in preventing it savaging your own cat, you would be liable to prosecution by the owners. You could attack the cat with water which might deter it from coming on your premises and which would do it no physical harm. Also, there are products on sale for keeping cats off flower beds, such as Foxorine. This is an evil-smelling product, but if you fix strings soaked in Foxorine across points of entry, this might keep it out.

Trespass – Cattle

I have received a complaint from my farmer neighbour about the state of the fence between our properties, and, as he has invoked the local N.F.U., I should like to have the legal side clear. He complains that his cattle can stray through it, and this is possible, though only one has done so in the two years I have been here. I had an idea that responsibility for keeping cattle, etc., within their fields was the responsibility of the farmer, but perhaps I am wrong. I do not at all want to be on bad terms with my neighbour, but I would first of all like to have the legal side clear. The fence is backed up on my side by quite a thickness of scrub, so that there is very little inducement for any animal to come through.

The general ruling is that everyone must prevent his own livestock from trespassing on to his neighbour's land. The only exceptions to this rule come under such heads as railway legislation, old common inclosure awards, and agreement between or binding neighbours. You can either sue for damages and claim an injunction ordering your neighbour to prevent further trespass, or you can seize and retain any animal in the act of trespassing and doing damage at the time, and keep it till the damage (and any cost of feeding incurred in the meantime) is paid for. But the damage must be only what is caused on the occasion by the animal seized, so if you want compensation for other and older damage you must bring an action.

Trespass – Cattle

I have suffered considerable damage as the result of a herd of cattle breaking out of a field through a totally inadequate fence on the public highway and thence on to my property via my private drive.

Could you tell me whether or not the owner of the cattle is liable for the damage in view of the fact that the cattle entered my property from the public highway as opposed to other private property?

The onus is on the owner of cattle to keep them in, and not on other property owners to keep them out. The owner of cattle is, therefore, liable for any damage subsequently caused when negligence is involved.

Trespass – Cattle

I find opinions on liability for cattle trespass very conflicting. Can you clear up who is liable for damage or loss under various circumstances?

1. Cattle trespassing from a public highway:
If they enter by a gateway left open and do damage to private land, in the absence of negligence on the part of the drover of the cattle, the loss lies wherever it falls—i.e., on the owner or occupier of the land. If negligence can be proved the loss is against the owner of the cattle.

When cattle similarly stray through open gates, damaging crops, the liability for such loss lies upon the owner of the cattle, and negligence need not be proved.

2. When cattle trespass on private land, and by doing so, sustain injury, the loss lies where it falls—i.e., upon the owner of the cattle. Again when they have entered from adjoining private land resultant loss from damage attributable to such trespassing falls upon the owner of the cattle.

Trespass and Damage – Children

I would be most grateful if you would give me advice regarding a problem which I feel may also be facing other members.

My house, although when I bought it 15 years ago was in the country, has now for the past six years or so had a council estate built in fields opposite the entrance.

Children, sometimes as many as 20, from the estate have formed a habit of playing on the hedge of my field.

I have continually chased the children off and have also asked the local police to prevent them trespassing and damaging my property. Some 200 yards from the estate there is a proper children's playing field with swings, etc.

The police have occasionally, usually at my request, come and talked to the children, but they say that, as most of them are under 15 years of age, they can do nothing. They admit they can prosecute the parents but are obviously not keen to take this action. What should I do, as when I go away they will obviously trespass on my property? Also the continual screaming and shouting—especially at week-ends—is a great nuisance.

While you have our sympathy, the more so because we can afford little towards the solution of your problem, there is almost nothing that can be done about it.

The police are impotent in the matter except that they could bring the children known to have done malicious damage before a juvenile court, and that is hardly likely. And, as you will agree, a civil action for trespass against the children would be a futile and absurd waste of money. A talk by you with the probation officer at your nearest court might possibly bring some improvement.

As the parents of the children are council tenants, you could start a campaign for reduction of rates because of loss of amenities. Councils are sensitive to such threats of loss of revenue.

Trespass – Dog

Has a farmer a legal right to shoot dead a trespassing dog found attacking his sheep? If the answer is in the negative, what legal steps should the farmer take to prevent such attacks?

To kill, shoot or injure another man's dog without legal justification is an actionable wrong in common law. It is no justification if it was trespassing. In order legally to justify such an act it must be proved that it was done under necessity for the purpose of protecting the person or saving the property in peril at the moment of the act. Property in such case includes cattle, sheep or poultry.

Trespass – Dog

For the past two or three years, three dogs belonging to a neighbour—who keeps many dogs and has ample ground round her house for exercising them — have constantly hunted in one of our pheasant coverts, half a mile from the neighbour's house and grounds. This has had—and continues to have—a seriously detrimental effect on our pheasants.

The neighbour has been asked several times to keep her dogs under control, but merely replied, 'What can I do? My dogs must have exercise.' She refuses to take any further steps to prevent her dogs hunting in our woods. Have we any redress? Is there any further action we can legally take in the matter?

The best way to answer your query is to quote from an excellent little book called *Animals and the Law*, by T. G. Field-Fisher, which states:

'Although an action for an involuntary trespass to another's land has not been possible in respect of the act of a dog since at least 1700, since a statute of 1865, re-enacted in the Dogs Act, 1908, their owners are liable for injury caused by the worrying of cattle without proof of the owner's knowledge of the animal's tendency to do so. This provision has been extended to the worrying of poultry by the Dogs Act. 'Cattle' includes horses, mules, asses, sheep, goats and swine. So the position now seems to be that an owner will be liable for damage caused by his trespassing dog to all cattle as defined above and to poultry without proof of 'Scienter,' but not for any other form of damage which arises as a direct result of a trespass by the dog. It will be

otherwise, however, if the owner knows of its tendency to attack or worry other animals. It should be noted in passing that it is no defence that the cattle or poultry were themselves trespassing at the time.'

'But if a man should deliberately send his dog on another's land in pursuit of game he is liable for the trespass although he himself remains on his own land. And it has been decided that to allow a dog to roam at large which the owner knew had a mischievous propensity to chase and destroy game was a trespass for which the owner was liable.'

Trespass – Horses

A riding school has been started in a field adjacent to my property.

In the recent cold weather, three horses have entered my property—presumably through hunger—and grazed on the grass in my orchard, but have also run across lawns and flower beds and left innumerable deep hoof marks.

I strengthened the boundary fence immediately adjoining the riding school, but despite this the horses have found their way in again and have done further damage.

On complaining rather heatedly on the second occasion, the owner of the riding school concluded that exchange by remarking that it was my fence.

I would be interested to know what the law is—e.g., is it incumbent on the owner of the property to keep animals out or is it the responsibility of the riding school to keep their horses in, and could I claim for costs of making good the lawns?

The owner of the horses is liable, and probably knows it very well, for the damage done by the trespass of his horses. This liability is strict; he has no defence in an action in showing that he took every reasonable precaution to keep his animals in. The liability is independent of the owner's negligence. It is also independent of whether or not the owner of the land invaded had a cattle-proof fence, or indeed, any fence at all. The obligation to keep his cattle in is upon the owner; no obligation lies upon the owner of private land to keep them out.

What you should do is to claim against the owner of the horses for the damage done by previous trespasses and to tell him that, in the event of further trespasses you will seek an injunction ordering him to take such steps to prevent further trespass.

Trespass – Peacocks

What is the legal position with regard to a neighbour's peacocks, which come into my garden, perch on the roof, and keep everyone awake with their cries, and also do damage in the garden and scare the dogs? There are a number of neighbouring cottages affected in the same way. The owner of the birds has been requested to keep them under control, but refuses to do anything about it.

What is the position should we succeed in catching the birds up and disposing of them, or handing them over to the police? Would we be in our rights to do this? If not, what can we do by law?

Peacocks are in the same category as domestic pets and cannot be disposed of by shooting or injuring them in any way. The R.S.P.C.A., whose opinion we asked, suggested a campaign of douching them with buckets of water or the garden hose which would eventually dissuade them from coming on to your property. Whilst you are within your rights to incarcerate them if you can catch them on your property with a view to extracting payment for damage caused, it seems to us that this will not really help matters.

Peacocks are notorious strayers, but we would have thought a simple answer would be to ask the owners to clip their wings so that they cannot get on to your premises by flying.

(But see Poultry Trespass)

Trespass – People

What is the law regarding people walking through one's garden or parkland in England?

English law is strict in respect of any entrance, without the occupier's permission, into a man's garden or parkland. To enter, to walk through, indeed to interfere with the possession in however slight a manner, is a trespass. As such it is an actionable wrong for which damages may be claimed; it is also a wrong to restrain which the sufferer may obtain an injuction from the court. The law also justifies self-help in respect of trespass; the occupier has a right to expel the trespasser, using, however, no more force against that trespasser than is necessary.

The occupier may give permission—licence—for entry; but a withdrawal of the licence turns the licensee into a trespasser. Moreover, when a licensee exceeds the right accorded to him by the licence—when, for instance, he damages the land by rooting up plants—he becomes a trespasser liable to expulsion.

If the owner of land tolerates unauthorised entry over a period of 20 years the trespasser may be able to establish an easement, giving him a right of way over even private land.

Trespass – Poultry

I have been told that when the farmer's cows and bull get into your garden from the lane (public highway) along which they are being driven, that it is my worry and that I should fence against them. Can I in an equally carefree manner house poultry on my land, but allow them to go through my stock-proof fence and eat the grass on the farmer's field? If he objects can I tell him that he must fence against them? I have an obligation to maintain a stock-proof fence between his land and mine, but no obligation so far as I am aware to maintain a poultry-proof fence.

What you have been told about cattle lawfully on the highway is not entirely correct. If they stray on to neighbouring land, without any negligence of the person in control of them, there is no liability for trespass. The justification for putting cattle in such privileged position is the practical hardship to their owners of adopting any other rule.

The exemption from liability, however, has no application to cattle straying from private land. The owner of the cattle is liable whether or not he exercised care to keep his cattle in. That is what constitutes the strictness of the liability.

Unluckily too, from the point of view of your housing poultry and allowing them to feed in the farmer's field, the definition of ' cattle ' for the purpose of ' cattle trespass ' includes poultry. The term ' cattle ' coincides with the old word ' avers,' and covers horses, oxen, sheep, swine, asses, goats, fowls, geese, ducks, and possibly also peacocks and turkeys.

Your stockproof fence therefore is not adequate unless it is ·proof against the escape of your poultry.

(*See also* Animals Act 1971, page 157.)

Trespass – Tree – 1

I should be much obliged if you would advise me on the following point of law. The boundary between my garden and my neighbour's is marked by a fence made up of strands of wire approximately one foot apart. A tree has grown from my neighbour's garden, at an angle, through the fence and leans over into my garden. Is my neighbour allowed, without my permission, to lop the branches of the tree which are well inside my garden although the tree actually begins to grow from his side of the fence?

The tree to which you refer is the property of your neighbour because it is growing on his land, and all of it, even that part on your side of the boundary, is his. That does not entitle him to come on to your land without your permission to lop the branches of the tree. This is a trespass, in the same way the tree is to a certain extent trespassing on your land itself, and you are entitled to cut back any part of it intruding on your space.

Trespass – Tree – 2

My neighbour has a large elm tree standing very close to an old stable and garage of mine. The crown of this tree spreads over the roof and several branches, of which two or three smaller ones are dead, hang within a foot of the tiles. In high winds these branches scrape the roof, and one or two small branches which were dead have fallen on to the roof. The roof has deteriorated and there were large gaps in the tiles when I bought the property last September. The tree itself appears to be perfectly sound and healthy. Wishing to repair the roof, as it is now in danger of collapsing in places, I asked my neighbour if she would have it pruned by tree surgeons, and obtained a quotation for her. In the meantime she took advice from an estate agent and solicitor, and informs me that they both advised her that she had no responsibility in the matter whatever but that I could, if I wished and entirely at my expense, remove any branches which were over my property.

I will be glad to know if you agree with this legal interpretation as I feel that she must accept some responsibility for damage done, and which may be done, by the branches of her tree.

We agree with you that your neighbour must accept responsibility for her tree and the damage which its branches do in trespassing over your property. You can quote a case (*Caminer v. Northern and London Investment Trust 1950*) which was specifically on the subject of an elm and its owner's liability to damage. The owner of a tree is answerable for the damage it does. Whilst you might have difficulty in proving that the branches caused damage prior to your occupation of the house we consider you are in a position to insist that these offending branches are cut back at your neighbour's own expense. This is especially so in view of elm's evil reputation for dropping its branches without warning for no known reason.

Once you warn your neighbour that you consider the top hamper on this tree dangerous she becomes liable for any damage that occurs as a result of its shedding any branches. If she continues to be uncooperative inform her you will have to take out an injunction against her and if that does not do the trick instruct a solicitor on your behalf.

Trustee – Retirement of

I am a reluctant co-trustee of a small family

trust—I don't recall whether I was consulted when the appointment was made but, no doubt, the fact that I have functioned in that office (somewhat ineffectively, I fear) indicates that I accepted the burden.

It would be better, I think, if I gave up—could you please advise if this can be done and, if so, what steps I should take.

Under the provisions of Section 36 (1) Trustees Act 1925 a Trustee who wishes to do so may retire from that position but another Trustee should be appointed in place of the retiring Trustee. It is quite usual in Trust Deeds or Wills for a clause to be included nominating a person or persons who have the power of appointing new Trustees in the case of a vacancy occurring through retirement, death, or any other cause.

It is often difficult to find a private individual to accept a Trusteeship unless they have a particular interest in the family or beneficiaries of the Trust, so it is sometimes advisable to appoint a professional Trustee such as The C.G.A. to take the place of the retiring Trustee assuming that there is not already a professional Trustee acting. One difficulty may arise in this connection that there may be no charging clause included in the Trust Instrument whereby a professional Trustee can be remunerated for his services.

This problem can obviously be solved, and we suggest that your first step is to discuss the matter with the Trust solicitors.

Unadopted Roads

The county council recently named an unmetalled bridle-way 'Heath Lane', but did not add 'unadopted' to the name plates. Does this omission mean that, if the road is ever made up the county council accepts responsibility, and cannot call upon householders for contributions towards the cost?

Many of the householders' solicitors have failed to find out the legal owner of the road.

The naming cannot of itself affect the status of the way. If it is shown in the statutory map compiled by the county council as a 'public road', there is no need of formal adoption, and it is maintainable by the public at large. If not so shown it is a 'private street' in the

ownership, under the control of, and to be maintained by, the frontagers. Adoption of such is now governed by Part IX of the Highways Act, 1959, and under this, a necessary preliminary would be a resolution of the highway authority. This would be a matter of public knowledge.

Its ownership as a private street is in the owners of the land fronting it, so that, if the way cuts through two properties then, apart from evidence to the contrary, the ownership of each is to the mid-point of the road.

If, as your letter allows us to think, the way remains private, the naming of it by the county council for the benefit of users is a work of superogation.

Upkeep – Compulsory

Am I correct in thinking that about a year ago the Government brought out an order saying farmers must keep up old farm buildings and cottages regardless of whether they wanted to or not— and even if they were no use for modern farming methods.

I am afraid that we do not know of any general order such as you mention and would suggest that if it had been issued it must have come through the Ministry of Agriculture. Therefore, we would advise you to get in touch with the local Ministry.

Local authorities do, from time to time, make preservation orders on buildings of architectural or historical value, and if you contact your local council they would tell you if any buildings of which you are the owner are covered by such orders.

Views – Lost

I have a problem which you may be able to advise me on. Briefly, it is the erection of a large house and garage within four feet of my garden, or approximately thirty-two feet from my cottage. In my considered opinion it will have the effect of devaluing my property, in depriving me of a certain amount of privacy and also of blanking out a fine westward view of the South Downs.

The position with regard to the erection of buildings on neighbouring property is that no one is legally entitled to a view. This of course is highly irritating for those who lose their view.

If you wish to prevent the building taking place – we are not clear as to whether it has already commenced – you should make representations to the planning authorities concerned, which is presumably your local RDC.

The other concrete thing you could do is to submit a proposal to reduce your rates because of the effect these building operations will have on the value of your own property. Local authorities are always sensitive to demands for reductions in rating valuations and if matters have not gone too far they might amend the plans for your benefit.

Vermin Shooting

What conditions, if any, apply to the shooting of vermin and what is included in this term?

Vermin can be shot at any time. Feathered vermin are: rooks, crows, magpies, jackdaws, carrion crows, jays, and woodpigeons. Animal vermin are: rats, squirrels, stoats and weasels. Foxes and rogue badgers are also classed as vermin, but there may be local antagonism if they are shot.

Vicar's Wife as Vicar's Warden

Can you please tell me whether it is legal for the wife of a vicar to be 'vicar's warden'? It seems to me to be wrong because if a son or daughter were 'people's warden' there would be a closed shop and not at all according to the idea of wardens.

No legal impediment affects the appointment. It was held in *Gordon v Hayward* (1905, *The Times* Law Reports) that a woman is eligible for the office of church warden; and no bar is upon the incumbent's wife. Certainly, whenever possible the wardens should be chosen by the joint consent of the parochial church council and the incumbent; only when this is not possible should the council choose one, the incumbent another. However chosen they have the same functions; and there is no legal precedence between them.

Water – Provision of

On the division of a property in 1951 the seller, who continued to live in part A, sold to the buyer of part B on condition that the ram used to supply water to both A and B should be maintained by B in perpetuity. At the time there was no mains water supply to the village but when the supply became available B (who was now the son of the former owner) took advantage of it but A (the property had changed ownership some four times) refused to be connected to the supply.

The ram now requires renewing and A still refuses to change to the mains supply. The cost of renewal would be high. Would you kindly advise me if the fact that the mains water is now available would make any difference to the 'in perpetuity' clause.

The governing and inescapable fact in respect of this query is that the land occupied by the successor of 'A' has attended to it and running with it the easement of water from a specific source in 'B's' land; and that it is wholly worth his discretion to relinquish his easement.

Obviously the present availability of an alternative source does, as you ask, make a difference. For it provides 'B' with a potent argument, and this, augmented by 'B's' expression of willingness to bear the cost of obtaining the alternative, and his statement that an adequate supply of pure water by the Water Board could be more relied upon than from the ram, should be effective to induce 'A' to accept the alternative.

The trouble is that no legal means exists of compelling 'A' to act as a reasonable man would; no court would order him to give up his easement. If, like Shylock, he is persistent in holding on to his strictly legal right, 'B' has no Portia to alter matters.

The hope seems well grounded, however, that 'B's' persuasive power will prevail. His objection of 'A' may be that he will be subject to water rates; a reasonable payment by 'B' would overcome that. It would be pleasant to learn that agreement has been reached.

Weeds

I would be grateful for your advice. Adjoining my garden is a field with a group of trees in the centre. On the far side of this is another garden and a house. The field and the house belong to a trust – and the house is sometimes let on short tenancies: sometimes used as a holiday home for missionaries. The field is covered with nettles and brambles and provides fine cover for vermin. The brambles and nettles spread to my garden and I have lost a considerable number of hens and bantams to foxes. Is there any way of enforcing – I have *failed to persuade – the trustees to look after the field properly?*

The Agricultural Holdings Act of 1948 states you must, in the management of your land, conform to the rules of a good estate management. You can complain to the local offices of the Ministry of Agriculture, but we have found that it is often more effective to go to the Local Authority quoting Section 36, Town and Country Planning Act, 1962, complaining of injury suffered from your neighbour's land.

The Local Authority should serve a notice on the owner requiring him to take steps to abate the injury. We hope that you will be successful.

GENERAL

*This section provides a useful selection of
addresses where one can get others to provide
the services one is unwilling or unable
to provide for oneself*

Adoption Societies

Can you give me the address of an Adoption Society?

The Church Adoption Society, 4a Bloomsbury Square, W.C.1.
National Adoption Society, 47a Manchester Square, W.1.
National Children's Adoption Association, 71 Knightsbridge, S.W.1.

Agricultural Benevolent Institution – Royal

Could you send me the address of what used to be the Agricultural Benevolent Society—or perhaps it never had exactly that name? I want to make inquiries about their homes for the elderly, and though I have asked Directory Enquiries am told it cannot be found.

The address of the Royal Agricultural Benevolent Institution is Vincent House, Vincent Sq., London, S.W.1. Perhaps you would like to write to the Secretary giving as many details as possible. They like to know how many years the applicant has been working on farms, their income, etc.

Agricultural Correspondence College

Do you know of any place that runs a correspondence course in Agriculture?

We suggest you contact: Major A. E. Bruce-Fielding, Agricultural Correspondence College, Warborough, Oxford.

Courses in Agriculture

Can you give me a short list of Universities or Colleges in England and Wales which give courses in agriculture?

A very short list of Universities is:
Cambridge.
Durham.
Leeds.
London (Wye College, Ashford, Kent).
Nottingham.
Oxford (School of Rural Economy).
Reading.
Wales (Aberystwyth).
N. Wales (Bangor).

Colleges:
Harper Adams, Newport, Salop.
Royal Agricultural College, Cirencester, Glos.
Seal-Hayne, Newton Abbott, Devon.
Studley College, Warwicks (women only).

Information on Agricultural Training for Young Farmers

Does anybody publish a general pamphlet on how a young man can train professionally to be a farmer?

The Royal Agricultural Society of England publish a leaflet (No. 2 New Series) entitled "The Training of the Young Farmer" obtainable from 35 Belgrave Square, London S.W.1.

Amateur Dramatics – Societies

My daughter would like to join an Amateur Dramatic Society. Can you give me an address?

You could try the British Drama League, 9 Fitzroy Square, London, W.1, or The National Operatic and Dramatic Association, 1 Crestfield Street, London, W.C.1.

Animal Homes

Can you let me have the address of the association which looks for homes for aged donkeys, horses, ponies, etc., as we have space here and can provide a home for one animal or possibly two.

The Association is the Blue Cross, 1 Hugh Street, London SW1. This association has a home for horses and donkeys at Northiam, Sussex.

Antiques – Books on Looking After

Can you recommend a book on looking after antiques?

The Repair and Restoration of Furniture by John Rodd, or *Care of Antiques* by J. M. Mills.

Antique Collectors' Club

Can you give me the address of the "Antique Collectors' Club"?

It is: A. C. C. Clopton, Woodbridge, Suffolk. They publish the Antique Collectors' Magazine and the Price Guide to Antique Furniture, and ditto Silver.

Antique Dealer – Leicester

I live in Leicester and would like to know the name of a reputable Antique dealer in these parts.

We suggest you contact: Walter Moores & Son, Wellington Street, Leicester.

Antlers

I have some stag horns which I would like to have made up into knives, do you know of anybody who undertakes this kind of work?

If you would like to contact Air Commodore Tindall-Carill-Worsley, Edrington House, Berwick on Tweed, he will be able to help you as he makes stag horns into cheese knives, butter knives, etc.

Archaeology

I have become interested in Archaeology and wonder whether you know of any society from which I might obtain more information on this subject?

We suggest that you contact the Royal Archaeological Institute of Great Britain, c/o London Museum, Kensington Palace, London, W.8, or alternatively The Council for British Archaeology at 8 St. Andrews Place, London, NW1.

Archery

I would like to take up Archery and wonder if you know of any club in my area which does this?

If you contact the London Archery Association, 14 Close Road, Barnes, London, S.W.13, they will be able to let you have the name of a club near to where you live.

Armour

I have recently come into possession of a suit of armour and would like to know more about what period it is, etc., do you know of anyone who could tell me this?

If you would like to contact: Peter Dale Ltd., of 12 Royal Opera Arcade, Pall Mall, London, S.W.1, giving him full details of your suit of armour he will be able to help you.

Coat of Arms

I have in my possession a small copy (about 6 in. by 4 in.) of a "Coat of Arms" which came to me some years ago on the death of my father. Unfortunately documents relating to it were lost during the war. I should like to obtain some details of the meaning and origin of the Coat of Arms and whether I or other members of the family are entitled to display it. Could you tell me to whom I should write please? I think it is probably of Irish origin as my family appears in "Irish Pedigrees" written by O'Hart in 1878.

You should write to the College of Arms, Queen Victoria Street, London EC4, since they will be able to provide all the information you require.

Art Exhibitions

Can you let me know of any society that would be able to inform me of the different Art Exhibitions that would be on in London?

If you would like to contact the Art Exhibition Bureau, at 6½ Suffolk Street, Pall Mall East, London, S.W.1, they will be able to help you as they act as a general secretariat for all the art societies in London. They will also find artists to paint portraits, etc.

Arthritis Cure – Book on

A short time ago I saw an advertisement for a book on the cure of arthritis by means of dieting. I cannot trace this now. Can you help?

The Arthritis and Rheumatism Council say that they do not know of this book. They do, however, recommend an up-to-date book on this subject called: *Arthritis and Rheumatism*, by W. S. C. Copeman, published by Evans Bros. Ltd., Montague House, Russell Square, London, W.C.1.

There is a book called *Arthritis and Folk Medicine* sold at a health food store in London called Cranks Health Food Shop, of 8 Marshall Street, London, W.1. This apparently contains some advice on diet. The price is $17\frac{1}{2}$p.

Art Packers

I wonder if you know of any firm of reputable Art Packers.

We suggest you contact: Messrs. Pitt & Scott Ltd., of 1 St. Paul's Churchyard, London, E.C.4, who will be able to help you.

Art Valuations

Do you know of anybody who values paintings, furniture, jewellery, fine art silver, etc., for probate insurance.

We suggest you contact Christie's of 8 King Street, St. James's, London, S.W.1, or Gurr Johns, 50 Pall Mall, S.W.1.

Art Restorers

I have some Antique Bronzes that I would like to be restored, can you suggest anyone who might be able to do this?

A firm of art restorers are: The Tortoiseshell and Ivory House, Ltd., 24 Chiltern Street, London, W.1. They are specialists in the restoration of jades, hardstones, ivories, ceramics, enamels, tortoiseshell, antique bronzes, ormolu, snuff bottles, marbles, and general works of art. They also renovate and rebristle brushes in any material and supply to your requirements.

Art Work and Restoration

I have a painting that I would like to be restored. Do you know of any reputable firm who could do this?

We suggest you contact The Art Workers Guild, at 6 Queens Square, London, W.C.1.

Association – Over 45's

I wonder if you could give me any help in tracing an association which was formed four or five years ago in order to assist in employing men over 45 years of age made redundant by takeovers or similar causes, aiming to help ex-company directors and executives?

We believe that the association that you are thinking of is: Senior Executives Development Association Ltd., 11 North Road, London, N.7. Tel.: 01-607 7811. Or possibly: Over 45's Association, 217a Kensington High Street, London, W.8.

Astrologer

Can you please recommend me a reliable astrologer?

We have spoken to Mrs. Julia Parker who works at the College of Astrological Studies, and she says if you would like to write to her she would be able to write a horoscope report for you. She really prefers to see the people before doing this, but she does not have a qualified astrologer in the Channel Islands on her lists. Her address is 37 Campden Hill Tower, London, W11. This College which has been going for twenty-one years, and runs courses for learning astrology, after which a diploma is given.

Universal Aunts

Can you please put me in touch with

an organisation who could provide the services of a reliable person to meet my two children at Exeter airport on a particular day next August, take them to Exeter station and see them safely on board a train to Bideford?

Contact Universal Aunts Ltd., 36 Walpole Street, London, SW3, since they specialize in this type of service.

Au Pair Students

Do you know of any society that makes arrangements about au pair students?

We suggest you contact Rospilgiosi Bureau, of 4 Marylebone High Street, London, W.1.

Society of Authors, Playwright and Composers

Do you know of any society for authors?

The one you require is: Society of Authors, Playwrights and Composers at 84 Drayton Gardens, London SW10.

Autographs – Sale of

I have a very nice studio portrait of Field Marshal Smuts, which is autographed. I understand that there are autograph collectors. Do you think this would be of interest?

We have spoken to a firm called W. A. Myers Autographs Limited, and they say they might be interested in buying it. Perhaps you could take it into their offices at 35 Dover Street, London, W.1, when you are next in London, and they will be able to value it for you.

Autographs – Valuation

Recently an autograph of Lord Nelson has come into my possession and I wondered whether you knew of anyone who could tell me how much it is worth?

We suggest you contact: W. A. Myers Autographs Ltd., 80 New Bond Street, London, W.1, who will be able to help you.

Wooden Balls

I read recently of an appeal for wooden balls for a country fete. It is too late now, but the inquirer might be interested to know that the nearest Polo Club always has old and chipped polo balls which they would sell, donate, or even loan for such a purpose.

Barbeques

I would like to purchase a Barbeque and its accessories, do you know where I might be able to obtain them?

You can get a Swedish Barbeque Grill at Liberties and sizzle charcoal briquettes at any store, but if you have difficulty Thomas Hill-Jones, Lee House, London Wall will advise stockists. Harrods supply bags of charcoal but it can also be bought from most coal merchants.

The *Daily Telegraph* Saturday small ads have a cheap portable affair which works very well.

You can make your own by digging a shallow trench for the fire and setting oven grids over the top but you have to use pans for this method.

Baracuta Raincoats

Can you let me know where I might obtain Baracuta Raincoats?

If you contact A. Woodcock, Manager, Baracuta House, 1/7 Beswick Street, Manchester, 4, they will be able to help you. Their London Agent is George West Ltd., 445 Oxford Street, London, W.1.

Barometer – Tube Replacement

Can you suggest where I might obtain a glass

tube for an old mercury barometer—a U tube, the main part being a capillary with the top and the open end at the bottom being of larger diameter?

I have found a firm in Liverpool who would fill it, but they are unable—or not sufficiently interested to find anyone to make a tube.

Thank you for your letter inquiring about suppliers of glass tubing. We would suggest you contact the following address: Scientific Glassblowing Co., 95 Gray's Inn Road, London, W.C.1. They specialise in glass tubing and laboratory glassware.

Other firms who specialise in renovating barometers, etc., and in the tubes are Garner & Marney Ltd., 41/43 Southgate Road, London, N.1, and R. W. Jennings & Co., Scientech House, Main Street, East Bridgford, Nottingham.

Bees

Do you know of any association that will be able to give me information about keeping bees?

We suggest that you contact the British Bee-Keepers' Association – their Secretary is Mr. O. Meyer, 55 Chipstead Lane, Riverhead, Sevenoaks, Kent.

Bellringers

I would be grateful if you would tell me whether there is a society for Bell-ringers?

Yes there is – it is the Ancient Society of College Youths, whose address is obtainable from Church of England H.Q.

Bells

Where might I obtain information about Bells, also do you know of a Bell-maker?

The Victoria and Albert Museum, South Kensington, London, S.W.7, will be able to give you all the information you require.

A firm of Bell-Makers are: Whitechapel Bell Foundry, 32 Whitechapel Road, London, E.1.

Betting Disputes – Settlement

Who can settle a dispute I am having over a bet?

Tattersalls Committee, 7 Hatherley Road, Reading, Berks.

Bird Boxes

Where can I obtain information about Bird Boxes?

Try contacting the Essex Bird Watching and Preservation Society, whose secretary is Mrs. P. V. Upton, Park Lodge, Margaretting, Ingatestone, Essex.

Birds Eggs

I have recently come into possession of a collection of Birds' eggs and wondered if you know of anyone who could tell me what they are and if it would be possible to sell them?

We suggest you contact the Editor, *Oologists' Record*, Five Magpies, Newnham-on-Severn, Glos., who will be able to tell you what they are. But we must point out that the 1954 Act and later amendments forbid the sale of the eggs of *any* birds known to nest in the British Isles, irrespective of the date at which the eggs were collected, and there is not much market for eggs of birds not nesting in this country.

Blue Cross, The

I know of some donkeys who will be destroyed if they are not found somewhere to "retire" can you help?

We suggest you contact The Blue Cross, 1 Hugh Street, London S.W.1. They have an Animal Hospital and Home for Donkeys and Horses. There is such a home at Northiam, Sussex.

Books – Antiques

Can you tell me of a firm who sell

antique books, also one where I might be able to sell some old bird books that I have?

A famous antiquaria bookseller is: Maggs Bros., 50 Berkeley Square, London, W.1.

Beachs Bookshop in Salisbury will buy old books, especially ones about birds.

Book Auctioneers

Do you know of a firm of Book Auctioneers?

Such a firm is Hodgson & Co., 115 Chancery Lane, London, W.C.2.

Book-Binding

Some time ago I wrote asking for advice as regards the binding of a quantity of magazines of historical interest into book form. I explained that I had already at that time approached several firms in the Home Counties without any success. You replied that I should take the magazines to W. H. Smith & Sons Ltd., who undertook this kind of work. Very soon after I had received his letter I approached the organization mentioned only to be told that they had discontinued this kind of work. Can you help again in any way? It seems peculiar that it is impossible to get these magazines bound.

We suggest that you contact Mr. R. G. Shillingford of The Book Jacket Company Limited, 307 New Kings Road, London, S.W.6. He will undertake all book-binding work, including leather if you wish.

Book Plate – Engraver

I wonder if you could recommend me a firm or an individual who could engrave me a book-plate?

There is no necessity for getting plates engraved these days. It is much cheaper to use the photo-litho process, which any competent printer can provide.

I got roundly seen off for this answer. A second attempt did better.

You should go to Mr. G. Holt, 6 Dyus Buildings, Holborn, E.C.1. Tel. 242 8682.

He was engraving one currently for Lord Mountbatten.

Rare Books

Can you put me in touch with any firm or firms interested in the purchase of old and relatively rare books?

Amongst other books I have in my possession the seven complete volumes of Lord Lilford's "Birds of the British Islands" in good condition with beautiful coloured plates, which I should be prepared to sell at a reasonable price.

We have spoken to Mr. Radcliff of Bernard Quaritch Limited of 11 Grafton Street, London, W.1, and he said that if your set of Lord Lilford's *Birds of the British Islands* is in good condition and not too spotted he would be interested in buying it. Its value would be about £40. As it is not possible for him to come to you, he suggests you send him just one volume, and if possible pick out the worst one.

This firm do specialize in rare books, but they would be interested in your other old books. Foyles in Charing Cross Road would no doubt also be able to give you a price for them.

Books – Unusual – Outdoor Variety

Can you tell me of any firm who have out of print unusual books?

Such a firm is St. George's Gallery Books Ltd., 8 Duke Street, London, S.W.1.

Is there any special bookshop that supplies books about gardens, plants, animals, etc.

There is such a shop and it is called: The Landsman's Bookshop, and is at Buckenhill, Bromyard, Hereford – it has books on trees, weeds, plants, gardens, farm animals, angling, etc.

Do you know of anywhere in London that has a large variety of books of all kinds?

We suggest you contact: W. & G. Foyles Ltd., 119 Charing Cross Road, London, W.C.2 (437-5660) or Hatchards of 187 Piccadilly, London, W.1 (734-3201).

Books – Valuations of

Heffers of Trinity Street, Cambridge, second-hand valuations and rare books, and John Walter Hellens, Much Marcle, Leadbury, Hereford, specialists in valuations of country-house libraries and rare books.

Bottles – Cutting

We used to make tumblers at Tobruk very effectively by the following method. Put water and then a layer of oil in the bottle. Plunge a red hot poker in. The difference in conducting qualities of oil and water cause the bottle to break off cleanly at the point of contact where water and oil meet.

See p. 6.

Boules – Where to Get

Can you let me know anyone who could supply me with a set of boules? These are used for a game played in Corsica and consist of at least eight spherical iron balls size 74 mm. diameter and 700–725 gms. weight. Designs are engraved on each ball to distin-·guish pairs (i.e. four designs for eight balls). There is also a wooden marker ball about the size of a tennis ball.

We contacted Lillywhites of Piccadilly, London, S.W.1, who say they can supply sets of boules. The metal ones cost £3.75 each for a pair of two.

Brass Lacquering

Can you tell me where I could get some Brass lacquered to prevent it tarnishing?

A firm which will undertake to lacquer brass is: John Wilkins & Co. Ltd., 231 St. John Street, London, E.C.1. BRU 1344.

Brass Mountings

I would appreciate your advice on how to obtain some particular brass mountings for a rather decayed Pembroke table.

There is a marvellous shop called J. D. Beardmore, of 4 Percy Street, London, W.1 (Tel.: 01-636 1214), and they can match almost any decorative handle, knob, or hinge, and they will reproduce anything in brass. Perhaps next time you are in London you could call in there, as it is rather difficult to describe exactly what you want in a letter.

Brass

Can you tell me where I could obtain some brass ornaments?

We suggest you contact: Jack Casimir Ltd., The Brass Shop, 23 Pembridge Road, Nottinghill Gate, London, W.11. Tel.: PAR 8643.

Brass fittings can be obtained from: Cluse Ltd., Brass Founders – Art Metal Workers, 4 Percy Street, London, W.1. MUS 4811.

Bread Making – Source of Rye Meal

We have for years been making our own bread with stone ground flour, plus a small quantity of Rye meal which has been supplied by Prewett's, of Horsham—but this firm has now discontinued stocking Rye meal owing to lack of demand—they offer me Rye flour instead, but this does not help, as it is the texture which is lacking—I cannot find any firm which can supply it, and so, if you cannot help me here, can you alternatively suggest where I can get whole Rye in small quantities, say 7 lb. at a time, and either find someone to grind it locally, or perhaps do it myself in an electric mixer, if you think that feasible? Years ago I knew a woman who grew a little on her farm just for this purpose, and had it ground, but that was before the last war when one could still get things done to one's individual requirements.

A wholesale corn and flour merchant in London has said that if you could possibly collect it from their premises, there would be no problem, except that one might have to buy 28 lb. (although he says they have sold as little as 7 lb. before). Their name and address is Baker, Sons & Dickson, 34 Crutched Friars, London, E.C.3.

They were very helpful and suggested that you try the Southern Counties Agricultural Trading Society Limited, at Northgate House, Staple Gardens, Winchester. They might be able to put you on to a supplier, and we believe they have a retail shop in Salisbury.

The only other possibility would be to buy the whole rye from a local corn merchant and to grind it yourself in an electric coffee mill. According to some of the shops I have contacted, this is what people do, and for small quantities, it is quite practicable.

We have tried many health shops in London, and they all seem to be supplied by Prewett's, and are, therefore, in the same predicament as you.

Bronze Plaque

I have been asked by our local Parish Council to find out how to set about getting the plaque on the north side of the War Memorial cleaned. It was put up in 1945 but has become very stained and weather beaten and looks in far wcrse condition than the other two plaques which date from the First World War. Can you advise?

Bronze corrodes very easily. This corrosion occurs readily in air, when a light green surface deposit is formed, usually referred to as "air patination." On the whole it is undesirable to tamper with corrosion. It is only necessary to remove any adherent loose material, and in fact, removal of the products of corrosion often reduce the value of an object, since the type and extent are useful indications of age. However, in the case of your plaque one needs to read the writing and the removal of the patination can be done with careful flaking with small tools such as a penknife and a *brass* wire brush. Do not use an iron or steel wire brush. When cleaning has been completed, a coat of clear varnish will preserve the surface from further corrosion. If it is desirable to use chemical means, probably the safest method to adopt is to clean the object with a solution of 10 per cent acetic acid in water, and to follow this with copious washing in clean water. The green carbonates of copper will disappear leaving red copper oxide which will be soft enough to remove with a little trouble.

Bronzes – Books on

I have a number of bronzes which I feel are slowly becoming more valuable. Is there any book similar to, say, one on old silver, which would help me to assess their worth?

According to Sothebys, the following list of books should prove helpful: *Bronzes* – in the "Pleasures and Treasures" series, by Jennifer Montague. A useful book which deals with bronzes from the Renaissance period onwards. *Italian High Renaissance and Baroque Sculpture* by Pope-Hennessy, published by Phaidon Press. This book also deals with bronzes. *Piccoli Bronzi Italiani di Rinascinento,* by Leo Planiscig (in Italian). Available at London libraries.

The following books deal with ancient bronzes: *Greek and Roman Bronzes,* by Mary Lamb. *Greek Bronzes,* by Charbonneaux. *Bronze Antiques de Haut Provence,* by H. Rolland, Supplement de Gallia (in French).

If you have any difficulty in obtaining these books, you could try contacting St. George's Gallery Books Ltd., 8 Duke Street, London, S.W.1, who specialize in getting hold of unusual books. Sothebys themselves could offer you advice, as could the Department of Metalwork at the Victoria and Albert Museum.

Brushes – Hair – Rebristling

Are there any firms who will rebristle hair brushes. I have a set of silver backed hair brushes and the bristles need renewing?

There are several firms who do this work but you should inquire the cost of having it done because it can be expensive.

Richard Ogden, 28 Burlington Arcade,

London, W.1 ; W. Brandt & Son, 9 Old Bond Street, London, W.1 ; Richard Attenborough, 142/144 Oxford Street, London, W.1 ; Army and Navy Stores, Victoria Street, London, S.W.1.

Budgerigars – Homing

Information on Homing Budgerigars?

The book available is Homing Birds by L. G. Collins and the Duke of Bedford (not the present one). This is available from the Cage Birds Society, Dorset House, Stamford Street, London, S.E.1, or good booksellers.

If you require any further information we suggest writing to the Budgerigar Information Bureau, Orchard House, Orchard Street, London, W.1.

Buildings – Cleaning of

Do you know of a firm that will clean buildings?

We suggest you contact: Peter Cox & Partners Ltd, 15 Addington Square, London S.E.5.

Old Buildings – Preservation

I have an old Cotswold barn near my house which various people have informed me would be worth preserving. I know nothing of these matters myself. It distresses me to see it falling into disrepair but it is of no use to me and I cannot afford to maintain it for its beauty.

I am wondering if you can tell me of anyone who would be able to inform me if it really is worth preserving and, if so, if there is any organization who might be able to assist in its maintenance.

We suggest that you write to the Historic Buildings Council, Century Buildings, Great Smith Street, London, S.W.1, giving them all the details of the building and its state of condition.

Buildings – Historic Council

We would like to know whether our house could be counted as an Historic building?

We suggest you contact: Historic Buildings Council, Century House, Great Smith Street, London, S.W.1. Grants can be obtained for the restoration of buildings of historic or architectural value.

Butlers

Where might I obtain a well trained Butler?

An Agency which train them themselves is: Belgravia Bureau, 35 Brompton Road, London S.W.3.

Butterfly Farm

Do you know of anywhere where I could obtain butterflies?

A Butterfly farm is: Hugh Newman, Esq., 41 Salisbury Road, Bexley, Kent.

Butterflies

Do you know of anyone who could help me identify some butterflies that have come into my possession?

One place you might try is: Watkins & Doncaster, 110 Park View Road, Welling, Kent.

Buttons

Do you know of any firm that has a large selection of buttons, I am particularly interested in Hunt ones?

You could try: The Button Queen, 23 St. Christopher's Place, London W.1. Or a firm that specialises in Hunt and Club Buttons is: Huntsman, 11 Savile Row, London W.1, they have Hunt and Club buttons in stock or they can be made to specifications.

Hansom Cabs

Could you, by any chance, suggest to me where I might be able to procure a hansom cab?

You should contact the following firm, which hires out all sorts of hansom cabs and horse-drawn vehicles. They should be able to tell you where to buy one: Alfred Jacobs & Sons, 343 Mile End Road, London E.1.

Candlestick Cleaning

Can you tell me where I could get a pair of candlesticks cleaned?

We suggest you contact: Chas. Farris Ltd., Bishopsgate Works, Hounslow, Middlesex.

Cane Chairs – Repairs

Can you give me the address of firms which recane chairs?

T. J. Draper, 37 Gt. Pulteney Street, W.1.
Mrs. E. A. Alliott, Rosemount, E. Hoathley, Lewes, Sussex.
Cooks Ltd., Market Place, Reading, Berks.
G. Holt and Sons, Oak Mead, High Wycombe, Bucks.

Cannons – 1

I have recently come into possession of an old cannon and wondered whether you could suggest anyone who could give me some information about it.

We suggest you contact: The Master of the Armouries, The Tower of London, London, E.C.3.

Cannons – 2

I have a pair of cannon models which I have been told by the Armouries at the Tower of London are mid-17th century, probably Dutch or German. The wooden carriages are probably also original, and the guns are very nice of their kind.
Can you let me know of any reputable

authority who might be interested in acquiring them?

We have spoken to Peter Dale, who has an armoury firm at 12 Royal Opera Arcade, Pall Mall, London, S.W.1. He is in fact a C.G.A. member, and we have had dealings with him before, and we know he is very knowledgeable on the subject. We suggest you contact him.

Cannons – 3

I have two cannon reputed to have been salvaged from the 'Santa Catalina', a Spanish galleon which was wrecked a few miles south of here in 1588.
The cannon are of cast iron, having an overall length of just over four feet and a bore of around two inches.
Can you give me any idea of their value and how one would dispose of them to the best advantage?

We have been in touch with Sotheby's who are very interested in your cannon and suggest that you take a photo of them and send it to them. They cannot give a value at the moment as they have not seen them, and a lot will depend on the condition of them.

Send your photo to: Arms and Armour Department, Sotheby's, 34 New Bond Street, London, W.1.

Caravans

Where might I obtain information about Caravans?

We suggest you contact either: The Caravan Club, 65 South Molton St, London, W.1, or Caravan Information Service, 3 Heathcock Court, Strand, London, W.C.2.

Cats

Is there any Society that looks after and advises about cats?

The organization you are probably thinking of is: The Cats Protection League and Tailwavers, 435 Caledonian Road, London N.7. This Society was founded in 1927 to raise the status of cats and it looks after and advises on the welfare of cats through Britain and N. Ireland.

Caves – Speleologists

Could you kindly put me in touch with some 'pot holing' club or organization, who might be interested in exploring a very old and extensive underground stone quarry, but which has not been worked for over two hundred years.

We would suggest that you get into touch with the British Speleological Association of Duke Street, Settle, Yorkshire, who might possibly be able to assist you.

Chair Seats – Repairs

I have some rush chairs I would like to repair myself. Can you suggest somewhere where I can get materials?

Dryad Handicrafts of 22 Bloomsbury Street, London, W.C.1, will provide both detailed instructions and materials.

Chandeliers

Where could I get a chandelier repaired?

We suggest you contact: Cecil Davis, 3 Grosvenor Street, New Bond Street, London, W.1.

Charities

Where can I get some advice about contributing to charities?

The National Council of Social Services run a Charities Aid Fund at 26 Bedford Square, London W.C.1. A person may enter into a covenant with this fund and they will distribute the income, after recovery of income tax, on his instructions throughout the year.

Chess Sets

I would like to purchase a set of ivory chessmen. Can you advise me where I should try?

Chess specialists are: Mackett Beeson, 22 Lansdowne Row, London, W.1.

Children's Clothes – Second Hand

Where can I get cheap but good-quality second-hand clothes for my children?

Children's Market, 29 Holland Street, London, W.8.
The C.G.A. Magazine operates an Offers and Wants section which can give you a contact.

Repairing China – Book on

Can you recommend a book on repairing china?

You could try " The Art of Repairing and Rivetting Glass, China and Earthenware," by J. Howarth.
A firm in Newbury, J. J. Davies & Sons (Newbury) Ltd., of 63 Northbrook Street, issue a manual on " The Art of Repairing China, Glass and General Pottery Wares."

China and Glass Repairs

Do you know of a reputable firm that carries out china and glass repairs?

We suggest you contact Jennifer Davies, 75 Walton Street, London, S.W.3. (01-589 8519.)

China Repairs – Glass

Can you advise me where I could get repairs to China carried out?

We suggest you contact: Valentine Pirie. 11 Westmoreland Place, London, S.W.1, or: Dorien Gough Studios, 38 Silver Street, Salisbury, Wilts.

Chinese Arts and Crafts

I wish to buy a genuine Chinese fan and wondered if you knew of anywhere that might sell these.

We suggest you contact: Arts and Crafts of China, 89 Baker Street, London, W.1.

Christmas Card Printing

Where might I get some Christmas cards printed?

We suggest you contact The Favil Press Ltd., 152 Kensington High Street, London, W.8 ; they also print bookplates, letter-headings, prospectuses, stationery, invitations, etc., and are reasonable Might we add it is considered non-U to have the name of the sender printed inside.

Christmas Cards

Can anyone suggest what can be done with Christmas cards after use?

They are welcomed by the Lord Roberts Memorial Workshops, 74 Upper Parliament Street, Liverpool, who put them to good use.

Christmas Tree Decorations

Where might I obtain a large quantity of varied Christmas tree decorations?

We suggest you contact either Fancy Papers Ltd., Polyfoil Papers, Polyfoil Works, Packington Road, Acton, W.3, or Wilner Products Ltd, 66 Dollis Hill Lane, London N.W.2.

Church Clocks

Do you know of anyone who could advise about Church clocks?

We have three addresses you might try. They are: Gillett & Johnson (Clocks) Ltd., Woodside Place, Mount Pleasant, Alperton, Middlesex. E. Dent & Co. Ltd., 41 Pall Mall, London, S.W.1. T. N. Hartley, Silchester Common, Nr. Reading (Silchester 21), these deal with Turret clocks as well.

Church Furniture

Could you suggest anyone who might be able to give me some information about Church Furniture?

We suggest you contact: G. Marle & Son Ltd., 10–12 The Borough, Canterbury. Canterbury 61296. They also supply woodwork, stained glass and Bronze tablets.

Churches Spires – Lightning Protection

I would like to advise about lightning protection for our church spire. Do you know of anyone who could help me?

We suggest you contact: A. J. Robb, Esq., The Bird Sanctuary, Drumaness, Co. Down, N. Ireland. He will be able to help you about church towers, spires, lightning protection, church bells, carillions and clocks.

Cigarette Cards

Can you suggest anyone who might be able to give me information about Cigarette cards.

A firm that sells cards is: The London Cigarette Card Co. Ltd., Cambridge House, 30 Wellesley Road, Chiswick, London, W.4.

Clay Pigeons

I am interested in finding out more about Clay Pigeon Shooting and possibly joining a club, I wonder if you can help me.

We suggest you contact: Clay Pigeon Shooting Association, Eley Estate, Angel Road, London, N.18. They are very helpful and will supply a list of clubs in any area.

Clock Glass Domes

Where might I obtain a glass dome for a clock?

Try Beech & Son Ltd., Swanley, Kent (Swanley 3211).

Clock Domes

I have an antique skeleton clock which

has had its glass cover or dome broken. I would be grateful if you would inform me of the name and address of a firm which is prepared to make one of these to pattern. Or, alternatively, a shop which stocks them.

We have now consulted our experts, who inform us that it is impossible to get a new dome made today. We understand that the firm who made these domes was bombed during the war and did not open up again. They can only suggest that you try and find a dome covering a stuffed animal in an antique shop or alternatively have a square frame made and put glass in the sides. The latter suggestion would keep the dust out of the clock.

Long-Case Clock

Can you please suggest a firm who are willing to undertake repairs to the mechanism of our antique long-case clock, and successful and reliable at such work?

We suggest you contact the firm of F. B. Boyer-Collard, 124 Cromwell Road, London, S.W.7. (Telephone Fremantle 0319.)

Clocks – 1

Do you know of anyone who could give me some information about clocks that I own?

We suggest that you contact: The Clock Room, British Museum, if you give them all the details of the clocks they will probably be able to help you.

Clocks – 2

Where might I get advice about clocks?

You could try: Meyrick Neilson, Tetbury, Glos., or The British Horological Institute, or: A. A. Osborne & Son, or: *Horological Review*, 258 Grays Inn Road, London, W.C.1.

Residential Club for Women

Do you know of any residential clubs in London for women?

We suggest you contact The English Speaking Union, 37 Charles Street, London W.1. (01-629 7400.)

Coats of Arms (Carved and Painted)

Do you know of anyone who can give me some information about Coats of Arms?

We suggest you contact: Peter Dale (Insignia) Ltd., Royal Opera Arcade, Pall Mall, London, S.W.1, or you could try College of Arms, Queen Victoria Street, London, E.C.4.

Coins

Do you know of anyone who would value my collection of coins and medals and advise me how to dispose of them?

We suggest you contact Spink & Son, 5/7 King Street, St. James's, London, S.W.1, or you could try A. H. Baldwin & Sons, 1 John Adam Street, London, W.C.2.

Bone Combs

I have a relative in Australia who has asked me to purchase a bone comb which I understand are no longer available in Australia. I have enquired at the fashionable chemists in Tunbridge Wells and I have been offered ivory or horn combs. Can you please tell me where I might obtain a bone combe?

We have tried several places without success, and the chemists say that it is not possible to get one. Harrods have ivory and horn combs which they say are very good but have never had bone ones. Perhaps your relative meant ivory as this would look similar to bone.

Commonwealth Families and Friendship Association

I have heard of an Association that offers reduced travel, and wondered whether you knew the name of it.

We believe that you must be thinking of The Commonwealth Families and Friendship Association, and we suggest you contact: Mr. C. J. Luke, 45 Mayesbrook Road, Dagenham, Essex. They offer reduced travel, charter flights, etc., for visiting relatives abroad. You would have to become a member and wait for six months.

Computers – Finding Homes

I have heard of an organization that finds homes for people by means of a computer and wondered whether you could tell me more about them.

There are two organizations that do this, they are: Home Search Ltd., 5 Queens Street, London, W.1, and: Home Seekers Computer Services Ltd., 7 Buckingham Gate, London, S.W.1.

Conkers – For Sale

I have a large number of conkers from my chestnut trees each autumn. Are they of any commercial value?

If they have been kept cool and fresh the following nursery might purchase them for sowing: E. F. G. (Nurseries) Ltd., Forestry House, Berkhamsted, Herts.

Consumers Association

Address: 14 Buckingham Street, London, W.C.2.

Cooking Queries

I have a rather tricky cookery problem and wondered if you knew of anyone who could help me.

We will forward your letter to Miss Winifred Graham, 1 High Path, Mid-hurst, Sussex, who is always pleased to answer cooking questions *re* recipes, etc.

Copper Pans

Where might I obtain copper pans?

You could try: P. C. L. German, 125 Edgware Road, London, W.2, or: Jack Casimir Ltd., 23 Pembridge Road, London, W.11.

Copper – Problems

I would like some advice about some copper ornaments that I have, can you suggest anyone?

We suggest you contact: Copper Development Association, 55 South Audley Street, London, W.1.

Copper Scuttles – Relacquering

Where might I be able to get a copper scuttle relacquered?

The Chalk Farm Plating Co., 21 Chalk Farm Road, London, N.W.1, do cleaning and relacquering.

Corn Dollies

I am desirous of obtaining some information about 'Corn Dollies' and wondered if you could help me through your columns.
Most counties have their own 'pattern' for a 'dolly', e.g., Cambs—a bell. I have heard that the Bedfordshire one is called a 'Jack and Jill', but cannot find out what form this takes. Can any of your readers help me, please?

The New Golden Dolly, by M. Lambeth, published by the Cornucopia Press, 22 Stonebridge Lane, Fulbourn, Cambs., may be of interest.

Mrs. Sandford, of Eye Manor, near Leominster, Herefordshire, is an authority on corn dollies, and runs three-day courses for people wishing to learn the art of making them. A short booklet, *Corn dollies and how to make them*, by Lettice Sandford and Philla Davis, is published by the Herefordshire Federation of Women's Institutes, 43 Broad Street, Hereford, price 12½p.

Cottage Crafts

I am seeking information and tuition in cottage crafts, and wonder whether you can help. In particular, I am interested in weaving, pottery, hornwork and stone polishing, with the object of producing craft work for sale. Can you please suggest where short intensive courses on these subjects are available.

We strongly advise you to get in touch with the Rural Industries Bureau, at 35 Camp Road, Wimbledon, London, S.W.19. This is a Government-financed advisory organisation set up to help country businesses in England and Wales, and the Bureau should be able to put you in touch with a college which specialises in this sort of thing. You could also inquire at the Craft Centre, 43 Earlham Street, London, W.C.2. (Tel. 240 3327.) Here you can buy such things as hand-woven fabrics, engraved glass, carvings, etc. You could also try Dryad's, at 22 Bloomsbury Street, London, W.C.1 (Tel.: Museum 0234), where weaving materials, pottery tools, and handicrafts equipment of all kinds can be obtained.

With reference to your reply to 'Cottage Crafts' I should like to point out that the information you gave was quite incorrect. Information on crafts in Scotland is obtained from the Scottish Country Industries Development Trust, 27 Walker Street, Edinburgh 3. The member from Argyll in suggesting weaving pottery, hornwork, and stonework appears to think that all four crafts can be mastered by short intensive courses, whereas it would take a number of months or probably years to become efficient in one of these crafts. My advice would be to study each craft by visiting the various workshops (addresses from the Development Trust) and make a decision to study one of them. Weavers can have instruction on commercial looms free of charge at the Highland Home Industries Centre at Morar, near Mallaig, but have to apply to the Development Trust in Edinburgh. As a professional weaver, I shall be pleased to answer any queries, if the member from Argyll cares to write.

Crafts – London

Do you know of any place in London that could advise on various types of craftsmen?

We suggest you contact Craft Centre, 43 Earlham Street, London W.C.2. (01-240 3327.) They will put people in touch with various types of craftsmen.

Crafts – Scotland

I would like to obtain some information about cottage crafts in Scotland. Do you know of any organisation that can help me?

We suggest you contact Scottish Country Industries Development Trust, 27 Walker Street, Edinburgh 3. They will help with information on cottage crafts and tuition in weaving, etc.

Cramp

Can anyone suggest a cure for cramp?

For variety these members' suggestions are hard to beat!

1. To alleviate cramp put some ordinary bottle corks into your bed. I generally keep a small cotton bag handy containing six or eight corks and put this near my legs. It relieves the pain in a few minutes.

2. Another plan is to stand bare-footed on a cork bath mat, but this has the disadvantage that you have to get out of bed and may catch cold in the process.

3. I find that a dessert tablespoonful of powdered glucose, stirred up in a little water, gives me quick relief, and I always have some of this commodity in my bedroom. It can be obtained from any chemist.

4. A friend quoted the case of his father who was cured by drinking salt water immediately after getting hot, the theory being that cramp is caused by loss of salt from the bloodstream due to perspiration. I toned this down and simply made a point of ladling generous help-

ings of salt on my food. I have seldom had cramp since doing this.

5. There is a simple suggestion which I have found of great help, which is to take a handkerchief, dip it into the coldest water available, and apply it to the limb in trouble as near as possible to the seat of the pain—it should be wrapped around and dipped again in the cold water until the pain ceases.

6. Regarding the alleviation of cramp, I myself have obtained almost unbelievable relief by taking, on retiring at night, one tablet of quinine sulphate—5 grains.

7. Get a bottle of Jamaica ginger from your chemist and put about a teaspoonful or less in a quarter of a tumbler of water, and drink when you feel an attack coming on.

8. A heaped teaspoonful of bisodol on going to bed, and if necessary repeated later on in the night. Either a circlet of corks to go around the leg or a cork tied on with a silk handkerchief or kept on with a silk stocking also helps.

9. Keep a jar of lump sugar by your bed. When you feel the cramp take two or three lumps of sugar.

10. On retiring to bed turn slippers upside down. This may sound farcical but is known to have cured sufferers and costs nothing.

A friend who suffered from cramp always filled her bed with corks. When she was taken ill the doctor called and found the corks. She was very crestfallen when he lectured her on the evils of drink.

Semi-long Term Credit for Farmers

I want to exceed my overdraft facilities temporarily in order to buy store capital. I believe there is an organization called the Agricultural Credit Corporation. Do you know anything about it and would it help me over my present difficulty?

The Agricultural Credit Corporation exists to guarantee excess borrowing over and above the normal overdraft which a farmer may have from a bank. The corporation guarantees the loan for two/ three and up to 12 years, but not for shorter periods. Your bank can be asked to approach the A.C.C. on your behalf.

Crests

Do you know of any books that deal with the subject of crests?

There are two books that are unfortunately out of print, but can be obtained from most large public libraries. They are: Fairbarns Crests of the Families of Great Britain and Ireland, published by Thomas C. Jack, 93 Princes Street, Edinburgh, and Armorial Families—A Directory of Coat Armour, in its 7th edition published by Hirst & Blackett Ltd., Paternoster House, London, W.C.4, in 1930.

Crystal – Regrinding

Inevitably valuable crystal glasses in use become chipped and so dangerous to continue using.
I should be grateful if you could advise me if there is any way of having brims of glasses re-ground and if so, the address of the firm carrying out such work.

We would suggest you contact either of the following addresses: Thomas Goode, South Audley Street, London, W.1; or R. Wilkinson & Son, 7 Temperley Avenue, London, S.W.12.

Curing Pigs

Can you tell me where I could get advice about curing pigs?

We suggest you contact Pig Industry Development Authority, Pida House, Ridgemount Street, London, W.C.1. (IAN 9174.)

Home Curing – Bacon and Hams

Mrs. Beeton has some good recipes for curing bacon and ham but I would like to try something different. Does anyone publish a book or leaflet on this subject?

The Ministry of Agriculture publish a booklet on this subject. It is called "Home Curing of Bacon and Hams" Bulletin 127 published in conjunction with the small Pig-keepers Council and

Where Might I Obtain a Well Trained Butler?

(See page 249)

issued by H.M. Stationery Office price 2s. 6d.

Curling

Where can I obtain information about curling?

We suggest you contact The Royal Caledonian Curling Club, 2 Coates Crescent, Edinburgh 3. Tel. 031-225-7083.

Paper Currencies

During the time when General Gordon was besieged in Khartoum he issued his own currency notes which I understand were later recognized by the Treasury and became legal tender. One of these notes has been passed down to me and I wonder whether it may be of value. Can you tell me of any organization or firm that would let me know the value of the note and how I should offer it for sale?

We contacted Spink & Son, who are one of the main dealers in paper currency. They said that it might be worth about £5 but they would have to see it first; if it has some value they will try and sell it for you, but will take commission on the sale.

They suggest that if you are interested in selling that you send it to them, addressed to Mr. D. Miller, Spink & Son, 5/7 King Street, St. James, London S.W.1. (Tel. 01-930 5275.)

Dampcoursing

Where can I get some expert advice about "Dampcoursing"?

We suggest you contact: Dampcoursing Ltd., 10 Dorset Road, London, N.15.

Damproofers

Do you know of a firm of damproofers?

We suggest you contact: British Knapen Gallwey, 16 Elvaston Mews, London S.W.7. (KNI 6379).

Damp Walls

Do you know of a firm who could give me advice about damp walls?

We suggest you contact: Newtonite Ltd., 12 Verney Road, London, S.E.16 (BER 1423).

Designers Representative Body

Is there a representative body or organization which looks after the interests of artists and designers?

The Central Institute of Art and Design is the body you are referring to. Their address is 41/42 Dover Street, London W.1.

Detectives

Where can I obtain the services of a Detective?

You could ask a solicitor to advise you or you could contact the Association of British Detectives, 2 Clements Inn, London, W.C.2. (HOL 1155).

Discs – Cure for Degenerated

Does anyone know of any method (apart from a ghastly operation, which I couldn't stand emotionally, and anyhow might not be a success)—to cure the nagging pain of degenerated, not slipped, discs? I am only 67, but hardly dare move.

We have had the following letter in reply to a recent enquiry for a cure for degenerated discs:

'For relief—try hanging *by the hands* from the floor above the stairs or any other convenient place for a minute or two several times a day.

'*By the neck*, if desperate, but that will be once only.'

The original enquirer was *not* amused.

Rag Doll's Faces

Where might I get the face of a rag doll renovated?

We suggest you contact the Dolls Hospital, 16 Dawes Road, London, S.W.6.

Domestic Bureau

Do you know of a good domestic bureau in London?

An address is: Maida Vale Bureau, 71 Chatsworth Road, London N.W.2.

Dowsers – Water Diviners

Where might I obtain the services of a water diviner?

We suggest you contact The British Society of Dowsers, Hon. Sec. and Treasurer P. B. Smithett, Esq., High Street, Eydon, Rugby, Warwickshire. (Byfield 525.) Or, if the enquiry is urgent, L. J. Latham, Esq., F.R.G.S., F.G.S., F.R.A.S., 49 Scarsdale Villas, London, W.8.

Earthworms

Do you know of any book about cultivating earthworms?

One book is " Harnessing the Earthworm," by T. J. Barrett, published by Faber & Faber.

(*See also* page 85.)

Education

Do you know of any association that will be able to advise about boarding schools, and one that can supply a list of colleges, schools and all diploma courses? Also I believe there is a society that gives advice about teaching at home.

The following are the addresses you should contact: (a) Educational Agency for Boarding Schools, 93 Chancery Lane, London, W.C.2. (Hol 6105.) (b) Department of Education and Science, Curzon House, 5 Curzon Street, London W.1. (c) Parents National Educational Union, Murray House, Vandon Street, London, S.W.1. (Abbey 7181.)

Eels – 1

Is there a reliable publication on eels, their habits and how to catch them?

The Ministry of Agriculture have a pamphlet on the " Capture of Eels." It is published by their publications department and is free.

Eels – 2

Could you possibly give me any assistance as to where I could find information on commercial eel farming in this country?

We think the best thing you can do is to contact Mr. Charles Marks, of H. Gade & Co. Ltd., 7 Lovat Lane, London, E.C.3, who is a wholesaler in live eels. Mr. Marks has just sold an elver station he had in the West Country. This, however, would only be for catching the young coming back from migration, and not rearing them.

Elephant Skin

I have some skin of an elephant which has been cured, and I would live to have a bag and suitcase made out of it. I was wondering whether you could tell me where I could find a leathercraft firm who might undertake this for me.

I have spoken to the Handbag Services Co., of Beauchamp Place, London, S.W.3, and they tell me they could make a handbag or some other sort of bag out of the elephant skin you have. They doubt if they could make a suitcase, but if you would like to take the skin into the shop, they will be able to give you an estimate for the work.

Employment – Over 45 Women

Do you know of anyone who can advise on employment for a woman of over 45?

You could contact any of the following: The Over 45 Association, 217a Kensington High Street, London, W.8. (937 6588.) Career Consultants Ltd., 29 Paddington Street, London, W.1. (486

1119.) Women's Employment Federation, 251 Brompton Road, London, S.W.3.

English Language – Association for

I would like to join an association that deals with English and its correct usage. Can you help me?

We suggest you contact The English Association, 8 Cromwell Place, London, S.W.7. (589 8480.)

Engraver

Do you know of a reputable engraver?

We suggest you contact Thomas & Son, 1 Great Pulteney Street, Regent Street, London, W.1.

Falconry – Association

I would like to take up falconry, and wonder if there is any association that deals with this subject?

There is the British Falconers' Club, whose Secretary is C. J. Morley, Esq., Hereford Stock Farm, Smarden, near Ashford, Kent.

Also Falconry Centre, Newent, Glos., who run courses etc.

Old Fans

I shall be grateful for advice on where to send some old fans (Regency and Victorian period) for repair and possibly mounting.

On the advice of the Victoria and Albert Museum we have been recommended to a Mr. Holness, who undertakes mending old fans privately. He does not do mounting himself, but this is not a specialised job and it should be easy to find someone to do this. The address is Victoria and Albert Museum, South Kensington, London, S.W.7.

Farm Holiday Guides

Where can I obtain information about holidays on farms?

We suggest you contact: Farm Holiday Guides Ltd., 18 High Street, Paisley Scotland, who publish a book called 'Farm Holiday Guide,' on sale at W. H. Smith at 3s 6d.

Farm Record Publications

Do you know of any firm which publishes farm record publications?

There is Robert Dinwiddie & Co. Ltd, Agricultural Printers and Publishers, Dumfries, Scotland, they will supply a complete list of their publications on application.

The NFU and ourselves also publish certain record books. Enquiries will yield details.

Farm Signs

Do you know of any firm that makes farm signs?

One firm is: C. G. Sales, Esq. 7 Grimstone Road, London, S.W.6 Makes easy to read signs in black and white lettering, in hard plastic.

Feather Dealer

Do you know of a dealer in feathers?

Veniards, 138 Northwood Road, Thornton Heath, Surrey. (653 3565.)

Feathers

I have a few hundred pinfeathers of woodcock and golden plover which I have collected through the years. Are they of any value, and is there any way of disposing of them other than the dustbin?

We have spoken to the well-known feather dealers called Veniards, of 138 Northwood Road, Thornton Heath, Surrey, and Mr. Veniard tells us that there is no commercial value for these feathers now. It does seem a shame to throw these feathers away—it might be worth while advertising.

Fencing Equipment

Where can I obtain equipment for

fencing?

We suggest you contact Leon Paul Equipment Co., 39 Neal Street, London, W.C.2. (836 6438), who are specialists in sports equipment.

Field Names

Where can I obtain information about the names of fields?

These are to be found in the tithe surveys of each parish, three copies of which were made by the Tithe Commutation Surveyor 1830 – one of which should be in the relative parish church chest, another at the relative Diocesan Registry and the third, at the Board of Agriculture in London.

They should be mentioned on Property Deeds and can often be discovered through the co-operation of Landowners and Solicitors.

British Fieldsports Society

Can you tell me the address of the British Fieldsports Society?

It is: British Fieldsports Society, 137 Victoria Street, London, S.W.1. (222 5407).

Fire-arms – Blunderbuss' Value

I have a blunderbuss alleged to have been carried by the Guard on the Dublin to Cork mail coach which bears the name Leonard (?the maker's name) on the trigger mechanism. It is a handsome piece with a walnut stock and a magnificent brass barrel. I understand that such weapons are in demand today but I have no idea of the value. Could you please tell me to whom I might turn for an opinion?

We have two addresses for experts on antique fire-arms and they are as follows: The Parker Gallery, 2 Albemarle Street, London, W.1, and P. C. L. German, 125 Edgware Road, London, W.2.

Fishing Book

Can you recommend a book about managing coarse fishing waters?

"The Management of Coarse Fishing Waters," published by John Baker, Royal Opera Arcade, London, W.1.

Fishing Lessons and Tackle

Can you recommend anyone who could give fishing lessons to my nephew?

We suggest you contact Hardy Bros. (Alnwick) Ltd., 61 Pall Mall, London, S.W.1 (930 7577), for individual lessons in Highgate ; they also sell fishing tackle.

Fishery Management Services

Do you know of anyone who can advise about fishery management?

We suggest you contact: Fishery Management Services, "The Rise", Brandon Village, Coventry.

Plaster Casts – Fish

Can you please advise me of one or two names of people who will make a plaster cast for a salmon? I have an outline on brown paper and the measurements, not a large specimen but caught on an 8 ft. 6 in. dry fly rod.

I have spoken to Mr. Hayward at the Natural History Museum, who tells me that he would be able to do this privately for you. Nowadays, they are making them out of fibre glass or hard rubber as plaster is so heavy and breaks easily, but you will have to discuss this with him. His address is: A. G. Hayward, Esq., Exhibition Section, Natural History Museum, Cromwell Road, London, S.W.7.

Fish – Indoors

Can you recommend a firm who supply and advise on indoor fish tanks?

Tachbrook Tropicals Ltd., 244 Vauxhall Bridge Road, London, S.W.1.

Fisheries – Trout

A river runs through my land which is only about a mile from the source. It looks feasible to make some pools and create some trout-fishing. Could you tell me who would advise me about this?

If you contact the Berkshire Trout Farm, Hungerford, Berkshire, they would send someone to come and inspect your river.

Fishing Valuations

Where can I obtain Fishing Valuations?

We suggest you contact: Mr. J. Illingworth, Stutt & Parker, Lofts & Warner, Berkeley Square, London, W.1. (493 7851).

Fishing in Windsor Great Park and Virginia Water

Where can I obtain information about fishing in Windsor Great Park and Virginia Water?

We suggest you write to The Crown Estate Office, Windsor Great Park. There is a certain allocation of tickets for the season.

Flat Earth Society

I believe there is a Society that has something to do with the earth being flat – do you know of its name and address?

You are probably thinking of: The Flat Earth Society, whose secretary is Samuel Sheriton, 24 Longon Road, Dover, Kent.

Flag Flying

Can you tell me on what dates the Union Jack should be flown from buildings?

Dates for flying the Union Jack can be found in Whitakers Almanack under Union. Also, each January *The Times* publishes a list of occasions for the forthcoming year. A list can also be found in the Services Diary.

Flags – Making up From Design

Can you tell me of anyone who would make a flag up from my own design?

Such a person is: Captain O. M. Watts, 48 Albemarle Street, London, W.1.

Floors – Damp

From much experience of damp cottage floors, especially those where tiles have been laid direct on Mother Earth, I do not feel your remedial advice was very sound. Firstly, it is most unlikely that the cottage referred to has any sort of damp-proof course in the walls; all that type of farm cottage were erected in the middle of the last century, before the advent of the damp-proof course in even good building. Even if there were, a fault in it would cause damp walls, not damp floors. The best remedy, and probably the cheapest in the end, would be to take up the tiles and scrap them. Then excavate the earth to 10 in. below finished floor level, and put in a 5 in. layer of hardcore, broken brick, etc. On top of this spread a layer of concrete, 4 in. thick, with a reasonably flat surface. Then spread a layer of Synthaproof over this as a damp-proof membrane; and finish off with a 1 in. screed of cement to sand 1:4. This could then be finished with lino, plastic tiles, or something similar. This may seem a complicated way of doing it, but it is the standard method, and best in the end; and do not let anyone be misled into thinking that concrete will be made waterproof by the addition to it of a water-proofing compound. This is a common misconception which always leads to trouble.

Floristry – Career in

My daughter wants to take up floristry professionally. How can she get some training? Would a shop take her on?

There is a school of floristry at 1 Ravenscourt Park, London W.6. and also the Constance Spry Flower School,

98 Marylebone Lane, London, W.1.

As for training in shops you could approach the British Flower Industry Association, 35 Wellington Street, London, W.C.2 for assistance.

Footpath Preservation Society

Is there a society that would be able to advise me on keeping a footpath open?

We suggest you contact: The Footpath Preservation Society, 166 Shaftesbury Avenue, London, W.C.2. 01-836 7220.)

Foresters and Forestry Societies

Addresses:

Society of Foresters of Great Britain, Sec.: E. W. March, 18 Northumberland Avenue, W.C.2.

Royal Scottish Forestry Society, 26 Rutland Square, Edinburgh, EH1 2BT.

Royal Forestry Society of England, Wales and N. Ireland, 102 High Street, Tring, Herts.

(*See also* Trees – Forestry Consultants, page 244.)

Forestry – Training

Where can I get information about Forestry training?

We suggest you contact: Royal Forestry Society of England, Wales and Northern Ireland, 49 Russell Square, London, W.C.1. (01-636 4892.)

Frame Cutter – Where to Get

I have been trying to purchase a steel picture frame cutter without success. The firm of Artistic Framing Ltd., of Holsworthy, Devon, told me yesterday that they had several such frame cutters on order from Sweden for many months, and they are still waiting. These cost £117. Do you happen to know any firm in this country who could supply one?

With regard to your inquiry about purchasing a steel picture frame cutter, may I suggest that you contact Mrs. H. M. Kent Jones at 69 Stanstead Road, Caterham, Surrey. Mrs. Kent Jones calls this a 'Morso' machine; it is foot operated and a spare set of knives and springs are included in the price of £112. She suggests that you send her some samples that can be tested on this machine to make sure that it will do the job you require.

Furniture – Buhl Cabinets

Where could I get a Buhl cabinet repaired?

We suggest you contact : H. J. Hatfield & Sons, 42 St. Michaels Street, London, W.2. (01-723 8265.)

Furniture – Doors Etc.

Do you know of any reputable maker of doors in the Middlesex area?

We suggest you contact: Bert Crowther, Syon Lodge, Busch Corner, Isleworth, Middlesex. (Isleworth 7978).

Furniture – Recaning

Where can I get some chairs re-caned?

Any of the following addresses would do this:

Mrs. E. Ann Alliott, Rosemount, East Hoathly, Lewes, Sussex.

Cooks Ltd, Agricultural Implements, Market Place, Reading.

G. Holt & Son, Oak Mead, High Wycombe, Bucks.

Furniture – Antique Repairs and Restorations – Oxfordshire

Can you suggest anywhere where I could get an antique chair repaired?

We suggest you contact: Benjamin Porter, Shill House, Alvescot, Oxon. (Carterton 393.)

Furniture – Veneers

Do you know of anyone who deals in veneers?

We suggest you contact: Aaronson Brothers Ltd., Towl Wharf, Wharf Lane, Rickmansworth, Herts. (Rickmansworth 74261).

Furs – Breeders Association

Could you advise me on the best fur to get in this climate?

We suggest you contact: The Secretary, Fur Breeders Association of the U.K., Beaver Hall, Garlick Hill, London, E.C.4 (01-248 9095), who will be able to give all the advice you require about furs.

Game – Advisory

I require some advice about Game, who should I contact?

Try: Eley Game Advisory Service, Fordingbridge, Hants. (Fordingbridge 2381). C.G.A. advise also and can put you in touch with a specialist: Major Willett of Sporting and Country Services.

Game Conservancy – Address

Fordingbridge, Hants. Fordingbridge 2381.

Game Farms, Pheasant Rearing

Where can I get advice about rearing pheasant?

We suggest you contact: Game Farmers Association, Manor Farm House, Micheldever, Winchester.

Game-keepers Association – Courses for

Pentridge, Hants. Tel. Handly 370.
These are run by the Game Conservancy at the above address.

Gardening – Correspondence Courses

Do you know any college that runs Gardening Correspondence Courses?

Try: Royal Horticultural Society,

Vincent Square, London, S.W.1 (01-834 4333).

Gardeners – Lady

Is there an association that deals with Lady Gardeners?

We suggest you contact: Womens Farm and Garden Association, Courtald House, Byng Place, London, W.C.1 (01-387 3651); or, Waterperry Horticultural College, Wheatley, Nr. Oxford.

Genealogists

Do you know of any Genealogists or where I could get some advice about the subject?

The Secretary, The Association of Genealogists and Record Agents, 6 Woodside, Vigo Park, Meopham, Kent, or The Society of Genealogists, 37 Harrington Gardens, London, S.W.7 (01-373 7054).

Gilt Chain – Cleaning

I have a small evening bag made of gold coloured gilt chain. This became discoloured and cleaning with ammonia has made it darker and even more discoloured. Can you let me know if there is any firm who would restore the fine gilt chain to its normal colour?

We should think that your bag will need to be electro-gilded. A firm that does electro-plating might be able to help you. One in London is Islington Metal & Plating Works, Torrens Street, London, E.C.1.

Blue Glass Linings

Do you know of anyone who can supply a blue glass lining for a mustard pot?

We suggest: F. W. Aldridge, Ltd., Leytonia Works, 2 Ivy Road, London, E.17 (01-539 3717). Or you could try: G. Garbe, 23 Charlotte Street, London W.1 (01-636 1268), both firms repair glass of all sorts.

Glass Blower

R. W. Jennings, Scientech House, Main Street, East Bridgford, Nr. Nottingham.

Glasses – Wine – Replacing Stems

Do you know of any firm that will mend wine glass stems?

We suggest: R. Wilkinson & Son, 7 Temperley Ave., London, S.W.12 (01-673 2626). They are a small family firm that mend broken glass and replace bits, e.g., stems of glasses, necks of decanters. They will get blowing done to specification and will cut the glass themselves. They also do engraving. Their speciality is Chandeliers.

Glasses for Candlesticks

I have two candlesticks designed to carry cylindrical glass funnels, like an oil lamp but not the same shape. Both are unfortunately broken. Can you tell me where I might be able to procure replacements?

I have spoken to a firm called H. K. Reichbach of 96 Gt. Titchfield Street, London, W.1, and they do have some candle tubes and glass funnels which might be suitable for your candlesticks. If they cannot find replacements, they say they can put you on to someone who they know would be able to.

Cut Glass – Replacing

The glass container (cut) of a Victorian biscuit box has been broken. Enough is present to see the shape, design, etc. It was held in a silver frame and had a lid of the same. Do you know any firm who would make and cut a glass container to take the place of the broken one?

There is a very good family firm who could probably make you another one called: R. Wilkinson & Son, 7 Temperley Avenue, London, S.W.12.

I know Mr. Wilkinson cuts glass himself, and if you send him the broken pieces, perhaps he can copy the original design.

Glow Worms

Do you know of any organisation which could give me information about glow worms?

We suggest you contact: The Secretary of the Henry Doubleday Research Association, Bocking, Braintree, Essex.

Broken Goblet

I have a nineteenth century heavy goblet which has a badly broken stem. The bowl and base are in clear and cased opaline. I wondered if any firm could undertake to make a new stem (about one inch thick), possibly with an opal twist, and re-fuse it to the bowl and base? Whilst on the subject, do you know of any local associations or gatherings interested in glassware?

We are afraid we do not know of anywhere that you could have a stem for the goblet made. We suggest that you write about this, and also about finding local associations which are interested in glass, to Antique Dealers and Collectors Guide, 167 Fleet Street, London, E.C.4.

Gooseberry Shows

I read an article recently by Trevor Holloway entitled 'Gooseberry Show and Tub Race' on which I feel that I must comment.

He writes about Gooseberry Shows and writes a lot of nonsense. He says, 'As far as is known, only one such show has survived – at Egton, near Whitby, Yorkshire. It is held early in August each year.' He also goes on to mention that the heaviest single gooseberry was nearly 4 oz. This I can assure him is quite impossible.

As the Honorary Secretary of the Mid Cheshire Gooseberry Shows Association I should like to inform Mr. Holloway that his statement is quite wrong. In our Association we have seven shows and there is also another show not in the Association. Members of these shows total at least 120 and live in the area bounded by Lower Peover, Over Peover, Marton, Lower Withington, Swettenham, Goostrey and Holmes Chapel.

For many years our members have been aggrieved by the information on gooseberry growing emanating from the Egton area, especially about the weights of gooseberries grown. Weighing there is by drams, whereas all our weighing is done in pennyweights and grains and there are 18 pennyweights and 9 grains to a grocer's ounce. Referring to the heaviest single gooseberry – in 1852 one named "London" weighed 37 pennyweights and 7 grains, which is a few grains over 2 ounces, and since then the heaviest one has been a Woodpecker, grown by Mr. T. Blackshaw in 1937.

I do hope that you will be kind enough to pass on my comments to Mr. Holloway, and if he wishes to learn something about gooseberry growing I am sure some of our members will gladly oblige.   W. Gordon Cragg.

Bespoke Gramophone Springs

Can you please advise me where I can get a new spring for a gramophone motor – the local music stores and clock repairers are unable to help.

The 1916 H.M.V. Table Model gramophone is part of a .collection of old musical instruments and the spring has recently broken – during a demonstration!

We suggest that you contact Pocklington and Johnson of 111 Clerkenwell Road, London, E.C.1. They have an enormous assortment of springs, and will make one to order for you. If you send the broken one to them they could match it up.

Grapes

Can you recommend a book about growing grapes?

A book on grape vines is the Amateur Gardening Handbook, 'Grapes, Peaches and Nectarines,' published by Collingridge.

Green Growth on Walls

Weedkiller Dimanin obtainable in tubes from the Baywood Chemical Co., Eastern Way, Bury St. Edmunds, Suffolk.

Guest Houses – Guide

I would be very glad if you could help me over the folowing. My eldest son – his wife and two children aged six and five years – have always had their holidays by sharing a bungalow in Wales. This has become too expensive for next year. I wonder if you could give me particulars and addresses of possible guest houses which are clean and offer good food and a pleasant atmosphere?

With regard to your son's holidays, there is a book published called Farm Holiday Guide on sale at W. H. Smith. We suggest that you buy this book as it gives a list, including prices, of guest houses and farms in the British Isles. If you cannot buy one, we suggest you write to the publishers: Farm Holiday Guide Limited, 18 High Street, Paisley, Scotland.

Guns

My son constantly points his gun at me and at people out shooting, and I would like to teach him the doggerel on this vice. Have you the full version? (He hasn't shot anyone yet, but it's a matter of time!)

A Father's Advice to His Son

If a sportsman true you'd be,
Listen carefully to me.

Never, never let your gun
Pointed be at anyone ;
That it may unloaded be
Matters not the least to me.

When a hedge or fence you cross,
Though of time it cause a loss,
From your gun the cartridge take,
For the greater safety's sake.
If 'twix you and neighbouring gun
Birds may fly or beasts may run,
Let this maxim e'er be thine:
Follow not across the line.

Stops and beaters oft unseen
Lurk behind some leafy screen ;
Calm and steady always be:
Never shoot where you can't see.

Keep your place and silent be:
Game can hear and game can see;
Don't be greedy, better spared
Is a pheasant than one shared.

You may kill or you may miss,
But at all times think of this:
All the pheasants ever bred
Won't repay for one man dead.
                Commander MARK BEAUFOY.

Alternatively you could buy him a record by Sonny and Cher called 'Bang! Bang!'

Guns – Sale of Antiques
Do you know of anybody who sells antique firearms?

Two addresses are: The Parker Gallery, 2 Albemarle Street, London, W.1, or P. C. L. German, 125 Edgware Road, London, W.2.

Guns – Cleaning of

Where can I obtain a leaflet about cleaning guns?

We suggest you contact: The Guntrade Association Ltd., P. Box 360, 75 Harborne Road, Edgbaston, Birmingham.

Gunsmiths

Can you recommend any gunsmiths, either in my area or London?

Some addresses are: J. Wheater, 27/29 Anlaby Road, Kingston-on-Hull (Hull 35698); Linsley Bros., Practical Gunmakers, 97 Albion Street, Leeds 1 (Leeds 22790); John Wilkes, 79 Beak Street, London, W.1 (01-437 6539).

Gun Dog Training

Can you recommend a gun dog trainer?

We suggest: Jack Chudley, Harper's Brook Kennels, Brigstock, Kettering, Northants (Brigstock 288). He is one of the best trainers and handlers in the country and is recommended by the Kennel Club. Specialises in retrievers, spaniels and labradors.

See also under Dogs—in Out of doors Section.

Hair Brushes – Rebristling

Do you know of somewhere I can get a pair of silver-backed hairbrushes rebristled?

We suggest you try either: The Tortoiseshell & Ivory House, 24 Chiltern Street, Baker Street, London W1 (01-935 8031) or Chalmers Ltd., 62 Pentonville Road, London N1. (01-837 3983).

Hall-Marks

Can you please tell me the title, price, and publisher of (i) a handbook with which to identify hall-marks on silver; (ii) a book with which to identify the makers of silver from the initials usually found on it?

We suggest that you write to the: Assay Master, Birmingham Assay Office, Newhall Street, Birmingham 3. They publish a free booklet all about hall-marks and initials on silver and gold.

Some other publications are: *A Pocket Guide to Hall-Marks* by F. Bradbury obtainable from J. W. Northends Ltd, Sheffield. *English Goldsmiths and their Marks* by Sir Charles Jackson is published by Macmillan & Co. *Hall-marks on Gold and Silver Wares* is published by the Worshipful Company of Goldsmiths, Goldsmiths Hall, London EC2.

Ham Radio

Can you advise me if a publication exists which gives a worldwide list of amateur radio transmitters and their owners, etc.?

We suggest that you write to *Short Wave Magazine*, 55 Victoria Street, London SW1. They tell me that they publish something called *The Call Books* which is an American publication which gives all the codes for amateur transmitters. I understand there are several volumes, one for the US list and one for the UK list.

Hams – Amateur Radio

I have become interested in amateur radio and wonder whether you know of any society that might be able to tell me more about this fascinating hobby?

If you contact the Radio Society of Great Britain at 35 Doughty Street, London WC1, they will be able to help you. They publish a monthly magazine, *Radio Communication to Members,* and the RSGB Call Book which lists all UK amateur call signs, and is the only official list that is approved by the GPO.

Handbags – Making and Cleaning

Do you know of a firm that cleans and makes handbags?

The Re-make Handbag Co, 183a Brompton Road, Knightsbridge, London SW3 (01-589 4975), cleans, repairs and relines handbags.

Handbag Services Co, Beauchamp Place, London SW3, makes handbags and other bags out of skin and will remodel bags, etc.

Handwriting – Book on

Can you recommend a book on character assessment through handwriting?

Yes. *Handwriting in Business* by Noel Currer-Briggs, Jane Paterson and Brian Kennett. Published by A.B.P.

Handwriting – Consultants

Can you give me the names and addresses of anyone who deals in graphology; that is, who reads character from handwriting?

We have the name and address of two handwriting experts. They are:

J. A. Conway, Esq., Moley House, Holborn Viaduct, London, E.C.1. Tel. 01-236 9904; and Mrs. Jane Paterson, Lipscombe, Lower Knaphill, Woking, Surrey.

Mrs. Paterson specialises in the use of graphology in personnel selection for industry and commerce.

Hansom Cabs

Where could I hire a hansom cab in London?

We suggest you contact: Alfred Jacobs & Sons, 343 Mile End Road, London E1 (01-980 3633)—they also have other horsedrawn vehicles for hire.

Helicopter – Hire of

Can you tell me where I can hire a helicopter in London to take me to the country?

B.E.A. have a helicopter charter service, which (for a helicopter carrying two passengers) costs £75 per flying hour. They calculate that to Herefordshire this will cost about £300, two hours there and two hours back, they have to charge for the return journey. They say that they do operate on an ad hoc basis, you need only give them a day's notice, if that, to obtain a machine. The person to contact is Captain Thompson at B.E.A. at Gatwick Airport—the telephone number is Crawley 28822, ext. 6434.

Herbs

Do you know of any society that could tell me more about herbs and their uses?

We suggest: The Society of Herbalists, 21 Bruton Street, London W1 (01-629 3157).

Historic Buildings Council

I believe there is some society that will be able to give me information about Historic buildings and their preservation. Can you help me?

You are probably thinking of the Historic Buildings Council, to get in touch with this contact: Ministry of Housing and Local Government, Caxton House, Tothill Street, London, S.W.1.

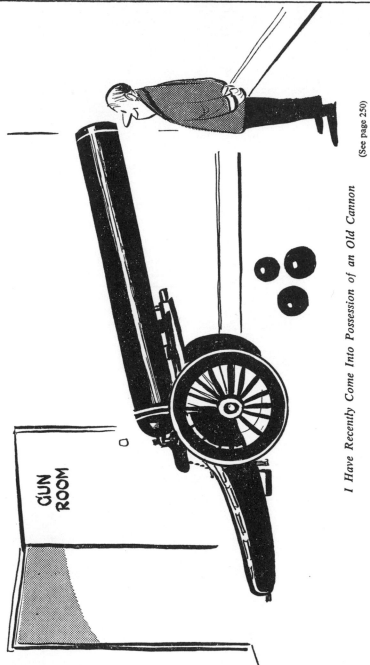

I Have Recently Come Into Possession of an Old Cannon

Union of Historic House Owners

I believe there is a Union of Historic House Owners, do you know how I can get in touch with them?

Yes, they can be contacted through the British Travel Association, 64 St James' Street, London SW1 (01-629 9191).

Hogarth Prints

About eighteen years ago my mother gave me some framed prints by Hogarth, of 'The Industrious Apprentice' and 'The Idle Apprentice'. She said that some day they would be valuable although some of them are not in good condition. At about that time I took one of them to art dealers in Bond Street, and was told that they are valueless and would be likely to remain so.

Since then I have stored them in my loft. Now with the considerable increase in value of many old articles, that only a few years ago were considered junk, have you or any member an opinion as to the value of these prints?

We have spoken to Sothebys about the Hogarth prints, and they say that if you have the complete set of twelve and they are in good condition they might be worth £30 or perhaps more.

Holidays with Children

Can you tell me where to get the holiday booklet 'Holidays with Children'?

We believe the publication to which you are referring is published by Haymarket Publishing Group, Gillow House, 5 Winsley Street, Oxford Circus, London, W.1, price 17½p. You may also be interested in the following two publications: *Children Welcome—The Happy Family Holiday Guide*, published by Herald Advisory Service, 23a Brighton Road, South Croydon, Surrey, price 20p; *Family Holiday Guide*, published by Lewis Publications Limited, 2–3 Fleet Street, London, E.C.4, price 15p.

Holidays for Children – Exchange Visits

Having four teenage children and wishing them to visit the continent in due course can you tell me are there any organisations that arrange exchange visits between children from families in the UK and on the continent?

We would suggest that you write to the Central Bureau for Educational Visits and Exchanges, 91 Victoria Street, London, S.W.1.

Homes for Old People

Do you have a list of homes, primarily for the elderly?

The Royal Surgical Aid Society, 1 Dorset Buildings, Salisbury Square, London, E.C.4 (maintain homes for elderly gentlefolk).

Mutual Households Association Ltd, 41 Kingsway, London, WC2. 01-836 1624. (They buy up large country houses and split them up into self-contained flats, with a communal dining room, for elderly people. One pays a loan of £1,000 on joining and then a weekly rent from £10 which includes everything. There is a waiting list of about a year.)

The Hampshire Old People's Housing Society, Beaconsfield House, Andover Road, Winchester, Hants. Winchester 4971.

Combined Household Association Ltd, Ridge House, Shenley, St. Albans, Herts.

The Elderly Invalids Fund, 34 King Street, London, EC2. 01-606 0877.

The Abbeyfield Society, 22 Nottingham Place, London, W1.

Hurst Homes, 9 Fladgate Road, Leytonstone, London, E11. (Homes in Hurst and Twyford, Berkshire.)

Mrs. Alan Rowe, Ixworth Abbey, Bury St. Edmunds, Suffolk. (She is forming an Association to provide flats for retired and professional people who wish to share a garden without keeping it up.)

Often the County Council of the area will be able to provide a list of homes locally.

Hops

Is there a society that will be able to tell

me more about the properties and uses of hops?

We suggest: The Hop Merchants Association, 10 Central Buildings, Southwark Street, London, SE1. (01-407 1008/2050.)

Horn Merchant

Do you know of anyone who purchases horns?

We suggest: Arthur Manning, 32 Gould Road, Twickenham, Middlesex. (01-894 4626.) He purchases raw horns from keepers and pays carriage.

Horns – Staghorns

Do you know of anyone who will make staghorns up into knives?

We suggest: Armstrong of Aberfoyle, by Stirling, Scotland, or Air Commodore Tindall-Carill-Worsley, Edrington House, Berwick-on-Tweed.

Horse Books

Do you know where I could see a large variety of horse books?

We suggest: J. A. Allen, 1 Lower Grosvenor Place, London, SW1. (01-828 8855.)

Horticulture

Do you know of an association that deals with Horticulture?

Royal Horticultural Society, London.
Kent Farm and Horticultural Institute, Swanley, Kent.

Hotel

I should like to run a hotel, and wondered if you knew of any books or an association that could give me some advice?

Practical Press Ltd, 1 Dorset Building, Dorset Rise, Salisbury Square, London, EC4 (01-353 1555), publish a booklet "Text Books for the Hotel and Catering Industry".
Or you could contact the British Hotels and Restaurants Association, 22 Upper Brook St., London, W1. (01-499 6641.)

Hotel Booking Service

Is there a Hotel Booking Service in London?

Yes: The Hotel Booking Service, 5 Coventry Street, Piccadilly Circus, London, W1. (01-437 5052.)

Houses Open to the Public

Is there a book that lists all the houses open to the public?

Yes: 'Historic Houses, Castles, and Gardens in Great Britain and Ireland.' Published annually by Index Publications, 69 Victoria Street, London, SW1. (01-222 4411.)

Horses – Arab

Where can I obtain information about rearing arab horses?

We suggest you contact: The Secretary, the Arab Horse Society, Lt. Col. J. A. Crankshaw, M.C., The Coach House, Cole Park, Malmesbury, Wilts.

Inventors

Is there an Institute of Inventors, if so, what is the address, please?

Institute of Patentees and Inventors, 207/208 Abbey House, 2/8 Victoria Street, London, SW1. (01-222 1616.)

Ivory

Do you know of any reputable firm that will buy ivory and/or restore it?

Dealers in ivory are: Puddefoot, Bowers & Simonett Ltd, Clarendon House, 11 Clifford Street, London, W1 (01-493 2060), or: W. Barrett & Sons, 9 Old Bond Street, London, W.1 (01-493 1996), or: The Tortoiseshell & Ivory House, Ltd, 24 Chiltern Street, London, W1 (01-935 8031). They are specialists in the restoration of jades, hardstones, ivories, ceramics, enamels, tortoiseshell, antique bronzes, ormolu, snuff bottles, marbles, general works of art. They will also rebristle and renovate your toilet brushes in any material and supply to your requirements.

Ivory – Use of

I have for disposal an ivory tusk from a Nigerian elephant. Can you advise me who buys such things? I have also an old pair of ivory-handled hairbrushes, the brush part of which is past use and the ivory chipped. Are they of any value?

We suggest that you contact E. Friedlein, of 60 Minories, London EC3. They are merchants in ivory and tortoiseshell, and might care to buy the tusk.

With regard to the hairbrushes, these do not seem to have much second-hand value, and especially as they are not in good condition. If you would like to have them rebristled, Chalmers Ltd, of 62 Pentonville Road, London N1, will do them for you, but this is very expensive, and we believe the cost would be not less than £4 each, in which case it would not be worth it unless you wish to use the brushes yourself.

Jigsaw Puzzle Library and Club

Where can I buy a Jigsaw puzzle suitable for adults?

The Secretary of the British Jigsaw Puzzle Library states that Harrods of Knightsbridge have the best selection of puzzles, and when buying a puzzle the best make are those called 'Victory' puzzles. For further information on this subject we suggest you contact the Secretary of the above club at 25 Kidbrooke Grove, Blackheath, London, S.E.3. Tel. 858 4668.

I thought you might be interested to know that there is a Jigsaw Puzzle Club, the charge of which is £4.10 per year, exclusive of postage. The address is 20 Haling Park Road, South Croydon, Surrey, Tel. 688 5320, and the person to contact is Miss G. Jones.

Insurance Companies

I for one would welcome advice on how to protect ourselves from bogus insurance companies of which there seems to have been an upsurge in recent years. Insurance of motor cars particularly, but of course farm buildings, property, in fact, the lot. Plausible young enthusiasts arrive at one's front door and offer what appears to be the best of bargains and the lowest premiums ever – how is one to protect oneself from being deluded by one such individual?

The basic protection for any member is not to entertain unsolicited salesmen. but to seek the advice of a reputable insurance broker. The cheapest policy many people have learnt to their cost recently, is not necessarily the most advantageous. Members can obtain advice on all aspects of insurance from the CGA (Insurance Brokers) Ltd.

Kennel Club

I would like to know how to go about breeding Alsatians. Is there anyone who will be able to advise me?

Yes: The Kennel Club, 1 Clarges Street, Piccadilly, London, W1. (01-493 6651.)

Lace – Valuing and Buying

Where can I find out the value of some old lace and a buyer?

The Embroiderers Guild, 73 Wimpole Street, London, W.1, will value.

Mrs. Price, 122 Durham Road, Wimbledon, London, S.W.20, will sometimes purchase.

Lacquering

I would be grateful for your advice on

where I can get scuttles and buckets cleaned and lacquered so that they will then require no further cleaning.

Any electro-plater in your area would do this job for you – if you do not know of one, perhaps your local chamber of commerce would let you know.

It is, of course, perfectly easy to do it yourself – clean the surface with cold water and a brillo pad, then dry it thoroughly and quickly so that it does not get oxidized (this is very important, as it is the air that tarnishes the metal) and then put on ordinary lacquer, which will seal the shine. This will last for quite some time without needing to be cleaned. It is the cleaning of the metal which takes the time, and the professional now use cyanide for this job, so that it is just a case of dipping the copper into it without scrubbing.

If you cannot find a local place, and do not want to do it yourself, Bartletts, of 97 Torriano Avenue, London NW5 would be able to get it done for you.

Lamps – Renovation of

Do you know of anyone who will renovate old lamps?

Yes: George Grou & Sons, 341 Goswell Road, London, EC1. (01-837 1639.) They renovate old coaching lamps and Veteran car lamps.

Land-agency – Book

I have taken over a small estate on my uncle's death. There is a resident Agent, but I would like a book to 'bone' up on the subject generally.

You want R. C. Walmsley's *Rural Estate Management,* published by the Estates Gazette Ltd.

Landowners' Association

I believe there is an Association which looks after the interests of Land Owners?

The Country Landowners Association of Swallow Street, London, W1, are the people you want.

Lead – Repairs

Use Plastic Padding obtainable from ironmongers.

Leaseholders Association of Great Britain

Their address is: 33 Ossian Road, London, N.4.

Leather

Do you know of anyone who will answer general queries about leather?

Try: The Leather Institute, 9 St. Thomas' Street, London, SE1. (01-407 1582.)

Leather – Preservation

Can you give me some advice about preserving leather?

Arthur Rich & Partners, Ltd, 42 Mount Pleasant Drive, Belper, Derbyshire, make a cream for this purpose. Or you could try Connolly's Hide Food made by a leather firm, which both restores and keeps leather as new. Sangorski & Sutcliffe, 1 Poland Street, London, W1, hand bookbinders, sell British Museum preservative formula made by the Museum, containing lanolin, etc., but they cannot post it as it is inflammable.

The British Museum have published a booklet called 'The Preservation of Leather bookbindings,' by H. J. Plenderleith, Keeper of the Research Laboratory of the British Museum.

Or if you wish leather to be restored by a firm of restorers we suggest: Leather Restorers Ltd., 22 Brompton Arcade, London, SW3. (01-589 1580.)

Leather Tools

Do you know of a firm that will supply leather tools?

Either: Wynn Timmins & Co. Ltd, Commercial Street, Birmingham, or: Joseph Dickson Tool Co., Batt Lane, Warsaw, Staffs.

Libraries – Postal

Do you know of any postal libraries?

Yes: Douglas & Foulis, 9 Castle Street, Edinburgh.
Tabard Inn Library, St. Edmunds Hall, Cornwall Road, Croydon, Surrey.
The London Library, 14 St. James' Square, London, SW1.

Line Breeding

Is it advisable to mate my pedigree Guernsey heifers with their sire?

Line breeding takes a lifetime to understand, and at this stage of your herd we would not advise mating the sire with his own daughters. You might breed some excellent cattle, but on the other hand things might go wrong. To practise line breeding with success you want to have a well-established herd.

2 Line Breeding

What is the fundamental difference between 'in-breeding and line-breeding'?

In-breeding is breeding from closely related stock such as from father and daughter, brother and sister, etc. Line-breeding, on the other hand, is breeding from animals which are not closely related although the pedigree contain the names of the same animals.

Lobsters – Pots and Books on

I want to buy some lobster pots. Could you tell me where I can obtain them and also some books on how to use them?

Lobster pots can be obtained from Mr. Legassick, Penlea, Hope Cove, Kingsbridge, Devon.
Books are: *Lobster and Crab Fishing* by W. Forsyther, or *Shore Fishing for Lobsters* by B. R. Farmthorpe.

London – Tours

Is there an association that organises tours around London?

Yes: Enjoy London Ltd, 40 Holland Road, London, W14. (01-603 4453.) They arrange outings of 'intimate' parties of about a dozen, conveyed in comfortable mini-buses. Will arrange or find out about anything and everything from a performance of Shakespeare in Stratford, see London by night, go down a coal mine (not in London!).

Lords of the Manor

Where can I obtain information about Lords of the Manor?

Try: Manorial Register, Historical Manuscripts Commission, Quality House, Qaulity Court, Chancery Lane, London, WC2.

Manorial Society

We recently read an article called Lords of the Manor and we would like to point out that the 'Manorial Society of Great Britain' mentioned in the article was formed privately by a small group of people in 1955 with the object as stated, but it became dormant, if not extinct, a few years later apparently owing to lack of support.

The original Manorial Society was formed privately in 1906, and at intervals published monographs about Lordships of Manors and their records until about 1925. At this date the changes in the Law of Property Act brought all manorial records under the care and superintendence of the Master of the Rolls, and a Register of Manorial Documents was commenced by the Public Record Office. This Manorial Society eventually merged with the British Record Society in 1929.

The Historical Manuscripts Commission took over the maintenance of the Manorial Documents Register from the Public Record Office in 1959. This Register shows the location of Court Rolls, etc., relating to Manors in England and Wales, that have been reported, together with the name of the Lord of the Manor where known. The Secretary of the Commission would welcome information from any Lord of the Manor who has recently acquired a Lordship, and who has not been in touch with him, so that the Register can be kept up to date.

Secretary, Historical Manuscripts Commission, Quality House, Quality Court, Chancery Lane, London, WC2.

Mantlepiece – Antique or Reproduction

Where can I obtain an antique mantlepiece or a reproduction one?

We have three addresses you could try. They are:

T. Crowther & Son, 282 North End Road, Fulham, London, SW6.

H. Crotty & Son Ltd., 74 New Kings Road, London, SW6.

H. W. Poulter, 158 Fulham Road, London, SW10.

Market Gardening Correspondence Course

Do you know of any place that does correspondence courses in Market Gardening?

Two places are: The Horticultural Correspondence College, 9 Priory Park Road, Dawlish, S. Devon and The International Correspondence Schools Ltd., 40 Parkgate Road, S.W.11.

Face Masks

I wish to contact a firm which might be able to rent me a face-mask and uniform to be worn by someone imitating one of the leading political figures in Europe.

The place to go for a face-mask is Barnum's of 67 Hammersmith Road, London, W14. They have a catalogue devoting three pages to face-masks – you do not say which political figure you want to imitate but no doubt Barnum's will be able to help you.

Matchbox Labels

Some years ago when living in North America I started to collect book matches, and over the years have acquired some 500–600. Whilst the majority are of North American origin, I have a number from European countries, both books and boxes. I believe there are serious collectors in this field, and I would be grateful if you could put me in touch with any member or a society who might be interested in acquiring these.

We would suggest that you contact the Secretary to the British Matchbox and Label Society, whose address is: J. H. Luker, Esq., 283/285 Worplesden Road, Guildford. He will be able to advise you upon who would be most interested in your labels.

Mayors – Civic Ceremonial

Do you know if any books have been published about Mayoral procedure, and Civic Ceremonial?

Here are a selection of books on this subject:

'Civic Ceremonial, a Handbook of Practice and Procedure' by J. F. Garner, published 1957 by Shaw & Sons Ltd., 7/9 Fetter Lane, London, EC4.

'The History, Law, Practice & Procedure relating to Mayors, Aldermen & Councillors,' by R. Tweedy-Smith (out-of-print?) pub. 1934 by Jordan & Sons Ltd., of Chancery Lane. Can be obtained second-hand.

Butterworth's 'Encyclopedia of Local Government Law under Mayors.'

Metal-work

Where could I get some metal work done to my specific order?

Either: Art Metal Workers, Ltd., 4 Percy Street, London, W1, or: Old Metal Craft Shop, 194 Brompton Road, London, SW7.

Milling

Information on mills and milling can be obtained from P. R. Stenning, 89 Barrington Road, Goring-by-Sea, Sussex.

Mirrors – Where to Get

Mirrors of all sizes vast to minute and looking glasses at 'Through the Looking Glass', 563 Kings Road, S.W.6 (World's End).

Monarchist League

I would be pleased if you could tell me the address of the Monarchist League or any other organisation that supports the Royal Family.

The address of the Monarchist League is as follows: 29 York Street, London, W.1. Tel. 01-935 3381.

Mottes and Baileys

Can you recommend some books about English Castles and their histories?

Some books on this subject are:
'English Castles,' R. Allen Brown, published 1962, by Batsford.
'Early Norman Castles,' by Mrs. E. S. Armitage, published 1912.
'Castles, a History of Fortifications, 1600 B.C.–1600 A.D.,' by Sidney Foy, published 1939.
'History of the King's Works,' edited by H. M. Colvin – three volumes have been published to date by the Stationery Office.

Museum of Machinery

We should be glad if you can advise us as to whether there is a museum or other similar institution which is interested in old agricultural machinery. We shall shortly have to demolish a very old timber horse gear, and we feel it will be a pity that it should not be preserved if there is anybody to take it. It consists of a big oak crown-wheel and yoke for horses and the various other parts for operating machinery in a barn.

We think that the Reading Agricultural Museum will be interested in old implements and we suggest that you write to the Curator and give him full details of the machinery for disposal.

Musical Boxes – Repair

Where can I get an old musical box repaired?

Try: Messrs. S. F. Sunley & Co., 81 George Street, Portman Square, London, W.1 (01-935 4700) – they are specialists in the repair of old music boxes.

Mushrooms

Can you recommend a book on growing mushrooms?

The Mushroom Growers Association recommend 'Mushroom Growing Today,' published by Faber & Faber, which can be obtained from any bookseller or from the M.G.A. This book in the opinion of the Association is most reliable and gives instructions in actual growing, the types of houses required, including the conversion of existing buildings, marketing, etc., and also lists firms which supply the necessary sundries required by the grower. But go and talk to the Association, because failure to find good outlets or a glut on the market has ruined many substantial growers. Don't be content with any vague reassurance on this particular aspect.

Books on Weaving Netting

Can you oblige me with the name of any book and where I am likely to buy it, which gives instructions as to how to make or weave netting and describes the tools or shuttle required.
I have a fruit cage with fine Terýlene netting and some of this has got badly torn. I have a bobbin of Terylene twine with which to repair it.

We suggest that you write to Dryads Handicrafts of Northgate, Leicester, who publish an illustrated book called *The Textbook of Netting.* They also publish leaflets (No 92 on *Netting*, and No 127 on *Cord Knotting*). Also you could buy from them a knitting needle made of wood, steel or vulcanite, but it would probably be best to write to this firm explaining that you want to repair some netting and they could probably advise you on the best needle and book.

Norfolk Reed – Supplier

Where can supplies of Dutch or Norfolk reed be got from?

We suggest you get in touch with a firm of thatchers who cut their own reed and supply reed. They are: Norfolk Reed Thatchers, 3 Herbal Hill, Clerkenwell, London, E.C.1. Tel. 01-337 1423. They say that they do not import any Dutch reed as this is more expensive than Norfolk reed. They will be cutting reed at the end of December and so they will not be able to supply it until after Christmas.

(*See also* Thatching, page 296.)

Oakleaf Enterprises Ltd.

Do you know of any association that finds rooms in country houses for visitors from overseas? We would like to entertain Americans (at a price).

Yes: Oakleaf Enterprises Ltd, 15 Pall Mall, London SW1. (01-839 4289.)

Objets D'Art – Advice on Sale of

I have a quantity of Objets d'art, paintings, antique furniture left me, which I cannot house and would like to explore the possibilities of disposing of them. I don't want to pay enormous fees for valuations and that sort of thing. Can you advise me what to do?

Christies will give you free advice on saleability and opinions on items brought to their premises in King Street, St. James, London SW1. We are sure they will be pleased to help you.

Officers Association –
Over 45's Association

Do you know of any association that would assist a retired Army officer to look for employment?

There are two such associations that

might be able to help you. They are:

The Officer's Association, 28 Belgrave Square, London W8, and The Over 45's Association, 217a Kensington High Street, London W8.

Oil Paintings – Cleaning

I have a small oil painting and panel in a gilt frame, the whole of which has been varnished many years ago. I should like to clean these and should be grateful if you would advise on the best solvent.

This is best left to an expert, but there is a method that you can do yourself, it is:

'To use a damp piece of cotton wool and distilled water, this can do no harm at all, it is not advisable to use detergents or strong acids, as these can damage the painting.'

But we would suggest that rather than do the job yourself, you get in touch with: The Secretary, The Association of British Picture Restorers, 43/44 Albemarle Street, London, W.1, who will be able to put you in touch with a suitable restorer at far less cost than if you approached a picture dealer.

Orchids – Advice on Growing

Where can I get advice about growing orchids?

Try: Orchid Review Ltd, 93 The Avenue, Greenacres, Aylesford, Kent, or: Mansell & Hatcher Ltd, Crag Nurseries, Apperley Bridge, Rawdon, Leeds. They are ready to supply information on orchid growing and send a printed booklet. The Orchid Society could be helpful. Their address is 87 Brookman's Avenue, Brookman's Park, Hatfield, Herts.

Orders and Decorations

Where can I obtain information about orders and decorations?

We suggest you contact: Central Chancery for Orders of Knighthood, 8 Buckingham Gate, London SW1.

First Ordnance Survey

I wonder if you can kindly tell me if I

am correct in thinking that the original Ordnance Survey maps were issued in 1805, and that these can be seen by the general public at the British Museum, or elsewhere.

The first map done by the Ordnance Survey was of Kent in 1801, but this was not published by them. A few years later they started publishing their own, and the first editions can be seen in the British Museum. You can acquire photo-copies of these maps from the Museum.

Ordnance Survey Maps

I believe one can purchase photocopies of the first ordnance survey maps, can you tell me where? Also where they are now published?

The First Ordnance Survey Map was of Kent in 1801. A few years later they started publishing them, and the first editions can be seen in the British Museum. Photocopies of these maps can be bought from the Museum. They are now being published by David & Charles Ltd, South Devon House, Railway Station, Newton Abbot, Devon.

Oriental Rug – Repair of

I wondered if you would be so kind as to give me the name and address of any firm you know, either in London or locally, which could undertake the specialist repair of oriental rugs which have become frayed at the edges.

We suggest you contact A. Bernadout, 199 King's Road, London, S.W.3.

Orkney Chairs

I have just seen a letter about repairing an Orkney chair.

These chairs were designed by a Mr. Kirkness at the beginning of this century, one of the specific purposes of which was to give employment to Orkney crofters by employing them to make the characteristic oat straw backs. Considerable success was gained in this, with the notable result that a number of the crofters were enabled to buy their crofts.

About the time of the second world war production of these chairs ceased for about twenty years, and Mr. Kirkness has since died, I believe, but a number of years ago Mr. Eunson, on retirement from the Fleet Air Arm, bought the business and recommenced the making of these splendid chairs in the same premises at Kirkwall, Orkney.

As there is a special method developed for making the backs of these chairs I think it is most unlikely that a chair caner would be able to repair them as you suggest. I should think the most satisfactorly thing for your correspondent to do would be to measure the back of his chair (there are three sizes of them made) and to order a new back for it from Mr. Eunson. It would then be a relatively simple matter to ask a craftsman furniture maker or a competent upholsterer to fit it exactly as the old one.

Orkney – Chair Caner

I have an Orkney or 'beehive' arm chair in my possession. I should be most grateful for any help you could give me as to the address of anybody or organization, preferably near London, who would be prepared to remake the beehive backing of the chair.

There is a chair caner called Mr M. South, of 37 Quarrendon Street, London SW6, and he will apparently go anywhere in London on receipt of a postcard, and I believe does the work by the roadside. Perhaps if you cannot find anyone local, you might have a friend in London who would house the chair for you whilst being mended.

(*See also* page 251.)

Ormolu

I should be grateful if you can advise me on regilding ormulo. I have been cleaning old wall brackets with soap and ammonia. In a few places the nice deep ormolu colour has turned brassy. Can I buy some ormolu solution to touch them up? If so, where?

Once the gilding has started to go patchy through years of cleaning, as you say, the only thing to do is to have the brackets re-gilded. It would be best to have this done professionally, and if you cannot find somewhere locally, there is a place in London called The Tortoise-shell & Ivory House Ltd at 24 Chiltern Street, London W1.

Taking up Ornithology

My son is interested in taking up orni-thology. Is there a club he can join?

The Royal Society for the Protection of Birds runs a thriving Young Ornitho-logists Club for those aged 18 and under. It also publishes a magazine. We suggest you write to the R.S.P.B., The Lodge, Sandy, Bedfordshire.

Ornithology

Do you know of any clubs or associa-tions that are interested in ornithology?

The Trust for Ornithology, 2 King Edwards Street, Oxford.
British Trust for Ornithology, Beech Grove, Tring, Herts.
Dr Jeffrey Harrison, Hon Sec, The Ornithological Club, Merriewood, Seven-oaks, Kent.

Overseas Relatives – Travel Facilities

I would ask if you can put me in touch with, or give me the address of, an association which is open to people who have relatives overseas and provides facilities for reduced price travel when visiting them.

Below is the address of an Association which offers reduced travel for visiting relatives in Commonwealth countries. We understand one has to be a member for five months before taking advantage of this. Mr. G. J. Luke, Commonwealth Families and Friendship Association, 45 Mayesbrook Road, Dagenham, Kent.

Ox-roasters

Do you know of anywhere where I can get an ox roasted?

J. Barran, 8 High Street, Buckingham.
Mumford Cooke, Mumford Arms, Ospringe, Faversham, Kent.
B. Harris, High Street, Henley-in-Arden.
P. Hobbs, 290 Myton Road, Warwick.
George E. Short, The Wimbledon Hill Hotel, High Street, Wimbledon, London SW19.
F. Tyler, 17 Glebe Road, Stratford-on-Avon.

Impressionist Painters

Do you know of a gallery in London that specialises in showing works of impressionist painters?

Yes: The Zwemmer Gallery, 26 Litch-field Street, Charing Cross Road, London, W.C.2. (01-836 1793.)

Paintings – Identification of Oils

I believe that the National Gallery will identify oil paintings. Have you any information about this?

Yes, they will identify oils on Wednes-day and Friday afternoons between 2.30 and 5 p.m. For further details contact them at National Gallery, Trafalgar Square, London, W.C.2.

Painting Restoration

I have a few oil paintings which need repair and restoration. I wonder whether you can put me in touch with a reput-able firm in my locality who can under-take this type of work at reasonable cost.

We do not think you will find any-body locally who is sufficiently competent to undertake this work. You might like to try contacting Mr R. M. Hoare, 27 Holland Villas Road, London W14. An article on the subject of picture restoring by Mr Hoare appeared in the November issue of the magazine. He has been recommended to us by one of our mem-bers, who states that he is an expert at his job and thoroughly reliable.

Papier-maché

Can you tell me of any books dealing with the preparation of papier-maché, and the making of articles out of this material.

There is a very good book called 'Papier Maché and How to do It,' by Anderson, published by the Oaktree Press at 15s, and obtainable at W. & G. Foyle Ltd, 119/125 Charing Cross Road, London WC2.

Parish Councils

Is there an association of parish councils?

Yes: The National Association of Parish Councils, 99 Great Russell Street, London W.C.2. (01-636 4066.)

The Parrot Society

Their address is: 17 De Parys Avenue, Bedford.

Application for Patent

How do I apply for a patent to be granted?

The first thing you should do is call, if you possibly can, between 10 a.m. and 4 p.m., or write to the Patent Office, Southampton Buildings, Chancery Lane, London, W.C.2, stating that you wish to make application for a provisional patent, and asking for the explanatory pamphlet. A Provisional Patent will protect your invention while you make arrangements for it to be put into production, and you can then make application for the patent. There are patent agents who will advise and patent items for you. The London Classified Telephone Directory has many addresses.

Patents

I believe there is an Institute of Patentees. Can you supply me with their address?

The Institute of Patentees and Inventors, 207/8 Abbey House, 2–8 Victoria Street, London, S.W.1. (01-222 1616.)

Peat

I have always appreciated the smell of peat, particularly as found in hotels in the north country and Scotland. Could you please advise how I can buy peat in this part of the world?

Peat for fuel can be obtained from the CGA Ltd, Letchworth, Hertfordshire.

Pebbles – Polishing

I have an assortment of interesting pebbles collected from various parts of the East Anglian coastline and would be most grateful if you would advise me where I can get information on the method and materials used for polishing them.

We suggest that you write to the Gemmological Association of Great Britain at St. Dunstan's House, Carey Lane, London, E.C.2, they can give you the addresses of where to buy the necessary equipment. It is apparently quite expensive and one has to be prepared to spend some money as one needs fast-rotating brushes, diamond dust, etc.

Pebble Polishing – Book on

I would be grateful if you would suggest suitable reading on the subject of amateur stone (pebble) polishing. The information required should include equipment required by the amateur for hobby-work at home, methods and materials and, if possible, an indication as to suitable 'hunting-grounds'. I am particularly interested in beaches in the N.W. of Scotland and in Norfolk and Suffolk.

There is a book that covers this whole subject called *The Pebbles on the Beach* by C. Ellis.

Paying Guests – Holidays

I believe there is an organization called 'Oakleaf Enterprises', which arranges hospitality in country houses up and down the country, but chiefly I understand in England. This hospitality is, I believe, mainly for visitors from overseas.

I am anxious to get in touch with this organization, and I should be very grateful if you could find out their address for me.

The address of Oakleaf Enterprises Ltd. is 15 Pall Mall, S.W.1. We understand that they are looking for suitable country houses in Argyll at the moment, and if you could write to them and let them know how many guests you could accommodate, some details about your house, and if possible a photograph, they would be very grateful.

Pensions for Disabled Farmers

I believe there·is a charity which grants pensions to disabled farmers. Can you tell me its name and what qualifies them for a pension?

The charity concerned is the Royal Agricultural Benevolent Institution, of Vincent Square, London, S.W.1.

Those applying for pensions must have depended upon farming exclusively for their livelihood for 20 years. Private means (exclusive of State pension) should not exceed £150 per annum or £200 in the case of a married couple applying together. Wives and widows qualify through their husbands, sons and daughters (unmarried) who assisted in the farm qualify through their parents. Candidates are eligible at 65, or in cases of permanent ill-health at 45.

Penny Blacks

An envelope dated 1846 has been found in an old bureau, the stamp on which I think must be a 'Penny Black'. I would be glad to know with whom I can get in touch to verify this, value it, if authentic, and sell it for me.

We have contacted David Field Ltd, of 42 Berkeley Street, London W1, who tells me that this could well be a 'penny black', and they would have to see it before giving you a price. He says the price seems to range from 5s to £5 for one in good condition.

This is a very reliable firm, and we suggest you might send it to them by recorded delivery. They could value it for you. You would probably get a higher price selling the stamp in London rather than Edinburgh.

Old Pennies

I have a quantity of pennies and half-pennies collected over the last twenty years. I have heard some may be valuable according to the date. Would you kindly inform me if this is so?

With regard to the coins you have collected, according to the information given to us by Baldwins, a well-known coin specialist, pennies and half-pennies are only valuable if they are in brilliant, uncirculated mint condition. Of course, these are quite rare. Even if yours are dated the early 1800s this still applies.

Perfume Making

Can you recommend any books on perfume making?

There are several books on the market to do with perfume, but the ones which would probably be helpful to you are *Chemistry of Perfumery Materials* by Moncrieff (published by United Trade, 30s) or *History of Perfume* by Ellis, published by Secker & Warburg. If you cannot obtain these from your local bookstall, we suggest you write to Hatchards, of Piccadilly.

Pet Shop

Can you recommend a pet shop in Scotland that sells talking mynahs?

Yes: We suggest you try The Pet Shop, Baker Street, Stirling, Scotland.

Pewter – Books on

Do you know of any books about pewter and its marks?

Two books on this subject are: *New Pewter Markings and Old Pewter Ware,* by Markham, and *Old Pewter Its Makers and Marks,* by Howard Herschel Cotterell.

Pewter – Repair and Manufacture – 1

Can you recommend a firm that will repair a pewter tankard?

Englefields Ltd., Reflection House, Cheshire Street, London, E.C.2 (01-739 3616), will do repairs to tankards, etc. They also make new pewter goods. If things are posted to them, make sure to pack them well, as pewter is a soft metal and easily damaged.

There are other firms that will restore pewter: Felix Hilton, 18 Boston Place, Dorset Square, Marylebone, London, N.W.1, and The Pewter Shop, Burlington Arcade, London, W.1.

Pewter – Repair and Manufacture – 2

I wonder if you could let me have the name and address of any firm specialising in the manufacture of Pewter goods? Pewter seems to be neither the province of jewellers nor ironmongers and I have had difficulty in finding who makes it.

Specialists in pewter goods are: J. Casimir, 23 Pembridge Road, London, W.11, and The Pewter Shop, 18 Burlington Arcade, Piccadilly, London, W.1, either of these shops should be able to supply anything you require.

In reply to a query of mine you were good enough to send me the names of three firms who might repair a glass-bottomed pewter tankard.

I thought you would be interested to know that I have had no success in this matter. The Veri-Best repair service said that owing to illness they were too busy catching up; Jack Casimir didn't reply, and the Pewter Shop in Burlington Arcade said that they only repaired their own things but advised me to write to Englefields Ltd., Cheshire Street, E.2. These people too said that they only repaired their own manufactures, so I am back to square one. I feel that there must be, somewhere, some 'little man round the corner' who could tackle the job.

Pewter – Repair and Manufacture – 3

Whilst attending a rural industries fair in Sussex I got into conversation with a coppersmith whose letterhead proclaimed that he could repair pewter goods. The address is: The Studio, Glynleigh Farm, Pevensey, Sussex. Tel. Hailsham 358.

Pewter – Valuation

Can you recommend a firm that will value pewter?

Yes: Casimir, 142 Brompton Road, London, S.W.3.

Picture Cleaning

I have a painting by Ludovici dated 1861 of my mother as a child. It measures 15 in by 13 in and needs cleaning. Can you tell me how to do this or where I could get it done and approximately the cost?

We suggest that you take the painting into W. Holder & Sons of 60 Brook Street, London W1, who are a firm specialising in picture cleaning and restoration. They tell me that it would be very unwise to undertake this work yourself.

Ornamental Pheasants

Do you know of a breeder of ornamental pheasants?

Yes: F. E. B. Johnson, The Grove, Stagden, Bedford. (Bromham Green 345.)

Aerial Photographs

Can you recommend a photographic agency that takes aerial photos?

Yes: Skyport Fotos, 227 Sipson Lane, Sipson, West Drayton, Middlesex. (01-897 8947.) Specialist Photographic Agency for Travel and Landscapes.

Photographic Agencies

Have you a list of photographic

Can Anyone Suggest a Cure for Cramp?

(See page 255)

agencies? I want some illustrations for a book I am writing.

Fox Photos	405 6851
Press Association	353 7440
Reuter	353 7440
Associated Press	353 1515
Keystone	353 9634
Pictorial Press	353 6677
Hulton Picture Library	353 3272
Central Press	353 6600
Barnaby's Picture Library & Associates Co.	580 8821

Photos for Covers

Do you know of any agencies worth contacting for covers?

Barnaby's. (01-636 6128.)

Photos of London

Where can I obtain pictures of London?

From: G.L.C. Press Office, County Hall, Westminster, London S.W.1.

Piano History

Would you kindly let me know of any society or body which deals with the history of grand pianos. There are numbers and marks indented on the frame of my piano. Such people would probably know what they represent.

We understand from Chappell & Co Ltd, 50 New Bond Street, London, W1, who have a large piano department, that it is possible to discover who the makers of a piano are from the numbers, but only in the case of well-known makes. However, we regret that there is no society which deals with this type of enquiry.

Picture Restorers

Have you a list of recommended picture restorers?

List as follows: R. M. Hoare, 17 Holland Villas Road, London, W.14.

(01-603 8040.) Col. J. W. R. Dugmore, Airieland, Kippford, Dalbeattie, Kirkcudbrightshire. Mr. J. Wilkinson, The Studio, Harold Grove, Frinton on Sea. E. Jerram, The Grove House, Droxford, Southampton. William R. Drown, 45 Dover Street, London, W.1.

If none of these is suitable we suggest you contact: The Association of British Picture Restorers, 43/44 Albemarle Street, Piccadilly, London, W.1.

Pigeon Breeder

Can you give me the name and address of a pigeon breeder?

We suggest you try: J. N. Abbot, Thuxton, Norwich. (Mattishall 220.)

Pigeons – in Towns – Discouragement

Do you know of any firm that specialises in getting rid of pigeons in London? One can hardly blaze away at them with a shotgun!

We suggest: Rentokill Ltd., 16 Dover Street, London, W.1. (01-493 0061.) They will gladly give advice on how to get rid of these pests. They "treat" balconies and window-ledges to dissuade perching.

Place Names

I am very interested in tracing the names of some neighbouring villages. Can you suggest anyone who might be able to help me?

We suggest: English Place-Name Society, University College, Gower Street, London, W.C.1.

Plating – Electro

Where could I get some plating done?

We suggest: Astral Engineers Ltd., Electro-Forming & Electro-Plating Division, 41–43 Gatwick Road, Crawley, Sussex. (Crawley 25241/5.) They have a Platton process which will cope with the electro-plating of most base materials and with any type of deposit—i.e., gold, silver, rhodium, palladium, and platinum, etc. They will also regild ormolu.

Playing Fields

We want to create a public playing field in our village. Can we get a grant or some financial aid for this project?

The National Playing Fields Association, 57b, Catherine Street, London S.W.1, will advise you. We suggest you contact them.

Water Pollution

Can any organisation help me with a problem we have locally due to fishing being spoiled by water pollution?

The Anglers Co-operative Association undertakes to deal with cases of water pollution on behalf of its members. Their address is 53 New Oxford Street, London, W.1.

Porcelain

Can you recommend a handbook, at a reasonable price, on porcelain and china?

There are two very good books dealing with this subject. The first one is *Pottery and Porcelain,* by Frederick Litchfield, published by Black at £3 10s., which deals with both Continental and English pieces. and *The Illustrated Encyclopaedia* of *British Pottery and Porcelain,* by Godden, published by Herbert Jenkins at £7 7s. There are probably many more books dealing with this subject, but these seem to be the ones that cover the widest field.

Portraits – From Photos

Can you please direct me to a firm or individual who paint portraits primarily if not entirely from photographs?

We suggest that you contact Maurice

Bradshaw Esq, Art Exhibition Bureau, 6½ Suffolk Street, Pall Mall East, London SW1 (Telephone 01-930 6844). This Bureau act as a general secretariat for all the art societies in London, and we have spoken to Mr Bradshaw on the telephone. He says he would like to see the photographs you have, to see whether it would be possible for an artist to paint entirely from these ; he would also like to have some indication of the fee you want to pay, as these can range from £50 to £5,000, and the size of the portrait. He will then be able to give you some names of artists who could do it.

Portrait Painter

I am anxious to have my portrait painted. It is for family record purposes and I want a head and shoulder portrait about 25 in. × 30 in. of reasonably modern style. I am not prepared to pay more than £50. Could you recommend a suitable artist?

We rather hesitate to suggest anyone personally because so much can go wrong between a sitter and an artist. Under the circumstances you could contact M. B. Bradshaw, Esq., Secretary to the Royal Society of Portrait Painters, 6½ Suffolk Street, W.1. This society should be in a position to recommend a suitable artist. Alternatively artists sometimes advertise their portrait painting services in the personal column of the *Sunday Times.*

Potholing (see Caves, p 251.)

Pottery – Staffordshire

Can you recommend any books about Staffordshire pottery?

Three such books are: *Staffordshire Pottery Figures of the Victorian Age,* by Thomas Balston, published by Faber & Faber. *Early Staffordshire Pottery,* by Bernard Rackham, published by Faber & Faber. *Animals in Staffordshire*

Pottery, by Bernard Rackham, a King Penguin book.

Bespoke Pottery

Could you please direct me to a firm which would make me a china teapot, cups and saucers, and a tray, to my requirements?

I have in mind a teapot based on the quaint eighteenth century round-tower block-houses on the Old Thames and Severn Canal between Lechlade and Stroud.

A local firm would obviously be best, otherwise photographs could be supplied.

We have made enquiries and have spoken to the Managing Director of the Chelsea Pottery, at Radnor Walk, London SW3, as I am afraid we do not know of any potteries in your area.

Chelsea Pottery suggested that if you would like to write to them direct, they might be able to help you.

Prints – Specialists

Can you tell me of any art dealers that specialise in prints?

Fores & Co., 123 New Bond Street, London, W.1. (01-629 5319.) The Fine Art Society Ltd., 148 New Bond Street, London, W.1. Thomas H. Parkes Ltd., The Parkes Gallery, 2 Albemarle Street, W.1. Christie, Mansen & Woods Ltd., Spencer House, 27 St. James Place London, S.W.1. Sotheby & Co., 34 New Bond Street, London, W.1.

Prints and Watercolours – Paper for Storing

Where can I buy sheets of chemically treated paper to place between watercolours and prints to prevent discolouration and spotting?

We contacted the British Museum, who suggested that you should use sheets of paper impregnated with Sanzabrite to store your prints. If you cannot obtain the sheets already impregnated with Sanzabrite, you can make a solution of 1 dessertspoonful of powdered Sanzabrite to 1 pint of water and impregnate good-quality blotting paper with this, then allow to dry.

Powdered Sanzabrite can be obtained from John Lyons, Tottenham Court Road, London, W.1.

Property Owners

Are there any associations that protect the property owner?

Yes: The Property Owners' Protection Association, Coventry House, South Place, London, E.C.2; or National Federation of Property Owners Ltd., Temple Chambers, Temple Avenue, London, E.C.4.

Fencing of Public Paths – Society to Prevent

A large public company has taken over the "Big House" in our village as a training college and has adopted a policy of fencing off public paths or diverting them in a flagrant way. We obviously need some help.

We suggest you call in the Commons, Open Spaces and Footpaths Preservation Society, 166 Shaftesbury Avenue, London, W.C.2.

Public Speaking

With my new appointment I find that I shall have to do quite a lot of public speaking, and wondered whether there is some organization that could give me advice about this?

We suggest you contact: The Abbey School for Speakers, 9 Curzon Place, London, W.1. (01-499 2760.)

Publishers – Information on

Are there any associations that can give information about publishers?

The Publishers Association, 19 Bedford Square, London, W.C.1 (01-580 6321) and Publishing & Distributing, 177 Regent Street, London, W.1 (01-734 6534.)

Removals Abroad

Can you suggest any firms that would be able to help me with a removal abroad?

Either of the following firms will be able to help you:
Pitt & Scott Ltd, 1 St. Paul's Churchyard, London EC4 (01-248 6474).
Pickfords, 205 High Holborn, London WC1 (01-405 4399).

Replating Cutlery

Do you know of a firm that will replate cutlery?

We suggest you contact: B. J. S. Electro Plating Co, 345 Kilburn High Road, London NW6 (01-624 6796).

Replating and Resilvering

Could you please advise me of a reliable firm which will undertake re-silvering of cutlery, vases, etc, and also a firm which will re-silver mirrors.

We suggest you contact one of the following: Cutlery: Mappin & Webb, 172 Regent Street, London W1. Mirrors: J Preedy & Sons Ltd, 4a Ashland Place, London W1.

Restoration of Antiques

Can you suggest any publications about restoring antiques?

'The Repair and Restoration of Furniture,' by John Rodd, published by Batsford (this is out of print, but copies can be obtained from specialist booksellers or libraries).
'Care of Antiques,' by J. M. Mills, published by Arlington.
'The Art and Antique Restorers Handbook,' by George Savage, published by Barry & Rockill.

Restorers Objets D'Art

Do you know the addresses of any restorers of objets d'art?

There is G. Garbe, 23 Charlotte Street, London W1 (01-636 1268).
Also Felix Hilton, 18 Boston Place, Dorset Square, Marylebone, London NW1 (01-262 3637).

Rhinoceros Horns – For Sale

Can you please tell me where we can sell rhinoceros horns?
I understand that there is a demand for them.

The following is the name of a Bone, Horn and Ivory Merchant, who might possibly be interested: W. Barrett & Son Ltd., 9 Old Bond Street, London, W.1.
We also have the names of two Bone, Horn and Ivory workers, whom you could contact: A. T. Clifton, 32 Lambs Conduit Street, London, W.C.1; and Morris and Forndran Ltd., 10 Heddon Street, London, W.1.
If all else fails ring the Saudi Arabian Embassy. Arabs are mad about rhinoceros horns!

List of Riding Establishments

Does anyone publish a list of Riding Establishments in the U.K.?

The British Horse Society, 35 Belgrave Square, London, S.W.1, do.

Ringed Birds – Tracing

Recently entering a disused room I found a dead bird, white, smaller than a pigeon, with a ring on one leg, and would be obliged if you could give me the address of the registry through whom I might be able to communicate with its owners.

I suggest that you contact the Royal Homing Union at 22 Clarence Street, Gloucester. If you write to them giving the ring number they should be able to trace the owner.

River Bank

I would like advice on the maintenance of an eroding river bank which is subject to sudden and extensive flooding.

We believe there may be a leaflet on this subject available from H.M. Stationery Office, Cornwall House, Stamford Street, London, S.E.1. Alternatively, we think that this is a matter on which you should consult your local water conservation authority, since they may be in a position to undertake this work without cost to yourself.

Rugmaking

Can you recommend a source of information on rugmaking or some books on the subject?

The National Federation of Women's Institutes, 31 Eccleston Street, Victoria, London SW1, have a booklet on Surrey Stitch Rugs. They recommend also the following books:

'Rugmaking Craft,' by Edith L. Allen, published by Manual Arts Press, USA.

'Woven Rugs,' by Ronald Grierson, by Dryads Ltd, 93 Great Russell Street, London WC1.

'The Countrywoman's Rug Book,' by Ann Macbeth, published by Dryads Ltd.

Rug-making

Do you know of an association that might be able to give me some information about rug-making, or do you know of any publications on the subject?

The Embroiderers' Guild, 73 Wimpole Street, London W1, might be able to help you, or there is a book on the subject called 'Needlemade Rugs,' by Sybil I. Mathew, published by Mills & Brown.

Rural England

Is there a protection association for the countryside?

Yes. The Council for the Protection of Rural England, 4 Hobart Place, London, S.W.1. Tel. 01-235 4771.

Rural Industries Bureau

Do you know of any association that will be able to give me information about Rural industries?

Yes: The Rural Industries Bureau, 35 Camp Road, Wimbledon, London SW19.

Sailing – Information on Learning

Apply for details to Central Council of Physical Recreation, 26 Park Crescent, London, W.1. Courses are run at the National Sailing Centre, Cowes, Isle of Wight.

Salmon – Smoked

Where can I obtain smoked salmon in large quantities?

Try: S. Baron Ltd, 9 Assembly Passage, London E1, or Essay Smoked Salmon and Pure Foods Co, 11 Back Church Lane, London E1, or Messrs. M. Barnett & Son, Frying Pan Alley E1, or Salmon Smoking Co Ltd, Moston Road, Middleton Junction, Manchester.

The Salmon and Trout Association

I believe there is an Association which can help owners of fishing rights.

The Salmon and Trout Association, Fishmongers Hall, London Bridge, London EC4, are the people you want. It has representatives on the fisheries committee of the British Field Sports Society, Flyfishers Club, Anglers Cooperative Association, etc.

Saw-dust as a Fuel

I believe there is a Government department experimenting with the use of sawdust as a fuel for domestic heating purposes?

The Department of Scientific and Industrial Research, Fuel Research Station, Blackwall Lane, East Greenwich, London SE10, will be glad to advise you.

Schools Exploratory Expeditions

Could you please let me have details about the organisation which runs an expedition each year for young people? The expeditions are of an exploratory nature and undertake tasks such as mapping, collection of scientific data, etc.

We believe the organisation you are thinking of is: The British Schools Exploring Society of Temple Chambers, Temple Avenue, London, E.C.4.

Scottish Agricultural Associations

Can you tell me what Agricultural Associations there are in Scotland?

National Farmers' Union (Scotland), 17 Grosvenor Crescent, Edinburgh 12, Scotland.

Scottish National Trust, 5 Charlotte Street, Edinburgh, Scotland.

Association for the Preservation of Rural Scotland, 15 Rutland Square, Edinburgh 1, Scotland.

Scottish Association of Young Farmers' Clubs, 11 Rutland Street, Edinburgh, Scotland.

Agriculture for Scotland (Government Department), St Andrew's House, Edinburgh 1, Scotland.

Farm Management Association, Room 219, Edinburgh School of Agriculture, West Mains Road, Edinburgh 9.

Scottish Council of Social Service

Can you tell me what the Scottish Council of Social Service do?

Its main object is to promote 'Better Living' in the countryside. This is through the provision of village hall facilities, Rural Industries, Citizens' Advice Bureaux, County Music Committees, Old People' Welfare. Alas, free whisky is not included.

Sea Fishing – Book on

Can you recommend a book on sea fishing?

Two good modern books on sea fishing are: 'Sea Fishing,' by Major D. P. Lea Birch (A. & C. Black), which deals especially with fishing from the shore, and 'Modern Sea Fishing,' by Eric Cooper (A. & C. Black), which pays more attention to fishing from a boat.

Seasons – Game

I am always getting into a muddle of when things are in 'season'. Can you give me a rough guide?

Salmon: Feb 2–Nov 1 (Wales and England); Feb 11–Oct 31 (Scotland).

Trout: Mar 2– Oct 1 (Wales and England).

Flat Racing: End of March–Nov 22.

Otter Hunting: Mid-April–Mid-Sept.

Freshwater Fish: June 16–Mar 14.

Stag Hunting and Shooting: Aug 12–Oct 12.

Grouse Shooting: Aug 12–Dec 10.

Cub Hunting: Aug 4–Nov 1.

Fox Hunting: November to April.

Fallow Deer, Moor Game: No close season.

Stag-horns – Salad Servers

My son shot his first stag recently. It was only a switch with unpointed antlers about 15 in. long and 1 in. diameter at the base. He is anxious to make something of them, salad servers or something of the sort. Can you proffer any advice or suggest who might?

We have been in touch with Mappin & Webb, of 172 Regent Street, London W.1, on your behalf. If you were to write to Mr. Mann (ref. RT65), giving details of design, he would be very happy to help you, provided, of course, that you decide to have silver handles, to the salad servers, or silver blades to the carvers.

Seaweed

I have recently taken over an hotel which is adjacent to a small, stony beach which is covered with considerable areas of seaweed. Can you advise me whether there is any method (other than manual labour, which we have tried and abandoned) by which we can eradicate this weed or, at least, loosen it from the rocks so that it can be gathered up and disposed of without excessive labour costs?

We know of no effective method of removing areas of seaweed, short of cutting it back continually, and we imagine there must be many councils of seaside resorts who would have developed such a technique if one could have been found.

Farm Secretaries

I have a granddaughter of 15½ who wants to train as a secretary to a racing stable or a farm secretary. Could you give me the name of an advice bureau who could tell me what subjects she should get instructions in for such posts?

There are special courses for farm secretaries at some colleges, but we would have thought that a basic secretarial training would be quite adequate, especially as she lives on a farm herself and must have some knowledge of what goes on in a farm office. The subjects which are essential are shorthand, typing and book-keeping.

Dressing of Sheepskins

Could you give me the name of any firm who undertake the dressing of sheepskins?

We think either of the following should be able to help you: J. A. Fischer Ltd, 24 Bracey Street, Hornsey Road, London N4, or C. W. Martin & Sons Ltd, 68 Upper Thames Street, London EC4.

Skins should be properly air-dried before sending. The following method is recommended: Cut the skin open quite flat as soon as it is off the animal. Pin out on a board – using plenty of drawing pins and stretching well but not unduly into a good clean oblong shape. Leave it in a cool place until it is quite dry.

Sheep Skins – Curing

From time to time I have sheep skins, some of which I have cured successfully, but I always seem to experience difficulty in getting a satisfactory suppleness.
I should be most grateful for any practical hints which would help towards this end.

J. A. Fisher Ltd., a curing firm in London, have given us the following hints although they do say that this is a job which should be tackled by skilled craftsmen.

The main problem is washing off the skins thoroughly, and cleaning the fur and scraping off the inner skin (known as 'fleshing'). This is a very difficult process without the proper machines, but presumably as you have already done some curing, you have managed to do this successfully.

For the tanning, make up enough pickle to immerse the skin, in the following quantities:

Water	100
Salt	10
Sulphuric Acid ...	1

If you have been using a mixture of alum and salt this would make the skins heavy and hard, but with the above mixtures the skins should become supple. Leave the skin to soak in the pickle for twenty-four hours, then dry it off, but it is important not to dry it off completely, and a small moisture content must be left in order to allow the skin to stretch and remain supple. The last stage is to smear the skin with oil, either vegetable or animal (lard would be all right), and this should leave the leather quite supple.

Shells

Where might I obtain shells in large quantities?

The Eaton Bag Co Ltd, 16 Manette St, London W1, sell shells wholesale, or you could try: The Rothesay Seafoods Ltd, Ladeside St, Rothesay, Bute.

Shoes – Handmade

Do you know of anywhere that will make shoes by hand to fit?

There is Lobb, of 9 St James' Street, London SW1, or: McAfee, 38 Dover Street, London W1.

Shooting and Fishing Rentals

Do you know of any firms that will arrange shooting and fishing rentals?

There are: Strutt & Parker Lofts & Warner, 41 Berkeley Square, London W1; or C. W. Ingram & Son, 90 Princes Street, Edinburgh 2; or Messrs Curtis & Henson, 5 Mount Street, London W1.

Shooting Rents – Standards

Can you give me some indication of rentals being obtained for shoots at the present time?

The rent payable for a shoot depends entirely upon supply and demand in the district where it is available; in other words, if you want the ground badly it is likely to be worth much more to you as a border shoot than it might be to an outsider.

Without seeing the shoot or knowing the local rents prevailing, we cannot possibly give an exact estimate – all we can say is that before the war shooting in this part of the country might possibly have been obtained for 1s an acre, and today you might have to give up to four times as much. As it stands, and provided no one else is after it, the ground sounds as though it is not worth a great deal; on the other hand, to you as one whose shoot marches with this, it may represent a much greater value, and we can only suggest that you must consider it in the light of whether it is a loss or nuisance to you, if you do not rent it; or how much of an asset it might be to your existing shoot.

We appreciate that this all seems a little vague, but it is only the man on the spot who can judge the value of sporting rights in his neighbourhood.

Shooting Schools

Can you let me have the address of a shooting school in Middlesex?

We suggest you contact: Holland & Holland Ltd, 13 Bruton Street, London W1 (01-499 4411), who have a school at Ducks Hill Road, Northwood, Middlesex. Or you could try: West London Shooting Grounds, West End, Greenford, Middlesex (01-845 1377).

Show Jumping

Is there an association which will be able to give me information about Show Jumping?

There is the British Show Jumping Association, whose address is: 35 Belgrave Square, London SW1, or you could contact: The National Equestrian Centre, Kenilworth, Warwicks.

Silhouettes

Do you know of anyone who will copy silhouettes?

We suggest: Josephene Harris ARWS, 37 Melville Road, London SW13, who is recommended by the Academy of Arts.

Silk – Cleaning

I have recently bought a dress made of Thai silk and heavily brocaded. I understand it needs a special form of drycleaning, presumably by hand. Can you please advise me of experts who can be fully relied upon to make a first-class job of this in Kent?

We are assured by their head office in London that Flynn's, of Tunbridge Wells, will be able to do this job for you.

Silkworms – Source of

Lullingstone Silk Farm, Salisbury Hall, London Colney, St. Albans, Herts.

Modern Silver

I have some silver, not antique, that I wish to sell. I would be most grateful if you could help me by giving me the names of suitable firms within easy reach.

Modern silver is best sold through a jeweller and not an antique dealer, and it might be better to bring the silver to London rather than try locally where there may not be the quality of jewellers which one could go to.

Skin Curing

Can you tell me of a place where they will cure and dress sheepskin, and also other skins?

Baileys, of Glastonbury, Somerset, will cure and dress sheepskins. For curing other fur skins try Whaley, Hampton, Middlesex they also remodel coats.

Skin Curing – Mink

Can you suggest anyone who will cure mink skins?

We suggest: J. A. Fischer Ltd, 440a Hornsey Road, London N19. He will also cure snake skins.

Skin-diving

I want to take up skin-diving. Can you give me the address of a club I could join?

The British Sub-Aqua Club, 160 Great Portland Street, London W1.

Skins – Animal Curing

From time to time I have an animal skin I would like cured, but I never know where to send it. For instance, we found an otter dead in the road and also a badger. I could skin these myself, but this is as far as I could manage. If I wrapped up a skin well in old newspaper and sent it at once, is there any firm who would cure these skins for me?

Rowland Ward Limited, of 64 Grosvenor Street, London W1 will cure them for you. They are very large taxidermists, and have animals sent in from all over the country. Tel. 01-493 4501.

Snake-skins – Making up

Would you please oblige and let me have per return the name of any firm you know that would be able to make up shoes and a hand bag out of snake-skins supplied.

We are afraid this seems to be a most difficult thing to find. Most of the old craftsmen who used to do this are now employed by firms and cannot undertake work of this kind. We have spoken to a shoemaker in Gloucester Road, who tells us that about twenty years ago he was doing just that, but now it is too expensive to make special patterns just for a few articles. He thought the only possibility would be to find a man working on his own out of the centre of London.

As regards the handbag, there is a firm called Handbag Services Co, of Beauchamp Place, London SW3, who will make handbags from skins provided. If you send them the skins they will give you an estimate.

Soil Association – Address

Houghley Research Farms, Houghley, Stowmarket, Suffolk.

Speleologists (see Caves, p 251.)

Squab Farming

Can you give me some addresses of people engaged in Squab farming who might advise me?

L. Holman Esq, 14 Washington Road, Maldon, Essex. (Breeder.)

G. W. Drake Esq, 1 Exeter Road, Braunton, Devon, 'Polish Lynor pigeons.'

A. Feltham Esq, 111 Sotheby Road, London N5. (Breeder and showman.)

Red Squirrels

Could you or any member give us any assistance or advice as to where we could obtain a pair of brown or red squirrels? Not for pets but to try and breed wild in our garden and countryside around. We have many trees surrounding the house and at present have a family of greys.

Red squirrels can be obtained from Ravensden Zoological Co Ltd, Hollington, Kimbolton Road, Bedford.

We believe that people mostly have them for pets nowadays as, of course, if they are wild the grey squirrels will destroy them immediately. It would be possible to keep them in your garden in a cage to protect them. Another place that supplies red squirrels for pets is G. E. Bunting, Bestwood Drive, Clay Cross, Derbyshire.

Stamp Dealers

Can you supply me with the names and addresses of some stamp dealers either in London or on the South Coast?

Perhaps some of the following can help you:
Veaseys, of Whitstable, Kent.
David Field Ltd, 42 Berkeley Street, London W1 (01-499 5252).
H. R. Harmer Ltd, 41 New Bond Street, London W1 (01-629 0218).
Robson Lowe Ltd, 50 Pall Mall, London SW1 (01-839 4034).

Stamp Prices

I have a small collection of British colonial stamps, Cape of Good Hope, Grenada, St Helena and New Zealand. Could you please give me an idea of how selling prices would compare with the valuation given in a Stanley Gibbons catalogue?

David Field Limited, stamp dealers, inform me that they would be worth under half of Stanley Gibbons's quoted prices. The value depends on what countries they are, whether they are a complete set, and, most important, whether they are in good condition.

Stamps

I wonder if you could put me in touch with a suitable firm or institution to give me a valuation of eight books of stamps, or tell me where to obtain a catalogue to price the collection. I know nothing about stamps and have no idea whether they are worth a lot of money or very little.

We suggest that you write to the following organisation, which is an authority on the subject: Stanley Gibbons Ltd, Postage Stamp Dealers, 391 Strand, London WC2.

Cleaning Stone

One of the paraffin stoves which we use to heat our small church burst into flames some weeks ago and has left the wall in the vicinity very black. The wall is faced with a very porous light colour stone, not unlike sandstone. What should we do in order to clean without damaging?

We suggest you experiment by washing the surface of the stone with warm water containing 10 per cent ammonia. This should dissolve the grease in the soot into a soapy solution which can then be wiped off with clear water. Great care should be exercised in order not to damage the surface.

Deciphering Stone Inscriptions

A method advocated by J. E. Lee in his book on the Antiquities of Caerlon. 'The slab to be washed perfectly clean and well moistoned, a sheet of dry silver paper is then to be laid upon it, when a singular effect is to be observed every part which touches the wet stone partakes of its dark colour, whilst that part of the paper which is stretched over the hollows retains its original white appearance. In fact inscriptions that before were hardly visible seem by this process to start into existence as in a moment. The paper may then be pressed into cavities with a soft cloth and the letters traced in indian ink.'

Stone Masons

Have you got the names of any stone masons on your files?

Here are a selection:
Hornton Stone Quarries, Edge Hill, Nr. Banbury. They make stone balls.
E. M. Lander Ltd, 605–9 Harrow Road, London W10 (01-969 2211). They make memorial stones.
William Wright, Alexandria Road, London W13.
E. J. & A. T. Bradford Ltd, 61–63 Borough Road, London SE1. (They are stone sculptors and also do wood carving.)

Polishing Stones

Could you tell me who I should contact to obtain information about polishing my own pebbles and stones? Or perhaps you can recommend a book on the subject.

This is a very expensive process, but equipment can be bought – we suggest that you contact: The Gemmological Association of Great Britain, at St. Dunstans House, Carey Lane, London EC2, who will give you all the information you require.
C. Ellis has written a book called 'The Pebbles on the Beach,' which has chapters on pebble collecting, dictionary varieties and composition, etc, hardness, with short notes on sawing and polishing.

Steam Engine Society of Salop

I believe there is a Steam Engine Society in this part of the world, but unfortunately can't seem to find the name of it; can you help?

Yes: the address of the Rally Organiser is: D. W. Smith, 44 Sandford Avenue, Church Stretton, Salop.

Streets Lamps – Victorian

I would very much like to have a Victorian street lamp to grace my garden; do you know where I can obtain one?

Try: O. C. Summers Ltd, 960 High Road, London N12.

Students Abroad

Do you know of any society that could advise me about where I could send my son to study abroad or a family he might live with?

A very reputable firm called Gabbitas and Thring, of 6 Sackville Street, London W1, have an advisory service for schools etc, as well as lists of colleges abroad.
Or you could try an agency which finds families abroad called En Famille Agency Ltd, of 1 New Burlington Street, London W1, but they may have moved.

Agricultural Student – Payment

I intend employing a pre-Royal Agricultural student for a year. What should I pay him?

It is quite common for students doing farm work for a year to pay the farmer and not vice versa. In other instances they work for nothing or pocket money. If this alternative does not appeal to you we suggest you contact your local NAAS at the Ministry of Agriculture and ask them for advice.

Sun-dials

Do you know of anybody in Kent who makes sun-dials?

A. A. Holt, Burton Holt Ltd, Goudhurst, Kent (Goudhurst 280) is a specialist in making and erecting sundials.

Air Surveys

Can you put me in touch with a firm which carries out air surveys?

We suggest you try Aero films Ltd, of

29 Old Bond Street, London W1, or Aerofilms, of 6 Elsten Way, Boreham Wood, Herts.

Swords and Daggers

I have a ceremonial sword from Bhutan and a valuable Arab dagger, the blades of both of which, through ill-use and neglect, have become stuck in the scabbards.

Could you advise me to whom I could send these to have the blades eased out and re-united with the hilts.

We have asked Wilkinson Sword Ltd, of 16 Pall Mall, London SW1, if they were able to do this for you, and they say that if you would like to send them by post they will be able to tell you if it is possible. They do say that there is a danger of damaging the hilts when unsticking them, and with native daggers and swords it is impossible to replace the materials. They were hesitant about re-uniting the blades with the hilts, but easing the blades out would be possible.

Tape Typing and Hire of Tape Recorder

Do you know where I could hire a tape recorder and then a place where I could get the tape typed?

You can hire tape recorders from: Tape Recorder Centre, 18 Blenheim Road, Chiswick (01-995 1661).

You will be able to get the tape typed at: Tape Typing Secretarial Agency Ltd., 12 Kingsley Street, London W.1 (01-734 6223).

Taxidermist

Can you suggest the name of a taxidermist in London? Also do you know of any either in North Wales or Lancashire?

The following list may be of help to you: Rowland Ward, 64 Grosvenor Street, London W.1 (01-493 4581). Mr. E. N. Hare, 60 Hamilton Road, Golders Green, N.W.11 (01-458 3954). Edward Gerard & Sons, Ltd., 85 Royal College Street, Camden Town, N.W.1 (01-387 2765). Specializes in lining rugs and skins. T. Salkeld, Over Kellet, Carnforth, Lancs. (Carnforth 2452), especially fox masks. Snowdonia Taxidermy Studios, Llanrwst, North Wales.

Taxidermy

Can you give any advice on taxidermy? Where should I go, or do you have special arrangements for C.G.A. members?

I am afraid there is no arrangement for members for taxidermy, but there is a very good taxidermist called Mr. E. N. Hare, of 60 Hamilton Road, Golders Green, London N.W.11, who specializes in fishes, but does all other animals as well. He tells us he has done everything up to elephants, but he will not touch pets.

His telephone number is Meadway 3954 in case you should wish to contact him. The animal must be posted off to him as soon as possible after its death, but we would suggest that you ask for an estimate before the work is done.

Telescope – Identifying

A friend of mine owns a telescope given to him by a Mr Weston over twenty years ago, who said it had been used at the Battle of Trafalgar.

There is no date on the telescope, but the following is just discernible: 'Stebbing, Portsmouth optician to the R.Y.S.'

I should be grateful if you would advise me where I can obtain authentic information about this telescope.

We have spoken to the National Maritime Museum, and they say that if you would like to take the telescope in to them when you are next in London they would be able to date it for you, as they have a list of opticians and the inscriptions they used. It is very common, they say, for people selling a telescope to say that it was used in the Battle of Trafalgar—and this they might well not be able to authenticate, but at least they will be able to tell you how old it is.

It would be very dangerous to put this in the post, so perhaps you could take it to: Mr. Stimson, Department of Navigation and Astronomy, National Maritime Museum, Greenwich, London, S.E.10. Tel. 01-858 4422.

It would be best to ring up first to make sure Mr. Stimson will be there.

Teazels-Source

I would be grateful if you could let me know where I can get some teazel-heads from. They are used to raise the nap of the cloth in the weaving, and used to be grown as a crop in the west country, but I have no idea where they come from now. I want big ones, full sizes ones are usually about 2½–3 inches long. I want them to make toys out of, and if the idea works I shall want a regular supply. Somerset and Gloucestershire used to be good districts for them.

We think you will have difficulty in obtaining these in small quantities, since they are usually grown on a commercial scale for cloth manufacturers in the counties mentioned in your letter. We suggest that you grow teazels yourself. The proper name is *Dipsacus Fullonum*, and they will grow almost anywhere. They are otherwise known as Fuller's Teazel, which is used industrially. The only other people who may be able to supply these in small quantities are home weaving organizations such as Art Needlework Industries Ltd., Ship Street, Oxford.

Preservation of Timber

We have a problem over preserving the timber in our Tudor house. Various commercial firms have advised unsuccessfully. Is there some organisation which carries out research to which we would turn?

The British Wood Preserving Association might be able to help. Their address is: 6, Southampton Place, London, WC1.

Thatching

Have you got a list of reed growers and thatchers in England?

We have various addresses. They are: Master Thatchers Association, c/o Rural Industries Bureau, 35 Camp Road, Wimbledon, S.W.19. Kent, Surrey & Sussex Master Thatchers Association, Secretary (Mr. S. F. Jarvis, 1 New Cottage, Ancton Lane, Middleton-on-Sea, Sussex. Norfolk Reed Thatchers, 3 Herbal Hill, Clerkenwell, London E.C.1. In the Essex area: R. C. Simmons, Rural Industries Committee, 79 Springfield Road, Chelmsford, Essex. F. J. Saunders, Esq., 14 Church Lane, Drayton, Berks. F. G. Cook, Esq., 2 Council Houses, Sherington, near Banbury. F. E. Davis, Esq., 49 Sutton, Eynsham, near Oxford. A. M. Brown, Esq., Oxfordshire Rural Industries Organisers, Oxford Rural Committee Council, Hadow House, 20 Beaumont Street, Oxford. Norfolk Reed Growers Association, 15 Chapel Field East, Norwich (Nor 65 E).

Thermometers

Do you know of a manufacturer of thermometers and scientific instruments?

Yes: Heath, Hicks & Perkin (Thermometers) Ltd., 8 Hatton Garden, London E.C.1 (01-405 1743).

Timber

Do you know of any associations that deal with the research and development of timber, and is there one for timber growers?

One of these might be able to help you: Timber & Research Development Association Ltd, 26 Store Street, London W.C.1 ; or Timber Growers Organisation, 35 Belgrave Square, London S.W.1.

Time, Gentlemen Please!

When, centuries ago, in many villages, there was only one time-piece, namely, the church clock, how did the parson know the time to set when the clock had been got going again?

Perhaps he consulted his sundial or The Maker!

Heresy of Heresies, perhaps no one cared all that much what time it was. Punctuality is after all said to be for kings. As for 'Time' pubs had no fixed hours until the reign of that uncomfortable King, George V.

Tobacco Grower – Curing

Can you give me any information, please, regarding 'authorized curing centres' for home-grown tobacco?

We suggest that you contact the secretary to the Scottish Amateur Tobacco Growers Association (unfortunately there is no English tobacco association), his address is: David Chalmers, Esq., 39 Milton Road, Kirkcaldy, Fife. This association provides plants, advice, and cures. One person can have 25lb. cured in one season, and it is illegal to sell this, give it away, or throw it away—it must only be for one's own use.

Tortoiseshell

Can you give any suggestion for cleaning and polishing a tortoiseshell pin tray, which has got very dull and rather scratched? Also blistered in one or two places, where an iniquitous guest used it as an ash tray but for this I imagine there is no remedy. A knowledgeable friend advised polishing with Brasso, and I have tried this, but without noticeable improvement.

We suggest that you contact: The Tortoiseshell and Ivory House Ltd, 24 Chiltern Street, London W1 (tel: Welbeck 8031). Perhaps you could take it in when you are next in town. We have spoken to them on the telephone and they tell us they could possibly restore this for you.

Translations

Where might I get translations done?
Try: Berlitz School of Languages, 321 Oxford Street, London W.1.

British Travel Association

Have you got the address of an association that deals with travel?
The address you require is: British Travel Association, 64 St. James Street, London S.W.1.

Travel – Reduced Rates

See *Commonwealth* Travel Association.

Commemorative Tree

We would like to plant a commemorative tree on our village green and wondered if there is someone who can advise us.

The Commemorative Tree Company was specially founded for this purpose. Their address is Monk's Vineyard, Nowton, Bury St. Edmunds, Suffolk.

Trees – Approved Contractors

Does any organisation publish a list of recommended contractors?

The Association of British Tree Surgeons and Arborists publish a list of approved contractors and consultants, which is as follows: B.C.R. Ltd., 6 High Street, Great Bookham, Surrey (Bookham 124). Beeching of Ash Ltd., Ash, near Aldershot, Hants (Aldershot 21415). Honey Bros. Ltd., 9 Woodstock Grove, Godalming, Surrey (Godalming 2406). The Southern Tree Surgeons Ltd., Crawley Down, near Crawley, Sussex (Copthorne 2215). Western Tree Surgeons Ltd., St. Burryan, West Cornwall (St. Burryan 374).

The above companies have been approved by the examining committee of the Association of British Tree Surgeons and Arborists as complying with and practising to the standard required by the Association.

This examination is based on B.S.I. Standard 17/79 landscape operations. The high standard required restricts the number of successful applicants. However, owing to the irrevocable nature of all operations concerned in tree care, this standard is jealously guarded.

All companies must provide a minimum of £50,000 third party and public liability insurance cover.

Trees

Do you know of a firm in Herts. that undertakes specialised pruning?

Yes: Countryside Tree Specialists, The Cottage, New Town, Codicote, Herts. (Codicote 558). They undertake specialised pruning, cavity treatment, stump removal, felling and fertilizing.

Walnut and Sycamore Trees in Wales

I have some sycamore and walnut trees that I would like to dispose of. Do you know of anyone who would be interested?

Yes, we suggest you contact: W. L. Cotton, Esq., Forestry Consultants, 50 Gerald Street, Wrexham, North Wales.

Trees – Forestry Consultants

Can you tell me the names of organisations which will recommend forestry consultants?

Society of Foresters of Great Britain, Secretary (Mr. J. J. Lawrie), 51 Colcokes Road, Banstead, Surrey. Royal Forestry Society of England, Wales and Northern Ireland, Secretary. 49 Russell Square, London W.C.1. Royal Scottish Forestry Society, Secretary, Room 10, 25 Drumsheugh Gardens, Edinburgh 3. Royal Institution of Chartered Surveyors, Secretary, 12 Great George Street, London S.W.1. Society of Consultant Foresters of Scotland, Secretary (Mr. J. Farquhar), 7 Station Road, Gordon, Berwickshire. Association of Professional Foresters of Great Britain, Secretary, Broad Oaks, Froxfield, near Petersfield, Hants. Timber Growers Organisation Ltd., Secretary, 35 Belgrave Square, London S.W.1. Scottish Woodland Owners' Association Ltd., Secretary, 6 Chester Street, Edinburgh. British Tree Surgeons, Mrs. Deller, Pembroke Cottage, Upper Hale, Farnham, Surrey.

Tropical Agriculture

I wonder if you know of anywhere where tropical agriculture is taught?

There is a college in the West Indies—this is the Imperial College of Tropical Agriculture at St. Augustine, Trinidad, West Indies.

Trout Fishery

There is a stream and lake on this estate which it is considered could have possibilities for developing as a trout fishery. Could you give me the addresses of a couple of firms who advise on such a matter?

Two places which supply fish and have consultants to come and do a complete survey and give recommendations for setting up a new fishery are: Berkshire Trout Farm, Hungerford, Berks; and Fishery Management Services, The Rise, Brandon Village, Coventry CV8 3HU.

Valuers of Books (see page 246.)

Valuers of Household Contents

Do you know of a valuer for insurance purposes?

Yes, Gurr Johns & Co. Ltd., 50 Pall Mall, London S.W.1, will value personal effects.

Veneers

Where can I see a good selection of veneers to buy?

Aaronson Bros. Ltd., Veneers Town Wharf, Wharf Lane, Rickmansworth, Herts. (Rickmansworth 74261).

Veterinary Book

Can you recomend a good veterinary book on cattle diseases?

We suggest that you obtain a copy of

Black's Veterinary Dictionary, which is published by Adam and Charles Black, and costs 50s. net.

Veterinary Inquiries

The Animal Health Trust, Houghton Grange, Houghton, Hunts, deals with these.

English Vineyards

I want to start growing outdoor wine grapes. I believe there are Viticultural facilities from whom, as a complete beginner, I can get information. Can you help?

I suggest that you contact The English Vineyard Association, c/o Mrs. Barrett, The Vineyard, Crick's Green, Nr. Felstead, Essex.

Walking Sticks

I have a blackthorn walking-stick which is still covered with the bark. This I have had for four years. Now the straight portion is becoming slightly out of straight and the crook is straightening out. I should be pleased if you could tell me what I can do to correct these conditions, bearing in mind that I do not wish to strip off the bark.

We contacted James Smith & Sons of 53 New Oxford Street, W.1, who are specialists in walking-sticks and umbrellas. They advised that you should keep the walking-stick out of all extremities of heat and cold as these do tend to affect its shape. To get it back into shape you should put it into hot water and bend it back.

Wart Cure – 1

Can you please advise a cure for warts? My little boy of four has them on his hands and had them removed by the doctor, but they have all grown back again, and there may be some country remedy.

Slice off small roundels of lemon peel and soak for 12 hours in a saucer of vinegar. Then place the lemon peel over the warts and secure firmly with adhesive tape. Change the lemon peel every 24 hours and continue the applications until the warts begin to disappear.

Other remedies—include: rubbing with castor oil; another recommended method is a 5% solution of brilliant green (can get this from chemist) and apply daily with a matchstick and cotton wool (do not spill it on carpets) or preferably apply it every 2 or 3 days keeping the wart covered meanwhile with waterproof sticking plaster, nail varnish durafix or something similar. This last cure is painful and only to be tried by people with masochistic tendencies.

Wart Cure – 2

With reference to the letter in your November issue:

The wart should be firmly covered with ordinary sticking plaster applied directly without lint. This covering should be firmly maintained for six weeks when the wart should come away cleanly leaving a neat hole. In short, cover with sticking plaster and forget it.

(Hants)

The immediate cure for warts is to apply the yellow juice from Greater Celandine and they usually disappear very quickly.

(Dorset)

My wife and I have found Posalfilin wart ointment to be really effective. It is made by Camden Chemical Co., 61 Gray's Inn Road, London, W.C.1, and costs 25p. per tube.

(Ayrshire)

Steal a small piece of raw beef from the larder, rub it on all the warts and then bury it in the garden. As the meat rots, so the warts rot.

How do I know? Many years ago my daughter, then aged 9, had 47 warts on both hands, and I spent pounds on treatment and medical advice, but to no avail until my mother asked me to try a witches' cure. I immediately said it was nonsense, but unbeknown to me she used to tell my daughter to go to the larder and steal a small piece of raw beef and rub it on all the warts and then bury it, but don't tell anybody she had done it. A few weeks later there was no sign of a wart on either hand, and has never been since. So amazed was I that I tried it on a wart that I had had for many years on a finger, and it disappeared. Recently I was telling a man about this cure for warts, and he said, 'Allow me to finish the story—I once had 10 warts on my hands and cured them by the same treatment.'

Years later my daughter trained as a nurse in one of the London teaching hospitals, but if you asked her how to cure warts, she would tell you 'the witches' cure'.

(Devon)

In reply to the appeal for a cure for warts, I can recommend the following: Paint the wart with water-glass (egg-preservative), allow this to dry. If possible the wart must be kept continuously coated.

This cure does not take many days. My daughter used this some years ago and the warts disappeared, leaving no scars. One that the doctor treated did!

(Berwickshire)

An excellent cure which I have never known to fail is dandelion milk. I have just cured a wart in 14 days by this method, merely squeezing the juice near the head of the stem liberally onto the wart. The wart will then blacken and the top layers will die off in a day or two. Reapply until it is obvious the skin is clear. The surrounding skin remains unaffected. The first application usually deadens the wart, which can be a very tender thing.

(Sark)

I have two cures for warts. The first was to touch the wart with an ordinary garden slug. Pin the slug to a tree trunk, then when the slug has shrivelled up the wart would have done likewise. The second cure was to dab the wart each morning with distilled malt vinegar.

Not feeling enthusiastic about the first method, I tried the second. I have tried it twice. On each occasion the wart disappeared in about three weeks.

(Derbys)

A doctor, who shall be nameless, when asked to cure warts asked despairingly, 'Have you tried hitting them with a Bible?'

Watch Repair

Can you suggest any books on watch repair?

"Practical Watch Repairing," "Practical Clock Repairing," both by Donald de Carle, obtainable from N. A. G. Press, Ltd., 226 Latymer Court, Hammersmith, London, W.6.

"Watch and Clock Making and Repairing" by W. J. Gazelry, obtainable from Heywood & Co., Drury House, Russell Street, London, W.C.2.

Water Diviner

I have a field on a hill and am certain there is water below. Could you advise me of someone who will examine the land and tell me where the water can be tapped in order to make a small stream and a pond.

The addresses you should contact are: The British Society of Dowsers, York House, Portugal Street, London, W.C.2. or J. C. Maby, Frocester, Stonehouse, Glos.

River Weeds

My problem is weed in a salmon river in Scotland. We have investigated the possibility of chemicals and it seems the river is too big for this. We have thought of dredging from a boat. I wonder if you have any ideas on the subject.

We suggest that you consider buying a Clearweed Water Weed Cutter. Alternatively, you could try contacting E. P. Barrus Ltd., of 12/16 Brunel Road, Acton, London W.3, who manufacture another from of underwater weed cutter, called the Jari. We do not advise dredging, as this may disturb the river bed too much.

Welsh Pony and Cob Society

I have recently purchased a Welsh pony and wonder if there is some organisation that might be able to tell me more about this animal?

We suggest you try: The Welsh Pony and Cob Society, whose secretary is: T. E. Roberts, Esq., 23 North Parade, Aberystwyth, Wales.

Wig Makers

Do you know of a wig-maker in the London area?

There is: Wig Creations Ltd., Stanley Hall, 25 Portman Square, London, W1 (01-486 0771).

Wildfowlers Association

I have heard there is a Wildfowlers Association, do you know its address?

Yes: The Wildfowlers' Association, Grosvenor House, 104 Watergate Street, Chester. (Chester 20344).

Women's Institutes – Nat. Fed.

Their address is: 39 Eccleston Street, London, S.W.1.

Wool Combings – Spinning

Do you know anyone who will spin wool combings and flax?

Miss D. M. Pennington, Weald Cottage, Old Heathfield, Sussex, will be able to assist you.

Yan Tan Tethera – 1

With reference to an article by David Gunstan, in Sussex, 40 years ago, our shepherds counted thus—*yan, tan, tethera, methera, pimp, sethera, lethera, hovera, devera, dick,* then *yan a dick, tan a dick,* and so on, notching the twenties on their sticks with incredible swiftness. Mrs. Wright, the author of *Rustic Speech and Folk Lore,* states that the numerals were Celtic, that our Anglo-Saxon forefathers never amalgamated with the Celts and the shepherds who became subject to the invaders were left to their hereditary occupations. The Celts took over their system of numbers which the shepherd associated with the sheep under his care. Be that as it may, I personally believe

this system of counting goes back beyond that, to our first farmers, the Bronze Age folk. I do know one thing. No Belgae, no Roman, no Saxon, Dane or Norman could have ever made a Sussex shepherd change his socks, even if he wanted to, let alone 'his times-without-number' method of counting. They are the most change resistant, obstinate, gloriously stubborn men on the face of the earth.

Yan Tan Tethera – 2

I think a trained philologist could trace the origin of the numerals used by the Sussex shepherds with certainty. I am far from being a trained philologist, but I have an amateur interest in language. The numerals certainly seem to be of Celtic (ancient British) origin. There is a resemblance to the Welsh numerals as used today. The pre-Celtic origin appears to be Greek; or if not actually Greek, then the shepherds' language and Greek have a very ancient common origin. There is also some likeness to the Romany numerals.

The shepherds seem to have transferred 'tethera' (Greek—tessares) from four to three. The likeness of the shepherds' numerals to the Welsh is far from exact, but a philologist would probably detect more than is apparent to the untrained eye. I have no knowledge of Basque, said to be the oldest language in Europe. Perhaps a line on shepherds' language could be taken from this source. However all this may be, the shepherds' numerals must be some of the oldest words in use in this country and I hope they still are in use. Beneath is a comparative table of Greek, Welsh, shepherds' and Romany numerals.

No.	Ancient Greek
1	Hen
2	Duo
3	treis
4	tessares
5	penté
6	hex
7	hepta

8   octo
9   ennea
10 dekem
11 ——-
12 ——

Welsh
  Un
  Dau
  tri
  pedwar
  pump
  chwech
  saith
  wyth
  naw
  deg
  un arr ddeg
  deuddeg

Shepherds'
  yan
  Tan
  ethera
  methera
  pimp
  sethera
  lethera
  hovera
  devera
  dick
  yan a dick
  tan a dick

Romany
  yek
  du
  trin
  hors
  pansh
  ——
  eft
  ——
  ——

——
——
——

Yan Tan Tethera – 3

This astounding survival from the past is of great interest to countrymen and deserves further consideration. The language, as has already been pointed out, is basically corrupt Welsh. It has nothing to do with Romany or Ancient Greek, but I must point out that all these languages are of the same Indo-European stock amongst which the numerals are strikingly similar. The Romany language is akin to modern Hindi, itself a derivation of Sanskrit which is closely allied to and of the same vintage as Latin, Greek and the Celtic languages. Basque is pre-Indo-European and quite different. It has some affinities with ancient Etruscan and modern Georgian. It is extremely improbable that this method of sheep counting survives from Roman times, though this has from time to time been proposed and it seems reasonably certain that it was introduced by Welsh shepherds, though how and when is quite unknown. It was, and to the same extent still is, common-place in the Lake District, Yorkshire and the East Coast as far south as Norfolk and possibly formerly in the Southern Counties, although there are considerable local variations. People tend to count and do mental arithmetic in their mother tongue, which probably accounts for its survival, as the Welsh shepherds would use their own language in this context long after they had become fluent in conversational English. The system goes to a pleasant swing and jingle, and for this reason is used on occasions to get tagged on to the end of nursery rhymes— 'This little pig went to market' would, for example, be followed by 'and this is the way to count the pigs—Yan, tan, tethera, etc.'

INDEX